*Reproductive Justice, Queerly*

REPRODUCTIVE JUSTICE: A NEW VISION FOR THE TWENTY-FIRST CENTURY

*Edited by Rickie Solinger (senior editor), Khiara M. Bridges, Laura Briggs, Krystale E. Littlejohn, Ruby Tapia, and Carly Thomsen*

1. *Reproductive Justice: An Introduction,* by Loretta J. Ross and Rickie Solinger
2. *How All Politics Became Reproductive Politics: From Welfare Reform to Foreclosure to Trump,* by Laura Briggs
3. *Distributing Condoms and Hope: The Racialized Politics of Youth Sexual Health,* by Chris A. Barcelos
4. *Just Get on the Pill: The Uneven Burden of Reproductive Politics,* by Krystale E. Littlejohn
5. *Reproduction Reconceived: Family Making and the Limits of Choice after Roe v. Wade,* by Sara Matthiesen
6. *Laboratory of Deficiency: Sterilization and Confinement in California, 1900–1950s,* by Natalie Lira
7. *Abortion Pills Go Global: Reproductive Freedom across Borders,* by Sydney Calkin
8. *Fighting Mad: Resisting the End of Roe v. Wade,* edited by Krystale E. Littlejohn and Rickie Solinger
9. *Fatal Denial: Racism and the Political Life of Black Infant Mortality,* by Annie Menzel
10. *The Pregnancy Police: Conceiving Crime, Arresting Personhood,* by Grace E. Howard
11. *Youth Organizing for Reproductive Justice: A Guide for Liberation,* by Chris A. Barcelos
12. *Queering Families: Reproductive Justice in Precarious Times,* by Tamara Lea Spira
13. *We Are Pregnant with Freedom: Black Feminist Storytelling for Reproductive Justice,* by Stacie Selmon McCormick
14. *From the Clinics to the Capitol: How Opposing Abortion Became Insurrectionary,* by Carol Mason
15. *Abortion and Reproductive Justice: An Essential Guide for Resistance,* by Marlene Gerber Fried and Loretta J. Ross
16. *Reproductive Justice, Queerly,* by Carly Thomsen

# Reproductive Justice, Queerly

Carly Thomsen

UNIVERSITY OF CALIFORNIA PRESS

University of California Press
Oakland, California



Cataloging-in-Publication data is on file at the Library of Congress.

ISBN 978-0-520-38534-4 (cloth)
ISBN 978-0-520-38535-1 (pbk.)
ISBN 978-0-520-38536-8 (ebook)

GPSR Authorized Representative: Easy Access System Europe, Mustamäe tee 50, 10621 Tallinn, Estonia, gpsr.requests@easproject.com

35 34 33 32 31 30 29 28 27 26
10 9 8 7 6 5 4 3 2 1

# Contents

# Illustrations

# On the Task at Hand

## A PROLOGUE

As I was putting the final touches on this book, I received a text from a friend asking if I had seen the most recent horrifying local news about a Houston midwife arrested for allegedly performing illegal abortions. I had, just moments before, and I was still reeling. It is the kind of news that stops you in your tracks. Makes it hard to remember what you were doing the moment before you received it. The kind that lodges itself in your body. That makes you fear we are on the brink. But, really, you know we are past the brink. We are living through the turning point. One rupture. Another rupture. They just keep coming. Far-right-wing conservatives now control all branches of the federal government, the courts, and various media channels. There has been a regime change, and we should not delude ourselves into thinking that any of this is temporary or easily reversible.

But—BUT!—this does not mean that our current situation is inevitable or that resistance is futile. On the contrary. In this heinous political moment, when new ruptures are shifting the contours of our political landscape on what feels like a daily basis, we must ask: What forms of resistance will make a difference? To whom? When? Where? What can we possibly *do* that could be adequate to the task at hand? Perhaps most pressing for someone in the trenches of finishing a book, what might a collection of words look like that can meet the demands of the here and now? It can feel impossible to know the answers to these questions. That's the point. It is too easy to feel overwhelmed by the magnitude of the political shitshow in front of us. The scale of ruptures in what was an already delicate social fabric is intentional, of course, a tool itself. It is how Trump 2.0 and aligned far-right conservatives are working to ensure we feel submerged. They have created and are continuing to create so many targets that we don't know where to aim our righteous energies. Conservatives are banking on dulling our capacities for resistance by overwhelming us, pulling us in so many directions, making the problems so big that any resistance we might be able to manage seems pointless. We cannot allow this strategy to work.

I want to be very clear about something up front: The questions I ask in the previous paragraph are not some armchair exercise. These are the questions all politicized people I know are grappling with right now, and they are life or death questions. Women are dying because they cannot access abortion. Nevaeh Crain. Amber Thurman. Candi Miller. Josseli Barnica. The causes of each of their deaths? Pregnancy. Miscarriage. Living in states that banned abortion. Each of these women needed a simple medical procedure—an abortion—which they could not get because politicians have made it such that doctors cannot do their jobs. The deaths of these women, mostly women of color, mostly mothers already, were preventable. We know maternal mortality rates are 62 percent higher in states that have restricted abortion.[1] And yet here we are. Twelve states have banned abortion outright and another twenty-nine have severely restricted it, with limited exceptions.[2] In the name of something antiabortion advocates ironically call "pro-life," women are dying. And more women will die.

But I should pause. This book isn't about maternal mortality or even primarily about abortion, miscarriage, or pregnancy. It is a book that invites you to bring queer theory and reproductive justice into deeper conversation with one another. You will, of course, experience this invitation within the context of our current sociopolitical moment. This context is grim. It is also different from that within which this book was conceived, nurtured, brought forth. In fact, I wrote most of these words before the

*Dobbs* decision was handed down and *Roe v. Wade* was overturned. That was three years ago. Three years! What, you might rightly be wondering, took me so long to hit send on the email to the press with my already finished book attached? Here is the raw truth: As things have worsened politically, I have become anxious about this book. It has come to feel inadequate, its concerns, dare I say it, silly and juvenile. It can now feel like a luxury to do the kinds of work that feminist and queer theorists have long undertaken: critically analyzing the discourses and ideologies circulating among those who consider themselves liberal, progressive, and leftist. Considering that Gender Studies departments (a predominant site for the production of queer theory) and all things reproduction are two key targets for the current Trump administration, is this really the moment to be asking critical questions of those committed to queer worldmaking and reproductive justice?! I have come to see the answer as a resounding YES! I hope that by the time you finish reading this book, you, too, will agree.

It isn't just what this book *does*—that is, the questions it asks, who it engages as its interlocutors, and the kinds of public interventions that have emerged out of it—that has encouraged me to pause. In fact, I have been far more anxious about what this book doesn't do and can't do than what it does do. This book will not bring back Nevaeh, Amber, Candi, or Josseli or prevent future deaths of people who need abortions and can't get them. This book can't bail María Margarita Rojas, the Houston midwife, or her two associates arrested alongside her, out of jail. This book will not quell the hunger of children who no longer have access to food because Republicans have slashed SNAP (Supplemental Nutrition Assistance Program) benefits. This book won't bring back the Palestinian children who starved to death as part of the long, coordinated US-backed Israeli occupation. This book won't generate resources so that Palestinian parents have access to basic medical tools necessary to give birth in the wake of Israel bombing their hospitals and decimating their infrastructure. This book will not get Black mothers, who are both arrested and incarcerated at disproportionate rates, released from prison so that they can raise their children. This book will not ensure that undocumented people are not deported and separated from their families. I could go on and on. The magnitude of reproductive injustices both in the United States and around the world makes it difficult to stop, in fact.

But no book does these things, and what I have written is a book, after all. Instead, and still importantly, books do other things—things we are in desperate need of right now. I have long found solace, inspiration, hope, and possibility in feminist and queer theory and related worldmaking projects, something that has, for the most part, only intensified in this political moment. I believe deeply in the necessity of queer theory and its ability to help us think otherwise about reproductive issues and to do reproductive justice otherwise, something this book demonstrates through reflecting on the queer art nights, art exhibitions, and reproductive justice mini golf course that emerged out of and alongside this book. That conservatives are targeting Gender Studies in ways we've never experienced before suggests that they too know that feminist and queer ways of thinking are powerful and, further, that classrooms are sites for undoing precisely the logics they are fomenting. We must remind ourselves that we have the power that conservatives believe we have. Moreover, we should not lose sight of the fact that conservatives are able to do their *political* work *today* because of the *cultural* work they've done for *decades*. Project 2025 did not appear out of nowhere. The feasibility of actualizing any leftist turn rests not simply on continuing to do the kinds of cultural work that scholars, activists, and artists have been doing for decades but *reinvesting* in our belief in its necessity and power. The development of new ways of thinking about old topics is part of that culture work. As my dear friend Ragini Tharoor Srinivasan said when I expressed my doubts about the usefulness of this book in this political moment, "We [scholars] have to do the thinking because every other place in society is not allowed or incentivized to think." She is right, of course. That I have worried that this kind of feminist and queer intellectual work is irrelevant in a political moment in which it is highly relevant reflects how deeply conservatives have sown the seeds of anti-intellectualism. They'll get us if we let them.

We cannot afford to succumb to conservatives' anti-intellectualism. We cannot afford to be debilitated. We must know who our targets are and who our interlocutors are, and here I want to be clear about who I see as mine. My targets are conservatives, although they are not the audience for this book. What I mean by this is that I do not imagine that conservatives will engage my work, and if they do—as in the case of public art exhibitions I write about in the epilogue or through a Fox News piece criticizing an article I published about crisis pregnancy centers in the *New York Times*—they do not do so with a desire to learn. While I don't envision a right-winger picking up this book, I do hope that it might give you, dear reader, more tools with which to talk to these very people. I hope it might make you feel less alone as you try to navigate conversations with people who don't agree with you.

I recently had an exchange with my mom that speaks to this point. I had been invited to contribute to an online forum reviewing Jessica Valenti's newest book *Abortion: Our Bodies, Their Lies, and the Truths We Use to Win*, and I asked my mom if she wanted to read the book alongside me and chat about it.[3] Our own little book club, if you will. In this conversation, my mom shared with me an exchange that she recently had with one of my aunts. It went something like this:

AUNT: I didn't vote, but if I had, I would've voted for Trump because of his positions on abortion.

MOM: [Our sister] would be dead if abortion wasn't legal! She needed one in the 1980s, after she had a miscarriage between her two kids.

AUNT: She didn't have an abortion! She had a D&C. She wanted that baby. Plus, you can still get abortions if there is a medical need like that one.

Most of us have someone like my aunt in our lives. And we find ourselves in conversations filled with so much misinformation that it is hard to know how exactly to start to respond. In this case, my mom tried to explain to my aunt that a D&C—short for Dilation and Curettage—*is* an abortion. An abortion is quite simply the name for a variety of medical procedures used to expel fetal tissue (wanted or unwanted) from a uterus. The procedure is not different based on how one felt about being pregnant, like my aunt suggested. Further, in states that have banned abortion, one often *cannot* access the procedure even if there is a medical emergency, despite my aunt's erroneous assertions. And this is precisely why women are dying.

These kinds of conversations make it easy to want to write people off, to think they are dumb or delusional or beyond reach. But Jessica Valenti makes a point that helped me feel empathy for my aunt and others like her. Valenti argues that conservatives have commandeered language with the goal of generating confusion, such that people do not know what is and is not an abortion and what is or is not allowed under the law. Learning that conservatives have systematically generated the very ideas that my aunt was parroting can help us sustain conversations, and even relationships, in moments that it can otherwise be hard to. I hope that this book provides some tools and inspiration for those who are doing the hard work of engaging with people whose positions differ from theirs and mine.

These people are not only conservatives. They are often, at least for feminist and queer theorists, people who see themselves as liberal, progressive, or even leftist but approach gender and sexuality in ways that run counter to the insights of our academic fields. As such, my interlocutors are fellow feminist and queer thinkers and doers and people who see themselves as politically liberal, progressive, or leftist. These are the well-meaning supporters of reproductive justice who increasingly call up an LGBTQ+ person, real or imagined, to index their progressive politics. The impulse here is admirable: to create a world that is more inclusive to LGBTQ+ people. But, as I show throughout this book, this impulse is being carried out in ways that ought to encourage us to pause. When reproductive justice supporters hail LGBTQ+ people their requests are often actually quite conservative, even reproducing the same racism, sexism, and classism that reproductive justice scholars and activists have long fought against—and, perhaps most disturbingly, all while deploying the language of queerness.

We must fight against this conservatism masquerading as progressivism, something both made possible and made difficult by the fact that it is everywhere, including in conversations about abortion, surrogacy, and parental leave, all topics this book takes up. Perhaps this is why my anxieties over the book's lack of relevance in this particular moment are especially senseless. That is, the discourses and ideologies that I began analyzing several years ago remain strangely present on the political left—even as the broader political climate has shifted. So, in that sense, anything I was writing five years ago remains relevant today. I have been reminded of this point repeatedly while I let this manuscript sit, and let my feelings about what it does and does not do fester.

Two brief anecdotes illustrate this point. I've recently been engaging in academic spaces where participants frame their concerns about reproduction in terms of ethics. The University of Texas Medical Branch in Galveston, Texas, hosts an annual Reproductive Ethics conference, the organizers of which are smart feminists with good politics, as were many conference attendees and presenters. On the second day, one of the few men in attendance gave a presentation entitled "A Philosophical Argument for Fathers' Rights," which was somehow even worse than what you'd expect from such a talk. He argued that because men and women each do half of the "work" of pregnancy, they should both have equal "rights" to the "property" that emerged out of that work (the fetus, that is). When pressed, he clarified that by "work," he meant "contributed half of the fetus's genetic material"—a far cry from work. He argued that if a man who impregnated a woman wanted the woman to carry to term a fetus she did not want, she should be legally and physically prevented from having an abortion, so long as he paid her some undisclosed wage to account for the work of pregnancy. That is, women should be forced to gestate fetuses so that men can purchase them.

Even our current world is not this dystopian. Unless incarcerated, detained, or institutionalized, women cannot (yet) be legally physically restrained from seeking abortions. While hearing such an argument presented at an otherwise largely feminist academic conference was shocking, what followed was equally bonkers, although in a different way. The question-and-answer period began with earnest clarifying questions from audience members, seemingly attempting to engage with these ideas as if they were legitimate and worthy of engagement. Finally, one brave audience member responded differently, noting that she found the talk not only misogynist but also homophobic and transphobic because the presenter was imagining that only women would be pregnant and that all couples would be heterosexual. The presenter responded, "Well, I don't believe in the trans thing. I believe in science. I believe in men and women." The audience audibly gasped, and rightly so. His comment was absurd, hateful, and violent. But it was no more absurd, hateful, or violent than the fifteen-minute monologue in which he argued that women should not be regarded as anything other than vessels for men's desires—something that did not compel the same kind of collective audience outrage.

Just a few months later, I was at a generative conference on reproductive research ethics at Rice University. The presentation by one scholar, who lives in and conducts research in Uganda, focused on the limits of the move to talk about pregnancy, birth, and postpartum care in gender-neutral terms by using phrases such as "pregnant people," "people with vaginas," "pregnant populations," and so on. She shared that she had experienced difficulty getting her research findings published in Western academic journals because reviewers and editors stated that they were opposed to her use of the word "women" to describe the Ugandan women with whom she was working. Not so incidentally, these same women had expressed hostility to the language the scholar was being asked to use to describe them; they felt that centering body parts (vagina, uterus) was crass and that referring to them as "people" or "populations" rather than "women" dismissed something crucial about their humanity. The presenter suggested that the assumption that Western ways of talking about gender travel easily or simply is a form of neocolonialism. The audience response to this presentation was the most divisive, critical, and animated of those at the two-day conference. One person implied that the presenter was transphobic and said that no one is being prevented from using the term "woman." (The presentation was literally about being prevented from using the term "woman.") Audience respondents were interrupting and talking over each other, so worked up that they were not waiting to use the microphone to respond, as was otherwise customary throughout the gathering. Others were rolling their eyes and sighing deeply, their agitation palpable. In an academic setting that was affectively otherwise for the reminder of our time together, these responses were noteworthy. Here we were in Texas, a state where women are dying from an inability to secure abortions, where the state's abortion ban will primarily impact low-income women and women of color, and scholars are arguing over the value of eliminating the word "women" from our vocabulary when talking about reproductive health, rights, and justice—and all from a fancy room with floor to ceiling windows at a university with a $9 billion endowment. It sounds like a *Saturday Night Live* skit.

Don't get me wrong: I do not believe that reproductive justice advocacy should only focus on women or that the reproductive health, rights, and justice concerns of trans people should be outside of the bounds of our work to create a reproductively just world. Rather, supporters of reproductive justice need to do *more* to address trans health, rights, and justice.

I take up this issue at length in chapter 3 and, to a lesser degree, the Introduction. Here, I will just briefly say that eliminating the word "woman" from our lexicon doesn't do the work that people on the political left think that it does, and further, that the demand for gender-neutral language cannot become synonymous with trans inclusion because actualizing trans justice and reproductive justice alike will demand far *more* from us than simple shifts in language.

Let me illustrate this point with an example from these same conferences. I was struck by how few times I heard the word "women" in presentations about topics that almost exclusively impact women, who were, in fact, the subject of the specific research being presented. Most presenters simply replaced the phrase "pregnant women" with "pregnant people," presumably as a way to index their trans-inclusive politics. When presenters did use the words "woman" or "women," they went to great pains to spell out that the reason they did so was because the specific individual to whom they were referring considers herself a woman. But this discursive shift did not actually reflect any shifts in their research questions or concerns; indeed, their research actually focused on women, whom they referred to as people, and, even more damning, not a single person presented research that centered trans people—at either two-day conference. The truth is that researchers and activists alike are not actually talking about trans people when they use the kinds of phrases that have come to index trans inclusion. This slippage makes it too easy to ignore that sexism and misogyny drive many of the problems that produce the negative reproductive health outcomes about which researchers write, and further that discursive inclusion does nothing to address the material health concerns of trans people, all points I expand upon in chapter 3.

What I hope these brief anecdotes make clear is that those of us who see ourselves as feminist, queer, liberal, progressive, and leftist could benefit from having more tools with which to discuss reproduction in moments where LGBTQ+ness is hailed. These discourses are circulating widely, put into effect by scholars, artists, activists, policymakers, content creators, and so on. As such, I necessarily imagine all of these people as interlocutors, and I tried to write a book that can speak to all of them. Of course, this means that everyone who engages with this work will likely be disappointed at points. More people have reviewed and responded to drafts of this book than anything I've ever written. I have been told that the book is far too theoretical, that it isn't theoretical enough, that the art included speaks to how amazing the project is, that the art is unimpressive and could be cut, that I engage with too many scholars, that I engage with too few scholars, that this is exactly the book we need right now, and that I should better articulate the political stakes of the project in this moment. To this I say: Yes! You are all right. If something here doesn't resonate with you, maybe it doesn't need to. Maybe it was written with someone else in mind. But, dear reader, please keep reading. Right around the corner, there is something else that *was* written with you in mind and that I hope will resonate with you. My greatest hope is that this book shifts how people concerned with LGBTQ+ issues and reproductive justice bring the two together such that what we are arguing for becomes far queerer than what is on offer in this moment. The gravity of the here and now means that we need all kinds of resistance. Op-eds, policy, medical care, protests, conversations, and direct action of all kinds, certainly, but also plays, social media posts, movies, books, and art—and perhaps above all, people in the struggle with you to reassure you that whatever you bring to the table is valuable, to remind you of the necessity of creative collective action, and to inspire you to keep fighting joyfully.

# Reproductive Justice, Queerly

## AN INTRODUCTION

Less than a week after the Supreme Court's summer 2022 decision to overturn *Roe v. Wade* was made public, *Time* magazine published an article entitled "How Employers Can Stand with Their LGBTQ+ Employees Post-*Roe*."[1] Immediately following the article's headline is a picture of two protestors at the New York City Pride parade, held two days after *Roe* was officially overturned. One of the protestors, who reads as a woman of color, is holding a red poster with the words "We Need Stonewall Energy Right Now" written in capital letters in black marker. The other, who reads as a white woman, is carrying a crinkled yellow poster with the message "They Won't Stop at *Roe*" written in block rainbow letters. Despite *Time* using an image of people invoking *Roe* at a Pride celebration, never once does the word *abortion* appear in the article. Instead, employers should "act now to protect the rights of queer employees," the article asserts, because of restrictions on trans youth access to gender-affirming care, ongoing discrimination against LGBTQ+ employees, and the "Don't Say Gay" bill, which Florida passed earlier in 2022 to prevent public school educators from discussing sexual orientation or gender identity in their classrooms. These, too, are real concerns. But what is perplexing here is that none of these issues are specific to a post-*Roe* world. Before the *Dobbs* decision was handed down, Florida legislators had passed the "Don't Say Gay" bill, trans youth had trouble accessing gender-affirming care, and LGBTQ+ employees faced discrimination. What specifically about the post-*Roe* world, in which 41 US states have banned or severely restricted abortion, might shift things for LGBTQ+ people? And what can employers do about this?

We ought to expect that an article linking LGBTQ+ employees to *Roe* would answer these questions. It does not. Instead, *Time* makes another point entirely: We should be worried about what the recent reversal of abortion rights means for LGBTQ+ rights—a point reiterated repeatedly in the news. Articles in *Forbes*, *The American Prospect*, *The Washington Post*, *NBC News*, and *Bloomberg* had titles including "Post-'*Roe*,' Transgender People Fear for the Future," "LGBTQ Community Braces for Rollback of Rights After Abortion Ruling," and "LGBTQ Americans Worry for Their Rights After *Roe* Reversal."[2] The fear that LGBTQ+ rights are on the chopping block was a consistent theme in conversations that attempted to bring LGBTQ+ness to bear on the news of *Roe*'s reversal. The same *Time* article begins, "Last week, Justice Clarence Thomas's concurring opinion for *Dobbs v. Jackson Women's Health Organization* confirmed the fears of LGBTQ+ advocates, allies, and community members. In it, he urged the court to reconsider other landmark civil rights cases of the past half century, including *Lawrence v. Texas*, which ruled anti-sodomy laws unconstitutional, and *Obergefell v. Hodges*, which enshrined marriage equality as the law of the land." *Time* was not alone in making such claims. In fact, Thomas's calling into question of *Lawrence* and *Obergefell*, two key gay rights cases, was referenced widely in conversations about *Roe*'s reversal.[3]

What was not conveyed in much of this discussion about what's next—about the future, that is—is just how bad things are *now* and *for whom* they are really really bad right now. Asking what the overturning of *Roe* means for LGBTQ+ rights before we could even know what the overturning of *Roe* would mean for those seeking abortions speaks to the lack of concern about patriarchy and misogyny that created the conditions for *Roe*'s reversal in the first place. Laurie Essig made this point in an essay entitled "U.S. Culture is So Deeply Patriarchal, We Can't Even Admit Overturning Roe is About Women." As Essig notes, "When . . . we move on from the deeply misogynist impulse [of outlawing abortion] to other presumably more important rights . . . we refuse to witness the horror of it by acting as if this particular form of state violence isn't enough, but could really have terrible consequences for other, more important groups of people than women."[4] We also ought to recognize that moving on so quickly from abortion to LGBTQ+ concerns perpetuates racism and classism. We know, of course, that *Roe*'s reversal—like all other abortion policies before it—does not impact all groups of people equally. Seventy-five percent of patients who obtain abortions are poor or low-income.[5] And Black women are five times and Latina women two times more likely to obtain abortions than white women.[6] Furthermore, as the numbers of abortion clinics and providers shrink, patients in the South and Midwest, as well as in rural areas across the United States, are forced to travel farther for abortions.[7] Clearly, who gets abortions and how they get them is racialized, classed, and shaped by location, and therefore restrictions on abortion exacerbate forms of oppression that transpire along racial, class, and geographic lines. These facts are so well-established that the centrality of race, class, and geography to the US abortion story is rarely disputed among those fighting for reproductive justice (although these aspects of the conversation are often left out when advocates move to "queer" reproductive justice, a point to which I return in chapter 3).

The same cannot be said about gender. In fact, how to talk about gender—and especially women, trans men, and nonbinary people—has become a key site of contestation among those of us committed to reproductive rights, health, and justice. Indeed, in the last several years, major reproductive and civil rights organizations, including Planned Parenthood, the National Abortion and Reproductive Rights Action League (NARAL), and the American Civil Liberties Union (ACLU), have begun to replace "women" with "pregnant people" and "patient," an ostensibly genderless reframing meant to be inclusive to trans and nonbinary people.

Such ostensibly genderless discourses are being repeated in a great deal of the liberal and progressive press coverage of reproductive issues—but not without pushback. Indeed, the battles over language used to advocate for reproductive rights and justice have been covered in major media outlets. An article in *Politico* titled "Texas Ban Spotlights Democrats' Generational Divide on Abortion and Trans Issues" has as its subtitle: "As the Left Tries to Stay United, its Different Factions are at Odds Over a Critical Word: 'Women.'"[8] Helen Lewis wrote two articles for *The Nation* on the topic: "The Abortion Debate is Suddenly About 'People,'" Not 'Women': What Progressives Lose When They Won't Name the Group Most Affected by Abortion Bans" and "Why I'll Keep Saying 'Pregnant Women.'"[9] Another article on the topic reflects on a tweet by the ACLU, which quoted feminist Supreme Court justice Ruth Bader Ginsburg:

> "The decision whether or not to bear a child is central to a [person's] life, to [their] wellbeing and dignity," the ACLU had Ginsburg saying. "When the government controls that decision for [people], [they are] being treated as less than a fully adult human responsible for [their] own choices," the quote continued. Most people's reaction upon seeing that tweet was probably the same as mine—not "Great comment, RBG" but "*What's with all the square brackets*?"[10]

The square brackets indicated, of course, that the words used in the tweeted quote did not appear in the original quote. The words that did: woman, women, she, her. The ACLU addressed their discursive decision in a post on their website entitled "Why We Use Inclusive Language to Talk About Abortion." Their reason: "Abortion access should concern everyone, and this ruling directly impacts everyone who can become pregnant. That's why so many LGBTQ+ people are deeply invested in the fight for abortion access."[11]

Despite the certainty with which progressive, liberal, and leftist organizations have talked about their move toward what they frame as inclusive language, other liberals aren't quite so sure how to talk about women when discussing abortion. Even members of the US Congress—not exactly the wokest bunch—are being informed by these debates. Or at least this point is true for Democrats. Republicans are certain that women are the ones who have abortions, something not disconnected from their belief that it must be outlawed. That is, it is precisely conservative understandings of women as a class, and their hatred of this class, that drives their antiabortion politics. In fact, they have no problem calling up women in abortion debates precisely because doing so allows them to mock liberals' so-called gender-neutral language to discuss abortion. This mocking reflects many Republicans' positions that trans people don't really exist—but conservatives aren't the audience for *Reproductive Justice, Queerly* so we'll just leave this point here for now. Back to the Democrats: In 2021,

Representative Judy Chu introduced HR 3755, otherwise known as the Women's Health Protection Act of 2021, which was intended "to protect a person's ability to determine whether to continue or end a pregnancy, and to protect a health care provider's ability to provide abortion services." Point eight in the bill's "Findings and Purpose" states:

> The terms "woman" and "women" are used in this bill to reflect the identity of the majority of people targeted and affected by restrictions on abortion services, and to address squarely the targeted restrictions on abortion, which are rooted in misogyny. However, access to abortion services is critical to the health of every person capable of becoming pregnant. This Act is intended to protect all people with the capacity for pregnancy—cisgender women, transgender men, non-binary individuals, those who identify with a different gender, and others—who are unjustly harmed by restrictions on abortion services.[12]

While the language of the bill focuses on women, the representatives who crafted it were aware enough of debates about gendered language to address their use of the term "women."

Alexandria Ocasio-Cortez, the youngest woman and youngest Latina member of Congress, known for working to push establishment Democrats to the left, has taken another approach. Just a few weeks prior to the "Women's Health Protection Act of 2021" appearing on the legislative calendar, Ocasio-Cortez shared via Twitter her thoughts about the language used to discuss reproductive issues. "Reproductive justice," she asserted, "is not just a 'women's issue,' it's an everyone issue. However, if you are angry with me for using gender inclusive language to discuss the dangers of Texas' abortion bounties, may I suggest this is a 'you' issue rather than an 'us' issue. Wishing you growth!" Ocasio-Cortez doubled down in later tweets. "Not just women! Trans men and non-binary people can also menstruate. Some women also *don't* menstruate for many reasons, including surviving cancer that required a hysterectomy. GOP mad at this are protecting the patriarchal idea that women are most valuable as uterus holders." In another tweet, she added "Trans, two-spirit, and non-binary people have always existed and will always exist. People can stay mad about that if they want, or they can grow up." Ocasio-Cortez's tweets went viral, garnering critique from conservatives and praise from progressives.

As these anecdotes show, it is no stretch to say that *how to talk about gender* has become a key question among those of us committed to reproductive justice. Or, perhaps more accurately, how to talk about gender has become a key point of contention among those of us committed to reproductive justice. So certain are reproductive justice advocates that gender-neutral language is synonymous with trans inclusion that questions can no longer be asked. AOC's tweets frame anyone who questions gender-neutral language as needing "growth" and to "grow up." In much the same way, advocates now explicitly tell people what to say and what not to say: Instead of X, say Y. The style guide put out by the Trans Journalists Association, for instance, instructs people to

> use the term 'reproductive health' instead of 'women's health' when writing about abortion, birth control, and other reproductive health issues. Additionally, use gender-neutral language like 'people who menstruate' when writing about people who get pregnant, menstruate, need access to abortion, and other related topics. These issues affect trans men and many non-binary people, so they are not just 'women's health' issues.[13]

Jack Qu'emi, the author of an *Everyday Feminism* post entitled "4 Ways to Be Gender Inclusive When Discussing Abortion," agrees. Qu'emi asserts that "Using 'women' as a catch-all term for 'people with active uteruses' is incredibly problematic (and also, don't reduce people to body parts)."[14] That the author doesn't see the parenthetical content as contradicting their assertion speaks to the difficulty of actually talking about those who get abortions in a way that isn't sexist and is inclusive of people whose genders are other than women—a complexity completely written over in these kinds of prescriptions.

For-profit doula companies, birthing justice community groups, and educational institutions are also stepping in line. Columbia University's Vagelos College of Physicians and Surgeons advocates for using "precise gender-related language," such as "'people with uteruses' instead of 'women' if the relevant point is about the presence of a uterus rather than the person's expressed gender identity."[15] The Boston University College of Health and Rehabilitation Sciences website implores us to "Refer to specific body parts if and when they are relevant to the discussion, such as uteruses or vaginas, rather than women's bodies or women's body parts.

This language is more specific as well as more inclusive, and ensures that vulnerable, minoritized individuals are not left out of our discussions regarding the health care that they need."[16] The reputable Bixby Center for Global Reproductive Health at the University of California, San Francisco now includes a "gender inclusive language statement" on its website with the following disclaimer: "Content made prior to 2020 may include gendered language, but as we create and update content moving forward we are prioritizing the use of more inclusive language. Our policy and language were informed by the work of GLAAD, The Midwives Alliance of North America (MANA), Abortion Access Front, NYAAF, and The EMA Fund."[17] Women, a category whose relevance ceased to exist in 2020, are officially a thing of the past. And as the string of feminist and LGBTQ+ organizations cited suggests, this move is supported by all of The Right People.

At the same time as it has become commonsensical among self-identified liberal and leftist supporters of reproductive justice to deploy discourses of queerness, queer theorists have said remarkably little about reproductive justice—despite the many useful tools queer theorists have developed for examining discourses and ideas that have become dominant within subcultural spaces, as well as the celebratory affects that "stick" to them, to use Sara Ahmed's formulation.[18] To be clear, queer theorists have discussed issues that we might think of as matters of reproductive justice or as helpful for actualizing reproductive justice—the problems with fetishizing the nuclear family, alternative kinship structures, the need to rethink the domestic sphere, applications of care, and so on—but they rarely frame their analysis of these very things in terms of movements for reproductive justice.[19] This point is not meant as a critique of the brilliant and crucial arguments scholars writing about these topics make. It is simply meant as evidence that queer theory has not engaged deeply or directly with *reproductive justice*, even when examining things like care, family, kinship, and home—all of which have ties to reproduction. This insight builds on Jennifer Doyle's reflections on queer theorists' lack of engagement with abortion, something Doyle describes as curious considering the field's ostensible commitment to sexual liberation.[20] Sexual liberation is, of course, impossible without abortion—although we wouldn't get that sense from engaging with queer theory.

Among the few scholars who frame their work as a matter of "queering reproduction," most focus primarily on the reproductive concerns of LGBTQ+ people. Laura Mamo's book *Queering Reproduction: Achieving Pregnancy in the Age of Technoscience*, for example, examines lesbians' use of fertility treatments.[21] In the introduction to a special issue of *Reproductive Biomedicine and Society Online* that brings together scholarship on "queer reproductions, reproductive justice, and stratified reproduction," the authors frame the key position of scholarship on "queer reproductions" as: "Identifying as LGBTQ+ should not place exceptional demands or restrictions upon one's access to reproductive care and services."[22] In "Queering Reproductive Justice: Memories, Mistakes, and Motivations to Transform Kinship," Lauren Silver, following Zakiya Luna, defines "nonnormative or queer family" in capacious ways, but her reflections on queering reproductive justice ultimately hinge on her experience of engaging in a transracial adoption with her wife.[23] In "Queer(ing) Reproductive Justice," Natalie Fixmer-Oraiz and Shui-yin Sharon Yam suggest that "the RJ framework applies to the reproductive health and social lives of queer people."[24] In another article titled "Queering Reproductive Justice," Marie-Amelie George notes that she uses "'LGBTQ' and 'queer' interchangeably because the legal issues are similar," even though she also acknowledges that "the two terms are not interchangeable."[25] Kimala Price's "Queering Reproductive Justice in the Trump Era" focuses on the ways LGBTQ+ individuals and the reproductive justice movement have "attempted to build solidarity and coalitions between their respective movements through hosting meetings and other activities, and through the strategic use of rhetoric."[26]

The conflation of "queer" and LGBTQ+ evident across these examples is one queer theorists have long argued against precisely because it ignores the politicized commitment to non-normativity long associated with queerness. That is, all LGBTQ+ identified people are not necessarily living in queer ways. Further, the use of "queer" to describe parenting ignores the ways in which parenting—regardless of the identifications of those doing it—often operates in the service of normativity. The position of *Reproductive Justice, Queerly* is that we should be cautious of any iteration of queerness that does not consider how it may serve to extend the positive affects associated with the heteronormative or homonormative nuclear family structure. In other words, we should push back against deployments of queerness in moments when we're talking about engaging uncritically in precisely the institutions and ways of thinking that produce dominant gender and sexual norms as inevitable. Beyond this, in many ways, it is obvious that transmasculine and nonbinary-identified people might want to give birth or may need abortions, LGBTQ+ parents may struggle to retain custody of their children, and LGBTQ+ people may experience difficulty adopting or accessing reproductive technologies—but all of these examples are built upon what queer theorist Lee Edelman calls "pronatalism" and "reproductive futurism," or the assumption that people want to reproduce and that supporting this desire should be central to LGBTQ+ organizing.[27] Considering that Edelman's *No Future*, in which he develops these concepts, is one of the most widely cited and hotly debated queer theoretical texts of the last two decades, why, we should ask, hasn't it inspired more queer examinations of abortion and reproductive justice more broadly? Taking up precisely this question, Jennifer Doyle asks us to consider an additional question: "What would it mean to absorb a radicalized position vis-a-vis abortion into discourse on queer sex politics?"[28] Why, we should ask, might we want to consider abortion—something that allows for sexual liberation and also halts reproduction—a queer act?

*Reproductive Justice, Queerly* takes up these questions as well as the inverse—that is: what would it mean to absorb queer theory into reproductive justice?—to contend that we need more complicated ways to discuss what it might mean to queer reproductive justice. We need, quite simply, reproductive justice done queerly—that is, reproductive justice as informed by queer theory as it is committed to addressing the materiality of reproduction, including the ways sexism, racism, classism, ableism, homophobia, transphobia, nationalism, and metronormativity contribute to this materiality in distinct and overlapping ways. *Reproductive Justice, Queerly* is the first book to bring queer theory into deeper conversation with reproductive justice scholarship and activism in a way that is in line with and extends both queer theoretical concerns and the critical work on reproduction. The book asks and answers the following questions: What does it mean to do reproductive justice queerly? How is it different from thinking about reproductive issues that LGBTQ+ people might face? What might an analysis of the now commonsensical discursive move to use less overtly gendered language reveal about cultural anxieties related to both women and transness? What might a queer analysis of gay men becoming the face of pro-surrogacy campaigns illuminate? How do feminist and LGBTQ+ demands for paid family leave traffic in heteronormativity? How can parenting be a site from which we enact queer futures? That's a lot of questions, I know. But in this moment, when discourses claiming to queer reproductive justice are becoming increasingly commonplace, there is a lot to question. Ultimately, *Reproductive Justice, Queerly* asks what a queer approach to reproductive justice might look like: one that does not focus primarily on children and families, that is relevant beyond individuals' reproductive desires, and that understands "queering" beyond examining an issue in relation to LGBTQ+-identified people.

In taking up these questions, *Reproductive Justice, Queerly* models what can happen to our thinking about queer and reproductive issues when we bring them together. In so doing, this book makes the simple point that queer theory and reproductive justice need one another—and now more than ever before. The arguments that I make in each chapter collectively allow me to make three interrelated points about moments in which reproductive justice advocates bring LGBTQ+ness to bear on reproduction. First: often, these discussions center men—sometimes gay, sometimes trans—and we ought to consider what it means, especially in this political moment, that men are being centered in discussions of concerns that continue to primarily impact women. Second, they often call up the LGBTQ+ person as a way to index progressive politics, making it difficult to see that what people are asking for is typically quite conservative, even reproducing the very racism, classism, and sexism that reproductive justice scholars and activists have long worked against. Third, they focus on discursive inclusion, ignoring what it would take to create material change in the world. *Reproductive Justice, Queerly* is a critical response to the increased discourses in circulation that tether LGBTQ+ness to reproduction; it asks us to bring the two together anew so that what we are arguing for can become far queerer than what is on offer in this moment.

## THOUGHTS ON "THE WOMAN QUESTION"

Because many of the ideas I'm questioning here have become commonsensical among those who see themselves as supporters of LGBTQ+ rights and reproductive justice, and because the issue of how to talk about abortion—as something that primarily impacts women or through ostensibly less gendered language, such as pregnant people, pregnant patients, people with uteruses, and so on—is so polarizing, it is worth articulating my position in the book's Introduction. I want to be clear up front that I do not see reproductive justice as specific to women, whatever that might mean, or as exclusive of trans concerns. On the contrary. As I noted in the preface, those of us concerned about reproductive justice should do *more* to advance trans justice. The demand for gender-neutral or gender-inclusive language cannot become synonymous with trans inclusion because actualizing trans justice and reproductive justice alike will demand far *more* from us than simple shifts in language. That is, refusing to use the words "woman" and "women" doesn't have the social or political impact that people on the political left believe that it does. This position should not be read as advocating for "decentering trans people in RJ," as one scholar erroneously suggested, a claim that reproduces the very conflation of abortion and reproductive justice that activists and scholars have long advocated against.[29] That is, I am not arguing for decentering trans people in conversations about *reproductive justice*; I am arguing that we cannot erase women in conversations about *abortion* and then equate this simple discursive move with reproductive justice for trans people. There are two reasons for this: Trans people disproportionately experience a plethora of material physical health issues, none of which will be addressed through rhetorical gesture; and abortion is not one of the health issues that trans people disproportionately experience. It shouldn't be surprising that most demographics of LGBTQ+ people seek abortion far *less* often than heterosexual women, especially those who are Black, Latina, or live below the poverty line. The single outlier: bisexual women, who are twice as likely as "exclusively heterosexual women" to have abortions.[30] Interestingly, we hear almost nothing about bisexual women in calls for LGBTQ+ inclusion in conversations about reproductive justice—issues I take up at length in chapter 3.

Here, I just want to say that I am certainly not the first person to reflect critically and carefully on what is at stake in calls for and critiques of this discursive shift, for both trans justice and reproductive justice. I take inspiration from the work of trans studies scholar Paisley Currah, who more than a decade ago reflected on the "disappearing women" in abortion conversations:

> It's entirely possible to point out that it's not just women who become pregnant *and* still keep in focus the bare political fact that abortion rights and access are gender issues, that it's almost only women who get pregnant and who need abortions, and that abortion rights and access are under assault all over the US precisely because it's primarily a "women's issue." Obviously, abortion access shouldn't be restricted by gender identity and providers should clearly communicate this in the messaging. Trans men need to know they can access these services. That said, taking "women" out of abortion rights rhetoric . . . has the faint reek of misogyny.[31]

In another essay, Currah expanded on this take, noting that "while it's certainly right to demand that providers of reproductive health services use trans-inclusive language, we lose important historical and analytical frameworks for understanding the restriction and possible ending of abortion as part of a war against women."[32]

The data on who gets abortions bears out Currah's positions. In 2017, the most recent year for which there is published big data on gender and abortion rates, between 462 and 530 trans or nonbinary people in the United States had abortions. Of the 862,320 abortions performed that year, then, between .05 and .06 percent were obtained by trans or nonbinary people. Two other studies of transmasculine and gender-nonconforming people assigned female at birth show that between 2 and 4 percent have had abortions.[33] Now, we should take these figures with a grain of salt because, as my friend Abraham Weil, a trans studies scholar and editor of *Transgender Studies Quarterly*, has warned me, data have a hard time capturing trans. At the same time, the data we do have on trans health make clear that trans people experience significant health disparities. Access to hormonal therapy and doctors competent enough to provide it, for example, remain serious issues for trans patients.[34] 42 percent of trans men in one study reported experiencing verbal harassment, denial of equal treatment, or physical assault at a hospital or clinic.[35] And 21 percent of doctors in another study reported that they are unwilling to perform pap exams on trans men to screen for cervical cancer.[36] Beyond this, trans-specific health needs are largely excluded from medical school curricula.[37] A survey of OB-GYNs showed that 80 percent received no training on trans health during their residencies.[38] And trans people are less likely than non-trans people to have health insurance.[39] These are all reproductive justice issues—all of which we hear far less about than the discursive inclusion of trans men in conversations about abortion.

The ramifications of these issues are serious. Trans people disproportionately experience a plethora of physical health issues including cardiovascular diseases, high blood pressure, insulin resistance, lipid derangement, liver damage, blood clots, stroke, and heart attacks (see chapter 3). Some of these issues are specific to being trans and to the process of transitioning. Trans people also experience health concerns that are common among non-trans people. Both of these points likely appear banal. It should be equally banal to say that trans people are also *less likely* to experience certain health care issues than are people of other genders. Abortion (as well as breast cancer, which I also discuss further in chapter 3), is one of these issues.

This said, it should be obvious that not everyone who has an abortion is a woman. We should recognize that some trans and nonbinary people, and people whose genders are something else entirely, can get pregnant and therefore can need various related reproductive healthcare services. We should also use language in the service of this recognition. At the same time, we should be able to recognize that the vast majority of people who obtain abortions and give birth see themselves as women, and further, that the root of legislative attempts to restrict abortion is misogyny and sexism, as Paisley Currah pointed out a decade ago. That is, the root of governmental restrictions on abortion is hatred and distrust of women, even though the ramifications of these restrictions will not be limited to women. We must be able to differentiate between the *roots* and the *ramifications* of social problems to effectively address them.

Being able to do so requires that we discuss women as a social category. Of course, this does not mean a single or simple category that everyone who is a part of experiences in the same way. Racism, classism, homo- and transphobia, ableism, and geography inform our experiences of our genders, as do our political leanings, upbringings, and personalities. But "women" remains a relevant category of analysis precisely because people who experience the world as such often have some overlapping experiences, and these similarities are rooted in the sexism and misogyny that various social institutions rely on and perpetuate. That is, our genders are not ours alone. They are informed by the (sexist) social worlds that surround us. This is, in part, what Judith Butler meant when they said that we are not only (gendered) subjects, but we are also (gendered) objects.[40] Further, women are the largest group of people who do not benefit from the current gender order, and, therefore, our ability to rethink our current world requires that we think *with* the category of women. To this point, those of us on the political left simply cannot allow "women" to become a dirty word, a word that signals one's supposed status as a trans-exclusionary radical feminist (TERF). We cannot cede the ground for talking about women, sexism, misogyny, and patriarchy to TERFs. Let me say it again: We cannot cede the ground for talking about women, sexism, misogyny, and patriarchy to TERFs! TERFs exist, and they are dangerous. Furthermore, TERF, as Mairead Sullivan explains, refers to an ideology, not simply people, and we need more tools to differentiate TERF from feminist ideologies.[41] Equating all discussions of women with transphobia prevents us from developing those tools.

In chapter 3, I reflect further on these points and ultimately make two interrelated arguments. First, expanding abortion access requires that we take seriously the sexism of antiabortion activism. Acknowledging that more than 99 percent of abortion patients are women—primarily women of color and poor women—need not be considered transphobic. We can recognize both that women are those who primarily get abortions and that women are not the only people who get abortions. Second, reproductive justice advocacy could do far more to advance trans justice through addressing trans health issues. The presence of ostensibly gender-neutral discourses makes it *more* difficult to address trans-specific health issues precisely because people believe that they've done the work necessary to index their trans-inclusive beliefs simply by using language they think of as gender-neutral when they talk about abortion.

To be clear, I am not suggesting that the trans and gender non-conforming abortion patients don't matter. Of course they do, regardless of whether they make up .05 or 5 percent of those accessing a procedure. And healthcare institutions should take care to meet the health care needs of trans patients. At the same time, we should not deceive ourselves into thinking that discursive recognition alone will effectively address the health issues that disproportionately impact trans people or increase abortion access. Equating language use or discursive or visual representation alone—that is, without accompanying structural change—with justice is a bankrupt approach.[42] Simply changing the language we use to talk about reproductive issues does very little and requires little from us, which is precisely why it has become something people demand. While misogyny and sexism are the root of antiabortion activism, we do not need to limit our responses to focusing on women. State-based legislative attempts to protect abortion access can and should be framed in such a way that they also protect gender-affirming care; both are, of course, about health care that allows for bodily autonomy. But we do not need to discursively disappear women in order to make this argument. We need coalitions that include trans people fighting for abortion rights alongside non-trans people fighting for increased access to gender-affirming health care for trans people not because either issue is likely to impact them personally but because both are crucial for gender and sexual liberation. Identity politics, as well as the overwhelming focus on abortion rights among reproductive rights advocates, have deadened our capacities to imagine the place of trans justice within reproductive justice, and vice versa.

## ABORTION, REPRODUCTIVE RIGHTS, REPRODUCTIVE JUSTICE

I want to back up a bit now to situate this book within a longer genealogy of work on reproductive justice. Throughout this book, I don't talk a lot about reproductive rights—that is, the legal right to the topic in question—preferring instead the framework of reproductive justice. Reproductive justice is an analytic developed by women of color activists in the early 1990s at a meeting in Chicago, Illinois, and it emerged in response to the limits of mainstream feminist reproductive rights work. As Loretta Ross and Rickie Solinger detail, those developing the reproductive justice framework argued for a more capacious approach, one in which demands for abortion *access* (not just rights) would happen alongside demands for resources that would allow women to have and raise the number of children they want.[43] For reproductive justice scholars and activists, an alternative to the pro-choice movement was and is necessary because the right to legal abortion will "not resolve the barriers to having children that many women of color and low-income women face."[44]

These barriers speak to the limits of the "pro-choice" framework, something women of color activists have pushed back against. Loretta Ross, one of the acclaimed founders of the reproductive justice movement, describes why the language of choice and the focus on abortion rights will never be able to address the myriad reproductive concerns women of color face. "If we made abortion totally accessible, totally legal, totally affordable, women would still have other problems. And so reducing women's lives down to just whether or not choice is available we felt was inadequate."[45] Reproductive freedom, then, requires the ability not only to prevent parenthood but also to have and raise children in safe and healthy environments. Barriers to reproductive freedom include limited access to food, health care, employment, and housing—issues reproductive justice advocates point out are both beyond the purview of traditional reproductive rights work and also disproportionately impact women of color and low-income women. These interventions have been and continue to be crucial to activists and scholars alike. As an analytic, reproductive justice helps us to move beyond concerns with law and policy—which have dominated feminist activism—to consider how ideas about reproductive issues circulate and become commonsensical. Many people have a general sense of how things are where they are, but most of us are unlikely to turn to policy to either better understand or push back against our current situations—a point that explains, in part, why reproductive justice as a framework demands that we move beyond thinking with policy, law, and rights.

Elsewhere, I've written about the limits of framing reproductive rights and reproductive justice as necessarily distinct, differences that are often articulated in terms of the movements' relationships to abortion.[46] "The main goal of the reproductive justice movement," Kimala Price argues, "is to move beyond the pro-choice movement's singular focus on abortion."[47] Here and elsewhere, abortion symbolizes the limits of a movement.

Disregarded in reproductive justice narratives that tether abortion to mainstream reproductive rights groups and frame abortion as the point "to move beyond" is that women of color and low-income women are also disproportionately impacted by abortion. On the one hand, this point speaks to the necessity of the reproductive justice framework and of addressing the issues that lead to abortions among those who would decide otherwise if their circumstances were different. On the other hand, racialized differences in abortion rates should encourage us to rethink those narratives in which middle-class white women, mainstream reproductive rights groups, and abortion exist in a one-to-one relationship, as do women of color, reproductive justice, and something more capacious than abortion.

I explore this dynamic in an article I wrote about Native women's fierce support for abortion rights when South Dakota lawmakers attempted to ban abortion in 2006. There, I outline the limits to binary constructions of reproductive rights and justice, arguing that such binaries position abortion as outside of reproductive justice and, thus, women of color, and further that Native women's engagement with the South Dakota ban calls for a complex reconceptualization of the relations between reproductive rights and reproductive justice frameworks. As I argue in that article, "The scapegoating of abortion, the using of abortion to stand in for the limits of a movement, ought to be rethought. That abortion may not be more important than other issues for actualizing reproductive justice need not suggest that it is any *less* important."[48] As such, I do not make any hard and fast distinctions between reproductive rights and justice, although I use the phrase "reproductive justice" throughout this book because, as reproductive justice scholars and activists have pointed out, abortion rights alone are certainly not enough to secure abortion justice, let alone reproductive justice more broadly.

It was nearly a decade ago that I articulated the position that reproductive justice advocates' and scholars' discursive distancing from abortion, a method used to mark the concerns of reproductive justice as distinct from reproductive rights, has harmful consequences for how we conceptualize reproduction and organize for justice. I noted that reproductive justice advocates' critiques of reproductive rights activists' focus on abortion might be less problematic if abortion were actually immaterial to the women being represented by the reproductive justice framework. The problem, I said then, is that dominant reproductive justice narratives make it difficult to view pro-abortion activism, as well as scholarship on abortion, as anything other than liberal, white, and uncritical. This framing of reproductive justice as "beyond" abortion has likely contributed to the disregard of abortion among critical race, queer, and poststructuralist theorists, as well as the erasure of the crucial involvement of women of color in abortion rights struggles.[49]

Today, I think a bit differently, mostly because the *Dobbs vs. Jackson Women's Health Organization* decision means that abortion is now front and center again among those of us committed to reproductive justice. Still, these narratives of reproductive justice remain in circulation, even in this moment. The irony is that it is precisely the fact that people equate abortion with reproductive rights and reproductive justice alike that has led us to the point where advocates are demanding we talk about abortion as a trans issue. That is, abortion is so front and center in conversations about reproductive rights and justice—indeed, there are many moments where abortion, reproductive rights, and reproductive justice are used synonymously, despite decades of women of color arguing against this very conflation—that many people have a hard time articulating reproductive rights and justice issues *other than* abortion. Trans people seek all kinds of reproductive health care, even if they are unlikely to seek abortions. There should be no shortage of ways to talk about what the reproductive justice movement could do to better support trans health and trans justice.

Further, I want to envision a day when abortion will be legal, accessible, and free across the world and feminists committed to abortion justice are not simply trying to survive and helping others to survive. And getting there will require that we are willing to engage in critical analyses of our own approaches. That reproductive justice has been produced as the critique has functioned to position it as that which is beyond critique—it is always already critical. In her analysis of feminist narratives about feminism, Clare Hemmings argues that "which story one tells about the past is always motivated by the position one occupies or wishes to occupy in the present."[50] The narratives that reproductive justice advocates tell about our movements, then, reflect the (critical) political position that we desire to occupy, rather than some inherent distinctiveness between reproductive justice and rights frameworks or how these terms are deployed. This isn't to say that there aren't some serious epistemological and material differences among reproductive rights and reproductive justice advocacy groups. Of course there are. But it is to say that our narratives, which root these differences in how both camps approach abortion, aren't sufficient. Our narratives are political, and we need better narratives that articulate this relationship between rights and justice, abortion and everything else, otherwise. Indeed, it is through generous critique that our movements and scholarship grow and flourish. The lack of critical engagement directed inward toward reproductive justice scholarship and activism is startling, precisely because reproductive justice is rooted in a belief in the necessity of social critique; it is not simply the mainstream in need of leftist engagement, without which it is too easy for reproductive justice scholars and advocates to lack the very capaciousness we critique elsewhere.

Lastly, I want to note that my critical reflections on reproductive justice narratives emerge from my participation in reproductive justice activism and are rooted in the belief that, as Laura Briggs argues, movements are strengthened via scholarly critique, while academic engagement in movements sharpens scholarship.[51] In order to better imagine leftist paths forward, then, we might ask: How might current queer reproductive justice discourses prevent us from engaging in vital self-reflection? What might happen to our thinking and to our activism if we paused in those moments when we're certain both that we're right and also that anyone who disagrees ought to be canceled?[52] And what lessons might fiction offer us for crafting new narratives that will allow us to approach reproductive justice queerly?

## INSIGHTS FROM *DETRANSITION, BABY*

Torrey Peters's best-selling and award-winning novel *Detransition, Baby* offers tools for answering this last question, in particular, through her articulation of a complex, beautiful, and queer relationship between transness and abortion that I have not seen elsewhere. Published in 2021, *Detransition, Baby* tells the story of Reese, Amy/Ames, and Katrina, three thirtysomethings living in Brooklyn, New York, and their interlocking lives. A quick sketch of the three main characters: Reese, a white trans woman, was previously in a romantic relationship with Amy. Amy is a white trans woman who has detransitioned to living as a man, Ames. After Amy and Reese split and Amy detransitioned to Ames, he started dating his boss, Katrina, a Chinese American woman. Ames gets Katrina pregnant, despite having told Katrina that he was infertile, something Ames assumed, incorrectly, due to his prior use of estrogen, although Ames had never explained to Katrina why he believed he was infertile and Katrina had never asked. Although Katrina didn't want kids and had felt relief at a prior miscarriage, her pregnancy opened her up to the idea of motherhood. When Katrina shares the pregnancy news with Ames, he doesn't respond with the excitement Katrina hoped for. In the following days, and unbeknownst to Katrina, Ames concocts a plan to invite Reese, his ex-girlfriend, to co-parent with Katrina and him. Ames knows how badly Reese wanted to be a mother, he misses having Reese in his life, and he misses being in proximity to transness—his own, Reese's, and more broadly. Reese agrees to give this queer parenting relationship a shot, only to find out that Ames has not yet pitched this idea to Katrina. At this point, in fact, Katrina is still unaware that Ames had ever been a trans woman, something Ames has to divulge in order for his proposal to invite Reese into their family formation to make sense.

In the conversation that follows, Ames explains why having Reese as a co-parent would change his relationship to the idea of having the baby. Ames is willing to become a parent, you see, but not a *father*. His interest in this configuration of family is less because it is outside the typical heterosexual nuclear family structure and more because Ames knows that Reese will never see him as a man. Therefore, through proximity to Reese, through being viewed through her eyes, Ames could be a parent without being a father. Much to Ames's and Reese's surprise, Katrina agrees. Reese and Katrina, the two potential future moms, begin to develop a friendly relationship. They go on a "moms date" to create a baby registry, Reese meets Katrina's friends and joins in a women's night out, and so on. Then, their plan implodes. At the women's night, it becomes clear that Reese is the mistress of Katrina's friend's husband. As a result, Katrina pulls away. Reese responds with an angry letter accusing Katrina of homophobia—of only wanting the good parts of queerness and not the messy parts. Reese knows that if she sends the letter Katrina will end their arrangement, and Katrina does. But Ames's involvement with Katrina's pregnancy was somewhat conditional on parenting in this trans way. So—and this is a huge spoiler!—Katrina decides to get an abortion, although the book's ending leaves ambiguous whether she actually obtains the procedure. In the end, Ames requests to join Katrina for the appointment. She finally acquiesces, and tells Ames to invite Reese, too. Reese refuses the invitation. Here is why, from Reese's perspective:

> In her mind she had given the baby up to Katrina, and now, it was with dismay—perhaps even horror—that she had to acquiesce that the baby's mother had the right to abort. That another woman could end the existence of a baby that she had come to imagine, softly, tentatively, at the center of her future life. She had found her emotions and, in the two days since Ames told her about the abortion, had veered in the direction of pro-life politics. Never before had she found her thoughts trending to the personhood of an unborn child. But after thinking about the invitation for a few hours Reese called Ames again. "Why would she invite me?" she wondered aloud to him. "Is it possible she wants us to talk her out of it?"... Even as she spoke, Reese could again hear the twisted conservatism of her position. She'd told other women to fuck off with their opinions about her body, her hormones.[53]

After reading this passage, in which a trans woman expresses antiabortion ideas and recognizes the irony of doing so, you might be wondering why I am suggesting that this book contains rich lessons for queering reproductive justice. Let me explain. In the only fictional account of abortion and femme transness that I know of, the connection between the two is not articulated in terms of an individual. Instead, a trans woman's dreams are being crushed by a woman who cannot imagine creating a family in such uncertain circumstances. This uncertainty is not connected to Reese or her transness, but it *is* connected to gender and transness. Katrina had expressed to Ames that she wanted stability, which for her included knowing that she could imagine to some degree what their future would look like. Ames responded that he couldn't promise that he would never transition back to being a woman, something Katrina read as lack of stability, and that ultimately led Katrina to decide to abort.

While Katrina's response is not exactly trans-affirming, viewing gender as inherently unstable and taking this instability seriously is a key feature of feminist, queer, and trans studies. So, too, is the idea that our gender is never ours alone—something we can see when Reese's motherhood dreams are smashed by someone else's unstable gender and another person's feelings about that instability. Peters is offering a model for thinking about abortion and transness alike in terms of intertwinement, rather than identity, which is in line with trans studies scholars' requests to imagine, as Abraham Weil says, "trans* as a collective mode of expression rather than a solitary confinement."[54] Peters's vision of that collective mode of expression is one that centers trans women, who are often missing from the conversations where people bring LGBTQ+ness to bear on reproduction, providing a counterpoint to what Paisley Currah describes as "the outsized role those on the trans-masculine side of the gender spectrum play in setting out the official gender line for trans politics."[55]

In offering this model of transness as collective rather than solitary, Peters takes on all of the hot button trans topics with stunning bravery. In interviews, she critiques trans rights advocates' focus on bathrooms, noting "it is incredibly undignified to have to stage your Human Rights Campaign about where you pee and it expends energy that could be used to build each other up positively." She admitted to feeling empathy for J. K. Rowling, who has expressed horrifying anti-trans ideas. And she noted she has "a lot of sympathy for people who detransition," arguing that the word should not be "weaponized" and that people who detransition should be able to do so without becoming politicized. As Peters says, "What I worry about is not so much detransitioning but if you create a precedent where you say you can't do this with your body; it opens the gates for all sorts of other precedents that affect everyone. The big one I think about is how it would affect abortion." Here, Peters frames conversations about detransitioning as potentially impacting how we think about abortion, rather than abortion dictating how we think about transness. In this deft maneuver, Peters connects abortion and transness by placing transness at the center, but not through individual trans people needing abortions or through de-gendering abortion—the typical approach, as I've suggested here and further explore in chapter 3. For Peters, abortion is about transness, which is about gender, but in ways that are impossible to see when we reduce the linkage to the level of the individual.

One might expect Peters to have been canceled for these kinds of statements. But I have not yet found a real critique of *Detransition, Baby* or of Peters's cultural commentary. Peters believes that this is because her work is fiction. "Unfortunately," she has said, "you can't really have those sorts of arguments intellectually and this is one of the reasons I write fiction and I don't write think pieces." But I desperately want to hold on to the possibility of having these arguments intellectually and also, like Torrey Peters and the other artists whose work appears in this book's conclusion, of finding creative outlets for them, as a way to begin to think about what it would look like to approach reproductive justice queerly.

## SOME QUEER SCAFFOLDING

I see approaching reproductive justice queerly as requiring theory as well as a commitment to inviting new people into reproductive justice work. I also see these two as interrelated. To actualize this invitation, we need to be able to translate theory so that it can travel in new ways, to new people, and to new places. Making academic theory accessible can look a lot of different ways. In my case it has included curating art exhibitions and building a mini golf course, as you'll read about in the book's epilogue, as well as incorporating assignments in my classes where students transform academic articles into board games, collages, jokes, and other creative cultural interventions. This book is another attempt at translation, at producing something that draws from and contributes to academic knowledge production while containing the capacity to move beyond academic circles. One of the more humbling critiques that I received on an earlier draft of this book was that it was still too theoretical and academic, getting too into the weeds of intellectual debates to be interesting to the vast majority of people.

I've tried to correct this impulse in many ways. One approach is worth noting. While I draw from hundreds of scholars throughout this book, there are two, in particular—Cathy Cohen and Lee Edelman—who pop up repeatedly, serving as a kind of messy queer scaffolding that functions as a through line for considering what it means to approach reproductive justice queerly.

This repetition, this mess, is intentional. One way for an idea to become familiar is to engage with it repeatedly. Another way is to engage with it in different circumstances or in relation to different contexts, especially, perhaps, those it was not designed to take up. Such an approach necessarily demonstrates theory's dexterity; understanding theory as dexterous, its promise lying in its promiscuity, is another tool for scholars, activists, and artists alike. Bringing forth the epistemological and political value of theory requires that we know it intimately, and repetition works in the service of intimate knowing.

Here, I want to spell out the arguments of Cathy Cohen and Lee Edelman, two scholars whose work has become foundational to queer theory, so that as you encounter my engagements with their work in later chapters it is already somewhat familiar. Let's start with Cohen, a political scientist and Black queer theorist. In her 1997 article "Punks, Bulldaggers, and Welfare Queens: The Radical Potential of Queer Politics?," Cohen outlines the problems transpiring within LGBTQ+ spaces that have limited their radical potential. First, Cohen says, there is a persistent lack of attention to the racial, gender, and class *differences* among LGBTQ+ people, and how these differences impact one's access to power. Second, the production of LGBTQ+ people as one kind of community in binary relation to heterosexual people makes it difficult to recognize that all straight people do not benefit from heteronormativity. Cohen argues that such approaches "misrepresent the distribution of power within and outside of lesbian, gay, bisexual and transgendered communities."[56]

To make these points, Cohen cites as examples the prohibition of heterosexual marriage between enslaved people, the moral panic around Black-women-headed households evident in the Moynihan Report, the forced sterilization at various times of Native and Puerto Rican women, and the demonization of so-called "welfare queens," who have been forced by the state to use birth control to access public assistance. These examples, Cohen says, speak to the "numerous ways that sexuality and sexual deviance from a prescribed norm have been used to demonize and to oppress various segments of the population," including some heterosexuals.[57] It is for this reason that Cohen pushes back against the queer versus straight binary LGBTQ+ activists invoke and, instead, distinguishes between "an upstanding, 'morally correct,' white, state-authorized, middle-class, male heterosexual" and "a culturally deficient, materially bankrupt, state-dependent, heterosexual woman of color."[58] Focusing on people's relationships to power vis-a-vis heteronormativity, Cohen says, can provide the "basis for radical coalition work." Put otherwise, so-called "welfare queens," always already presumed heterosexual due to their supposed hyper-reproduction, should be at the center of queer analyses and activism.[59] In many ways, Cohen is making the point that one can be LGBTQ+-identified and not be queer, just as one can be heterosexual and be quite queer. Ultimately, Cohen invites us to use this insight as a way to generate new coalitional approaches to LGBTQ+ activism that center eradicating racism, sexism, and classism and are queer in form and not just in name.

Like Cohen, Lee Edelman is concerned with the conservative ways that self-described queer activism has taken shape. In his polemical 2004 book *No Future: Queer Theory and The Death Drive*, Edelman, a literary theorist, suggests that we cannot understand how conservative LGBTQ+ politics have become or identify new, queerer ways forward unless we rethink the place of "the Child" in our movements. "The Child"—by which Edelman means the persistent deployment of images of children such that they operate beyond the calling up of any real, material, individual child—is hard to argue against, something that makes it seem like a potent political strategy. Indeed, we see those on the political right and the political left deploy children in their advocacy. But Edelman's work encourages us to exercise caution here precisely because the Child often represents conservative ideas and, even worse, "the fantasy subtending the image of the Child invariably shapes the logic within which the political must be thought."[60] The Child, Edelman says, is "the emblem of futurity's unquestioned value."[61] Queer politics needs to rethink its allegiance to the future and its deployment of the Child in the service of that allegiance. In fact, Edelman goes so far as to claim that "queerness name[s] the side of those not "fighting for the children."[62]

But what does this mean in practice? Edelman offers as an example singer, beauty queen, and anti-gay activist Anita Bryant, who ran an anti-gay campaign in Florida called "Save Our Children" in the late 1970s. LGBTQ+ rights activists responded to this variety of criticism that LGBTQ+ people posed a danger to children and to family life by claiming overtly that they value marriage, procreation, and family. In fact, in the years leading up to the 2015 *Obergefell* decision, advocates for LGBTQ+ marriage equality often made their demands by claiming that having access to a family recognized by the state would be good "for the children" of LGBTQ+ couples. They also argued that it would allow LGBTQ+ people access to the same benefits heterosexual people can access through marriage, such as tax breaks, citizenship, and health insurance.

At the time, queer theorists and leftist queer advocates argued against this line of reasoning, noting that this move would primarily benefit LGBTQ+ people who already had the most social and material capital. In order to access citizenship or health insurance through marriage, for example, one marrying person has to be a citizen or have health insurance already, and tax breaks tend to benefit the richest people. Making LGBTQ+ organizing synonymous with marriage equality, queer theorists and activists argued, was inherently conservative and anti-queer. While marriage equality broadened who can fit inside of culturally prescribed ideas of who and what are "normal," it did nothing to change the treatment of those who do not operate according to these cultural norms. Edelman's work created the foundation for these types of arguments by outlining how ideas that are being positioned as progressive can be quite conservative, and by demonstrating the centrality of the Child to this conservatism. Part of the reason that the Child can be hard to argue against, and why, therefore, it is seen as a slam-dunk political strategy, is that it represents the possibility of the future as something better than what we have now. But Edelman says the image of the future deployed in the name of the Child rarely veers far from the world we have now; instead, the Child is mobilized to uphold the current social order. By placing the Child at the center of our articulations of the future, advocates on the political left and political right engage in what Edelman terms "reproductive futurism," prioritizing their imagined future (which always already includes children) over addressing more immediate political situations.

Edelman's arguments have been widely criticized, and I also see the critiques his work has generated as useful for approaching reproductive justice queerly. José Esteban Muñoz suggests that Edelman's critique of the place of the Child in contemporary gay rights activism relies on a "figure of the child . . . as always already white."[63] That is, all children do not garner equitable concern, and ignoring this fact reproduces the very oppressions that queer theory should be dedicated to dismantling. Furthermore, all people don't have equitable access to the future—in figurative or real terms. "Racialized kids, queer kids, are not the sovereign princes of futurity," Muñoz writes. Reflecting on the value of Muñoz's reclaiming of the future, Gayatri Gopinath argues that Muñoz "lays claim to a futurity on behalf of those for whom it is systematically denied."[64] Ultimately, Muñoz wants us to "belong to a future that is often narrated as impossible but is nonetheless attainable and utterly necessary."[65]

It isn't just Edelman's ways of conceptualizing people and time (the future) without taking serious account of race that scholars have critiqued. Jennifer Doyle takes aim at the place of abortion and fetal imagery in *No Future*, noting that readers might find her position that "abortion plays a key role" in the book surprising for two reasons. First, *No Future* is "almost totally uninterested in female figures or questions of femininity" and, second, Edelman's reliance on fetal imagery to generate his arguments "has not been taken seriously in any of the critical responses." This latter point is interesting, Doyle says, because *No Future* is "perhaps the most hotly debated text in queer theory published in the past decade."[66] Indeed, Doyle was the first to ask queer theorists to consider what it means that a text that seems to be about the watering-down of queer politics through the symbolic image of "the Child" actually generates its rhetorical force through reflecting on a billboard with "an image of a fetus embedded in a woman's uterus, named by a slogan [on the billboard] as 'child,'" which is then re-narrated by Edelman as a "symbolic image of 'the Child.'" That is, neither Edelman nor his critics consider the implications of his slippage from fetus to child to Child. Doyle argues that critics' refusal to comment on the billboard scene or the unfortunate slippage from fetus to Child reflects queer theory's disinterest in abortion.

In making these crucial interventions, neither Cohen nor Edelman were attempting to queer reproductive justice. Nonetheless, their insights, along with the critical responses their work has generated, are surely valuable for doing so. Drawing from Edelman and Cohen, we ought to ask: What might queer and reproductive justice activism look like if it weren't fighting "for the children?" And what would happen to our ability to address abortion access if our queer coalitions moved beyond what people typically thought of as part of the LGBTQ+ umbrella and, instead, centered the welfare queen, a figure imagined as Black, poor, and hyperreproductive? Further, how can we do this centering without reproducing the stereotypes of "mothering while Black," as Jennifer Nash puts it, that tend to focus on suffering, trauma, violence, and death, rather than the rich vibrancy of Black motherhood?[67] And how do we do this work while being firmly attendant to the politics of the present without losing hope for something better than we can imagine in the here and now? I see Cohen's reclaiming of the welfare queen, which necessarily requires reimagining the affects that stick to Black mothers, and her argument for coalitions, as well as Edelman's critiques of the place of the imagined Child in current progressive politics and broader imaginings of the future, as crucial for approaching reproductive justice queerly.

## CHAPTER BY CHAPTER

To demonstrate what it means to queer reproductive justice, each of this book's chapters takes up a different reproductive justice issue—abortion, crisis pregnancy centers, surrogacy, parental leave, parenting—in a way that challenges now-commonsensical ideas in feminist and queer spaces about these very topics. Put simply, each chapter approaches a fairly typical reproductive justice topic in "queer" ways. I see the queer approach I use here as enabled by the messiness of the archive I have constructed, which includes analyses of various campaigns and nonprofit organizations, close reading of articles in the media, quantitative analyses, autotheory, art made by students, a roundtable with students, and another with feminist and queer parents. My approach here is indebted to the work of Martin Manalansan, who argues for seeing the value of mess, both in terms of what we allow into our archives and also our reading of our archives. For Manalansan, "mess, clutter, and muddled entanglements are the 'stuff' of queerness," and I have tried to honor—rather than resist—messiness in different ways in each of the chapters of this book.[68]

Chapter 1, "Surrogacy Without Surrogates: On Gay Men and Surrogacy," takes on commercial surrogacy, which feminist scholars have long debated. This chapter "queers" these prior debates by tracing the contradictory positions feminist and LGBTQ+ activists have taken in recent debates over surrogacy legislation. As New York's state legislature battled over a surrogacy bill in 2020, for example, prominent feminists, including Gloria Steinem, came out against commercial surrogacy, while prominent gay rights groups took a pro-surrogacy stance. Other self-identified feminist activists responded to Steinem with outrage, noting that "surrogacy is about bodily autonomy [and] feminists should embrace it."[69] Such a position ignores the many critiques of choice-based frameworks that have been developed by reproductive justice scholars and activists, though primarily in relation to abortion. As such, this chapter extends reproductive justice critiques of choice-based feminism by putting these critiques in conversation with surrogacy. In doing so, the chapter discusses the ethics of surrogacy and the question of whether everyone has the "right" to reproduce biologically through the lenses of queer theory and critiques of racial capitalism. How, in other words, do we square Black feminist critiques of the exploitative nature of surrogacy and its disproportionate impact on poor women, who are more likely to be Indigenous, Black, and Latina, with the fact that gay men and some people with disabilities would inherently be unable to reproduce biologically if we take such arguments to their logical conclusions? How might a queer reproductive justice politic help us to figure out when we center LGBTQ+ concerns and when we center (and I mean center, not reference) race, class, gender, disability, or geography? Through addressing these questions, this chapter suggests that critiquing that which has been largely celebrated is key to approaching reproductive justice queerly.

Chapter 2, "The Heteronormativity of Paid Parental Leave," examines discourses surrounding parental leave. US feminists discussing parental leave are critical of one primary issue: the lack of federally institutionalized parental leave policies. Few discussions that position themselves as feminist question the logics that drive support for parental leave or their ramifications. Queer theorists, by contrast, have said remarkably little about parental or family leave—despite the field's concerns with the nuclear family as a legitimate social unit through which sexual citizenship is granted, as well as the results of the affects that stick to this social formation. In taking a queer approach to parental leave, I am not advocating against government or employer paid leaves that compensate for the work of social reproduction. I am, however, advocating for a more capacious approach to paid leave as something that should be available to those who engage in many forms of social reproduction beyond childbearing and rearing.

Chapter 3, "The Woman Question, The Trans Question: On Abortion and Gender," takes on the cultural shift within self-identified liberal, leftist, and progressive circles away from discussing abortion primarily as a women's issue and toward the use of ostensibly less gendered terms. This chapter addresses this thorny issue by considering as a case study the production of the play *Jane: Abortion and the Underground*, which I co-produced with a trans student at Middlebury College in January 2020. The play tells the story of the Jane Collective, a group of housewives and college students who performed approximately eleven thousand illegal abortions during the late 1960s and early 1970s. This chapter reflects on students' discomfort with the play's attachment of abortion to women and addresses how we "queered" the play in ways that kept gender central.

Chapter 4, "Abortion as Gender Transgression: Reproductive Justice, Queer Theory, and Anti–Crisis Pregnancy Center Activism," tells the story of End Fake Clinics, a queer reproductive justice student club at the University of California, Santa Barbara, that worked with the student government to make UCSB the first university to ban crisis pregnancy centers from falsely advertising on campus. This chapter archives and analyzes End Fake Clinics' activism, ultimately arguing that approaching abortion as a form of gender transgression allows us to recognize deeper connections between queer and reproductive issues. Those who abort disrupt, and it is time we think of the abortive woman as a gender transgressor. In the case of End Fake Clinics, creating a queer reproductive justice politic was enabled by the deep affective connections developed through the group, as well as by participants' collective belief that their activism would be at its best when informed by feminist and queer theory. As such, End Fake Clinics provides us with more complicated ways to approach queering reproductive justice beyond the typical identitarian models plaguing liberal activism.

Chapter 5, "Queer Feminist Parenting," reflects on what it means to parent in feminist and queer ways. The chapter is composed of a roundtable with parents who practice feminist and queer parenting. Their insights are full of hope, vulnerability, beauty, and courage. The book's Conclusion, "Playing with Queer Theory: The Queer Potential of Art," also includes a roundtable, in which I reflect with two of my former research assistants on the political and epistemological benefits of art for queering reproductive justice. Each of the people contributing to these two roundtables are in my affective, political, and intellectual networks; they are fellow scholars, activists, mentors, and former students. But, most importantly, they are my friends. I note this point here because my approach is meant to draw attention to the ways in which the affects of queer kinship networks can enable the circulation of collaboratively created knowledge in decidedly queer ways. Indeed, I set out to create a book that is as queer in form as it is in content, and my queer networks enabled this project's queerness.

In addition to the kind of material typical in academic books, *Reproductive Justice, Queerly* includes a few, well, queer components. Beyond the collective insights generated through the two roundtables, the concluding chapter includes art made at events where students read drafts of each chapter of this book, talked about them, and then made art reflecting on the chapter or their conversation about it. Organized by my research assistants, mostly during the pandemic, each of these queer art nights took place over the course of an hour or an hour and a half. The point was to create a space for coming together and for practicing the generation of queer thinking about reproductive justice. Of the sixty attendees who participated in an art night, most did not think of themselves as artists, and creating art was, in fact, a byproduct of the process. Considering that the event structure meant that the art featured here was created in such a short period, some of it is really remarkable. But, again, the art was never really the point. The feedback from those who attended the art nights, which came to me via my weekly research team meetings, informed the shape of this book. In the book's conclusion, I reflect with former students on the queerness of the art nights and our process.

As the queer art nights suggest, my desire to queer reproductive justice extends far beyond this book. In the book's epilogue, I discuss two outgrowths of my attempt to do this work queerly, both of which represent my commitment to public feminism. In 2023, I facilitated two public feminism fellowships, both of which culminated in art exhibitions about reproductive justice, and I co-created Reproductive Justice Mini Golf, a playable course. This book also includes a companion website, which you can access at www.queeringreproductivejustice.com. There, you'll find even more art made at art nights, a downloadable Cards for Queering Reproductive Justice game (which was inspired by Cards Against Humanity), and a queer reproductive justice trivia game. These elements are meant to help this book's arguments circulate beyond its own contours and to increase interest in the book's ideas, even among those unlikely to read it. We might, then, see the first three chapters—on surrogacy, paid parental leave, and the use of gendered language to discuss abortion—as articulations of problems in contemporary conversations about these very topics. The final three chapters—on queer reproductive justice activism, queer feminist parenting, and the queer generation of art—as well as the epilogue, serve as examples of what queer solutions can look like. Mostly, I hope that this book inspires both increased interest in reproductive justice among those committed to queer justice and also increased interest in queer justice among those advocating for reproductive justice. We need one another.

# 1 Surrogacy Without Surrogates

## ON GAY MEN AND SURROGACY

Like the Kardashians, it seems like surrogacy is everywhere these days. Perhaps these two things are related. That is, maybe surrogacy's ubiquity can be explained, in part, because celebrities' use of surrogates is increasingly in the news. Far beyond Kim and Khloe Kardashian, both of whom have children through surrogacy, many celebrities have made headlines for using surrogates, including media personality Andy Cohen, news anchor Anderson Cooper, fitness professional Shaun T, actor Neil Patrick Harris, designers Nate Berkus and Jeremiah Brent, fashion and style expert Tan France, and musician Elton John—all of whom are gay men. Social reception has been largely positive. An article on the "Gay Parents To Be" website, entitled "LGBTQ+ Celebrities and Surrogacy: Why Representation Matters," even calls for *more* LGBTQ+ celebrities to make their so-called surrogacy journeys public. The article begins: "While images of 'traditional' pregnancy are always just a scroll away on social media, we're still working on making LGBTQIA+ family building (in all its forms) visible and normalized. The more we see different experiences of family building on our feeds, the more that queer people will feel encouraged to pursue the path to parenthood that best works for them. Surrogacy is one of those important family-building options for the queer community."[1]

Here, like elsewhere in conversations about surrogacy in LGBTQ+ spaces, surrogacy is celebrated. We're told that for "queer people" and "the queer community" surrogacy is an "important family-building option." But who, exactly, are these imagined "queer people," and who is in this imagined "queer community?" The "Gay Parents To Be" article doesn't address these questions directly, but it doesn't need to. Through its references, it makes clear who it imagines as in need of surrogates, and therefore as part of the "queer community" it invokes: gay men who are coupled and married. The article claims that Neil Patrick Harris and David Burtka, who had twins via surrogacy in 2010, "publicly normalized surrogacy in a way that hadn't been done before." And a decade or so later, when Tan France of Netflix's popular show *Queer Eye* and his husband welcomed a baby via surrogate, the couple said to "millions of young LGBTQIA+ people around the world that surrogacy is a normal, beautiful option for creating a family." We are meant to understand, of course, that this normalization is positive.

In this "Gay Parents To Be" essay, and, indeed, in many of the conversations about the use of surrogacy among LGBTQ+ people, women are rarely mentioned—either as people who might also want to use a surrogate or, more importantly for the purposes of this chapter, as surrogates themselves. In fact, the term "women" appears just once in the "Gay Parents To Be" article and is used to refer to a figure positioned in opposition to LGBTQ+ people who might use a surrogate: a heterosexual reproductive subject, just one among "thousands and thousands" of people posting photos of themselves on social media while "smiling and holding their bellies with their husbands or boyfriends beaming at them." But, the article continues, "social media can also be a great tool to make less traditional processes for family building visible, which can be particularly empowering for people who are outside of the 'normal' conception bubble." Here, the pregnant woman is the marker of the "traditional" reproductive process, an annoying normie. Equating the image of the pregnant woman with "traditional processes for family building" ignores that images of pregnant bellies rarely capture the processes by which the pregnancy transpired. Furthermore, those smiling women, holding their bellies, also could have used assistive reproductive technologies not so different from what the article is celebrating. Those smiling women, holding their bellies, could also be . . . gasp . . . surrogates.

That an article posted on a website dedicated to LGBTQ+ family-making does not recognize this point speaks to how little surrogates themselves are a part of the conversation about LGBTQ+ people using surrogacy. This chapter takes up this issue. It asks: What is said about surrogates in conversations about LGBTQ+ family-making? What is implied? When and where is the surrogate a ghost? The relationship between surrogates and intended parents is one that feminists have long debated, focusing on the ethics of commercial surrogacy and articulating positions that have historically coalesced around fears of exploitation and oppression, on the one hand, and agency and possibility on the other.[2] Regardless of their stance, surrogacy's opponents and proponents alike have used discourses of feminism to articulate their positions. This chapter both outlines these conversations and "queers" them through tracing how the figure of the gay man, and by extension, the so-called "queer" family, is informing contemporary debates over surrogacy. In short, I argue that the figure of the gay man functions to reduce the complexity of feminist critiques of surrogacy, namely those regarding its racial and class implications.

As this chapter demonstrates, gay men have become central figures in conversations about surrogacy. A 2018 *Washington Post* article notes that gay men—rather than heterosexual couples—are even imagined as the ideal client by some surrogates.[3] Christina Fenn, the surrogate profiled in the article, only carries for gay men, noting she is reluctant to be a surrogate for heterosexual couples because "they usually don't want contact with the surrogate after the birth and are notoriously controlling during the pregnancy," a sentiment Fenn has heard expressed frequently in her circle of fellow surrogates. Another article in *The Atlantic* speaks to this point: "Gay men are the favorite clients of many surrogate moms; one emotional complication is removed from the tricky relationship, because the gay intended parents don't suffer the understandable jealousy/inferiority issues that can plague infertile intended mothers."[4] Scholars have made similar points. Sociologist Heather Jacobson notes that while some surrogates might not want to work with gay men due to disapproval of gayness, others actually "wish to work with gay men because of what they see as gay men's positivity," a sense of optimism that is harder to generate among heterosexual couples or single women who are using surrogacy as a result of infertility. Other surrogates, Jacobson notes, seek out gay men to demonstrate their support for LGBTQ+ people.[5]

This chapter examines the relationship of gay men to surrogacy, in part, to analyze how a topic that has long been considered feminist emerged as an LGBTQ+ issue. That gay men have become the face of battles over surrogacy reflects the long history of LGBTQ+ movements becoming more conservative. Over the last few decades, LGBTQ+ advocates have increasingly made their political demands based on claims that LGBTQ+ people are normal and desire inclusion into social structures synonymous with normativity, key among them marriage.[6] Laura Briggs argues that "gay political demands for marriage, for protection for reproductive labor—from caring for children and sick or disabled partners to marriage" are part of a larger pattern of privatizing reproductive labor. As Briggs shows, "the gay married" are, in part, responsible for "the privatization of dependency."[7] That the use of surrogacy by gay men is celebrated both reflects and extends the homonormativity, as Lisa Duggan terms it, of so much contemporary LGBTQ+ culture and, with it, the shrinking nature of queer kinship creation.[8]

In what follows, I begin by providing a brief genealogy of feminist and queer scholarship on surrogacy. I then analyze two different case studies in which LGBTQ+ness comes into contact with surrogacy. The first is New York's "Love Makes a Family" campaign, which resulted in the Child-Parent Security Act, legalizing surrogacy in the state. The second is the surrogacy advocacy organization Men Having Babies. I then discuss how race and class do and do not appear in conversations about gay men and surrogacy by focusing, in part, on the industry that has popped up to support gay men using crowdsourcing to secure funding for surrogacy. In so doing, this chapter raises the question of whether everyone has the "right" to reproduce biologically. Put more provocatively: How do we square Black feminist critiques of the exploitative nature of surrogacy and its disproportionate impact on poor women, who are more likely to be from the Global South or (within the US context) Black, Indigenous, and Latina, with the fact that gay men and some people with disabilities would be unable to reproduce biologically if we take such arguments to their logical conclusions? How might a queer reproductive justice politic help us to figure out when we center LGBTQ+ concerns and when we center (and I mean center, not reference) race, gender, class, or disability?[9]

Addressing these questions is crucial in this moment not only because images of gay men couples are increasingly being used to generate positive affects around surrogacy but also because the surrogacy industry is growing. A 2016 CDC report on IVF trends in the United States shows that between 1999 and 2013, gestational surrogacy rose from 1 to 2.5 percent of all IVF cycles. During that time, there were a total of 30,927 IVF cycles with gestational surrogates, resulting in 18,400 live births in the United States alone.[10] Unfortunately, this is the best and most recent data publicly available. The CDC has not updated their information on Assisted Reproductive Technology (ART) and gestational carriers since 2016, except to note possible birth defects or links to autism related to using ART.[11] According to the Society for Assisted Reproductive Technologies, more than 1,000 babies are born annually in the U.S. via gestational surrogacy.[12] And, of course, the United States is just one part of the much bigger global commercial surrogacy industry, the value of which one scholar estimates at approximately $6 billion annually.[13] In cases where intended parents travel across borders, they are often trying to escape higher costs or more stringent regulations in their home countries—a form of border crossing that scholars, including Laura Harrison, describe as "reproductive tourism."[14] We do not know the exact number of people who engage in this kind of travel because this data is not publicly available, but we do know that surrogacy is on the rise, both in the United States and globally.

## FEMINIST POSITIONS ON SURROGACY

Such growth has transpired despite feminist critiques of surrogacy. For the last few decades, feminists have written extensively about surrogacy, taking positions that range from scathing rebukes of how surrogacy exploits women of color, low-income women, and women in the Global South to advocating for a full "parenthood market" wherein essentially everyone would be a surrogate and no one would raise the biological children they carried and birthed. Although a few pro-surrogacy feminist texts exist, most feminist scholarship on surrogacy is skeptical about the practice.

One of surrogacy's most notable critics is feminist legal scholar Dorothy Roberts. In her article "Race and the New Reproduction," Roberts argues that reproductive technologies, including but not limited to surrogacy, perpetuate both sexism and racism. As Roberts puts it, "IVF serves more to help married men produce genetic offspring than to give women greater reproductive freedom." She continues, "At least half of women who undergo IVF are themselves *fertile*, although their husbands are not. These women could conceive a child far more safely and inexpensively by using artificial insemination although the child would not be genetically related to the husband. Underlying their use of IVF, then, is often their husbands' insistence on having a genetic inheritance." Roberts makes clear that "the desire to have genetically-related children is influenced, if not created, by our culture." On this point, Roberts is in alignment with prior feminist arguments for "abandoning the genetic model of parenthood because of its origins in patriarchy and its 'preoccupation with male seed.'"[15]

What Roberts adds to these prior feminist critiques of surrogacy is a focus on race. In fact, Roberts argues that reproductive technologies, including surrogacy, "reflect and reinforce the racial hierarchy in America." That is, surrogacy is a practice that at once relies on underpaid labor by women of color (especially when we consider surrogacy globally) and is largely inaccessible to people of color—both because of its exorbitant cost and also because many people of color, particularly Black people, distrust genetic technologies due to a long history of being told they are genetically inferior. According to Roberts, many Black people "are skeptical about any obsession with genes" because "they know that their genes are considered undesirable." To support this point, Roberts notes that Black people "make up a disproportionate number of infertile people avoiding reproductive technologies." Perhaps these technologies are less important for Black people considering that their "family ties have traditionally reached beyond the bounds of the nuclear family to include extended kin and nonkin relationships," precisely the kinds of relationships that surrogacy produces as outside of "family." For these reasons, Roberts says we need to be critical of framings that suggest that ART is a way to "subvert conventional family norms." In fact, considering that these technologies are typically used to help mostly white, heterosexual, married couples reproduce biologically, "they more often reinforce the status quo than challenge it."

These technologies are, in short, more "conforming than liberating," as Roberts puts it. Ultimately, Roberts concludes that "these technologies are harmful and that their use should therefore be discouraged."[16]

Over the course of her esteemed career, Roberts has reconsidered some of these positions, notably how she earlier "contrasted policies that penalize poor Black women's childbearing with the high-tech fertility industry that promotes childbearing by more affluent white women."[17] "Rather than place these women in opposition" in what Roberts calls a "reproductive hierarchy," as she felt she had done in some prior work, Roberts began to take another approach: analyzing women of color and white women "together in relation to the neoliberal trend toward privatization and punitive governance." As she argues, "Both population control programs and genetic selection technologies reinforce biological explanations for social problems and place reproductive responsibility on women, thus privatizing remedies for illness and social inequality."[18] Notably, Roberts did not change her position on the conservative nature of reproductive technologies.

Extending Roberts's analysis of the racialization of surrogacy, Laura Harrison's *Brown Bodies, White Babies* examines cross-racial gestational surrogacy, that is, when the race of the surrogate differs from that of the intended parents and the fetus. In these arrangements, the intended parents are typically white, middle-class, heterosexual, married couples. As such, Harrison argues that these reproductive technologies are primarily available to those who already conform to "hegemonic and traditionally restrictive family formations," people who use these technologies as "mere aids to natural, heterosexual reproduction." These "mere aids" are, of course, humans whose labor has been, as Harrison says, "virtually ignored." In the case of the cross-racial surrogacy arrangements Harrison analyzes, those laboring are largely women of color and those paying are more financially secure white families.[19]

This kind of racialized reproductive labor is not new. Sociologist Amrita Pande notes that historically "women in socially subservient positions, including, for instance, slaves and domestic workers, have served as surrogates."[20] Alys Weinbaum's *The Afterlife of Reproductive Slavery* makes clear the extent to which these histories continue to permeate the practice today. In fact, Weinbaum notes that "Black feminist legal scholars studying surrogacy recognized slave breeding as a conceptual antecedent for surrogacy." Weinbaum argues that surrogacy is only possible because of what she terms "the slave episteme," which "renders the racialized capacity to reproduce human biological commodities thinkable."[21] As Weinbaum argues, "there are two periods in modern history during which in vivo reproductive labor power and reproductive products have been engineered for profit: during the four centuries of chattel slavery in the Americas and Caribbean and now, again, in our present moment."[22] What Weinbaum demonstrates is that "slavery is epistemologically central to biocapitalism even when biocapitalist processes and products do not immediately appear to depend upon slavery as antecedent."[23] Surrogacy is, for Weinbaum, one of those processes, and it produces one of those products that is not self-evidently connected to slavery but that actually is.

In addition to being distinctly racialized, the labor of surrogacy, feminists contend, is also clearly classed. As April Cherry notes, surrogacy contracts "most often involve working-class women who agree to act as surrogates because of their limited economic means and intended parents with large amounts of disposable income."[24] Feminists worry that surrogacy commodifies poor and working-class women's bodies, turning them into a good to be bought, sold, and used on the market in a way that is distinct precisely because, as Roberts notes, a surrogate's workday quite literally never ends. It is for this reason that some feminists have argued that surrogacy is unlike all other forms of labor under capitalism. Some feminists have equated surrogacy with sex work as a way to argue against both, but I find that often these linkages are rooted in three ways of thinking that feminists have long argued against: anti-sex ideology (the belief that sex is harmful to women); sexual exceptionalism (the belief that once sex is involved, the thing it is involved with changes; that is, sexual assault is imagined as necessarily worse than other forms of assault, sex work is imagined as necessarily worse than other forms of work, and so on); and gender essentialism (the belief that there are universal, biological, and fixed aspects of gender that make women and men different, and therefore, make sex work and surrogacy alike emotionally taxing for women).[25] The conflation of sex work and surrogacy also ignores many differences between the practices, including that a surrogate's workday never ends and that the intended outputs of the labor are distinct; sex work is meant to lead to sexual pleasure (among other things) while surrogacy is meant to lead to more (normative, biologically linked) families.

So, if we take seriously feminists' claims about the uniqueness of surrogacy labor, what, we might ask, would fair compensation look like for a job unlike any other? Minimum wage is a pretty low bar, but let's start there, even though minimum wage laws do not apply to surrogates. If they did, surrogates would make far more than they currently do. For instance, surrogates work anywhere between fourteen and twenty-two months, according to one surrogacy agency.[26] The first four to five months include completing an extensive application and screening process, acquiring medical records, matching with intended parents, drafting legal contracts, beginning a cycle and medication schedule, and, finally, transferring the embryo.[27] The cycle schedule and medication phase alone take about four weeks, while the embryo transfer and early pregnancy takes approximately six weeks. So, even prior to a successful embryo transfer, a surrogate's body is working non-stop for ten weeks or so. Add to that forty weeks of pregnancy and seven weeks of postpartum recovery. The total number of working hours for surrogates, then, is at least 9,576—a conservative calculation that does not account for the number of hours surrogates invest into the twelve to twenty-one week process prior to the medication phase, the length of time associated with any failed IVF attempts before the pregnancy sticks (and there are typically two to three),[28] or the extreme variations in postpartum recovery.

But surrogates are not paid even close to minimum wage for any of these 9,576 hours. In Georgia and Wyoming, the states with the lowest minimum wage at $5.15 per hour, the surrogate's salary would be more than $49,000—or nearly $22,000 more than the mean US surrogate's earnings of $27,162.80.[29] In California, where the minimum wage is $15.00 per hour, a surrogate's salary would be nearly $144,000. Even worse, surrogates often get paid nothing at all until the successful embryo transfer, and all payments stop if they miscarry.[30] Surrogates are guaranteed no income, regardless of how many hours they invest into their job.

The issue of monetary compensation for pregnancy labor is key to feminist discussions of surrogacy, an issue that becomes even more complicated when considering the transnational nature of the surrogacy industry, since intended parents from the Global North often hire women of color from the Global South to act as surrogates. A great deal of feminist scholarship on surrogacy focuses on how this dynamic has played out in India, in particular, because of the early centrality of India to the global surrogacy market, before it outlawed the practice in 2018.[31] Part of the reason India was attractive to intended parents from outside of the country is because, as Sara Ainsworth notes, Indian surrogates received quality medical care and the overall cost was significantly less than elsewhere because Indian surrogates' wages were lower than in the United States.[32] For example, in 2016 Aasima, an Indian surrogate, said she received 4,000 rupees (or $54) as a monthly stipend; upon delivering the baby, she would receive an additional 4 lakh rupees ($5,400).[33] Such figures suggest, as Fariyal Ross-Sheriff argues, that "the agreements drawn by medical tourism agencies and clinics protect the interests of the commissioning parents, the agencies, and the clinics over the interests of the surrogate."[34]

It is for these reasons that Serene Khader questions whether "transnational surrogacy is simply a 'worse' version of domestic surrogacy."[35] Indian surrogates, Khader says, were in an especially unique position because they were forced to deal with racist, sexist, and classist assumptions from both inside and outside their home country. But at the same time, Khader insists that we should not think of poor women in India as more easily exploitable than women in the West. In fact, Khader argues that "poor Indian surrogates are *less likely* to be taken advantage of than their Northern counterparts" [emphasis added] for two primary reasons. First, poor Indian women likely decided to become surrogates for what Khader describes as rational economic reasons, rather than due to the altruism messages communicated to surrogates in the United States. Second, they were able to benefit economically in ways that are not true of US surrogates because there was "no alternative form of employment [that] allows poor Indian women such a quick and large infusion of capital"—something that is not true in the United States, where minimum wage jobs that pay more than surrogacy are widely available.[36] Despite the influx of capital enabled by surrogacy, India outlawed the practice following debates about the ethics of paying for children and the exploitation of low-income women.

Such concerns have not been a part of recent conversations about surrogacy in the United States, as I demonstrate later in this chapter. Perhaps this difference accounts for the largely unregulated nature of surrogacy in the United States. One study found that wealthy European gay men often choose surrogates in the United States despite the higher costs—something even true among intended parents who live in countries where surrogacy is legal—because, as Heather Jacobson says, the US market allows for things restricted or prohibited elsewhere. These men are also drawn to the United States because their citizenship worries are "alleviated by U.S. legal clarity."[37] The lack of federal legislation regarding surrogacy means that what is perceived as legal clarity transpires at the state level and, therefore, regulation varies widely state by state. The company Hatch, which describes itself as the "the first and most established egg donor and surrogacy agency,"[38] posted an essay to its website entitled "Explore the Best U.S. States for Surrogacy in 2023." Not surprisingly, it is under the "Intended Parents" tab, rather than the tab for surrogates. "In the most surrogacy-friendly states," the essay asserts, "intended parents can receive the pre-birth orders regardless of their sexual orientation, marital status, and sometimes the genetic linkage to the baby."[39] Never once in Hatch's calculation of "surrogacy-friendly states" is the treatment of surrogates considered.

This context is precisely why feminists have been critical of the surrogacy industry. However, not all feminists oppose the practice. Often feminists seem resigned to the existence of the surrogacy industry, and rather than arguing for outlawing it, they advocate for better regulation. Legal scholar Martha Ertman, for instance, argues that we should see surrogacy as part of a broader "parenthood market" in which many aspects of parenthood are already commodified, and further, that we should see surrogacy compensation as a key component of this market. As Ertman notes, the surrogacy doctors, lawyers, and contract brokers who dedicate just a few hours to the process are allowed to get paid, and yet the surrogate, who "is on task twenty-four hours a day altering her nutrition and other behaviors, risking physical injury, undergoing profound emotional and hormonal changes, and also enduring extraordinary physical pain and hardship while giving birth" was not, in many places, able to get paid. And nowhere was she, or is she, paid an hourly wage comparable to the doctors, lawyers, and contract brokers involved with her case. Ertman describes the fact that the surrogate is "doing the most work in the transaction" while public policy forbade "her from receiving payment" as a paradox.[40]

Ertman's advocacy for compensating surrogacy labor was especially crucial in 2003, when she published her article, because, at that point, it was still illegal for surrogates to get paid in much of the United States.[41] (In 2025, compensated surrogacy is legal in all but three states: Michigan, Louisiana, and Nebraska.)[42] Despite advocating for paying surrogates, however, Ertman does not make an argument for what their compensation should be. As such, her article leaves unanswered the question that her analysis raises: How much is a pregnancy worth and who gets to decide? Instead of taking on this question, Ertman makes the argument for surrogacy's benefits by shifting her focus to intended parents, asserting that surrogacy is beneficial because it "facilitates formation of families on the basis of intent and function rather than biology and heterosexuality."[43] Ertman questions the idea that a parenthood market is necessarily a problem, arguing instead that it "furthers human flourishing by allowing gay and single people to become parents."[44]

Ertman's deployment of "gay" people in her discussion of surrogacy occurred more than twenty years ago. Since then, many other scholars have followed suit. Legal scholar Khiara Bridges is one of them. While Bridges carefully considers the positions of those who worry that surrogacy extends racism and sexism, she ultimately concludes that the current moment necessitates that these stances be reconsidered because surrogacy can "enable persons who are unprivileged by virtue of sexual orientation to have children." "The most significant shift that might merit a reconsideration of surrogacy," Bridges says, "is the increasing recognition and legitimation of lesbian, gay, bisexual, and transgender (LGBT) persons and the families that they have created and desire to create."[45] Bridges recognizes that current surrogacy trends, including "white couples' failure to look to US-born women of color for surrogacy services," reflect ongoing racism, and, therefore, that "those who are interested in racial justice" may still not be convinced to support surrogacy.[46] Still, Bridges concludes that "there are more desirable avenues for destabilizing racial hierarchies and undoing the marginalization of unprivileged persons and families. These avenues are more desirable because they do not involve limiting opportunities for LGBT persons, but rather expanding opportunities for poor people of color of all sexual orientations and gender identities."[47]

But it isn't "LGBT persons" who are at the center of studies about LGBTQ+ness and surrogacy. It is gay men. Take, for instance, Judith Stacey's examination of surrogacy, which focuses on "comparatively affluent First World gay men" intended parents in Los Angeles.[48] Or Marcin Smietana's research on "single men and gay couples who are forming families using surrogacy and egg donation."[49] Or Pablo Pérez Navarro's work on gay men in Madrid who hire US-based surrogates.[50] Or Heather Jacobson's analysis of how the US surrogacy industry markets itself to gay men. Jacobson even frames surrogacy as "a rights and justice issue that intersects with and takes shape within broader and multiple reproductive rights and justice issues.'"[51] Yet Jacobson's analysis of "LGBTQ participation" in surrogacy is limited to gay men, whose experiences with surrogacy, Jacobson says, deserve more scholarly attention. Perhaps this is why she decided that even if a surrogacy agency's website mentioned friendliness toward "same-sex" couples but showed photos of a lesbian couple, it would not count toward her tally of agencies friendly to gay men. In short, gay men are the center of scholarly analyses of LGBTQ+ surrogacy, even when LGBTQ+ness more broadly is invoked.

## WHO ARE SURROGATES? WHO ARE INTENDED PARENTS?

Feminist theorists' concerns about the exploitation involved in surrogacy make sense when one considers the social locations of surrogates alongside those of intended parents. Unfortunately, available demographic data on surrogates and intended parents in the United States are not easy to come by. More data exist about transnational surrogacy, especially in the Indian context, although since surrogacy is no longer legal in India, the usefulness of these data for understanding the current global surrogacy industry is limited. In short, there is a dearth of data-driven conversations about surrogacy. Still, when it comes to transnational commercial surrogacy, we often hear that the transaction involves, as one scholar put it, "white and/or monied intending parent(s) from wealthier countries hiring women of color from poorer countries and/or lower socioeconomic classes as surrogates, brokered by international agencies—although permissive states in the U.S. have also become major hubs for commercial surrogacy, with many white, middle-class women acting as surrogates."[52]

Who exactly are these "middle-class" surrogates? And even if they are "middle-class," are they still surrogates because they need money? Most middle-class people have jobs because we need income, after all. One study of surrogates in the United States found that their education, income, and employment status varied. Among the surveyed surrogates, 31.9 percent had high school diplomas or GEDs, 28.9 percent had associate's degrees, 24.5 percent had bachelor's degrees, and 14.7 percent had graduate or professional degrees. Household incomes varied too; 28.6 percent of surrogates had household incomes of $100,000 or higher, 18.7 percent were in the $75,000-$99,999 range, 27.6 percent were in the $50,000-$74,999 range, 21.2 percent in the $25,000-$49,999 range, and 3.9 percent had incomes less than $25,000. Finally, 7.4 percent had used public assistance in the last year.[53] Other data indicate, however, that surrogates in the United States are largely working class. According to one surrogacy agency, the average household income for surrogates is below $60,000.[54] Laura Harrison notes that 40 percent of surrogates are otherwise unemployed or receive financial assistance, or both.[55] One study found that 49 percent of surrogates reported being otherwise unemployed.[56] These facts persist despite surrogacy agency restrictions designed to remove financially precarious women from applicant pools. These restrictions might explain why the most financially precarious women are rarely hired as surrogates (they challenge the surrogacy industry's narratives of itself as altruistic), while capitalism might explain why the majority of surrogates are working class or lower-middle class (they need the money), points I return to later in this chapter.

Data on the race and ethnicity of surrogates are even less widely available. In a study of surrogates in Los Angeles, 52 percent were white, compared to 38.2 percent Hispanic/Latina and 3.4 percent Asian—a higher proportion of white people and a lower proportion of Hispanic/Latina and Asian people than in the population of LA County.[57] In another study, 92.6 percent of surrogates were white.[58] A 2005 review of twenty-seven empirical studies, cited in Laura Harrison's *Brown Bodies, White Babies,* similarly describes most surrogates as women "in their twenties or thirties, White,

Christian, married, with children of their own."[59] At the same time, cross-racial gestational surrogacy makes up a significant proportion of surrogacy arrangements. An ethnographic study by anthropologist Heléna Ragoné estimated that 30 percent of arrangements in the largest surrogacy programs were between surrogates and intended parents of different racial and ethnic backgrounds.[60] More specific data are hard to find because the CDC, which is the only governmental organization that collects nationwide data on surrogacy, does not collect data on race or ethnicity.

Similar data problems plague our knowledge of intended parents, although the general consensus is that, for the most part, intended parents' class position affords them social privileges, including access to surrogacy. Surrogacy agencies offer anecdotes that serve as evidence for this point. In an article in *The Atlantic*, one surrogacy agency describes their clientele as "usually older, richer, better educated, often with graduate degrees, and more likely to come from large urban cities like New York, Los Angeles, Paris, and Tokyo."[61] In fact, this agency says that approximately 50 percent of their clients are international,[62] a number significantly higher than the CDC's estimate that 15.7 percent of intended parents who hire gestational surrogates in the United States are not US residents.[63] Another study found that between 2006 and 2013, the percentage of gestational surrogacy cycles in the United States that involved intended parents from outside of the country rose from 6.3 to 18.5 percent, providing further evidence that transnational surrogacy is on the rise.[64]

The number of (gay) men who are intended parents is also on the rise. According to the CDC's 2016 report, 10.5 percent of intended parents were either single men or men in relationships with other men.[65] An informal 2016 study by Fertility IQ, a fertility data service, which includes data from fertility clinics in more than ten cities, found that 10 to 20 percent of donor eggs were going to gay men using surrogates—up 50 percent from just five years earlier.[66] Anecdotal evidence from the agency featured in *The Atlantic* notes that the majority of clients are heterosexual, but that there has recently been an increasing number of gay men couples, as well as single people, utilizing surrogacy services.[67] Data also show that gay men comprise a large portion of surrogacy clients in places beyond the United States. One Canadian study found that 37.4 percent of surrogates were birthing children for single men or gay men couples.[68] Another study estimates that gay men make up 70 to 80 percent of surrogacy clients in Mexico.[69]

What is unspoken in these discussions about gay men hiring surrogates is that their class status—which reflects their gender and race—enables their surrogacy transactions. Data from the US Department of the Treasury indicates that the average household income of two married men with children is $275,000, more than double the income for heterosexual couples with children as well as married women couples with children.[70] Census data confirm similar patterns: Gay men couples have the highest household income of any couples, although the census data, which do not account for children, puts the median household income for gay men couples at $123,600, which is more than 20 percent higher than that of heterosexual and lesbian couples. These numerical differences are likely partially explained by differences in average versus median income, but may also reflect the significant class differences between gay men couples who have children and those who do not.[71]

The short answer to the questions with which this section opens—Who are surrogates? Who are intended parents?—is that surrogates are people who need the $27,000 pre-tax income they will, on average, earn through surrogacy, while intended parents are people who can pay $100,000–150,000 to hire a surrogate. With this understanding in place, let's turn to a recent New York state campaign to legalize surrogacy and a pro-surrogacy organization to explore the place of gay men in contemporary discussions of surrogacy.[72]

## "LOVE MAKES A FAMILY" AND THE CHILD-PARENT SECURITY ACT

On February 11, 2020, Andrew Cuomo, then the governor of New York, launched the Love Makes a Family campaign, one goal of which was to "support LGBTQ individuals and people struggling with fertility [to] start families."[73] At the time, New York was one of a handful of US states that had not legalized gestational surrogacy, which Cuomo described as "shameful" and "repugnant," considering his view of his state as a "national leader on LGBTQ rights."[74] Cuomo's promotion of the campaign often invoked "LGBTQ equality" and focused on same-sex couples' "right to conceive."[75] One year after launching Love Makes a Family, the Child-Parent Security Act was signed into law.

Like Cuomo, the media often discussed the legal protections proposed by Love Makes a Family and the Child-Parent Security Act as a matter of LGBTQ+ rights, and LGBTQ+ rights advocates largely celebrated the legislation. An article titled "New York 'Love Makes A Family' Campaign Fights for Legalized Surrogacy, LGBTQ Rights" speaks to this point. The article suggests that legalizing surrogacy is indistinguishable from LGBTQ+ rights and quotes LGBTQ+ advocates praising the campaign. Kristen Prata Browde, president of the LGBT Bar Association of New York, stated that "surrogacy is how couples with fertility issues and LGBTQ New Yorkers get their families started." Glennda Testone, executive director of the Lesbian, Gay, Bisexual & Transgender Community Center, similarly noted that "LGBTQ New Yorkers continue to have to fight for the right to conceive by surrogacy," a right Love Makes a Family was intended to ensure.[76] Browde and Testone were two of the twenty-two members of the Love Makes a Family Council, which also included two celebrities who have used surrogates (Bravo TV host Andy Cohen and comedian and actress Amanda Buteau), lawyers specializing in family law and surrogacy law, and various leaders of nonprofit organizations—primarily those focusing on LGBTQ+ rights and infertility advocacy. Notably absent from the council were representatives of reproductive justice groups, feminists who have been outspoken about the problems with surrogacy (such as New York City resident Gloria Steinem), and surrogates themselves.

News coverage of this case was widespread, and Love Makes a Family council members were front and center in it. One *New York Times* article, published about five months after the campaign was announced but before the Child-Parent Security Act was passed, quotes several council members. Written by David Kaufman, a gay man who used a surrogate to father two children, the article characterizes surrogacy as part of a "fertility equality movement . . . led mostly by L.B.G.T.Q. people."[77] In the article, Ron Poole-Dayan, Love Makes a Family council member and executive director of Men Having Babies, suggested that the proposed legislation was "about society extending equality to its final and logical conclusion."

One of the stories that Kaufman featured to argue that surrogacy is a matter of "fertility rights" and "fertility equality" was that of Captain Aguilera. As a veteran injured in combat, Aguilera would qualify for the military's fertility benefits—that is, if he weren't gay. Unfortunately for Aguilera, the military's "policy dictated that the couple must not only be married, but also that one partner 'must have an intact uterus and one functioning ovary,' while the other 'must be able to produce sperm.'"[78] Kaufman and Aguilera frame this policy as necessarily targeting gay men. As Captain Aguilera put it, "But what about gay men? . . . Why aren't we on equal footing?"—a question that leaves aside that the policy also excludes single people of any gender, unmarried couples, and heterosexual married couples who do not have the eggs, sperm, or uterus required to create and carry a fetus.

The question also necessarily ignores all of the ways in which gay men—by virtue of being men—are on far more than equal footing. We might even say that gay men in a position to hire a surrogate have a third foot, especially compared to surrogates or even some heterosexual couples, who, on average, earn less than gay men couples precisely because women earn less than men. Put more directly, surrogacy costs less for gay couples than it does for anyone else—not in raw numbers, of course, but as a percentage of annual income or assets, a point I return to later in this chapter. What is perhaps most ironic about the critique of the military's policy is that the policy traffics in the same biological idealism as the article critiquing the policy for its unfair impact on gay men. Despite Kaufman's claim that the fertility equality movement "envisions a future when the ability to create a family is no longer determined by one's wealth, sexuality, gender or biology," his notion of "family" requires biological children and his notion of "equality" is limited to expanding access to the biological family unit.[79]

This centering of gay men in discussions of surrogacy is also apparent in the promotional materials for the Child-Parent Security Act. In one video interview, Assemblywoman Amy Paulin, who introduced the legislation, briefly addresses concerns about commercial surrogacy, stating that it had been outlawed in New York "in a time when they probably should have. There was a great deal of concern about making sure that women were not taken advantage of." But, Paulin notes, "times have changed." To support this point, Paulin references both reproductive technology—

which now allows for gestational surrogacy, where the surrogate is not biologically related to the fetus—and also advances in LGBT equality. As Paulin put it, "families who want to have a baby may only have [surrogacy] as an option . . . including same-sex couples. Two men."[80] Here and elsewhere, biology is imagined as that which enables bonds. The lack of biological connection between the surrogate and the fetus is precisely what allows supporters to locate the problems with surrogacy in the past. In much the same way, a surrogate is presented as the *only* option for having a baby, especially for two men, an assumption that rests upon an unstated belief in the paramount value of biological connection for family building. Such assertions suggest that, contrary to the campaign's rhetoric, it isn't love that makes a family, after all; it is biological children.

Assemblywoman Paulin's brief reference to hypothetical women who may have been "taken advantage of" in the past is one of the few moments when people connected to Love Makes a Family or the Child-Parent Security Act mentioned surrogates or critiques of surrogacy. Often, when surrogates were mentioned, they were grouped together with intended parents, and their unique positions or concerns ignored. A press release from Cuomo's office, for instance, claimed that Love Makes a Family will "provid[e] [the] nation's strongest protections for parents and surrogates."[81] How a law titled the Child-Parent Security Act would actually protect surrogates was unclear in both the promotion and coverage of the case.

One rare moment connected to this legislation when surrogates are discussed explicitly and at length is on the New York Department of Health website. On the page dedicated to the Child-Parent Security Act, the Department of Health notes that "although gestational surrogacy increases opportunities for family building, it also involves medical, psychosocial, fiscal and ethical considerations, as well as legal complexities."[82] The webpage goes on to offer information on "gestational surrogacy program licensure, surrogate registry, surrogacy screening guidelines, and surrogates' Bill of Rights." Throughout the subpages to which this page links, one can learn about these legal and medical complexities. Take, for instance, the surrogates' so-called Bill of Rights, which the Department of Health says "describes the rights gestational surrogates have as they relate to the health and welfare, right to independent counsel, health insurance coverage and reimbursement for related medical costs, life insurance and contract termination protections."[83] Nowhere here—or elsewhere on the website, for that matter—are the psychosocial, fiscal, and ethical considerations discussed again, despite the site's claims to the contrary. Perhaps most damning, nowhere is a surrogate's right to compensation listed, nor a range provided for what might be considered ethical compensation for the job. Perhaps we shouldn't be surprised that a law meant to provide "a simple path to establish legal parental rights for parents who rely on assisted reproductive technology (ART) to have children" is not terribly concerned about surrogates.[84]

We should, however, be concerned that images of LGBTQ+ people are being used in the service of ignoring issues surrogates face. The New York Department of Health's website speaks to the degree to which this is happening. Of the four images posted on the Child-Parent Security Act homepage, all feature couples.[85] Two of these couples are presumably meant to be read as LGBTQ+ and three of the four couples include at least one person of color. While liberals might be tempted to read this representational diversity as positive, we also ought to think about the limits of imagery that does not capture the reality of who primarily hires surrogates. Further, we should be critical of conversations about surrogacy that do not recognize the gross disparity in resources that surrogates and intended parents typically can access.

In fact, it was for precisely these reasons that one hundred prominent New York feminists, including Gloria Steinem, Eve Ensler, and Erica Jong, signed a letter to Governor Cuomo urging him to reject the bill. As Steinem wrote, "Under this bill, women in economic need become commercialized vessels for rent, and the fetuses they carry become the property of others." Steinem continued, "The bill ignores the socio-economic and racial inequalities of the reproductive commercial surrogacy industry, and puts disenfranchised women at the financial and emotional mercy of wealthier and more privileged individuals."[86] The debate around the surrogacy legislation was covered in a *New York Times* article entitled "Surrogate Pregnancy Battle Pits Progressives Against Feminists." Here, "progressives" is used synonymously with LGBTQ+ people and in opposition to feminism, a conflation that Deborah Glick, whom the article notes "became the first openly gay member" of the New York legislature in 1991, troubles. Responding to claims that the surrogacy bill was crucial for LGBTQ+ equity, Glick noted, "I'm not certain that, considering the money involved, that this is an issue for the broader L.G.B.T. community." She continued, "This is clearly a problem for the extraordinarily well-heeled."[87] Unfortunately, the circulation of these critiques was limited.

## MEN HAVING BABIES

Nearly a decade before the Child-Parent Security Act was signed into law, an organization called Men Having Babies was launched in New York. Growing out of a peer support network of "biological gay fathers and fathers-to-be," Men Having Babies is now one of the most well-known and far-reaching organizations offering surrogacy advice for gay men. Their resources and services include a robust website; a peer support Facebook page with twenty-one thousand followers; educational materials such as conferences, workshops, and webinars; a Speakers Bureau of gay parents; a research library of academic scholarship on gay men; and resource-oriented blog posts that include discussions of financial assistance, including grants Men Having Babies offers. Their grants program, called the Gay Parenting Assistance Program, annually facilitates more than a million dollars. Men Having Babies also participates in advocacy, including policy work, developing guidelines for best practices, and supporting academic research.[88]

When researching LGBTQ+ people and surrogacy, it is impossible to avoid Men Having Babies. They are everywhere, including on the Love Makes a Family Council. Other similar groups focusing on gay men and surrogacy often reference Men Having Babies, with one, Daddy Squared, describing the group as "the most well-known surrogacy grants giver created exclusively for gay men."[89] Daddy Squared goes on to say that "Men Having Babies' amazing work around the world has helped thousands of gay men learn about surrogacy."[90] Considering the respected position Men Having Babies occupies within surrogacy advocacy, the organization is a rich case study for considering the place of gay men in surrogacy advocacy as well as how surrogates are imagined by advocates.

The organization's mission includes helping "prospective parents who are gay, queer, or bisexual men, as well as transwomen (henceforth 'gay') achieve biological parenting."[91] The group's articulation of whose reproduction they are concerned with is, at first glance, baffling. Their inclusion of trans women, whom they describe as "gay," and exclusion of trans men, seems especially strange for an organization called Men Having Babies. It seems obvious that trans women wanting to reproduce biologically might not feel welcomed by an organization focusing on men and that trans men interested in becoming biological parents might want to hire a surrogate for reasons connected to their masculinity (or other reasons entirely). What the inclusion of trans women and exclusion of trans men suggests is that the organization is primarily concerned with those who do not have uteruses, and thus are incapable of carrying a pregnancy to term. Considering the organization's focus on "biological parenting" and "biological gay fathers," perhaps we should not be surprised by their focus—albeit unstated—on those who do not possess the organ required for biological reproduction. In fact, Men Having Babies unapologetically makes clear why their focus is what it is: "Due to biological and social constraints, gay men as a category face *the most obstacles* in their quest for parenting, not the least of which is financial" (emphasis added).[92] Men Having Babies even advocates for using the term "social infertility" to describe gay men's reproductive status.

It is not surprising that an organization framing gay men as the demographic category that experiences "the most obstacles in their quest for parenting" is geared toward gay men. But this assertion is woefully out of touch at best and racist, sexist, and classist at worst. Consider, for instance, that rates of maternal mortality for Black women are more than three times higher than those of white women.[93] And that Black women are disproportionately surveilled by the state and by medical providers, leading to disproportionate rates of incarceration and loss of their children to the foster care system.[94] These "obstacles"—racism and sexism and classism, that is—deeply inform the "quest for parenting" among Black women.

Considering the organization's disregard for women, perhaps we shouldn't be surprised that they also disregard surrogates, who are essentially absent from the Men Having Babies website. Take, for example, the "Framework for Ethical Surrogacy: Principles, Protocols, and Best Practices," the organization's only document that attempts to address surrogates' experiences.[95] Here, we might anticipate a discussion of, well, the ethics of surrogacy—one that centers surrogates and addresses feminist concerns about exploitation. This is not, however, what the document delivers. In fact, the document goes in the opposite direction, mentioning non-exploitative surrogacy relationships. "The ultimate test for a non-exploitative surrogacy arrangement," Men Having Babies asserts, "is the quality of the interaction between the parties, and the overall sense of accomplishment and gratification surrogates have during and after the journey." Apparently, the only thing intended parents need to do to avoid an exploitative relationship with their surrogate is to foster "quality" interactions. That financial compensation is not mentioned in relation to creating "non-exploitative relationships" speaks to the degree to which Men Having Babies positions surrogacy as outside of the employer/employee context. For most workers, the matter of compensation is central to feeling exploited or gratified.

Men Having Babies does not, however, ignore the issue of compensation entirely. As the organization notes, "Regardless of compensation paid to the donor and surrogate, keep in mind these individuals *want to help you have a child.* They are not service providers" (emphasis in original). Framing surrogates as "helpers" is a move Men Having Babies commonly deploys. In this same document on ethical surrogacy Men Having Babies describes the "surrogacy journey" as "a sequence of agreements, actions, services, and treatments with the aim of achieving a pregnancy *with the help of a surrogate,* for the benefit of [intended parents]" (emphasis added). In another moment, they state that "women everywhere should have the right to decide when, how and under which circumstances *they agree to help intended parents* by donating eggs and/or carrying a baby for them" (emphasis added).[96] Such discourse is in line with framing surrogates as "altruistic," an approach that offers a sly way around feminist critiques of the commodification of women's bodies inherent to surrogacy; surrogates are performing charity, after all. It is no wonder Men Having Babies encourages all surrogacy arrangements to be altruistic. In fact, the organization encourages the legal regulation of compensation so as to "avoid unreasonably large sums that may lead to overwhelming financial incentives."[97]

To Men Having Babies, surrogates are both those who are inherently helpful and altruistic and also those who could succumb to the lure of financial incentives. At moments in the "Ethical Surrogacy" document, surrogates appear mysterious, even suspect. In the document's twelfth principle, Men Having Babies suggests that "additional medical and social science research is necessary to better understand the motivations, experiences and outcomes of surrogates and egg donors so as to guide best practices across all professional disciplines."[98] At first glance this may look like a benevolent attempt to include surrogates' positions; in other words, we *should* consider surrogates when developing best practices. Yet, the implication is that surrogates are mysteries—something we do not yet understand and therefore that should be researched. Such assertions both ignore the vast scholarship that exists on surrogacy and kicks down the road concerns that surrogacy raises for surrogates: Once we research and understand surrogates, *then* we'll take them into consideration (meanwhile, we'll make surrogacy a more "normal," accessible practice). Such framings are convenient because, if we do not know surrogates' motivations, we can assign them.

Both depictions of surrogates—as altruistic helpers and as mysterious suspects in need of surveillance—benefit intended parents and the surrogacy industry more than they do surrogates. Put more directly, when surrogates are described as altruistic, rather than as workers, they need not necessarily be compensated for their labor; they are offering *help* that they *want* to provide, rather than labor that should be compensated fairly. At the same time, the framing of surrogates as mysterious or suspect encourages increased surveillance and control of surrogates' bodies. In various places in the Men Having Babies document on ethical surrogacy, parents are advised to compromise with surrogates, as if surrogates' goals are in opposition to those of parents. At one point, Men Having Babies claims that "balancing the surrogate responsibilities with her autonomy" can be difficult. "Health restrictions on the surrogate" can exist, but, Men Having Babies asserts, they must be reasonable. Examples of acceptable restrictions include bans on smoking, alcohol consumption, and, at certain points in the pregnancy process, sexual intercourse. Beyond that, Men Having Babies asserts that many intended parents "find that it is best to agree that the surrogate will maintain a healthy lifestyle suitable to pregnancy." As such, they advise that intended parents "avoid conflict and infringing on her autonomy by trying to control decisions such as use of certain cosmetics or travel. Adjusting expectations, curbing the need to control, and maintaining good communication are key, and a professional can help facilitate this and mediate when needed."[99] Here, surrogates are presented as wild women in need of being tamed—a far cry from the altruistic surrogate just out to help the world.

Throughout their nine-page document ostensibly outlining what "ethical surrogacy" looks like, Men Having Babies says remarkably little about what could make surrogacy ethical or how to best address the exploitative aspects of the practice. In fact, even here the vast majority of principles, practices, and recommendations focus on intended parents and how they can ensure their best outcome without crossing ethical lines. For example, recommendations focus on how intended parents can benefit from matching agencies, how those agencies can be fairly compensated without being overcompensated, how intended parents can utilize professional and legal services to communicate with surrogates, how intended parents benefit from knowing the identity of their donors . . . and the list goes on and on.

The "Framework for Ethical Surrogacy" presents surrogates as just one of "all involved" in the "surrogacy journey," alongside attorneys, medical providers, the surrogacy matching agency, and egg donors. In fact, surrogates and egg donors are often lumped together. "Special attention," the organization notes, "should be made to make sure candidates for egg donation and surrogacy are given access to independent medical and legal advice, and ongoing psychological and emotional support." Another principle advocates that "Steps should be taken . . . to limit the medical risks donors and surrogates are subjected to during the surrogacy process."[100] In nine of the twelve ethical surrogacy principles offered, surrogates and egg donors are referenced as a group, as if both parties necessarily experience the same concerns and therefore would benefit from the same "special attention," although the organization never spells out what this special attention might look like or how it might differ for egg donors and surrogates. And this is the rare case when Men Having Babies discusses surrogates at all.

## RACISM AND CLASSISM IN THE SURROGACY FUNDING INDUSTRY

Just as race and class are absent in most surrogacy data in circulation, so too are they missing in conversations surrounding surrogacy legislation and advocacy. In media coverage of Love Makes a Family and the Child-Parent Security Act, as well as on the Men Having Babies website, no explicit attention is paid to the raced and classed dynamics of surrogacy. This point should not suggest that surrogacy advocates ignore the topic of money. On the contrary.

Discussions of "financial barriers" to surrogacy are commonplace. David Kaufman, in his aforementioned *New York Times* article on "fertility equality," notes that "some would-be gay male parents see this high price of parenthood as a penalty for not being straight. (Sperm donation and intrauterine insemination, commonly used by lesbian couples, are comparatively inexpensive procedures)."[101] What Kaufman and other surrogacy advocates making these claims ignore is that gay men couples earn more money than any other couples. A 2017 study published in the *Southern Economic Journal* found that overall gay men make 10 percent more money than straight men who have similar educational backgrounds, experience, and job profiles.[102] Gay men also are paid far more than women of all sexualities because men in general are paid more than women. The National Committee on Pay Equity shows that in 2019 women workers were paid 81.6 cents for every dollar men workers were paid—numbers that haven't changed since 2017. The wage gap is even worse for some demographics of women of color. For every dollar paid to white men, white women were paid 79 cents, Black women 62 cents, and Latina women 54 cents. Asian women were paid more than any other group of women, at 90 cents per white man's dollar.[103] The pay gaps described here would be even larger if the income of these women workers was compared to the income of white *gay* men, in particular.

Despite the privileged class position gay men as a demographic occupy, an industry has sprung up around the notion that gay men's efforts to reproduce biologically constitute a form of financial oppression. The irony here, of course, is that the scope of this industry reveals that gay men are also understood as a lucrative target market. In fact, Jacobson's aforementioned study of surrogacy agencies' and clinics' online recruitment strategies found that 58.3 percent of agencies and 34 percent of clinics cater to gay men. Agencies have developed this "market for wealthy gay men" through "constructing a particular image of surrogacy that affirms the aspirations of gay men to become parents." "Gay men's procreative consciousness is encouraged," Jacobson says, "by seeing images and reading text supportive of gay fatherhood on clinic and agency websites." Despite being hailed, gay men, Jacobson argues, "may represent an untapped profitable market."[104]

Today, it seems, this market is being tapped. Many organizations, consulting firms, and law practices offer advice specific to gay men on acquiring funding for surrogacy, which include hiring consultants to secure "surrogacy grants" or developing compelling crowdfunding campaigns. The organization Gays With Kids (GWK) offers a "GWK Academy," which provides "unlimited coaching calls with GWK," consultations with "mentors," and discounts from GWK's surrogacy partners—"all for $99!"[105] Family Equality, Giving Tree Surrogacy, and Daddy Squared are organizations with similar goals. Family Equality's list of "LGBTQ+ Family Building Grants" includes several "grants" that require fees. One, for instance, requires that grant applicants "actively fundraise for [the granting organization] and . . . raise $3,800 before being matched with a clinic, and donate $55 or more annually with the [granting organization] community."[106]

Considering these stipulations, it is somewhat baffling who these organizations see as needing financial assistance. One question on the Men Having Babies' "Frequently Asked Questions" page asks, "Why do you ask for current Asset and Liability information?" Their answer is telling: "To get a full understanding of your current needs as well as helping you to identify potential financial sources that you may have not already considered. For instance, if you have a mutual fund, can you borrow any amount against that plan? Do you own a second home? If so, is that something you could sell in order to have additional cash on hand?"[107]

Advising intended parents to sell their second homes to pay for surrogacy reveals the imagined socioeconomic status of Men Having Babies' target audience. On the other hand, while a great deal of concern surrounds intended parents' finances, little is said about surrogates' financial situations, including in journalists' writing that profiles surrogates. Instead, surrogates are portrayed as altruistically motivated. That the women featured are also often working class—and therefore likely taking on additional work because they need the money—somehow manages to escape discussion. In a *Washington Post* article that describes one couple's experience with surrogacy, the author draws several distinct contrasts between the surrogate and intended parents. "They're an unlikely foursome: two gay men from the Upper East Side of New York and a small-town husband and wife who met when they both were 20 at a Dunkin' Donuts." The gay couple both have white-collar jobs in the city and the surrogate runs a restaurant with her husband. Even after establishing these differences, the author argues that the surrogate is not in it for the money. She merely likes being pregnant. Further, the author asserts, money is too small of a driving force. "There has to be something bigger, given the intense emotional and physical effort" involved. When you break down the hours, the author notes, surrogates don't actually make that much.[108] Rather than being evidence of a problem, this point is used to confirm that surrogacy is not exploitative because people don't do it for the money anyway.

Similar approaches are evident in an *Atlantic* article entitled "Who Becomes a Surrogate?" In this case, too, there are class differences between the featured surrogates and those hiring them. Note the article description: "There are often 'have' and 'have not' differentials at play in the surrogate-intended parent relationship. The surrogates already have the ability to create babies; the intended parents have money. They are usually better educated, and far more economically secure. Sometimes these dynamics can create subtle tensions."[109] Despite acknowledging the class differences, the author downplays them by saying they only "sometimes" can cause "subtle tensions"—while implying that wealthy gay parents are actually the "have nots." The article opens with an administrator of a surrogacy company, Sherrie Smith, describing what she sees as "the biggest misconception about American surrogates." Her answer: "That they do it for the money." Quelling fears about surrogates' financial motivations, Smith asserts "it would be easier to get a job at McDonald's" than to become a surrogate. Furthermore, "working at McDonald's or temping as a law firm receptionist can't compare to being a wealthy, educated couple's savior," the author asserts.[110]

That working as a temp or at McDonald's are the two alternative jobs mentioned speaks to how surrogates' job opportunities and class statuses are imagined. Further, never does the article dare to imagine that perhaps surrogates have no desire to be a savior to wealthy folks but see a unique opportunity to work two jobs simultaneously—as a surrogate, that is, and whatever other job they have, including perhaps as a receptionist or fast-food worker. This reality cannot be named because it questions the narratives of altruism that surrogacy advocates rely on. One surrogacy firm featured in the article rejects a surrogate's application if it seems she is too motivated by money, a practice common among surrogacy agencies. Turns out you can't do it for the money if you aren't hired in the first place.

Some promotional materials for Men Having Babies even suggest that intended parents must worry about surrogates exploiting them by scamming them into paying too much. On Men Having Babies' Instagram page, Luis and Ron, a gay couple who used surrogates twice, advised others that the "biggest challenge on our journey was finding true partners who were genuinely interested in helping us and not trying to charge maximum rates and exploit the process."[111] This sentiment villainizes any surrogate seeking maximum rates for their labor, something that white collar workers, such as Luis and Ron, are not only likely to do but are encouraged to do.

At times, surrogates' own testimonies are used to rebut the claim that surrogates "do it for the money." In Kaufman's *New York Times* article on "fertility equality"—where we might rightly expect attention to questions of race and class, considering the article's focus on "equality"—only one surrogate is quoted one time. This surrogate, Michelle Pine, states, "while there are certainly opportunities for exploitation, working with agencies or groups that offer some regulation help take away that piece."[112] This single quote is used to downplay feminists' concerns about surrogacy's potential for exploitation, despite the fact that the practice involves "wealthy people paying less wealthy people," as pro-surrogacy feminist Sophie Lewis is also quoted as saying in the article.[113]

Critiques of Kaufman's argument went viral. In tweets responding to the article, people expressed concerns about the exploitation and commodification of women through surrogacy, as well as the use of "equality" and "rights" discourse to shroud such exploitation. Pointing out the irony of this "equality" framework, one tweet asked, "So fertility equality means your right to use a woman's body to have a child?"[114] Another stated, "There is no such thing as 'fertility equality.' Fertility or parenthood is not a right. This article obfuscates the reality of surrogacy and refers to women as 'carriers.'"[115] Another said, "Imagine thinking that you have the human right to rent a woman's womb though. Imagine thinking you're oppressed because you can't financially coerce women into bearing and birthing your spawn. If you ever needed proof that gay men can be just as misogynistic as straight ones."[116] Feminists, too, took up critiques of the article. In an article published in the *Hastings Journal on Gender and the Law*, Isa Elfers references Kaufman's article to argue that "a 'right' to the organs and reproductive labor of other people cannot exist under any circumstances, even in the name of enabling LGBT couples to have children biologically related to them."[117]

About seven months after Kaufman's article was published, the *New York Times* published another article on surrogacy. Entitled "Meet the Women Who Become Surrogates," this one features four surrogates. Aretha Cagno is one of them. Cagno had promised her sister that she would carry her children for her. After Cagno's sister died from complications from lupus, Cagno decided that she wanted to fulfill her promise to her sister by being a surrogate for someone else. That Cagno is Black is never mentioned—something only evident in the article's two images of her—and neither is her class status. What is mentioned: that the intended parent of the fetus Cagno carried is a gay man. In fact, three of the four surrogates featured in the article carried for gay men. Niki Renslow, one surrogate, claimed that she began considering surrogacy after talking with gay men friends. So, she broached the subject with her husband, asking "If we can help other people who this doesn't come as easy to, why not?"[118]

Here, as elsewhere, the motivations of surrogates are framed as largely altruistic, which, it turns out, is by design. Lisa Wippler, another featured surrogate, now works as the director of surrogacy admissions at a California agency. There, she ensures that applicants who are "deemed overly dependent on the compensation provided, including those who receive government assistance, are screened out as surrogates."[119] Despite such assertions, the aforementioned study of surrogates in Los Angeles found that 49 percent were otherwise unemployed.[120] Considering these numbers, as well as Wippler's claim that just 1 to 1.5 percent of surrogates applying are accepted, we might assume that a large number of people applying for the job want it for the money—like most jobs, not so incidentally. Interestingly, the *New York Times* article does not mention if either of the two surrogates it features who are currently pregnant have additional jobs. Readers do learn that the two women featured whose pregnancies had concluded both work for surrogacy agencies. Presumably, these women are paid for their work at the agencies. That their paychecks come from the surrogacy industry does not seem to call into question their ability to do their work—an assumption that is not extended to surrogates themselves.

Considering the lack of acknowledgment of the classed relations that enable surrogacy, one might not be surprised that surrogacy's racial dynamics are also largely ignored in popular conversations about surrogacy. In short, race is almost never mentioned in discussions about gay men and surrogacy. Apparently, the industry is not bothered by the fact that white gay men couples and their children are the primary image of families produced through gestational surrogacy. The Instagram account of Men Having Babies is evidence of this point. Of the 200 most recent posts on the Men Having Babies Instagram page, 188 include photos of fathers with their children. Of these photos, 130 are of two white men (69.1 percent) and 23 are single white men (12.1 percent). Twenty-four photos include one man of color and one white man (12.7 percent), while just two are single men of color (1 percent). Only 7 of 188 posts, or 3.7 percent, include the surrogates who birthed the babies, one of which does not show the surrogate's face. Five of the surrogates appear white and one Asian.[121] While the racialized nature of the imagery deployed by Men Having Babies reveals a great deal, so too does their lack of explicit discussion of race. In fact, race is almost never mentioned on their website, including in their Ethical Framework document or in multiple advice articles related to surrogacy matching, moments where one might expect attention to race. One "Ask the Expert" article titled "Tips for Successful Surrogate Match Meeting" mentions race only once, when the "expert"—a founder of a surrogacy agency—advises intended parents to avoid making racial slurs toward surrogates.[122] A remarkably low bar.

Other websites and articles look similarly white and take a similarly color-blind approach. The American Surrogacy website, for instance, asks, "Does Race Matter When Choosing a Surrogate?" It pointedly answers: "No." In fact, it asserts that "of the many things to spend serious time thinking about, race is not one of them."[123] In a similar, though less egregiously colorblind approach, the *Atlantic* article engages with race only once, briefly noting that "Black surrogates carry babies for white families and vice versa," with no discussion of whether Black surrogates disproportionately carry babies for white families (or vice versa), the percentage of surrogates who are Black, or how Black surrogates are treated in relation to other surrogates.[124] A *Yes Magazine* article about Black women and infertility is helpful for thinking about *The Atlantic*'s omissions. Black women, the article asserts, are "twice as likely to experience challenges achieving or sustaining a pregnancy—and less likely to seek assistance." And while surrogacy is on the rise, this is not true among Black women. "The number of Black surrogates and Black intended parents remain low," something that the article attributes to both current costs and history. Likening surrogacy to slavery, the article suggests that Black women may hesitate to be surrogates for white families, who would then own and control Black women's wombs.[125]

Despite the overwhelming lack of discussion of race in surrogacy advocacy as well as related media coverage, racial anxieties are present, something especially evident in cross-racial surrogacy. Take, for instance, the video entitled "World's First Black Woman to Give Birth to Two White Babies" and the article "I'm a white woman but I've become a surrogate mother for an Asian couple."[126] As the titles suggest, both sources sensationalize the racial differences between surrogates and the fetuses they are carrying. At the same time, they attempt to alleviate the very racial anxieties they produce by emphasizing the genetic and racial similarities between the intended parents and intended children. A white surrogate, Karen Streeter, notes, "I never thought of it as my baby as I had no genetic link with it." But it isn't just genetics at play. Race is too. As Streeter says, "I don't know how any surrogate could keep a baby who isn't even biologically theirs, especially when it is of a different race." In another article about the same case, Ian Craft, the director of the London Fertility Centre, suggests that cross-racial surrogacy can alleviate the "major risk . . . that the surrogate mother may not want to yield the child" to the intended parents, because a surrogate "is unlikely to want to keep a child of a different race. . . . That is just human nature."[127]

Sylvia Wynter's work is useful for questioning these claims, which rely on the kind of biocentrism Wynter has long worked to disrupt. Biocentrism, following Wynter, refers to understandings of the human as a "universally applicable conception" and as a primarily "biological being."[128] "Race and racism," Wynter says, "are logical outcomes of the biocentric conception of the human."[129] Wynter helps us understand that the fetishization of biology evident in the comments made by Karen Streeter and Ian Craft spills over into how we understand humans' relationships to others. That is, biology becomes not just the basis for our individual human bodies but for our relationships to others' bodies, including, in this case, the fetus one grows and the child one raises. For Wynter, the function of biocentrism, which includes an overinvestment in DNA and genetics, "is to legitimate the structure of the order."[130] While this social order is clearly racist, it is also post-racial, something evident in Karen Streeter's claims. That "[the intended parents] were a different race just didn't come into it. As far as I'm concerned everyone on this planet is exactly the same. We have the same blood running through our veins and we all want the same things in life—to love and have children. White, black, Asian, it makes no difference to me at all."[131] Except, of course, that it does, evident in Streeter's own statement that surrogates are unlikely to want to keep babies they birth if they are not biologically related, and especially if their race differs from the surrogate's.

## QUEERING SURROGACY

"Queer," as I outlined in the introduction to this book, is not synonymous with LGBTQ+-identified people. Clearly, there are a lot of LGBTQ+-identified people who are acting in ways that are not necessarily queer if, by queer, we mean intending to uproot dominant social systems and their attendant affects. In this chapter, I suggest that queering surrogacy necessarily involves critically examining the practice in a way that takes seriously that LGBTQ+ness has been deployed to downplay the significant concerns surrogacy raises.

But, as I found myself encountering the kinds of positive cultural representations of surrogacy I examine here and their featuring of gay men, I wondered how deeply my archive was influenced by the algorithms used by my news apps. As I clicked on stories about surrogacy from left-leaning sources, was I fed more stories about surrogacy written from what the authors see as a liberal or progressive perspective? To answer this question,

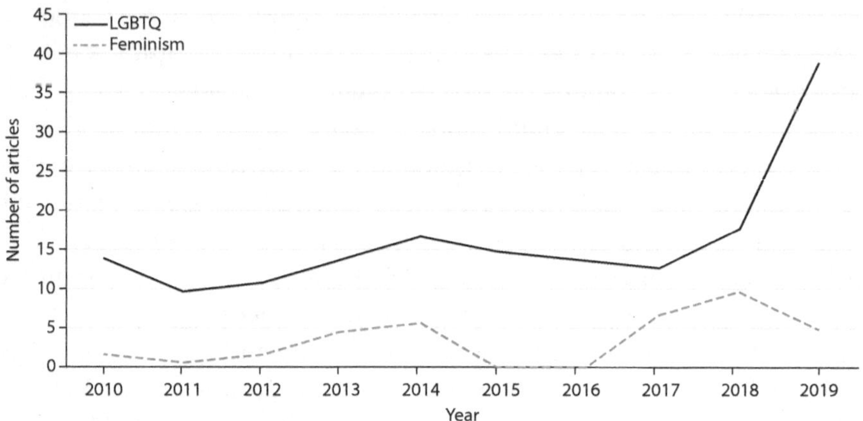


Surrogacy in the media over time.

I quantitatively analyzed every article about surrogacy that was published between 2010 and 2020, appeared in one of four major national newspapers (*The New York Times, The Wall Street Journal, USA Today*, and *The Washington Post*), and included the terms "LGBTQ" or "feminism" or derivatives of these terms.[132]

I found that, yes, indeed, LGBTQ+ness has appeared more frequently in discussions of surrogacy in recent years. Of the 532 articles about surrogacy in these newspapers, "LGBTQ" appears in 165, or 31 percent, of them. Meanwhile, terms connected to "feminism" appear in just 38, or 7 percent, of articles about surrogacy. As telling, of the 38 articles on surrogacy that include the words "feminism" or "feminist," 28, or 74 percent, mention the "surrogate" specifically. By contrast, the term "surrogate" appears in just 43 percent of articles that mention LGBTQ+ness. I also measured the tone of articles and their positive or negative valence. Articles with LGBTQ+-related terms have a tone score of 0.16, while articles that do not include such words have a tone score of 0.04. This finding demonstrates that articles with terms related to LGBTQ+ness are more positive than those without such words.

Such quantitative findings should encourage us to ask: How we can make sense of these affects? And, further, what we do with this information, especially if we want to develop queer approaches to surrogacy? The goal of queering surrogacy must be to disrupt the celebratory affects swirling around surrogacy enabled by the figure of the wealthy, often white, gay men couple or family, something necessary because of the ways in which the practice extends racism, classism, and sexism. Beyond this, we must contend with the fact that surrogacy is, in many ways, a mechanism for bolstering normativity via not only contributing to dominant ideas regarding the value of the nuclear family formation but also the idea that this formation is most desirable when rooted in biology. Queering reproductive justice vis-a-vis surrogacy requires questioning both positions.

And yet, many scholars writing about LGBTQ+ people who use reproductive technologies to create children biologically related to them (including but not limited to surrogacy) describe the process as queer. Heather Jacobson, for instance, frames her analysis of the surrogacy industry's marketing to gay men as in alignment with broader attempts at "queering reproductive justice." Marcin Smietana and France Winddance Twine describe the ways that gay men parents select egg donors and surrogates to create "racialized resemblance" between them and their children as "queer decisions."[133] Like Smietana and Twine, who see their work on gay men intended parents as contributing to the scholarship on "queer family formation," other scholars also describe LGBTQ+ people's family formations in terms of queerness. Laura Mamo—who describes lesbians' use of fertility treatments, such as in vitro fertilization and sperm donation, as a matter of "queering reproduction"[134]—is concerned with the ways that "seeking fertility services constituted new subjectivities: lesbian mothers, gay fathers, and queer families."[135] In their analyses of the use of reproductive technologies among LGBTQ+ people, these scholars offer many provocative and useful insights regarding transnational capital circulation, racial formation, and the gulfs between queer theoretical insights and LGBTQ+ individuals' desires as well as the paradoxes these desires create. Mamo, in particular, takes up this last point. In working to "queer" the fertility clinic, Mamo pushes back "against the domestication and displacement of lesbian mothers in favor of only seeing the radical in gay men parenting or a fetishization of masculine pregnancy and parenting."[136] Instead, Mamo asks, "Why not see both the radical in all queer family forms as these traverse the fertility clinic (or choose not to and seek adoptions, foster parenting, and other family formations) and theorize how these at once queer and also perpetuate normativity?" While Mamo rightly urges us to see relations among lesbian/gay/queer, we also ought to question what is lost when we conflate lesbian/gay and queer, especially for our ability to analyze what exactly makes the building of biological families, even when done by LGBTQ+ people, queer.

Judith Stacey took up precisely this point in her comments at the 2016 Making Families symposium. As Stacey notes, "there has been a striking increase in emphasis on genetic and biological family creation in queer and lesbian, gay, bisexual and transgender kinship practices, in contradistinction to earlier emphases on escape from the norms and demands of heteronormative patriarchy. During the gay liberation movement, older concepts of 'families we choose' were not defined by (nor meant necessarily to include) the creation of children as kin." Today, this is no longer the case. In fact, Stacey suggests that "the utterly dramatic gains in public acceptance that gay sexuality and family life have since achieved in so many contemporary societies also represent a *retreat* from queer family visions" [emphasis added].[137] Turning to surrogacy, Stacey argues that "Generally, the types of families created through transnational surrogacy are not queer families in the affirmative sense. Reproductive justice discourse reveals the racism, colonialism and imperial relations involved in making kin ties we could still perhaps call queer, although they by no means embody the vision of the liberatory queer movement."[138]

How do we retain the visions of these earlier queer movements that advocated for re-thinking family as key to queer liberation, especially in a moment in which surrogacy is being framed as a method for rethinking family and even for actualizing queerness?! This is, in fact, precisely Sophie Lewis's argument in *Full Surrogacy Now: Feminism Against Family*, in which Lewis makes two interrelated points. First, surrogacy is work and we should approach it as such. Second, the family needs to be abolished because it is a conservatizing force that makes it more difficult to create dispersed networks of care and queer kinship networks. Neither argument is actually new. Lewis's contribution to scholarship on the family and on surrogacy is in bringing these positions together. Ultimately, she argues that every pregnant person should be a surrogate. We should all be birthing kids, swapping them, and raising them without any regard for which children we birthed. Doing so, Lewis says, is in the service of developing "feminism against family," a phrase she coins in an attempt to undermine the heteronormative biological family. But, unfortunately, it is in attempting to link and expand upon these two aforementioned arguments that Lewis's argument falls short, something that I suspect is the case because there is no link between the arguments.

Put more directly, calling surrogacy work and ensuring that it is remunerated does nothing to disperse networks of care or to help us abolish the family. In fact, expanding surrogacy, which Lewis calls for, does precisely the opposite. Even if people were not raising their biological children, they would be raising their own children. Surrogacy, as articulated by Lewis, as well as those who see LGBTQ+ people reproducing through surrogates as fundamentally queer, becomes another way to feel like we're queering a social formation that has long trafficked in and continues to traffic in normativity. The family is enabled by surrogacy; family abolition is not enabled by surrogacy. In short, surrogacy will not help us to undo the family. Undoing attachments to the family could, however, help us to approach surrogacy differently—that is, to queer surrogacy.

By way of closing, I want to make two simple points. First, we should take seriously that surrogates themselves are rarely centered in discussions of surrogacy, including those that focus on LGBTQ+ people. The solution is not to make surrogates "more visible" for the sake of the ostensible value of representation itself. Queer theorists, including myself, have warned against beliefs in the social value of visibility.[139] At the same time, the lack of surrogates in conversations about surrogacy is particularly surprising, given the degree to which all pregnant bodies are surveilled, sites of public interest, and hyper-visible, as many feminist scholars have argued.[140] Surrogates are so outside of legible pregnancy that their bodies are sites of state surveillance—evident in New York's legislation—without being present almost anywhere in discussions of surrogacy by nonprofit organizations, the media, and politicians. Centering surrogates, rather than those who hire them, would help us to acknowledge the materiality of surrogacy, such that the practice can be taken more seriously as a job and surrogates could be paid fairly for their labor. If people considering using surrogacy to reproduce understood the material conditions that lead people to become surrogates as well as the materiality of surrogacy, I would like to believe that fewer people would decide to reproduce in this manner.

This belief leads me to my second point: We ought to be working toward a world with *less* surrogacy—both because of the ways in which it reproduces racism, classism, and sexism and also because it operates in the service of hetero- and homonormativity. On that note, we should stop describing surrogacy as "queer." We ought to be working toward a world in which people can imagine and live fulfilling lives outside of the nuclear family formation. A world where would-be surrogates earn a livable wage at their place of employment such that they do not need a second job—surrogacy or anything else—to be able to meet their basic needs. A world that prioritizes adult women over fetuses. Moving toward this world requires a great deal, including, perhaps most simply, that we push back against the celebratory affects that get attached to surrogacy in the name of extending queerness.

# 2 The Heteronormativity of Paid Parental Leave

Maternity leave. Paternity leave. Parental leave. Family leave. Whatever you want to call it, it seems like virtually all feminists—as well as vaguely progressive people and even some conservatives such as Ivanka Trump, who made it her signature issue during her father's first presidency—agree that such forms of leave are socially valuable. In their 2021 holiday card, Prince Harry and Meghan Markle noted that they made donations to "several organizations that honor and protect families—from those being relocated from Afghanistan, to American families in need of paid parental leave."[1] Just a couple of months earlier, Markle released a public letter in conjunction with the organization Paid Leave for All addressed to Sen. Charles Schumer (D-NY) and Rep. Nancy Pelosi (D-CA), which encouraged them to enact a federal paid parental leave policy. In the letter, Markle, who noted that she was writing to the politicians "as a mom," advocated for a "new era of family first policies." She boldly asserted, "In taking care of your child, you take care of your community, and you take care of your country."[2]

Harry and Meghan aren't the only celebrities to comment on the United States' parental leave problem. Markle's close friend Serena Williams, one of the all-time greatest tennis players, has discussed the difficulty of being a new mom with an outside career: "I'm telling you, it's so hard to be a mom. I have my own job and I make my own schedule, but even then I still have commitments, and I can't imagine moms that get two weeks off and have to go back to work."[3] Actress Anne Hathaway also has addressed the issue of paid parental leave, noting in a United Nations speech on International Women's Day,

> American women are currently entitled to twelve weeks unpaid leave. American men are entitled to nothing. . . . Somehow, [my husband and I] and every American parent were expected to be "back to normal" in under three months. Without income. I remember thinking to myself, "If the practical result of pregnancy is another mouth to feed in your home and America is a country where most people are living paycheck to paycheck, how does twelve weeks unpaid leave economically work?" The truth is, for too many people it doesn't. One in four American women go back to work two weeks after giving birth because they can't afford to take any more time off than that. Twenty-five percent. Equally disturbing, women who can afford to take the full twelve weeks often don't because it will mean incurring a "motherhood penalty."[4]

It's easy to see where these celebrities are coming from. The United States is one of the few countries in the world that doesn't offer paid leave to new mothers, a global outlier.[5] Advocacy group MomsRising makes clear why this is a problem: "Paid family and medical leave combats poverty, gives children a healthy start, and lowers the wage gap between women and men by providing structural support to balance work and family." MomsRising supports these claims with statistics: Paid leave reduces infant mortality by as much as 20 percent; 25 percent of poverty spells in the United States are due to having a baby; yet, just 17 percent of people in the United States have access to paid family leave through their employer, while fewer than 40 percent have personal medical leave through their employer. The current Family Medical Leave Act (FMLA), which allows employees to take up to twelve weeks of *unpaid* leave and return to their jobs after, only covers about 60 percent of US employees.[6] Yet even among those eligible for unpaid leave through FMLA, many cannot afford to take it. Data show that just 39.5 percent of wage-earning parents are both eligible for and can afford to take parental leave under FMLA, a number that breaks down along racial lines: 35.7 percent of

Black parents, 33.4 percent of American Indian/Alaska Native parents, and 26 percent of Latino parents can afford to take leave under FMLA.[7]

The number of parents with access to *paid* leave is even lower. In 2019, just 15 percent of US workers had access to employer-sponsored paid family leave.[8] Furthermore, access to and use of paid leave—like unpaid leave—differs along racial and class lines. Low-paid and part-time workers were less likely to have access to paid family leave.[9] A study by the Bureau of Labor Statistics, which drew data from four nationally representative data sets, found a nine-percentage-point difference in access to paid parental leave between Latino and white workers, even after controlling for various demographic and employment characteristics.[10] Another survey of mothers in the San Francisco Bay Area examined disparities in access to and use of paid parental leave. It found that, compared to white women, Black, Latina, and Asian women received 3.6, 2.0, and .9 fewer weeks, respectively, of full pay during their paid parental leaves.[11] Furthermore, women of color are less likely to have access to *any* form of paid leave, including parental leave; 37 percent of Black women, 44 percent of Latina women, and 40 percent of Asian American women had no access to any form of paid leave, compared to 36 percent of white women.[12] Data on Indigenous women's access to paid leave is extremely limited, although one study found that Aboriginal teen mothers in Canada were less likely to be eligible for parental leave programs.[13] The economic consequences of such disparate access to paid leave is clear: it is estimated that Black women with family caregiving responsibilities spend 41 percent of their annual income on caregiving-related expenses, compared to white caregivers, who spend 14 percent of their annual income on these same expenses.[14]

It is not surprising, then, that feminists largely and uncritically support paid parental leave. But, as it turns out, so too do the vast majority of Americans. Polls show that 73 percent of US adults support federal funding for paid parental leave. This support transpires along partisan lines: 90 percent of Democrats, 72 percent of independents, and 50 percent of Republicans support federal funding for paid parental leave.[15] And the value of such leaves is especially taken-for-granted among liberals and within feminist and LGBTQ+ spaces. There is not, in fact, a single leftist queer critique of paid parental leave published and in wide circulation.

In the rare moments where critiques of paid leave are articulated, they are almost entirely connected to the language we use to discuss this leave—do we call it maternity, paternity, parental, or family leave?!—rather than the premise of the leave or the ideas that such leaves traffic in. The article "Ditch Maternity Leave for Parental Leave—Here's Why," posted to the website of the human resources firm Insperity, speaks to this point. The essay's key argument is that we should swap maternity leave for parental leave, which, ostensibly, would allow parents of any gender time off work to bond with a new baby. For an article so concerned with the language used to talk about policy, it is telling that the author slips between describing this form of leave as "parental leave" and "family leave."[16] This conflation reveals a great deal. Today, we can have parents and families without mothers and fathers, but we still cannot have families without parents, and we certainly cannot have paid leave without parents and families.

But why not?! Why can't families without parents or children be structurally recognized? Why are paid leaves limited to parents? How do feminist and LGBTQ+ demands for paid leave reproduce the same heteronormativity evident across calls for paid leave more broadly? In this chapter, I take up these questions. In so doing, I develop a queer critique of parental leave (which includes, at least in practice, maternity leave, paternity leave, and family leave), outlining the epistemological limits of familial discourse central to imaginings of and calls for paid leave. To be clear, I am not advocating for obliterating paid leave. In fact, I am advocating for *expanding* it, but in queer ways. I am arguing for a material shift in the conditions that allow workers to access paid leaves, for forms of paid leave entirely disconnected not just from the family form but also from any dependents one might already see themselves in relation to. I suggest that this queer reconfiguration can occur by moving from family or parental leaves to care leaves, and, crucially, not just in name.

This argument is meant to queer how people advocate for paid leave as well as scholarly conversations about social reproduction—especially those happening in feminist, queer, and trans spaces—by outlining the significant political and epistemological limits of familial discourses evident in discussions of paid leave. In so doing, I move beyond analyzing social reproduction in terms of so-called invisibilized labors of the home, which has been precisely the site of feminist demands to recognize and compensate these labors.[17] I also add to the scholarship that complicates feminist efforts to reward and value the work of unpaid and underpaid care alike.

To be clear, I believe, of course, that care workers, overwhelmingly US-born and immigrant women of color, should earn a livable wage—as should all workers. My queer complication of Marxist feminist approaches is rooted in concerns that valorization of care compels additional and almost always uncompensated labor in ways that transpire along predictable racial, classed, gendered, and sexual lines. I recognize, of course, that the provision of additional care-related resources can ease the double days of individual women and stop the hemorrhaging of women from the labor force at a time when racial capitalism continues to demand the naturalization of this very labor. Considering that women, and disproportionately women of color, continue to provide the vast majority of both paid and unpaid care labor, I understand why Marxist feminist scholars and activists have advocated for care to be central to policy agendas. At the same time, as I demonstrate in what follows, current discussions of care rely on heteronormative assumptions regarding where this care occurs (the family), disregarding the many forms of social reproduction that transpire beyond the family structure. As long as we promote care through an affective evocation of family, I argue, it will be difficult to enhance living otherwise.

This position extends prior Marxist feminist critiques of work. Kathi Weeks, for instance, cautions that in fighting for equal pay, decent working conditions, and the need to recognize unpaid work as valuable, Marxist feminists have spoken of work in largely positive terms.[18] Heather Berg argues against the feminist tendency to frame women's work as worthy or socially necessary precisely because it can be harder to resist one's working conditions when one's work is imagined as crucial for someone else's existence.[19] I extend these Marxist feminist insights by asking what might happen to our understanding of care if we brought concerns about social reproduction into more serious dialogue with queer theory. I turn to the place of the imagined family in conversations about social reproduction to raise a series of questions: How has positioning social reproduction as a Marxist feminist—not queer Marxist—concern limited understandings of these very labors? How might queering social reproduction allow us to both account for the materiality of the world in the here and now and reflect what José Esteban Muñoz describes as the horizons of queer utopic thought?[20] Does Lee Edelman's plea to say "Fuck the Child," as part and parcel of a queer uprooting of the heteronormative reproductivist social order, necessarily mean "Fuck childcare"?[21] How can institutional investments in care infrastructure—childcare tax credits/stipends, expansion of affordable and quality childcare, paid family and medical leave, and so on—overcome inherent assumptions about the subjects and objects of care and the social relations through which and spaces within which care occurs?

In this chapter, I suggest that queer theory is useful for approaching both parental leave and social reproduction otherwise. While scholars have demonstrated just how good Marxism and queer theory are for one another, little scholarship considers what it might mean to queer social reproduction—even though Marxist feminists have been at the forefront of developing social reproduction theory, and feminist and queer theory are themselves in deep conversation.[22] At this point in the book, readers will not be surprised that I do not attempt to queer conversations about paid leave by centering LGBTQ+ people. Such an approach runs counter to the demands of queer theory, which asks us to think past identitarian lines and also demands challenging institutions, rather than asking for incorporation into them.[23] In many ways, there is nothing more normative than using one's time to build a life in relation to a nuclear family. As such, there is something decidedly queer about destroying the expectation that we do so, as well as the institutional practices—including parental leave—that further these very expectations.[24]

This chapter's argument unfolds as follows. First, I outline how paid leave is being talked about among self-identified feminists and progressives, offering some critiques of these contemporary discourses in circulation. I then share a series of encounters that collectively comprise a queer autoethnographic archive and that speak to how one's imagined home creates expectations in the workplace, extending feminist and queer critiques of the so-called public/private split. Next, I draw from discourses surrounding child-free workers' experiences to outline the conservative gender ideologies driving calls for paid leave, which also appear throughout feminist articulations of social reproduction theory, or the labors of life making. I close by thinking through what it might mean to queer social reproduction, and suggest that doing so requires far more than incorporating "chosen family" into the care matrix, the discursive move for which LGBTQ+ supporters often advocate. I also offer a queer proposal, which is at once a queer critique of paid family leave and an argument for broadening it: the utopian, aspirational model of "Fuck the Child" as a new way to interrogate and move past the public/private split and familialism that haunt discussions of care. This move, I argue, is essential for caring in a way that does not reinforce the heterosexual order.

## CONTEMPORARY CONVERSATIONS ABOUT PAID LEAVE

In early 2022, when it seemed possible that the US Senate would pass Build Back Better—the Biden-Harris administration's policy proposal described as comparable to Franklin Roosevelt's New Deal—feminists rejoiced. In a *Ms. Magazine* article, longtime feminist activist Kathy Spillar championed the bill, noting that it "includes elements that feminists have worked literally decades for: historic investments in child care, paid family and medical leave; universal pre-kindergarten for every 3- and 4-year-old in the country; and an extension of the child tax credit that has already cut child poverty in half this year."[25]

Overwhelmingly, feminists' excitement about the proposed policy, and its nearly $2 trillion budget, circled around its provisions for paid family and medical leave, childcare tax credits, and money for childcare. Senate Majority Leader Charles Schumer asserted that "one of the most important planks [of Build Back Better] is family leave."[26] *Ms.* headlines initially read: "Building Back Better for Women and Families," "Build Back Better Would Achieve Feminists' Long-Deferred Dream of Affordable Childcare," and "The U.S. is in Urgent Need of Childcare Solutions. Build Back Better Would be a Game-Changer."[27] As we learned that the Senate likely would fail to enact the bill, headlines began to read: "Why Is the Senate Failing to Build Back Better? Blame Sexism," "Build Back Better is in Peril. Low Income Families Can't Afford to Lose It," and "Death of Build Back Better Will Hurt Women and Kids the Most."[28] As these headlines suggest, mothers, women, and families were central to the feminist media coverage of the proposed bill.

But others have pushed back on this framing, arguing explicitly that paid leave is not just a mothers' issue. In her aforementioned United Nations speech, Anne Hathaway made precisely this point.

> The deeper into the issue of paid parental leave I go, the clearer I see the connection between persisting barriers to women's full equality and empowerment, and the need to redefine and in some cases, destigmatize men's role as caregivers. In other words, to liberate women, we need to liberate men. . . . Maternity leave, or any workplace policy based on gender, can . . . only ever be a gilded cage. Though it was created to make life easier for women, we now know it creates a perception of women as being inconvenient to the workplace. We now know it chains men to an emotionally limited path.[29]

This sentiment is shared by Serena Williams's husband, Alexis Ohanian, who wrote a *New York Times* essay titled, "Paternity Leave Was Crucial After the Birth of My Child, and Every Father Deserves It." Williams agreed that parental leave is "so important for both parents."[30]

These celebrities are in step with Insperity's call to "ditch maternity leave for parental leave." It is worth noting that by the time Insperity demanded this discursive shift from maternity to parental leave in 2022, it had already largely been actualized. The figure below represents every article about parental leave published between 2010 and 2020 in one of four major national newspapers (*The New York Times*, *The Wall Street Journal*, *USA Today*, and *The Washington Post*).[31] This graph highlights that the number of articles using the language of "parental leave" rather than "maternity leave" has increased over the last decade, with an important shift occurring in 2019, when the number of articles mentioning "parental leave" eclipsed those mentioning "maternity leave."

Back to Insperity, which is particularly concerned with how paid parental leaves "for fathers lag far behind." The essay notes that the average maternity leave is forty-one days while the average paternity leave is twenty-two days. "To correct this imbalance," Insperity says, "Many companies moved to a seemingly gender-neutral parental leave policy. Companies offer the bulk of paid time off to a designated primary caretaker and a lesser amount to the secondary or supporting caretaker. But this practice often results in mothers getting more time off. Often, men can be discouraged from identifying themselves as primary caregivers

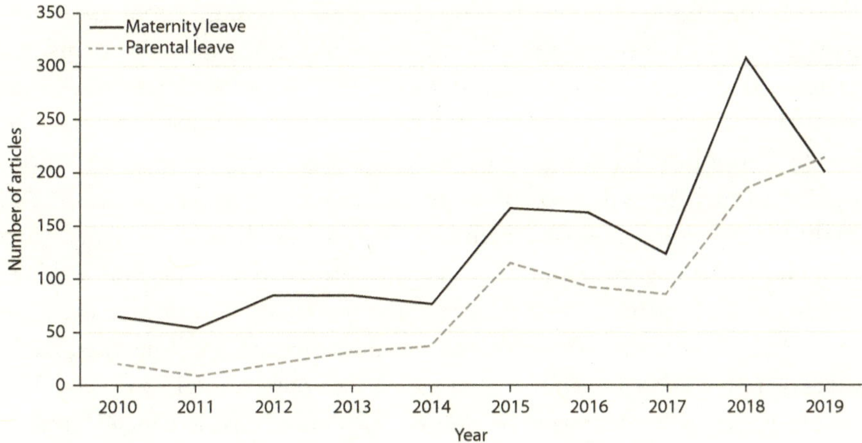


Family leave in the media over time.

(either by their employers or because they've fallen victim to the pressure of long-entrenched gender norms)."[32]

These long-entrenched gender norms must be disrupted, in part, Insperity says, because nowadays "mothers and fathers share parenting duties more equitably."[33] Despite Insperity's confidence, they are, unfortunately, incorrect. A Gallup poll shows that women continue to do the majority of household and childcare labor. In fact, the only areas where men do more work than women are in terms of making decisions about investing or finances, car maintenance, and lawn care. All other forms of domestic labor—laundry, cleaning, cooking, grocery shopping, washing dishes, paying bills, and even "caring for children on a daily basis"—are still disproportionately performed by women. And this disparity cannot be accounted for based on the idea that women are less likely to work outside of the home. In fact, even in households where both parents work outside of the home, men still only "shoulder slightly more of the burden of chores than do men in single income households."[34] We also know that LGBTQ+ relationships and families often reproduce similar domestic dynamics; scholars have argued, for instance, that women partnered with transmasculine people often do outsized household and emotional labor.[35]

Despite the widespread and deeply gendered disparities in who is saddled with domestic labor, advocates for paternity leave increasingly frame their demands in terms of feminism. Proponents argue that paternity leave is feminist because it works to disrupt traditional gender norms. An article titled "Here's Why Paternity Leave Is a Huge Feminist Issue" suggests that allowing fathers to take on more caregiving responsibilities can create "more fluid" definitions of fatherhood and motherhood and more opportunities for public displays of fathering.[36] Another article, "The Fight for Paternity Leave is a Feminist One," similarly sees paternity leave as a challenge to gender norms and assumptions about masculinity, suggesting that the gendered expectation that men work and women caregive hurts men who *want* to be more involved in caregiving. Thus, the article asserts, paternity leave allows men to "choose parenthood," a choice they would apparently otherwise be denied.[37] (This choice is complicated, it would seem, by the fact that where women incur a "motherhood penalty," fathers experience the opposite, a so-called "fatherhood bonus," which refers to the fact that men with kids are paid more than men without kids.)[38] One father, who noted that "paternity leave set[s] us up for visible father-in-public time," even went so far as to describe "marching the stroller to the grocery store" as "the most feminist thing [he's] probably ever done."[39] Parallel arguments appear in a *Hasting Women's Law Journal* article that frames its approach to paternity leave as feminist. In critiquing the FMLA for "promot[ing] the stereotypical 'traditional family' structure and undermin[ing] the role of fathers in the home," the article asserts that expanding paternity leave provisions will disrupt typical family formations.[40]

But beyond upending gender norms and benefiting fathers, paternity leave, advocates often claim, also benefits women because it allows mothers to get back to work. When fathers take paternity leave, a section of the *Instyle* article aptly titled "Paid Paternity Leave is Good for Women's Careers" argues, it creates the grounds for a more equal division of care labor between parents (always already assumed to be one man and one woman). When mothers' caregiving loads are lightened, the thinking goes, they can get back to work more quickly, overcome the "motherhood penalty," and generally have more successful careers.[41] Such ways of thinking are also evident in an article in *The Atlantic*, which frames paternity leave as a solution to the gendered division of care labor and thus the wage gap, warning that without paternity leave, "those tasks continue to fall to women, whose careers suffer as a result."[42] As evidence for this position, one article cites a Swedish study showing that mothers' earnings rose 7 percent for each additional month of paternity leave that her spouse (assumed to be a man) took.[43] Another notes that countries with the highest percentage of women in leadership tend to have more paternity leave.[44] And yet, underpinning this argument is the same conflation of "woman" with "mother" that advocates claim paternity leave disrupts. In other words, paternity leave does not benefit *women*; it benefits *mothers*.

The interchangeable terminology here, which positions all women as mothers and the only women who might need support as mothers, was paralleled in commentary on Build Back Better. Upon the House passage of Build Back Better, C. Nicole Mason, the President and CEO of the Institute for Women's Policy Research (IWPR), commented, "Access to affordable child care is a fundamental need for women in today's workforce."[45] Melissa Boteach of the National Women's Law Center similarly noted, "COVID has only exacerbated these inequalities and families are getting left behind—particularly Black and Latina women and mothers."[46] And Rep. Brenda Lawrence (D-MI) asserted, "With the president's newly-announced Build Back Better Framework, we are making historic, transformational investments in women and families across the country."[47] The singling out of women here ("women and families") both assumes that children's concerns are women's concerns are feminists' concerns and also suggests that these issues are not men's or fathers' concerns. Moreover, while it is clear how Build Back Better is an investment in mothers and families, it is unclear how exactly it is an investment in women who are not mothers. In much the same way, affordable childcare may be a fundamental need for mothers, as Mason asserts, without it being a fundamental need for women.

A similar conflation of women and mothers is pervasive in the work of advocacy group "A Marshall Plan for Moms." Its website opens by asserting "We need a Marshall Plan for *Moms*—a historic investment in *women*'s economic recovery and empowerment" (emphasis added). Later, in a section titled "Finishing the Fight for *Women*'s Equality," the group states that it is a "national movement to center *mothers* in our economic recovery from the pandemic and value their labor. We advocate for public and private sector changes to expand choices for *women* and to remove barriers

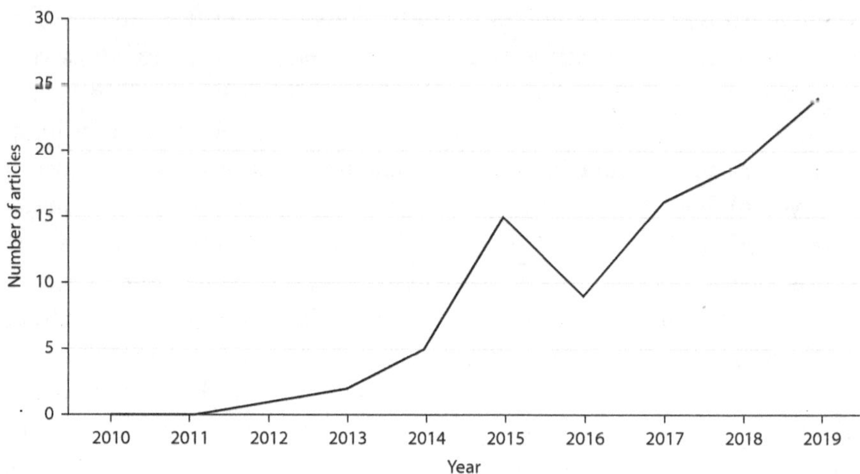


LGBTQness in articles about parental leave over time.

to equality" (emphasis added). These kinds of slippages also are apparent when the organization talks about families, something evident on the organization's Instagram account, where it shares mothers' stories.[48] One of these stories featured Raena Joy, who described how her male partner's family leave improved their relationship and made the time immediately following the delivery of their child less of a burden, even though he had to sacrifice pay. "It has been an investment in our family, and only possible because my employer offers paid leave," she declared, encouraging others to call Sen. Schumer to demand paid leave for "ALL families."[49] The assumption here that ALL families should have access to paid leave rests upon the assumption that ALL families have children. Those oriented in feminist and queer ways should be pushing back against the conflating of women/mothers and families/those who have children.

Put otherwise, queering parental leave requires more than ensuring that LGBTQ+ families are considered a part of "ALL families" and therefore have access to paid leaves. But such an invoking of LGBTQ+ families has been the primary discursive move to connect LGBTQ+ness and parental leave. The figure above demonstrates the dramatic increase in the use of terms related to LGBTQ+ness in articles about parental leave.

Gay men are often at the center of concerns about parental rights. Anne Hathaway's United Nations speech called up the figure of gay men to make the point that maternity leave "cannot serve the reality of a world in which there is more than one type of family. Because in the modern world, some families have two daddies. How exactly does maternity leave serve them?"[50] In one of the previously mentioned articles about paternity leave, a Nashville city councilor discussed a resolution to grant maternity and paternity leave to city workers, saying, "Don't forget about dads and LGBTQ couples too." In his view, the resolution was "inclusive" because it included paternity leave and thus LGBTQ+ (men) couples.[51] In its critique of using the term "maternity leave," Insperity also notes that moving from maternity/paternity to parental leave is important because it "includes adoptive parents and same sex couples."[52] And in a *Newsweek* op-ed titled "The Fight for Paid Parental Leave is a Fight for Queer Rights," David Doge, the Executive Editor of *Gays with Kids*, argues that "queer men, in particular, are disproportionately impacted" by the current lack of federal paid leave policies.[53] We ought to be asking why, in moments when parental leave is framed as an LGBTQ+ issue, the subject consistently invoked is a gay man and his family. We also ought to be asking how we might do better in our attempts to bring LGBTQ+ness—with an emphasis on the Q!—into conversation with paid leave.

## THE PERSONAL IS POLITICAL: A QUEER AUTOETHNOGRAPHIC ARCHIVE

Before I moved to Houston, Texas, for a job at Rice University, I worked for eight years at Middlebury College, a small private liberal arts school in a little town in Vermont. The combination of rural life with liberal arts life—by which I mean that one key thing the college sells in its pitch of itself is access to faculty and the unique faculty-student relationships that result from this access—means that many of my former students knew a great deal about my faculty colleagues and about me. My students knew, for instance, that I am decidedly child-free. They also often knew when faculty had new babies and were on parental leave. Students often babysit, petsit, and housesit for faculty. What I want to focus on here is how this intertwinement between work life and life outside of work impacts different workers differently. In some ways, this enmeshment happens in many kinds of academic spaces, especially, perhaps, feminist and queer classrooms where faculty and students alike share things about our lives as a way of relating to course material. But it is often more pronounced in small departments at small schools in small towns, like the one I was institutionally located in.

A few years ago, I co-taught a Gender, Sexuality, and Feminist Studies (GSFS) course with a colleague and close friend whose PhD is in Black Studies. She is a married lesbian who, at the time, had one child. After a student in our co-taught class requested a letter of recommendation from me, I asked if she also had requested one from the course's other professor—an important question because, had the answer been affirmative, I would have worked with my colleague to avoid duplicating material in our letters. The student responded by saying that she did not ask the other professor because she had a young child and wouldn't have as much time to write a letter as I would. Another student once asked me if I could email them a PDF of an article assigned in a course taught by another faculty member. With some confusion, I asked why they wouldn't ask the other faculty member. They commented—publicly and during our Politics of Reproduction class, no less!—that this faculty member has a five-year-old child and, therefore, no time. The implication, of course, is that, as a child-free person, I had endless time to give to work and should even be willing to do others' work. These kinds of encounters are more common than people with children might think.

They are also not limited to students. In fact, the ways that ideas about children and families structure one's working environment also get institutionalized in discriminatory ways. I learned from a colleague and friend, who was pregnant at the time, that an administrator authorized an extension of her start-up research funds—money that incoming faculty are given to conduct research—because traveling internationally became inadvisable due to her pregnancy. Earlier that same year, I had been involved in a serious accident that left me unable to walk for several months. As I prepared for surgery, I emailed the same feminist-identified administrator to ask if I could have a similar extension. I thought I had a good case. I quite literally could not walk, was in an enormous amount of pain, and had spent the last several months doing intensive rehabilitation in preparation for surgery, leaving little time to adequately prepare for a research trip. Traveling to conduct research and spending my research funds on the timeline given when I started my job—and could not have predicted that I would become temporarily disabled for nearly a year—became extremely difficult. The same administrator who approved my pregnant friend's extension denied my request. When I asked for clarification regarding the criteria upon which these decisions are made, the administrator responded by email, "I am not at liberty to discuss the personal circumstances of another faculty member. Given that you clearly already know some details about those circumstances, I'm confident you would agree that that is a unique personal/public health situation with time- and space-specific constraints *unlike any other*. It is, therefore, not comparable to your request" (emphasis added).

Considering that both requests emerged out of unanticipated changes to our bodies and physical health that would make fulfilling job expectations difficult, the circumstances are, in many ways, exactly equivalent. My pregnant friend smartly joked in response to the administrator's comment, "The only difference between our situations is that I know when my disability will end!" All jokes aside, the notion that we can think of pregnancy as temporary disability is rooted in the work of feminist legal scholars who, in the 1980s, linked pregnancy to other conditions that inhibited one's work to argue for leaves for a wide range of temporary medical issues. Incidentally, this strategy still allowed employers to deny leaves for pregnancy if they also denied leaves for other temporary conditions.[54] Of course, in our case, mutual denial of our requests was not how the scenario played out. My colleague's extension and the denial of my extension stood. While this situation is not exactly about parental leave, the college administrator commented that I had not applied for any formal leave due to my disability, which is true. I didn't know that I *could* have gotten a leave to deal with my medical situation, and further, following my accident, I was too depressed to figure out which institutional hoops I needed to jump through to make this happen. It did not matter to the administrator that my colleague also had not yet applied for maternity leave at this point in her pregnancy. Her pregnancy itself was enough to confer legitimacy to her need for leave and, by extension, a reconfiguring of her access to work-related resources.

I have learned through complaining about these encounters that I am not alone in my frustrations. Fellow child-free colleagues have bemoaned that others in their departments routinely invoke their children to assert why they cannot do certain things (teach a late afternoon class, be available for a morning meeting, and so on), implying that those without children should accommodate the parents' schedules—even when doing so comes at significant personal expense. And, of course, none of us child-free folks get anything at all for doing additional work when our colleagues take their parental leaves or, later, when they are presumed unavailable precisely because they have children. A brief story to illustrate this point: I attended an open meeting about faculty compensation, which is less at Middlebury than at Middlebury's peer schools. The person representing the institution commented that while it is true that Middlebury faculty salaries are lower than those of most of its peers, faculty members' total financial compensation was about average when you include things like daycare subsidies, reimbursement for college tuition for dependent children, parental leave, and so on. I raised my hand and commented that those forms of "compensation" do not benefit all employees equitably. I also asked how much the college spends reimbursing faculty members $25,000 annually for each of their children's college tuitions and how much the college spends on parental leave.

Leaving aside the question of college tuition reimbursement, a dean cheerfully responded that the college spends very little on parental leave because those positions are almost never replaced. The institutional representative running the meeting followed up to say that they'd get back to me with specific figures—which I never received, despite asking multiple times over the course of multiple years. A faculty colleague with children then responded to my comment by saying that we should be focused on differences between the earnings of Middlebury employees and those of other institutions, rather than focusing on the differences in compensation among Middlebury employees. After the meeting, two child-free colleagues approached me to express their frustrations with the way that conversations about "total compensation" require that we ignore significant differences between parents and non-parents and, further, that pointing out these differences was perceived as threatening, even at a meeting about faculty compensation. Collectively, this queer archive of encounters and exchanges speaks to the difficulty of thinking about the labor of reproduction, where it happens, and how it should be compensated, especially if our attempts to do so are meant to be oriented in feminist and queer ways.

## IT'S REALLY NOT ABOUT ME: CRITIQUES FROM CHILD-FREE WORKERS

While feminists have long advocated for paid leave, they have said far less about the mechanics of those leaves, including how to reduce the burdens of parental leave for the workers who are left behind. It seems ideal that those workers taking leave would be replaced, but often they are not, and even if they are, someone has to do the labor of hiring, training, and welcoming their replacements—typically without any additional compensation. It is no surprise, then, that tensions between wage-earning parents and child-free workers have erupted in many workplaces, a dynamic intensified during the COVID-19 pandemic.

A *New York Times* article, "Parents Got More Time Off. Then the Backlash Started," discusses precisely this scenario.[55] After several major tech companies implemented new pandemic-related leave policies, primarily geared toward parents—including, for instance, twenty weeks of paid leave at Facebook—child-free people began to express their exasperation. They noted, for instance, that their colleagues' paid leaves meant that they were "being asked to shoulder a heavier workload" without any increase in pay. Such sentiments were widespread. Two thousand Facebook employees voted to ask Sheryl Sandberg, Facebook's Chief Operating Officer, "what Facebook could do to support nonparents, since its other policies had benefited parents." The *Times* article reporting on this story closes with a quote from Erin Kelly, codirector of MIT's Institute for Work and Employment Research: "A question that we might ask the employees who are feeling some frustration about their co-workers being on leave is what do you think is going to happen if that person quits? You're going to actually be stretched further."[56] Such a response to complaints about workplace culture makes clear the degree to which the expectations associated with work are connected to how a person's home life is imagined. It also makes clear that only certain people are allowed to have their complaints taken seriously.[57]

These people are, of course, not child-free. In her UN speech advocating for the social value of paid parental leave, Anne Hathaway invoked such non-parents:

> I don't mean to imply that you need to have children to care about and benefit from [paid leave]—whether you have or want kids, you will benefit by living in a more evolved world with policies not based on gender. We all benefit from living in a more compassionate time where our needs do not make us weak, they make us fully humans. . . . Paid parental leave is not about taking days off work; it is about creating freedom to define roles, to choose how to invest time, and to establish new, positive cycles of behavior.[58]

Hathaway invoked non-parents to suggest that interest in this topic should not be limited to parents since everyone will benefit from living in a less prescriptively gendered world. But non-parents quickly become ghosts. "We all," Hathaway said, benefit from policies that allow us to have needs.[59] However, the only needs Hathaway gestures toward are related to time away to care for one's own children. As such, only those people with children who get time away from work are imagined as in need of the freedom to create new roles and to choose how to invest their time. Because of widespread entrenchment of normative gender ideologies, many others—including both those who are child-free and those who have grown children—could surely benefit from time off work to rethink the gendered roles they have long assumed and to establish new behaviors.

It was precisely the desire for new behaviors and for developing the capacities to push back against typical gendered stereotypes that led author Meghann Foye to take a "meternity" leave from work.[60] At thirty-one years old, and a decade into her demanding career at a prominent magazine, Foye was feeling burned out, something she attributed, in part, to not having access to any of the socially acceptable (and highly gendered!) leaves from work precisely because she hadn't gotten married or had kids. "For women who follow a 'traditional' path," Foye says, "this pause often naturally comes in your late 20s or early 30s, when a wedding, pregnancy and babies means that your personal life takes center stage.

But for those who end up on the 'other' path, that socially mandated time and space for self-reflection may never come." Foye continued, stating that she

> couldn't help but feel envious when parents on staff left the office at 6 p.m. to tend to their children, while it was assumed co-workers without kids would stay behind to pick up the slack. . . . It seemed that parenthood was the only path that provided a modicum of flexibility. There's something about saying 'I need to go pick up my child' as a reason to leave the office on time that has far more gravitas than, say, 'My best friend just got ghosted by her OkCupid date and needs a margarita'—but both sides are valid.[61]

So, Foye took a "meternity" sabbatical from her job, and she wrote a novel about a woman who also took a "meternity" leave.

After the right-wing *New York Post* published an article about Foye's book, conservative commentators responded with the kind of vitriol that *Salon* described as reserved for the "spoiled, entitled, childless woman."[62] In a scathing article titled "Parents Should Be Worshiped by Their Childless Co-Workers," conservative author Kyle Smith opened with some questions for Foye and, by extension, all child-free workers:

> Have you recently had your body split open by a screaming, red, nightmare-lump of writhing humanity? Or taken on the hair-raising responsibility of parenting a little one with less ability to manage for him- or herself than a newborn kitten? Then, sorry. You don't qualify for maternity leave. . . . Giving birth is like "pooing a train," someone explained on Twitter this week. Take your lower lip and pull it over your forehead and you'll be in the ballpark, some say. Compensation for this is in order, along with time off to adjust to the less intense, but much more emotionally challenging, process of getting the kid acclimated to existence on Planet Earth—especially given that parents suffer so that society as a whole may prosper (or at least continue).[63]

It might appear at first glance that this conservative writer and the conservative newspaper he's publishing in have become—even temporarily—concerned with women, but deconstructing this post reveals gendered ideologies at play here that feminists have, in other moments, contested. Smith implies that maternity leaves should be connected to the physical act of birth, an idea that would necessarily preclude adoptive parents from paid leaves, as well as fathers. Considering this position, Smith's claim that parents "deserve a little work break (though mommies are far, far more deserving than daddies)" doesn't hold up.[64] If physical recovery is the point of parental leave—and I am sympathetic to this argument—then there should be similar support for other kinds of short-term leaves meant to heal one's body after other kinds of traumatic events. But this clearly is not the case. (Even if short-term disability leave is available to workers, how one accesses it is rarely made as obvious as is how one accesses parental leave.) Furthermore, it is unclear if, for Smith, mothers are more deserving of parental leave than fathers because, in most cases, they are the ones who have given birth, or because Smith correctly identifies that women do more domestic labor than men and he believes either that this should be recognized as labor or that women should have time off work because they *should* be doing this disproportionate domestic labor.

What we do know is that, either way, Smith's assertions contribute to the glorification of the production of families with biological ties. This glorification rests on insulting child-free people. "Non-parents should fetch us lattes daily and offer to do light housekeeping, preferably while doing some 'Downton Abbey' groveling and calling us 'Madam' or 'M'lord'—though I personally would prefer 'Your Excellency.'" For Smith, "Wanting to order a case of chardonnay and settle in to binge-watch the new season of 'Unbreakable Kimmy Schmidt' isn't in the same category. If you've got a case of the sads, or sudden-onset reflectivitis, that's just a personality problem—not a reason to take off work."[65] While Smith doesn't name women here, he doesn't have to. His references to "Downton Abbey" and "Unbreakable Kimmy Schmidt," which are often lauded for their female-led casts, as well as to white wine, are clearly gendered.[66] Just note that "feminine" was third in *Wine Enthusiast* magazine's list of top wine terms because of its widespread use to describe wines that were "light, refined and delicate."[67] But caring about women, their post-birthing bodies, and the disproportionate domestic labor they do was never Smith's concern. If it were, he would not so flippantly describe "a case of the sads" as a personality problem that doesn't justify taking time off work[68]—especially considering that one in seven women suffer "a case of the sads" following giving birth. It's called postpartum depression.[69]

Unsurprisingly, Smith does not acknowledge what I see as the most convincing of Foye's points: that when people have children it creates more work for their coworkers and that this labor not only is uncompensated but also cannot be spoken of. In the few articles in circulation that do reference those workers left behind, the toll of leave-taking on remaining workers is so seemingly obvious, so commonsensical, that authors do not even feel the need to support their argument with facts or figures quantifying how many additional hours are worked as a result of coworkers taking parental leave. Several articles mention workers' loads doubling. A *Washington Post* article entitled "What You Need to Know When Covering for Someone on Maternity/Paternity Leave" offers as a piece of advice that "it's simply not realistic . . . to do two jobs in the same amount of time" and that workers "can't pull off multiple 80-hour weeks without seriously damaging [their] own work-life balance."[70]

In making such claims, journalists acknowledge tension and resentment between parents and nonparents in the workplace. At the same time, the same journalists work to make clear that those not on leave respected parents' needs, were "pro-leave," and were "willing to do their parts." To explain why coworkers are—or should be—pro-leave and happy to pick up their coworkers' slack, the *Washington Post* article states, "Remember: Supporting employees when they need to take maternity, paternity, or other forms of personal leave is a benefit to you, even if you're not the one taking the leave. You never know when you'll be the one who needs help from your colleagues." Such sentiments frame all workers as always already parents. When *you* have kids, your colleagues will help you, too. Of course, not all workers will have children. And securing "help from your colleagues" if you don't have kids, especially in some kind of structurally supported way, seems improbable, since the concept of paid leaves disconnected from the family formation does not widely exist.

Why, we should ask, should child-free workers be expected to support everyone else around them while knowing that they will never be entitled to the same kinds of flexibility to build the kinds of lives they imagine for themselves? This question is important for workplaces to consider for many reasons, including that the number of people who are not having children is increasing. Data show that 16.5 percent of adults aged fifty-five and older do not have biological children.[71] And more people are also asserting that they do not intend to become parents. A 2021 Pew Research Center study found that 44 percent of non-parents aged eighteen to forty-nine say it is not too or not at all likely that they will have children, up seven percentage points from 2018.[72] For unmarried women, as well as LGBTQ+ people, these numbers are even higher. In 2008, 13 percent of "ever married" women were child-free, compared with 56 percent of "never married."[73] And just 24 percent of women couples and 7.2 percent of men couples have children, far fewer than heterosexual couples.[74] Perhaps most crucial for thinking about how parental leaves do not work for LGBTQ+ people, just 12 percent of heterosexual women report caring for someone else's child, compared to approximately 23 percent of lesbian and bisexual women—the latter far less likely to get a paid leave for their care labor precisely because the children for whom they are caring are not imagined as "theirs."[75]

A 2014 study of twenty-five thousand workers in the United Kingdom suggests that the concerns of child-free workers are well-founded. In fact, two-thirds of child-free women between the ages of twenty-eight and forty felt that they were expected to work longer hours than those with children—a statement with which 40 percent of mothers also agreed.[76] Another study, which focused on faculty in the University of California system, measured the number of hours faculty members spent working, caregiving, and doing housework. The study concluded that women without children put in more hours at work than anyone else, including men without children and both men and women with children.[77] On average, faculty without children worked 6.05 more hours per week than those with children. More specifically, women without children worked 8.6 more hours per week than women with children, as well as 4.2 more hours than men with children.[78]

These figures suggest that we need more complicated ways of assessing and compensating the work of social reproduction and thinking through the place of child-free adults in this equation. Child-free workers work additional hours at work so that their colleagues can devote time to what is recognized as a family. The latter receive parental leaves for their labor while the former receive no recognition whatsoever, let alone the tax breaks or other structural support parents receive. It's not surprising that many child-free workers feel overlooked, taken-for-granted, and disregarded.

Contributing to these feelings are conflicting narratives in circulation regarding the social responsibilities of nonparents. We are told repeatedly that "it takes a village to raise a child," on the one hand, and on the other, that child-free people should avoid offering parenting suggestions to parents. These tensions are apparent in the different responses to questions that comprise *Slate*'s "Care and Feeding" parenting advice column—a surprising number of which are submitted by child-free people. "Child Free but Not a Child Hater" wrote in to ask about opportunities she and her child-free husband, who "have no desire to be parents," could explore to "interact with and help kids."[79]

> I think children are members of the community, and so are child-free people, so why not support each other? Every responsibility shouldn't fall on people who have to deal with the kids the rest of the time. But that isn't really the societal norm, and I feel weird trying to volunteer at a school or after-school program as an adult without children of my own. Is there a place for me to volunteer with kids? As a volunteer tutor, helping at a school, finding a cool outdoor or skills program? My husband and I don't want to be the annoying child-free people everyone hates or thinks of as creepy for inserting ourselves in how other people are raising their kids. Plus, I wouldn't even know where to start. How could we pursue this? Should we?[80]

The *Slate* advice columnist responded:

> I strongly agree with you that child-free adults have the *same responsibility* to children in their community, and the *same duty* to protect and support children in general, that is typically associated with those of us who are parents. There are many ways in which children (and their parents) could benefit from the time and energy you and your husband can offer, and you shouldn't deny them that, nor yourselves, simply because it isn't the norm for us to care for our neighbors in our selfish, capitalist society (emphasis added).

Other "Care and Feeding" advice columnists suggest that, perhaps, "same responsibility" isn't quite the right framing. "Terrorist Kids" wrote in to ask for advice regarding how she might support her friend whose children are disrespectful to their mother.

> Let me start by saying that I am not a parent. My best friend "Megan" is a single mom with two kids who are 8 and 4. I love Megan with all of my heart, but her kids are awful. They yell at her to give them snacks, buy them

> toys, or whatever else they want in a given moment. She rarely puts her foot down which results in her kids having a ton of expensive toys and eating cupcakes and candy at 6 a.m. just to shut them up. Again, I'm not a parent . . . Should I tell her that her kids are out of control?[81]

The Slate columnist confirmed what all child-free people already know: "You're right: few parents want to hear parenting advice from non-parents. That's not to say that you're wrong about what you're witnessing, but even if she's your best friend, she may not be open to your critiques about her children. I usually believe that as long as the kids are safe and not in imminent danger, then we should keep our thoughts to ourselves."[82]

Similar sentiments appeared in response to "Anti-Racist Aunt," who wrote in to ask about how she can help instill anti-racist beliefs in her niece and nephew, especially when her more conservative brother has asked her explicitly to avoid "talk[ing] politics" with his kids.[83] Recently, "Anti-Racist Aunt" noted that she had given her niece a doll with Brown skin and the child responded that "the doll would be prettier with lighter skin."[84] The *Slate* columnist responded:

> This is tricky, because as I've said before around here—unless the kids are in serious danger, your job isn't to save other people's children. I know you love your niece and nephew and want what's best for them, but their parents have the final say. However, I can't help but roll my eyes whenever white parents say they want to "protect" their kids from current social and political events by not talking about them. Hell, I was called the N-word by a white person as a 9-year-old. Who protected me from that? I have the same belief that you do in the sense that the only way to truly fix this dumpster fire of a country we find ourselves in is to have uncomfortable conversations with our kids about racism, politics, social issues, and more. It truly is the height of privilege to have the luxury to not concern yourself with those topics, when people like me have to deal with them every day whether I want to or not. . . . I think what you're doing is spot on. Continue to introduce the kids to diverse people who are making the world a better place through books, kid-friendly movies, etc.[85]

These conflicting pieces of advice raise many questions: Do child-free people really have "the same" responsibility to kids as their own parents do? Some other kind of or level of responsibility? A responsibility to adhere to parents' wishes . . . but with wiggle room when those wishes are racist? And yet no avenues for sharing reflections that emerge out of those responsibilities? What these questions make clear is that we need more complicated ways of thinking about where the labor of reproduction occurs, what it looks like, who does it, and how. Much of the labor of childrearing happens outside of the home and is performed by people who aren't parents to the child in question, and yet it often seems as if the labor of raising children must only be discussed in terms of the labor individual parents do in relation to their own children—something that impacts not just child-free people but also care providers.

This tension is evident in another exchange on the "Care and Feeding" advice column. "Mom of a Hugger" wrote in because her two-year-old son's teacher informed her that her child has personal space issues.

> Basically, he gets too close to the other kids, and sometimes the other kids cry. He does not hit them, he does not steal their toys, and he does not do anything to physically hurt them. He sometimes tries to hug them, but his teacher said most of the time he just wants to stand really close to the other kids. I am not sure how to fix this or what I can do about it. . . . My son is very cuddly and affectionate with my husband and me, and I love this about him. Every day that I pick him up from class the teacher tells me that she is still working with him on respecting personal space and that she hopes I am too. I want to help, but the only time he exhibits this behavior in front of me is with family, and I don't want that behavior to change. A part of me thinks that this is ridiculous, but I don't want to be the mom that ignores teachers. I want to have a great relationship with them and have up until this point. Any advice?[86]

The Care and Feeding advice columnist responded that Mom of a Hugger should "Rejoice!" because she has an "excellent opportunity to not worry about something."

> You are in great luck here. Your kid has a teacher who is working with him on this behavior. . . . Toddlers are so wonderfully weird, and they try out all kinds of absurd behaviors. I suspect that you know this on some level and that you don't think your son has a significant problem. The real sore spot for you, then, is the sense that your kid's teacher is judging you for not bringing this close-standing to heel in a timely fashion. As tough as that feeling is, I wouldn't worry too much about whatever shade you're feeling from her because a) you don't even know what she really thinks, b) you're doing everything you can anyway, and c) honestly who cares about snide comments from one

> stressed-out teacher? All due respect to stressed-out teachers—but she doesn't get to make you feel bad about your parenting when you're doing your best![87]

Mom of a Hugger, the columnist asserts, is off the hook for dealing with their child's behavior because someone else is doing that labor for them—despite the fact that a person we can assume is an underpaid worker (precisely because daycare provision is labor gendered feminine) is asking for help with a situation that is creating increased work for her at work. Aside from the recognition that this teacher is likely stressed out, there is no recognition here of her position as a worker, indeed precisely the type of low-paid, racialized worker who is unlikely to have access to paid parental leave herself. Notably absent from this discussion is the sentiment that "it takes a village to raise a child"—which is common elsewhere in the Slate parenting advice column—and any recognition that this childcare provider is key to that village. This is not terribly surprising. Even scholars analyzing the use of the village formulation for discussing childrearing approach the sentiment rather uncritically, noting that the role of different villagers is to "provide direct care to the children and/or support the parent in looking after their children. . . . Inherent in the concept of the village is the notion that caring for children is a shared responsibility amongst many."[88] Here and elsewhere, the village exists, it is imagined, to support children and parents—rather than to create a robust environment that supports life making in all kinds of ways and for all kinds of people.

These examples illustrate the degree to which we are meant to understand parenting as labored and nonparenting as nonlabored, even when it is being done by workers providing the kinds of care associated with parenting. They also speak to the ways that forms of social reproduction that occur outside of the home—and those who provide them—are dismissed. And they make clear the necessity of disrupting dominant ideas about the family if we want to develop feminist and queer ways of caring for one another.

## DISRUPTING THE FAMILY

Feminists have long made precisely this point. In an article published more than twenty-five years ago, Maxine Baca Zinn suggested that "the concept of family is an ideological concept, which conceals varied meanings and configurations."[89] Common among feminist activists in the 1960s was the belief that "the family was the primary site of women's oppression."[90] Rallying calls included "smash monogamy" and "abolish the nuclear family." Later feminist scholarship and activism worked to complicate these positions. Turning to the experiences of women of color and poor women, feminists, including Baca Zinn, argued that "in the absence of outside support, many women found collective strength in family life. Some women joined forces with husbands, brothers, and other community men to forge political struggles against racial and class-based oppression."[91] At the same time, the women of color feminists making these arguments did not reproduce a rosy or uncomplicated image of the family. Baca Zinn, for instance, acknowledged that "most families were indeed patriarchal."[92] And Bonnie Thornton Dill made clear that the opportunities of certain (white or upper class) families often rely on the disadvantages of other (non-white or poor/working-class) families.[93] In short, feminists have long pushed back on the positive affects tethered to the family formation, arguing instead that the family is a site for reproducing racial and class inequalities, encouraging normative gender and sexual desires, and policing those who step out of line.

The family and the home are also front and center in Marxist feminism, which has long critiqued classic Marxism for its inability to account for the specificity of women's oppression under capitalism. Marxist feminists have argued that sexism is responsible for the collective social refusal to recognize as work those household and domestic labors typically gendered feminine, including intimate, affective, and reproductive labors. We can think of these labors, scholars suggest, in terms of "the activities and attitudes, behaviors and emotions, and responsibilities and relationships directly involved in maintaining life, on a daily basis and intergenerationally."[94] It is through analyzing these forms of unrecognized and repetitive labors that Marxist feminists have developed social reproduction theory, the "fundamental insight" of which is that "human labor is at the heart of creating or reproducing society as a whole."[95] In her introduction to *Social Reproduction Theory*, Tithi Bhattacharya explains that "social reproduction theorists perceive the relation between labor dispensed to produce commodities and labor dispensed to produce people as part of the systemic totality of capitalism."[96] That is, we cannot understand capitalism without understanding the gendered labor required to produce workers themselves.

This unpaid or underpaid labor is imagined as primarily occurring in the home and in relation to the family formation. Bhattacharya contends that the family serves as a locus for capital accumulation insofar as creators of commodities "are themselves produced outside the ambit of the formal economy, in a 'kin-based' site called the family."[97] Kathi Weeks also focuses on the institution of the family, noting that the current wage system

> depends on a second institution, namely, the privatized family that serves as the primary locus for the reproductive labor necessary to reproduce workers on a daily and generational basis. So the wage-and-family-work system includes the major systems of production centered on the realm of waged work and of reproduction organized around the household and held together by the institution of the family as the means by which many of us are recruited into these typically unwaged and gendered relations of reproduction. So as feminists have long argued, we need a broader mapping of a capitalist economic system that can account for all the work, both waged and unwaged, that is involved in sustaining that system.[98]

For the most part, this "broader mapping" for which Weeks has called has not extended terribly far beyond the family, despite many Marxist feminist critiques of the nuclear family.[99] In fact, in defining and mapping processes of social reproduction, Marxist feminists return repeatedly to labor done in the household, a location theorized in opposition to the factory and other sites where commodity production occurs.[100] In *Women and the Subversion of Community*, Mariarosa Dalla Costa focuses on the role of the housewife in social reproduction, describing it as "the work of giving birth to, raising, disciplining, and servicing the worker for production."[101] In other words, household labor is precisely that which allows husbands to work and children to grow to be workers. Here and elsewhere, social reproduction is understood as those forms of labor that flow in one direction: from a woman to her husband and/or child(ren). Within this formulation, home quickly becomes synonymous with the family; both are sites where social reproduction occurs.

To be fair, not all scholars of social reproduction theory focus solely on the family. Bhattacharya, for instance, notes that labor power is reproduced through the school, the hospital, and other social institutions. She also recognizes that replenishment of labor occurs through slavery and immigration, in addition to birth.[102] Despite conceding that some social reproduction transpires outside the home, Bhattacharya describes these forms of labor as "even murkier" to analyze and returns to her focus on the domestic sphere.[103] Even as social reproduction theorists attempt to move away from the family, they hearken it back. And the family and the home remain the dominant sites of analysis for scholars of social reproduction theory.

The focus on family here speaks to the heteronormative nature of a great deal of scholarship on social reproduction. Equally worrisome for those of us trying to create queer paths for caregiving in this largely straight world is the focus on, as Bhattacharya puts it, making "visible labor and work that are analytically hidden by classical economists and politically denied by policy makers."[104] In pushing labor studies scholars and related activists to take seriously the labor of domestic, intimate, and reproductive care by calling it work, whether or not it was waged, Marxist feminists continued the Marxist project of making labor "visible." Bhattacharya's belief in the power of making labor "visible" is apparent in the vast majority of Marxist feminist scholarship. Dalla Costa laments that women's labor "remained invisible because only the product of her labour, the labourer, was visible," which she sees as the reason women were "trapped within pre-capitalist working conditions and never paid a wage."[105] While most Marxist feminists assume that making women's household labor "visible" is inherently valuable, Kathi Weeks discusses the paradoxical qualities of visibility, noting that even as Marxist feminists work "to make domestic labor visible as work and part of the valorization process," we must also "insist it is not something to celebrate or revere." Weeks notes that

> This is a very difficult thing to do: to gain its recognition as socially necessary labor (that requires, for example, more time off from waged work to accomplish), but not to overvalue it as such—to insist rather on its demystification, de-romanticization, de-privatization, de-individualization, and of course, de-gendering. As work, it too is something to struggle against becoming the whole of life. As I see it, this means struggling against—to name only a couple of things—the gender division of this work, the appall-

> ing conditions of so much waged domestic work, as well as forms of work intensification such as the ideology of intensive mothering. It also involves the invention of new ways of organizing and sharing work and of making it meaningful.[106]

Just as Weeks advocates against feminist approaches to work that frame it as an inherent social and political good, we must challenge feminists' beliefs in the value of making work visible. Such approaches speak to the long-held assumption within both Marxist feminist as well as LGBTQ+ spaces that visibility ushers in progress or is itself a representation of social and personal liberation—a belief that might just be the most commonsensical and taken-for-granted position in LGBTQ+ circles. Queer theorists have pushed back against such celebratory beliefs about visibility politics.[107] Elsewhere, I critique LGBTQ+ activists' calls for visibility, cautioning that the promises of so-called visibility have been oversold. I argue that we should be wary of the belief that achieving visibility will necessarily achieve anything else and suggest instead that visibility politics can actually thwart possibilities for collective political engagement precisely because the political project of LGBTQ+ movements is too often reduced to encouraging visibility. Queer justice will never be achieved if all one needs to do to be liberated is to "come out" and be "visible," precisely because building a world wherein queer life is possible will require far more than this simple discursive act.[108] We might extrapolate from such queer critiques to consider the limits of Marxist feminist attempts "to make visible labor and work"[109] as well as activist calls for workers to come out of the shadow economy. Put otherwise, making care labor visible will not on its own do anything at all to increase structural supports for ensuring that this labor is treated differently than it is now.

## QUEERING SOCIAL REPRODUCTION

The time to queer social reproduction has come. By queering social reproduction, I mean something other than stirring LGBTQ+ people into the pot of concerns regarding care. This is, in part, because the evocation of family and home evident in Build Back Better, social reproduction theory, and the other cultural texts I've referenced throughout this chapter are also evident in LGBTQ+ spaces. Put more directly, the language of family has long been deployed rather uncritically within LGBTQ+ spaces. Referring to fellow LGBTQ+ people as "fam" (short for family) or celebrating one's "chosen family" or "queer family" are, indeed, common practices.[110] Further, such familial discourse is prevalent in LGBTQ+ conversations about caregiving and receiving. In one discussion of Build Back Better, the LGBTQ Research and Communication Project at the Center for American Progress argued for including "chosen family" in paid family and medical leave. "An essential component of a comprehensive, inclusive paid family and medical leave policy," the authors note, "is an updated understanding of which individuals count as family."[111] Because, the article asserts, the majority of LGBTQ+ people have strained relationships with "their families of origin" and are unmarried, they are unable to rely on blood relatives or spouses for care. In addition, LGBTQ+ people often have difficulty accessing paid family leave; either their jobs fail to provide such a benefit, or they cannot take family leave because current leave policies do not recognize as family those who they would care for or be cared for by. "To ensure that LGBTQ individuals are included in paid family and medical leave policies," the authors argue, "lawmakers must design the policies to cover diverse family relationships and allow for caregiving of chosen family."[112] They note that models already exist for doing so, citing the "expansive definitions of family, including chosen family" in the paid family and medical leave policies being implemented in New Jersey, Connecticut, Oregon, and Colorado.[113] While this article advocated making Build Back Better more expansive and inclusive, it still relied on the trope of the family—both biological and chosen—in order to do so.

During the pandemic, claims about the importance of "chosen family" for LGBTQ+ people became even more pronounced. See, for instance, articles entitled "'Chosen Families' Ruptured: How Covid-19 Hit an LGBTQ Lifeline," "Between the Binary: On the Gratitude I Feel to My Chosen Family," and "How My Queer Chosen Family Got Me Through COVID."[114] Funders for LGBT Issues, a philanthropic organization, put out a statement encouraging employers to offer paid time off for staff who "must devote time to caring for ill family and chosen family."[115] A report entitled "LGBT Older People & COVID-19: Addressing Higher Risk,

Social Isolation, and Discrimination," written by The Movement Advancement Project, SAGE: Advocacy and Services for LGBT Elders, and the Center for American Progress, mentions chosen family nine times.[116]

Recent discussions of care in trans studies are helpful for considering familial discourses—whether connected to biological or chosen family. In *Trans Care*, Hil Malatino argues that "We need [care] especially when our lives fall in the gaps between institutions and conventional familial structures."[117] But Malatino does not deploy the family uncritically. He notes that "both hegemonic and resistant cultural imaginaries of care have depended on a heterocisnormative investment in the family as the primary locus of care."[118] While Malatino describes the alternative "network of support" or "care web" he envisions as "a family of choice, a family constructed through consent rather than accident and forced relationship," he also underscores that "the word, the construct, the ongoing practice of building one" will "outstrip the mythic purported providential reach of the family."[119] Following Martin Manalansan, Malatino argues for shifting the geographies of care to the spaces where "trans and queer care labor occurs: the street, the club, the bar, the clinic, the community center, the classroom, the nonprofit, and sometimes, yes, the home—but a home that is often a site of rejection, shunning, abuse, and discomfort."[120] Malatino's rethinking of the place of home and family in geographies of care speaks to the complexity, messiness, and paradox of the family formation for LGBTQ+ people as well as queer and trans politics.

As this discussion of Malatino's insights makes clear, references to "chosen family" in queer and trans spaces need not be entirely hetero- or homonormative. For this to be the case, however, "chosen family" should not be a simple replacement for the biological family. Chosen family, in Malatino's formulation, might be a site for developing new ways for thinking about care—not simply receiving care typically associated with family from someone to whom one has no biological relation. "A resilient care web," Malatino argues, "coheres through consistently foregrounding the realities of burnout and the gendered, raced, and classed dynamics that result in the differential distribution of care—for those receiving it as well as those giving it. A care web works when the work that composed it isn't exploitative, appropriative, or alienated."[121]

Such articulations are crucial for developing queer approaches to social reproduction. As we work to develop these queer approaches, we might consider the limits of the race-class-gender formulation that cuts across feminist discussions and is especially pronounced in conversations about social reproduction. This is not simply an argument for expanding the trilogy to recognize sexuality for the sake of including LGBTQ+ people, but because one's sexuality—including whether or not one has children—deeply informs one's home life, one's work life, and the care one both does and is expected to do in both spaces. In addition, we ought to consider the political and epistemological possibilities that can open up if we refuse to see and describe our networks of care as familial, chosen or otherwise.

Aren Aizura's analyses of queer and trans reproduction provide a basis for beginning to think through how moving beyond the family-as-care formulation can contribute to the dismantling of the heteronormativity that continues to plague so many discussions of care. While Aizura suggests that it is possible that "trans and queer understandings of family look different, whether through the nonbiological bonds of 'queer family' or through queer and trans parenting, pregnancy, and child-rearing," he also makes clear that "we must refuse to exceptionalize the queerness and transness of reproduction. It is not sufficient to claim that queer and trans reproduction—whether social or biological—is radical."[122] Indeed, following Talia Lewis, Aizura states that "queering reproduction may mean abolishing the family form altogether."[123] In what follows, I offer a queer proposal for how we might queer reproduction by advocating for care resources that extend beyond the family formation.

## A QUEER PROPOSAL: FUCK THE CHILD

This queer proposal requires an extension of the widespread critique of the public/private binary as dangerously simplistic, as that which makes it even more difficult to recognize how unpaid labors enable paid labors and thus capitalism. In response to the devaluing of the home and the largely unpaid labors that transpire there, feminists have argued that domestic labors are valuable and, as such, ought to be waged or recognized in systems of social security. We know, of course, who the subject of these labors typically is: the wife/woman/mother (who is always already one and the same). We also know who is imagined as the object of these labors: children, the home's wage earner/man/husband (who are, again, one and the same), and, less often, elderly family members or those with disabilities. What would happen to normative formulations of the home, of work, of workers and their objects if we took more seriously Edelman's call to say "Fuck the Child"?[124] Even in the scholarship that attempts to "queer" social reproduction, Edelman has been largely ignored—a curiosity considering that his polemical approach to "the Child" (always already with a capital C!) could allow us to consider how the imagined "Child" is precisely the object that haunts social reproduction theory and has made it difficult to bring together queer and feminist approaches to rethink social reproduction and theories of it.

As I have insisted, queering feminist approaches to paid leave requires more than a removal of the word "family" from the care lexicon. It requires dismantling the centrality of the imagined family in visions of care, including but not limited to care policies. It requires actively pushing back against heteronormativity and grappling with how feminist discourses can work in the service of precisely the things feminists need to disrupt. In this case, we might consider paid family leave as an example of what Lauren Berlant describes as a "relation of cruel optimism," which refers to moments when the thing we desire is also an obstacle to our flourishing.[125] Following Berlant, how, we should ask, can we advocate for paid leave without exalting the value of work, parenthood, children, and the family—ideas related to which have long created problems for women and for feminists?

I have a queer answer. I am advocating for a more capacious approach to paid leave as something that should be disconnected from normative ideas about where and how care occurs. We need more than a shift from family leave to care leave, which, in a handful of states, is already available for those providing forms of care to non-family members. We need paid leaves to be available to those who engage in any form of social reproduction. Some examples of community care labors that could be socialized through paid leave from one's employer: Starting a garden to feed one's community, completing a mechanic training program and providing a certain number of free automobile services monthly, pickling and preserving foods to distribute to those in need and teaching others how to do so, plowing the snow from the driveways of those living nearby, leading weekly Pilates classes in the park or yoga classes through Zoom, getting a massage therapy certification and providing a certain number of free massages each month afterward, and teaching feminist, queer, or critical race theory at the local library, prison, or shelter. Each of these examples would allow us to decouple paid leaves from the heteronormativity that drives them and that they drive. In addition, this proposal collectivizes the provision of care and broadens its potential reception.

Admittedly, my proposal, like every policy ever proposed or implemented, has limits. Namely, it imagines paid social reproduction leaves as transpiring through the same institutions and mechanisms that support paid family leave: the employer. Tethering paid leave to employment is a serious drawback for actualizing its queer potential for many reasons, including, but not limited to, the fact that so many employers are not required to provide any kind of leave at all, paid or unpaid. So, this proposal is essentially limited to employers already offering paid parental leave, and will benefit those employees who have the luxury of access to these leaves. At the same time, this move is precisely what makes the current proposal implementable in the here and now, enabling the disruption of the heteronormativity baked into current approaches to paid parental leave. Its implementation will, however, raise new and different questions: How many social reproduction leaves can one get from their employer during their tenure as an employee? Might a cap on social reproduction leaves lead to a cap on the maximum number of paid family leaves one can take? Do paid family leaves count toward one's number of allowable paid social reproduction leaves? Perhaps most importantly, who decides whether one is granted a social reproduction leave? What if deciders reject the purpose of the leave as unworthy? These questions are answerable. But they are harder to grapple with than those that root the solution to our current care crisis in achieving visibility of women's care labor—a problem, it turns out, that extends beyond Marxist feminism and is apparent in recent conversations regarding queer care, as well. A 2021 Duke University "Queering Communities of Care" event, for instance, asked: "How do we make care more visible?"[126] Implying that making care more visible is essential to queering care reproduces the same missteps of Marxist feminism. We need something far more radical to queer care. We need to see that providing care to one's family is no more valuable than providing other forms of care, including those not directed toward individual people with whom one already imagines they are in relation.

I see this proposal as the queerest possible policy solution within the current context, given that such solutions necessarily take shape within existing social and political formations. Our current context is not, of course, terribly queer. It is one in which the Build Back Better Act, hailed as the greatest feminist policy proposal in US history, failed to pass. Further, we are still reeling from the first presidency of Donald Trump, whose daughter's most significant policy work included extending paid family leave to federal employees.[127] Obviously, things have gotten so much worse since then, such that the heteronormativity driving Ivanka Trump's policy proposals feels quaint. Considering the shape of our current world, I'm tempering my queer dreams for implementing any sort of post-work imaginary, including a world wherein everyone has a basic income, where work is not at the center of our lives and everyone has access to paid care leaves. But I also want to keep that dream alive and I see this proposal—which asks us to value forms of care rarely thought of as care, at least in part because they transpire in places not associated with care provision—as working in the service of that dream.

We can work toward this world through queering social reproduction in smaller quotidian ways, as well. We ought to recognize, for instance, that how a person's home life is imagined directly impacts their work life. Put otherwise, the heteronormativity that drives celebrations of paid leave informs expectations of employees *both before and after* one would be eligible to take family leave, as well as those non-procreative employees who are never eligible for paid leave. Indeed, ideas about families structure the lives of those who work really hard to eschew these very ideas. Paid leave from employment can become a tool, like basic income, that can untether reproduction from production. It can allow for uncoupling community activities from commodification and even worthy work from pleasure and joy. Taking a Fuck the Child approach, I suggest, is required for this reimagining, which would allow us to see that in order for paid leave to be utilized for queer purposes, we must sever it from childbearing and -rearing altogether.

# 3 The Woman Question, The Trans Question

## ON ABORTION AND GENDER

In January 2020, Planned Parenthood released the documentary *Ours to Tell* in honor of *Roe v. Wade*'s forty-seventh anniversary. The short film follows four individuals who, according to Planned Parenthood, "live full and empowered lives because they had the freedom to access abortion." The documentary asserts that the stories of these individuals—two Black women, a Latina woman, and a white transgender man in a relationship with a white transgender woman—are particularly timely because "communities of color, LGBTQ people, and many others are increasingly denied access to abortion—and [because] people across the country face an unprecedented assault on the legal right to access it."[1]

The contemporary abortion story told by the best-known reproductive rights organization reveals more about deep social anxieties on the political left than it does the materiality of abortion, including who actually has trouble accessing abortion care. Sure, collectively, we have experienced a well-coordinated assault on abortion rights, but this attack does not impact all people *equally*. It is notable, for instance, that Planned Parenthood does not mention poor or working-class people, who are the most likely demographic to seek abortions and also to experience difficulty accessing care. It is also notable that people in rural areas, where abortion access is even more limited than elsewhere, are ignored. Furthermore, the linkage of "communities of color" and "LGBTQ people" tells us more about Planned Parenthood's attempts to connect with the social justice concerns of the moment than about who is denied abortion care. While the organization's invoking of "communities of color" to make a point about shrinking abortion access is partially accurate, considering that some demographics of women of color are disproportionately likely to seek abortions, it is hard to make sense of their point that LGBTQ+ people are "increasingly denied access to abortion." LGBTQ+ people, like "people of color," are not one homogeneous group, and, as such, its subgroups do not seek abortions at the same rates as one another. In fact, most demographics of LGBTQ+ people actually seek abortion far *less* often than heterosexual women, especially those who are Black, Latina, or live below the poverty line.

The single outlier, according to the Human Rights Campaign: "bisexual women and heterosexual women with a history of same-sex partnering," who are twice as likely as "exclusively heterosexual women" to have abortions.[2] Interestingly, we hear little about bisexual women in discussions of the need to shift language to be more LGBTQ+ inclusive. Perhaps this is because it isn't so surprising that women who have sex with men who produce sperm—even if they also have sex with other people—can become pregnant and therefore may need abortion care. Or perhaps it is because bisexuality is rarely front and center within LGBTQ+ spaces. Regardless, we hear very little about LGBTQ+ people and abortion, with the exception of transmasculine people, trans men, and nonbinary people, gender demographics for whom there is little abortion data. One 2018 survey of 450 trans and gender-nonconforming people who were assigned female at birth concluded that 2 percent of the study's respondents had experienced abortion.[3] In another 2018 study of 197 masculine-identified people assigned female at birth, 3.5 percent had experienced abortion.[4] A 2020 study found that just under 4 percent of its 1694 transgender, nonbinary, and gender-expansive respondents assigned female or intersex at birth had experienced abortion—although the study also notes that it relied on convenience sampling and its findings are not generalizable.[5]

But this important new data—which focuses on the percentage of transmasculine and/or nonbinary people obtaining abortions—doesn't tell us much about the percentage of people obtaining abortions who do not consider themselves women. (We also cannot extrapolate from these numbers to discuss trans *people*, considering that trans women, who make up a slightly higher proportion of trans people than do trans men, do not need abortions, a point to which I return below.)[6] Up to this point, just one study has taken up this issue. Researchers found that in 2017, the most recent year for which big data on the genders of people obtaining abortions has been published, between 462 and 530 trans or nonbinary people in the United States had abortions. That same year, 862,320 people—or just under 862,000 women—had abortions. To put this in statistical terms, then, between .05 and .06 percent—or 1/20th of 1 percent—of abortions were obtained by transgender or gender-nonconforming people in 2017.

There is good reason, trans studies scholars tell us, to be skeptical of big data in general, and there is certainly good reason to be skeptical of this variety of data, which conflates trans, nonbinary, and gender-nonconforming people. In the largest study of non-women-identified people and abortion, respondents' most common "gender identity was nonbinary (51%), followed by transgender man (39%) and gender-queer (39%)"—identifications that the study largely discusses as if they are interchangeable.[7] Work by Kadji Amin and Finn Enke is useful for articulating the problems with these conflations, as well as the study's requirement that eligible respondents must be "of TGE experience." What exactly does it mean to be "of transgender experience?" Enke's discussion of the limited ways in which we discuss the temporality of trans-ness—that is, if one is trans, then one must have always been trans and will always be trans—is helpful for addressing this question.[8] Enke suggests that producing gender as if it can ever be static as a way to suggest that you take seriously someone's transness is short-sighted; It is precisely this approach to gender as fixed that undergirds the questioning of trans people's genders in the first place. When it comes to abortion and transness, then, we need to be able to see (trans)gender as slippery and complicated. Many transmen and transmasculine people did not always think of themselves as trans and had other gendered lives before they transitioned. In this case, it is likely that some of these people who later became trans had abortions earlier in their lives, when they thought of their gender differently or experienced the world differently based on their gender presentation. Remembering a past abortion from a current social location as a trans person does not necessarily mean that this person was trans when obtaining an abortion. We don't know how many trans people are having abortions, in other words, in part because researchers are imagining transness as static.

We also don't know how many trans people are having abortions because of the conflations of transness and nonbinary-ness. Kadji Amin outlines the problems with this conflation. Amin argues, like Enke, that contemporary discourses of nonbinary-ness produce gender as simple for so-called cisgender people. As Amin says, "When we refer to normative cisgender, do we know precisely what we mean?"[9] No, he says, we don't. We can't. And that is because "cisgender is not and has never been a social identity. Like heterosexuality, cisgender is an opposite fabricated out of thin air."[10] "The notion of an alignment so exact between one's personal sense of identity and their assigned gender role . . . that there is no rub, no ambivalence, and no sense of constraint—is and has always been a fantasy. Nobody has ever felt that way."[11] This fantasy "cis/trans distinction," Amin says, "has birthed a third term, nonbinary," and "nonbinary discourse has just invented a new fictive opposite": so-called binary trans people and binary cis people.[12] These people, Amin and Enke argue, don't exist. Who, in other words, experiences their gender so simply that they never act out of alignment with the norms of their gender?

> We can drop the notion that gender is purely psychic and work instead toward creating a livable, valued, and legible social category for feminine male-assigned people (given the high cultural and erotic value of masculinity, a space for masculine female assigned people will likely always exist). Most importantly, we can stop idealizing (and attempting to name) some version of normal gender, and we can refuse to use the misleading terms binary and cisgender altogether. For just as there has never been a heterosexuality without homosexual desire, there has never been a cis- or binary gender free from cross-identification or gender atypicality. . . . We must, first and foremost, relinquish the fantasy that gender is a means of self-knowledge, self-expression, and authenticity rather than a shared, and therefore imperfect, social schema.[13]

If "nonbinary" is an identity being claimed by people who, Amin says, "look and behave in a manner indistinguishable from ordinary lesbians and gays, or even ordinary heterosexuals," and if no one really experiences gender in a binary way anyway, how do we make sense of the data on abortion that not only uses nonbinary as an identity category but also conflates nonbinary and trans?[14]

I want rearticulate here, as I did in the Introduction, that I am not arguing that the trans and gender-nonconforming people who obtain abortions don't matter. Of course they do, regardless of whether they make up .05 or .06 percent of abortion patients, as the data suggest, or .00001 or 5 percent. The question these figures raise for me, and that drives the remainder of the questions I ask in this chapter is: How do we make sense of Planned Parenthood's invoking of LGBTQ+ people while ignoring those groups that are far more likely to need an abortion or experience difficulty obtaining one? Answering this question requires that we talk about precisely that which Planned Parenthood and other reproductive justice groups have recently jumped through hoops to avoid: women. To this point, never once in Planned Parenthood's description of those who are increasingly denied access to abortion is the word "woman" used. In many ways, this discursive sleight of hand is even more notable than the organization's ignoring of poor people, rural people, and specific groups of people of color likely to need an abortion. Indeed, almost all people who obtain abortions experience the world as women and consider themselves women. More than 99.9 percent, in fact. These women are also disproportionately poor and of color. And yet, self-identified liberals, leftists, and progressives increasingly have moved toward using what they consider "gender-neutral" or "gender-inclusive" or "all-gender" language to discuss abortion. This chapter traces and reflects on this discursive trend, as well as the material consequences of the attempts to quell the (trans)gendered anxieties that undergird it.

I first experienced the depth of these cultural anxieties, as well as the affects that stick to assumptions about how to best address them, when I coproduced, along with a trans student, Paula Kamen's *Jane: Abortion and the Underground* as part of a class I taught at Middlebury College in January 2020. The play tells the story of the Jane Collective, a group of housewives and college students who performed approximately eleven thousand illegal abortions during the late 1960s and early 1970s. Considering the historical nature of the play, I found myself surprised by the degree to which the students in the course that put on the play, less than one-third of whom considered themselves heterosexual and nearly all of whom appear in the world as women, expressed discomfort about the play's attachment of abortion to women. That we were having these conversations in January 2020—precisely the moment that Planned Parenthood released the *Ours to Tell* film—suggests that my students' angst was both reflective of and informed by these broader discursive trends. Indeed, in the class period immediately prior to the release of Planned Parenthood's film, a student asked what she called "the woman question": What are we to make of a play that connects abortion to women? Is the play transphobic?! Are we transphobic for putting on the play?!

In this chapter, I take on "the woman question," or what might more accurately be called the "trans man question," and the cultural shift within liberal, leftist, and progressive circles away from discussing abortion primarily as a women's issue and toward using ostensibly less gendered terms such as "pregnant people," "people with uteruses," "patients," and "parents." In so doing, I ask the following questions: What is at stake in calls for *and* critiques of such discursive shifts? What are the material and embodied costs of this discursive shift for trans men, women, and our ability to address both misogyny and transphobia? What are the benefits and limits of tethering abortion to an ostensibly nongendered—and we might even say universal—subject?

This chapter addresses these questions, in part, by considering as a case study our production of *Jane*. To provide broader context for this case study, I first examine the recent shift to discussing abortion in "gender-neutral" or "gender-inclusive" terms, arguing that the concerns with visibility by activists on both sides of the debate are misplaced. I then outline the health care issues that disproportionately impact trans people, but that, despite their very real material consequences, have not compelled the same kinds of discursive shifts evident in abortion rhetoric. Finally, I discuss how we "queered" the *Jane* play in ways that kept gender central, suggesting that queering abortion discourses requires something far deeper than so-called "gender-neutral" or "gender-inclusive" language. In so doing, I make two interrelated arguments: The presence of ostensibly gender-neutral discourses makes it *more* difficult both to address trans-specific health issues and to counter antiabortion sentiment. Sexism, not transphobia, drives antiabortion activism, after all. Expanding abortion access, then, requires that we take seriously the sexism of antiabortion activism. At the same time, reproductive justice advocacy could do far more to advance trans justice through addressing the health issues that trans people do disproportionately experience. Ultimately, I suggest that demands for gender-neutral language do nothing to queer reproductive justice nor make abortion more accessible, including for trans men and gender-nonconforming people. Doing either would require that we address the material *differences* in manifestations of sexism and transphobia and move away from the self-congratulatory performative wokeness that increasingly appears in abortion justice activism.

## WOMAN *OR* TRANS: A NARRATIVE TIMELINE

Based on my engagement with reproductive justice activism and scholarship, I had a hunch that the assumption that gender-neutral language marked progress had become more widespread over the course of the last several years. But had it? Or were these rhetorical shifts largely being debated among those of us steeped in the reproductive justice world? To answer this question, I analyzed articles that mentioned abortion, appeared in one of four major national newspapers (*The New York Times*, *The Wall Street Journal*, *USA Today*, and *The Washington Post*) between 2010 and 2020, and included ostensibly gender-neutral terms, such as "pregnant people/person" and "patient."[15] The figure below demonstrates the increase in the use of what activists describe as "gender-neutral" terms in news coverage of abortion over the last decade. It also shows that trans people are increasingly mentioned in articles about abortion. To put a finer point on it, prior to 2019, "pregnant people" or "pregnant person" was used in these major US newspapers just three times. On its first appearance, in a 2014 op-ed in *The New York Times* primarily concerned with pregnancy discrimination in the workplace, the phrase appears to be used unconsciously.[16]

By 2019, mainstream news coverage of abortion had changed. As the figure shows, 2019 marked a sharp rise in the use of phrases such as "pregnant people" in abortion coverage; the phrase—which, again, appeared in

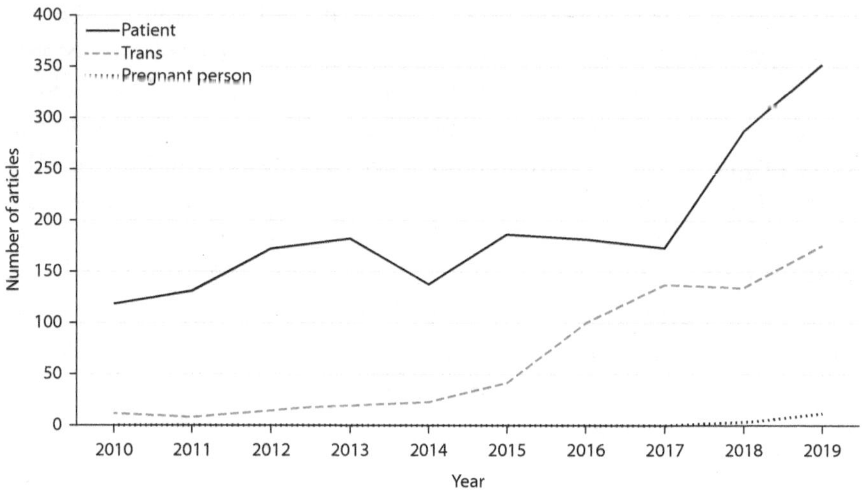


Gender-neutral terms in articles about abortion over time.

major national newspapers just three times between 2010 and 2018—was used in eleven articles in 2019. A 2019 op-ed in *The New York Times*, written by Rep. Pramila Jayapal (D-WA), was the first to use the term several times. In fact, Jayapal's op-ed uses a variant of the phrase "pregnant people" six times, never once using the term "woman," despite its focus on her own experience with having an abortion and its use of "Congresswoman" to describe the author. It seems clear that Jayapal deliberately used ostensibly gender-neutral language, as did others discussing abortion in 2019.

How did we get here? What was going on behind the scenes among abortion justice activists that led to such shifts in journalistic discussions of abortion? In what follows, I move from this bird's-eye view of mainstream news coverage to conversations happening among movement activists and in more feminist or leftist spaces. Let's begin just a bit before 2014, the year the phrase "pregnant people" first appeared in a major national newspaper.

In 2013, Lauren Rankin wrote an op-ed for *Truthout*, a left-leaning independent news site, entitled "Not Everyone Who Has an Abortion is a Woman—How to Frame the Abortion Rights Issue." Rankin's use of the phrase "pregnant people" to talk about those who have abortions marks the first time I can find the phrase in public, published writing, although the concerns motivating Rankin's op-ed were already being discussed within more left-leaning reproductive justice activist spaces at the time. Just a month before Rankin published her op-ed, Unite for Reproductive and Gender Equity (URGE) shared a blog post on its website regarding the need for trans-inclusive language, an issue the author notes the movement had been grappling with "in recent years." The post, written by Verónica Bayetti Flores, asks "How do we meaningfully integrate the perspectives and issues faced by gender non-conforming and trans folks into our work?"[17] Flores's insights are worth quoting at length:

> In a movement that has so long focused on cisgender women, how do we talk about the fact that there are also gender non-conforming folks seeking abortion? That trans women's reproductive health care needs differ, often dramatically, from those of cisgender women? That there are trans men looking to get on birth control? I ask specifically how do we talk about these issues because my central question revolves around language. In terms of analysis, it's not a difficult case to make: we know that trans and gender non-conforming folks face myriad barriers in accessing health care, including low rates of health insurance, refusal of treatment and high reported rates of violence while accessing care. We know that trans and gender non-conforming folks of color are especially hard hit. . . . So, what's the problem? The truth is, it's hard—How do we talk about such a deeply gendered issue as reproductive health while recognizing that it's not just cisgender women that have a stake in this? . . . Some of us have started to use gender-neutral terminology in our grassroots work; others of us aren't entirely happy with the ways this takes the focus off of the fact that gender oppression is at the center of this for women and gender non-conforming folks alike. There isn't an easy answer, or a one-size fits-all.

There is much to comment on here, in part because of the stark differences between Flores's careful approach and the often reactionary deployments of the figure of the trans person in more recent conversations about reproductive justice, as I demonstrate in the sections that follow. Never once in Flores's post is the phrase "pregnant people" used. Perhaps this is because the author is attuned to the materiality of transness and how this materiality informs reproductive health care needs. Trans women's needs may differ, Flores says, from those of non-trans women, while trans men might want to get on birth control. While this point should be obvious, so much of the conversation around gendered language and reproductive health and rights ignores how the ontological differences among people create different health care needs. Further, Flores never suggests that we ought to ban "woman" or "women" from the reproductive justice lexicon. And perhaps most importantly, Flores's post suggests that in 2013 reproductive justice activists were asking *questions* regarding *how* to talk about gender and reproductive justice in more complicated ways—rather than demanding prescriptive discursive shifts as if the answers to these questions are simple and obvious. They aren't. Flores's approach likely is informed by her being attuned to contestations within the movement regarding the value of ostensibly gender-neutral language and the concern that such terminology could, as Flores notes, take "the focus off of the fact that gender oppression is at the center of this for women and gender non-conforming folks alike." Put succinctly, Flores approaches a complicated issue in a complicated way.

Ultimately, Flores believes that thinking critically about the language we use is crucial. Immediately after stating that her "central question revolves around language use," she notes that "In terms of analysis, it's not a difficult case to make: we know that trans and gender non-conforming folks face myriad barriers in accessing health care, including low rates of health insurance, refusal of treatment and high reported rates of violence while accessing care. We know that trans and gender non-conforming folks of color are especially hard hit." In many ways, Flores is right. Trans people experience myriad barriers in accessing health care, have lower rates of health insurance, and often face transphobia when they do access care. And people of color have poorer health outcomes than white people in general, so there is no reason to think that trans people of color would exist outside of this trend. But there remains a key question we should be asking: How would shifting language use—Flores's central concern—address any of these very real and very serious issues? Flores does not answer this question.

Flores and URGE, the organization posting her blog entry, were not alone in expressing their concerns regarding overtly gendered language use. Between 2012 and 2015, other reproductive health and justice organizations made similar discursive changes. Midwives Alliance of North America (MANA) changed its "core competencies" to use the phrase "pregnant people" rather than "women."[18] The New York Abortion Access Fund edited "women" out of their mission, opting for terms such as "anyone," "every person," and "people who call" their hotline.[19] And Fund Texas Women changed their name to Fund Texas Choice, noting on their website that their name change was rooted in a desire to include "trans people who needed to get an abortion but were not women."[20] Clearly, the debate over gendered language use inspired significant changes among reproductive justice organizations.

By 2015, the debate had moved beyond conversations internal to the movement. In the op-ed sections of liberal and progressive news outlets, including *The New York Times*, *The Nation*, and *The New Statesman*, feminist-identified writers pushed back against the assumption that the move toward discussing reproductive concerns in gender-neutral language is necessarily positive or progressive.[21] Victoria Smith, writing as "Glosswitch," argues that we should consider gender not as a means of self-definition, but in terms of how it functions as a "class system." For Smith, discussing pregnancy in ostensibly gender-neutral terms "is a way of using language to create the illusion of dismantling a hierarchy when what you really end up doing is ignoring it. Pregnancy is a gendered experience, not because pregnant individuals necessarily feel like women, but because the pregnant body is externally managed within the context of its subordinate sex class status." She continues:

> One can argue over whether or not gender exists as an apolitical entity; whether to be a woman is to identify or be identified as one. Our most immediate challenge, however, concerns whether all pregnant individuals are seen as people, not whether all pregnant people are seen as women. In order to address this we need to talk about women as a class. Gender-neutral terms limit our ability to do this. Whatever our intentions, neutralising language is not a neutral act.[22]

Just as Glosswitch is concerned with the impact of what she and other activists call "gender-neutral" terms and the assumption that shifts in language use do anything at all to dismantle gender hierarchies, Katha Pollitt similarly argues that "removing 'women' from the language of abortion is a mistake. We can, and should, support trans men and other gender-non-conforming people. But we can do that without rendering invisible half of humanity and 99.999 percent of those who get pregnant. . . . It feels as if abortion language is becoming a bit like French, where one man in a group of no matter how many women means 'elles' becomes 'ils.'"[23] For Pollitt, the issue is not simply about language. She is concerned with abortion politics, including what she sees as the damages abolishing the term "women" can have on "political analysis." She ends her op-ed by asking: "How do you even talk about women's being underrepresented politically, or earning less than men, or being victims of rape and domestic violence? In an era where politics is all about identity, as a tool for organizing and claiming public space, are women about to lose theirs? Because after all we're all just people now."

Although Pollitt makes clear that "We can, and should, support trans men and other gender non-conforming people . . . without erasing women from the fight for reproductive rights," her op-ed was met with enough pushback that, a month later, *The Nation* published critical responses by two abortion fund activists. Rye Young was one of the respondents. At the time, Young served as the executive director of Third Wave Fund, a youth-led reproductive and gender justice organization. He writes:

> I believe language that doesn't equate abortion with women increases accessibility of services for trans and gender-nonconforming (TGNC) people, who, because of discrimination at clinics and because these clients are disproportionately low-income, homeless, and uninsured, face significant barriers to care. . . . Pollitt's article follows an insidious pattern in the history of mainstream feminism. She sets up an ultimatum: that to address privilege in the movement threatens women and therefore strengthens patriarchy. This approach silences and marginalizes feminists with the least power. Pollitt co-opts the narrative of "being erased" from those who actually *are* erased from the movement—women of color, trans people, poor women, etc.—while using her relative power in the movement to be a gatekeeper of abortion discourse.[24]

Just as Young doubles down on the idea that shifts in language use will address issues far larger than abortion access and invokes the past to suggest that resistance to this shift reflects longer problematic feminist histories of exclusion, so too does Alicia Johnson, the writer of the second retort published by *The Nation*. Johnson, who then worked for the Eastern Massachusetts Abortion Fund, argues that:

> Using gender-neutral language such as people doesn't make women invisible, but using women to describe people who need access to abortion does make trans and genderqueer people invisible. Reproductive justice activists, particularly young people, aren't relinquishing years of progress by being inclusive of all people who can become pregnant; we're improving the movement and remembering the people whom those earlier movements forgot. . . . The feminist movement has a long history of prioritizing the experiences and needs of straight, white, upper-class, cisgender women. We must work toward a feminism that uplifts all oppressed people—a shift that begins with inclusive language. If you stand for feminism and reproductive justice, you must demand equal access for all people, not just women.[25]

Neither Young nor Johnson, like Flores, articulate exactly how shifts in language use will "increase accessibility" of abortion services or "uplift all oppressed people." In fact, it seems more likely that changing language used within the movement would have little material impact on trans men's *access to* abortion—particularly on those who are homeless, uninsured, and poor, a point to which I return below.

Here, I want to reflect on what it means that both authors invoke "the movement" and who it has prioritized or erased to make their arguments. Johnson suggests that feminists have "a long history of prioritizing the experiences and needs of straight, white, upper-class, cisgender women," while Young argues that those who are "erased from the movement [are] women of color, trans people, poor women." Such comments ignore the reality of who has abortions. Upper-class white women are far less likely to get an abortion than are poor women, who are disproportionately Black, Latina, and Native. Even worse, these assertions also ignore the long and deep history of women of color working for reproductive justice, as well as the ongoing feminist activism of women of color.[26] This is not necessarily surprising, considering the wide circulation of similar narratives of feminism's past, narratives that feminist and queer theorists have taken on directly. Clare Hemmings, for example, suggests that feminists' narratives of feminism tend to erase its "complex past."[27] To make this argument, Hemmings traces how ideas related to progress, loss, and return imbue feminists' stories of feminism, and further, how these narratives require that we ignore the scholarship and activism that does not fit into a neat genealogy. In narratives of feminism's progress—feminism gets better over time!—Black feminism and women of color feminism of the 1980s are positioned as that which allowed us to address feminism's prior erasures and mistakes. One problem here, Hemmings says, is that "women of color feminism" becomes fixed in a decade a half-century ago, and, thus, it becomes difficult to see the important contributions of women of color feminism both far before the 1980s and in the decades since.

The erasure of feminism's "complex past" and the place of women of color in it—something exacerbated in current deployments of discourses of so-called "white feminism"—are evident in the claims made by both Johnson and Young. Such characterizations are not independent from activists' desires to appear progressive themselves. As Hemmings argues, the "story one tells about the past is always motivated by the position one occupies or wishes to occupy in the present."[28] For Johnson, the so-called ciswoman stands in for feminism's failures and becomes synonymous with a feminism we need to move beyond. Women are feminism's problem. But what is surprising, considering Young's demand to move beyond woman-centric language, is that he also uses the figures of certain women—"women of color, trans people, and poor women"—to make the argument that certain women "are erased from the movement" and that this is a problem. Young's slippage speaks to the paradox that women had become for feminist abortion justice activists by 2015: If we don't talk about women, we can't talk about poor women or women of color. But by invoking these women, indeed by using the word "women," we are excluding people who do not identify as women.

By 2019, questions about gendered discourse in abortion rights groups had moved beyond liberal news sites and had become much more mainstream, as the graph that opens this section suggests. In 2019 alone, *Forbes*, *GQ*, *MEL Magazine*, and *Allure* published articles about trans men who get abortions with headlines that read, for example, "Abortion Is an Issue for Transgender Bodies, Too" and "The Trans Men Who Get Abortions."[29] These stories, which emerged primarily in response to legislative threats to abortion at the state and federal levels in 2019, largely ignore concerns regarding what is lost in the discursive shifts for which the authors were calling. Caitlin Van Horn's *Allure* magazine article entitled "Trans and Nonbinary People Get Abortions Too: Why Does the Conversation Surrounding Reproductive Rights Exclude Them?" speaks to this point. The only people Van Horn could imagine being "resistant to updating their language" are TERFS, or trans-exclusionary radical feminists. Van Horn's main question is:

> Do you want people to get the care they need or not? What is your endgame if reproductive autonomy and unwanted pregnancies are acceptable collateral to getting there? Or, more baldly, do you hate trans and nonbinary people enough to spite them into pregnancy? My job is to make sure anyone who wants an abortion can get one. There is nothing about pregnancy or the termination of such that is unique to cisgender women, and letting language be a barrier between a pregnant person and their abortion is, frankly, dangerous.

Like those who came before her, Van Horn never spells out how exactly the language shifts she proposes will increase access to abortion care. Unlike those making similar claims six years earlier, Van Horn goes so far as to say that there is *nothing* about pregnancy or abortion that is "unique" to women. The flip side of this position is necessarily that there is nothing unique about pregnancy or abortion for nonbinary or trans people—an utterly preposterous thought, and one that runs counter to claims for the need for "gender-neutral" language. While it is unlikely that any two women or any two trans men or nonbinary people will experience pregnancy or abortion in exactly the same way, there are, of course, commonalities and differences across experiences among those within a group and between those in different groups. In fact, the *differences* between trans and non-trans people motivate a great deal of trans studies scholarship and related activism. If nonbinary and trans people do not experience anything unique about pregnancy, there is no discussion to be had here. Van Horn ignores these differences to make an argument for same-ness. That these ideas appear in *Allure*, a beauty magazine that describes itself as "an insiders' guide to a woman's total image," suggests that by 2019 these ideas had become totally mainstream.[30] The debate was over: Women-centric language is transphobic and ought to be removed from discussions of abortion.

This position had become so commonsensical that in July 2019 it appeared in the Democratic Party's presidential debate. Candidate Julián Castro attempted to show off his cognizance of trans issues when he responded to a question about reproductive rights by saying "just because a woman—or let's also not forget someone in the trans community, a trans female—is poor, doesn't mean they shouldn't have the right to exercise that right to choose."[31] As many news outlets pointed out, Castro was likely referring to transgender men. Trans women, of course, would not need an abortion. Castro rehashed his point on Twitter with a slight edit: "I don't believe in only reproductive freedom, I believe in reproductive justice. All women—and that includes the trans community—have the right to an abortion. #DemDebate."[32] In framing trans people as a subgroup of women, Castro's follow-up tweet still missed the mark.

Many media outlets picked up on Castro's blunder, but passed over it quickly in order to rave about trans people being publicly incorporated into the reproductive justice conversation, and especially on a presidential debate stage.[33] The headline of the *Huffington Post* article covering Castro's comment, for instance, was "Julián Castro Gives Nod to Trans Community While Sharing His Abortion Views," while *NewsWeek* titled its article "Julián Castro Earns Acclaim for Including Trans Community in Impassioned Call for Reproductive Justice."[34] Never mind that Castro was not sure *which* trans people might need abortions. His mere mention of trans people was enough to make him appear in-tune with trans issues, and thus to receive praise.

It was also in 2019, six years after URGE called for activist organizations to discuss their use of gendered language, that Planned Parenthood released its first statement regarding trans men and abortion.[35] A few months later, in January of 2020, NARAL Pro-Choice America announced their organization's new slogan: "Freedom is for EVERYBODY."[36] The changed slogan was reflective of NARAL's arrival to the gender-neutral language party. As NARAL president Ilyse Hogue noted, "Our conversation has rightly focused on the fact that when it comes to reproductive oppression or reproductive freedom, it affects a lot of different people—anyone who can get pregnant, trans people, non-binary people, people who need to access reproductive services."[37] While it's hard to argue with NARAL's claim that "freedom is for everybody," *every* body cannot get pregnant, and *every* body will not need abortion care.[38] What is perhaps most bizarre about this shift is that for many years NARAL's slogan was "Who decides?" While this question does not appear terribly gendered, how people answered it was: "women and their families" and "women and their doctors." What was once a commonsensical answer no longer is. Now it is problematic, evidence of the failures of past feminists, of feminism's past.

Several years before NARAL changed its slogan, Katha Pollitt lamented the death of phrases that have long been central to abortion rights activism and questioned how this death might inform our political analysis of abortion more broadly. Pollitt asked: "What happens to Dr. Tiller's motto, 'Trust Women'? There was a whole feminist philosophy expressed in those two words: women are competent moral actors and they, not men, clergy or the state, are the experts on their own lives, and should be the ones to decide how to shape them. It is because abortion gives power specifically to women that it was criminalized." Rye Young didn't buy Pollitt's point, arguing in response that Pollitt "rests on the threat of losing the rallying power of abortion slogans. Slogans are not a reason to abandon a community that is literally dying from a lack of visibility, healthcare access, and solidarity."

What is perhaps most interesting about this now decade-long debate among reproductive justice advocates is most succinctly encapsulated in Pollitt and Young's exchange. Activists who celebrate the banishment of the term "woman" from the abortion debate and those wary of this move actually share two fundamental premises: first, that visibility of a marginalized group of people is necessarily positive, and second, that shifting language use to increase or decrease visibility of the marginalized group in question is synonymous with addressing abortion justice. In her response to Pollitt, Alicia Johnson also used the language of visibility to articulate her concerns with how women-centered abortion discourses make trans people invisible: "Using gender-neutral language such as people doesn't make women invisible, but using women to describe people who need access to abortion does make trans and genderqueer people invisible." Young went further to suggest that trans people are "literally dying from a lack of visibility, healthcare access, and solidarity." Here, Young equated lack of visibility with healthcare access, suggesting that lack of visibility, like lack of access to healthcare, can "literally" cause people to die. (It quite literally cannot.) On the other side of the debate, feminists critical of the removal of the term "women" from abortion discussions similarly deploy discourses of invisibility and erasure. Katha Pollitt is concerned with "erasing women" and "rendering invisible half of humanity and 99.999 percent of those who get pregnant." The possibility of invisibility is precisely what troubles these activists, even appearing, at times, as the problem itself. Being "erased," then, becomes that which we must fix. Put more directly, for activists on both sides of the debate, visibility itself is both the problem and the solution.

But we ought to ask how *exactly* visibility translates into action or material changes, including but not limited to increased access to health care. Trans studies scholar Paisley Currah does exactly this in an article in which he considers two events related to transness that occurred simultaneously. In 2008, Thomas Beattie, the first trans man who became famous for his pregnancy and for giving birth, was all over the media, including on *Oprah*. It was at exactly this moment that Democratic US Senators cut trans people out of the Employment Non-Discrimination Act, which prohibits employers from discriminating against people based on their sexual orientation, with the belief that cutting gender identification from the language of the proposed legislation would help it pass. One of the things we can learn from this comparison is that the increased social visibility, if you will, of trans people, symbolized by Beattie, did nothing at all to ensure that trans people's legal rights would be protected, something that Currah describes as "of much greater significance to the lives of transgender people" than Beattie's pregnancy. As Currah put it in 2008, "That a man can get pregnant may be the central, and for many the only, fact that most people in the United States now know about transgender issues."[39]

Since 2008 other queer theorists, including myself, have expanded on Currah's insights, critiquing LGBTQ+ rights' advocates unsubstantiated beliefs in the political possibilities of what we term "visibility politics," evidenced most often in demands to "come out" and to be "visible."[40] In my book *Visibility Interrupted: Rural Queer Life and the Politics of Unbecoming*, I argue that advocates' demands for visibility can make addressing social and political issues *more* difficult, and indeed, can *foreclose* political engagement.[41] In a moment when discursive recognition is too often conflated with structural change, the positioning of coming out to become visible as political itself means that many LGBTQ+ people feel as if they've engaged politically by virtue of stating their sexuality or gender—although, as I demonstrate in my book, the evidence that coming out does much politically is shaky at best.

LGBTQ+ rights supporters are not, of course, the only culprits. Reproductive rights activists, along with activists addressing a range of contemporary social movements, call for visibility and bemoan erasure, assuming that visibility is a worthwhile endeavor in and of itself. But never do these activists spell out exactly how their proposed use of language—meant to ensure visibility—can increase abortion access. Considering that abortion clinics do not exist in approximately 90 percent of US counties and that the Hyde Amendment restricts federal funds from covering abortion costs, and therefore poor people's access to state resources for health care is determined by the state in which they live, increasing access to abortion will require far more than removing the word "women" from abortion debates. Indeed, such shifts will have no consequences for the vast majority of poor women and women of color who seek abortions—other than making it more difficult to recognize which women are most likely to need this form of health care.

But I also want to suggest that these shifts will be of little material consequence for trans men, both because trans men have relatively few abortions, and because those who do need an abortion are more likely to be impacted by lack of access to health care more broadly than by language use. In fact, it is far easier to make the argument for changing language around a procedure that is not likely to be experienced by the people in question than it is to actually address the health care issues that those same people *do* experience. But for the most part, people—including those advocating for language to include trans people in the abortion debate—are not calling for greater attention to the health care issues that trans people disproportionately face. In fact, in the current iteration of the debate over the erasure of women or trans people from reproductive justice conversations, two key points get lost: Access to abortion is dwindling, and we should be figuring out how to increase access—something true pre-*Dobbs* and even more crucial now. There is no harm in recognizing that the primary beneficiaries of this increased access will be people who see themselves as women, and further that these women will disproportionately be poor, Black, and/or Latina. But there is harm in not working to address the health care concerns trans people do experience. In fact, we might say that the overall focus on (trans)gender in recent conversations about abortion has been to the detriment of emphasizing trans health.

## THE MATERIALITY OF TRANS HEALTH

Medical research on transgender healthcare makes clear that significant health disparities exist for people who live their lives outside of dominant gender categories. Access to hormonal therapy and doctors competent enough to provide it, for example, remain serious issues for trans patients.[42] In one study, 42 percent of transgender men reported experiencing verbal harassment, denial of equal treatment, or physical assault during an encounter at a hospital or clinic.[43] In another study, 21 percent of doctors self-reported that they are unwilling to perform pap exams on trans men to screen for cervical cancer.[44] Beyond this, trans-specific health needs are overwhelmingly excluded from medical school and residency curricula, with trans issues typically relegated to one-time attitude and awareness-based interventions.[45] In fact, a survey of OB-GYNs showed that 80 percent received no training on trans health care during their residencies.[46] Additionally, trans people are less likely than non-trans people to have health insurance,[47] more likely to be excluded from cancer prevention outreach campaigns,[48] and less likely to be up to date on cancer screenings, including pap smears.[49]

It is no surprise, then, that trans people experience a plethora of physical health issues. Studies suggest that some hormonal therapies can pose long-term health risks, including cardiovascular diseases, high blood pressure, insulin resistance, lipid derangement, and liver damage, as well as blood clots, stroke, and heart attacks.[50] Health risks associated with hormone therapy also differ between trans men and trans women. Trans men are at increased risks of "erythrocytosis, liver dysfunction, hypertension, excessive weight gain, salt retention, lipid changes, excessive or cystic acne, and adverse psychological changes," while for trans women, "key issues include avoiding supraphysiological doses or blood levels of estrogen, which may lead to increased risk for thromboembolic disease, liver dysfunction, and development of hypertension."[51] Testosterone hormone therapy is also associated with pelvic floor complications as a result of estrogen loss in genital tissues, which can become susceptible to irritation from sexual contact as well as bacterial infections.[52] Hysterectomies are often presented as a possible solution for hormone-related health problems, although the surgery also can come with complications, including those associated with pelvic floor pain.[53] To be clear, none of these potential health issues should be used as ammunition against the value of gender-affirming care. Over and over again, people make thoughtful health decisions that can have various side effects because they understand that the reward is greater than the risk; the decision to undergo gender-affirming care should not be approached differently.

Cancer in trans people has also been a concern among medical researchers, whose studies have come to vastly different—and even contradictory—conclusions. One study notes, for example, that LGBTQ+ people "bear a disproportionate burden of cancer," suggesting that one explanatory factor may be higher rates of exposure to HPV.[54] While this claim is not specific to trans people, other researchers suggest that trans people experience HIV- and HPV-related cancers at disproportionate rates.[55] Another study hypothesizes that trans men who have not received hysterectomies may be at an increased risk for uterine cancer, as well as for hormonal disorders such as PCOS.[56] Some researchers suggest that these risks can be mitigated by a hysterectomy, noting that "many transgender men desire hysterectomy and salpingo-oophorectomy for gender affirmation, cancer risk reduction, pelvic pain, or abnormal uterine bleeding."[57] Their findings conclude that "removal of the uterine corpus, cervix, fallopian tubes, and ovaries decreases the risk of carcinoma in a population where screening rates are significantly lower and may cause psychological harm compared to cisgender women."[58] The Committee on Health Care for Underserved Women recommends cancer screenings on the basis that "for patients using androgen therapy who have not had a complete hysterectomy, there may be an increased risk of endometrial cancer and ovarian cancer."[59] One problem with the findings and suggestions presented here, scholars have pointed out, is that they are largely based on anecdotes and small sample sizes. An article reviewing the published scholarship on breast and reproductive cancers in transgender people ultimately concluded that there is insufficient evidence available to estimate cancer prevalence among transgender people and, further, that gender-affirming hormones are not linked to cancer risk.[60]

As this review of medical literature on trans health care issues demonstrates, trans people experience a plethora of health concerns specific to being trans and that can accompany medical transition. Trans people also experience health concerns that are common among non-trans people. Both of these points likely appear banal to readers. It should be equally banal to say that trans people are also *less likely* to experience certain health care issues than are people of other genders.

Breast cancer appears to be one of these issues. One study demonstrates that both trans men and trans women are far less likely to have breast cancer than non-trans women, although they are also more likely to have breast cancer than non-trans men.[61] Headlines citing this study, however, read "Transgender Women Have an Increased Risk of Breast Cancer" and "Trans Women on Hormones Have More Breast Cancer."[62] These inflammatory headlines do not make clear who the referent is. "Increased risk" or "more breast cancer" compared to whom? The study compared trans women with non-trans men, and trans men with non-trans women. It turns out that trans women on hormones have an increased risk of breast cancer compared *only* to non-trans men—but, as the study notes, the increase is quite small. Perhaps more surprisingly, given these headlines, is that trans women and trans men both have *lower* rates of breast cancer than non-trans women. These headlines demonstrate the problems and panic that can emerge when the universal—but undisclosed!—referent is, once again, non-trans men.

Planned Parenthood also takes up the issue of breast cancer and transness, noting on the "Breast Cancer" page of its website that "While it's possible for anyone to be diagnosed with breast cancer, the disease occurs almost entirely in cisgender (cis) women. . . . After skin cancer, breast cancer is the most common type of cancer in cis women. When it comes to the breast cancer statistics, about 1 in 8 (women) will get breast cancer. It's also the second deadliest type of cancer for cis women."[63] In short, breast cancer is a disease experienced "almost entirely" by non-transgender women. Nonetheless, links between gender-affirming hormone therapy and breast cancer are often made—despite the lack of evidence for such claims. The New York State Department of Health, for example, claims that "trans men who have not had removal of the uterus, ovaries, or breasts are still at risk to develop cancer of these organs."[64] We ought to ask why state health departments are framing breast cancer as a trans-specific health issue, and note the dangers of doing so, especially for those who are interested in beginning gender-affirming hormone therapy. We also ought to ask why, in the medical literature on trans health care concerns, abortion almost never comes up. Even in a medical journal article entitled "Transgender Men and Pregnancy," abortion is not mentioned once.[65] While such absences certainly could reflect biases among researchers, it is also plausible that abortion does not come up because other issues are far more likely to impact trans men, and, as such, medical researchers have prioritized these issues.

As discourses connecting transness to pregnancy, and particularly, to abortion have become more widespread, this has begun to change, as the studies I reference earlier in this chapter demonstrate. But even those studies that set out to explore "Family Planning and Contraception Use in Transgender Men," as one article does, show that the pregnancies of trans men are less likely to end in abortion than are pregnancies of women. This point should not suggest that trans people do not need reproductive health care. They do. In fact, trans men are using "contraception at a rate comparable to the national average of 62%," and have higher rates of using the most effective forms of birth control—long-acting reversible contraception, such as IUDs and implants—than the general US population. However, when trans men do not use these forms of birth control, they cite as reasons their concerns with taking additional hormones or that the hormones could interfere with their hormone replacement therapy. What is worrisome about this position, the study's authors note, is that "there is no current research demonstrating positive or negative effects of low dose hormones from contraception on exogenous testosterone use."[66] The paucity of research on effects of hormonal contraception among transmasculine users, as well as the circulation of medical (mis)information about these effects, clearly represent reproductive justice issues—and yet we hear far less about the trans men needing contraception than we do about the trans men who get abortions or the trans women who get breast cancer. Planned Parenthood makes clear that breast cancer, with which one in eight women is diagnosed, is a *women*'s issue. Yet abortion, which is experienced by one in four women, is something that *patients* and *people* obtain.

As importantly, rather than pushing medical schools to broaden their curriculum to include trans healthcare or for universal comprehensive healthcare that would allow trans people to access gender-affirming care, liberals and leftists are demanding the discursive inclusion of trans people into conversations about a form of healthcare that trans people need way less often than other forms of healthcare. This is not what trans justice looks like. It simply can't be. We can and must do better. Let's turn now to an example of abortion activism that goes far beyond demands for discursive inclusion and emerged instead out of a desperate attempt to meet material needs as well as a deep recognition of the relationship between material conditions and social justice.

## JANE: HISTORY AND CONTEXT

In 1965—eight years before *Roe v. Wade* legalized some abortions in the United States—Heather Booth helped an acquaintance obtain an illegal abortion in Chicago, Illinois. The fact that Booth could be a source of information for others seeking abortions spread. Eventually the demand for abortion referrals increased beyond what Booth could manage on her own, so she enlisted the help of other women's liberation movement activists. In 1967, the Jane Collective, or Jane, was officially born. The group, which initially began as an abortion referral service, came to realize that one of the men to whom they had been referring patients was not actually a doctor. This information propelled Jane members to learn how to perform abortions themselves. Between 1967 and 1972, Jane, a group of housewives and college students, performed approximately eleven thousand safe abortions.[67]

In my Politics of Reproduction class, students learn about this remarkable history through Paula Kamen's play *Jane: Abortion and the Underground*. Importantly, my engagement with this play has not been limited to classroom conversations. In 2011, while a graduate student at UCSB, I collaborated with fellow graduate students as well as undergraduates to put on a production of the play—a story I share with my current students. After the class period in which we discussed *Jane*, one particularly bright, engaged, and motivated student activist, Taite Shomo, approached me about collaborating to put on the play at Middlebury College. While I was absolutely thrilled by this proposition, neither Shomo nor I had any experience directing a play. What we did have was a lot of excitement. We jumped right in. We decided that making our idea come to life would be most feasible—for both of us, as well as the students involved—if we could connect it to a course. I would serve as the producer (as I had at UCSB) and Shomo as the director.

But the world in January 2020, when we put on the play at Middlebury College, was not as it was in January 2011, the last time I had produced the play. We were three years into the presidency of Donald Trump, an overt fascist who had appointed another conservative to the Supreme Court, courted evangelicals with the promise of banning abortion, and encouraged brazen acts of racism, sexism, homophobia, transphobia, ableism, and xenophobia. For those of us on the political left, collective despair was in the air. And it shifted the contours of our activism. In 2011, the idea that abortion could be outlawed at the federal level at any moment was unfathomable, even though abortion was under threat at that time, too. And no one was discussing abortion as a trans issue. By 2020, things were different: LGBTQ+ groups had begun to center trans justice, reproductive rights advocates had begun to frame abortion as an issue of concern for trans men, and fears that *Roe v. Wade* could be overturned were palpable.

And it was not just the social world and political context that had changed in the last decade. Young people, including my students, are different. Just as they were in 2011, my students remain engaged, earnest, and excited about learning. But, in my experience, by 2020 they had become far more angsty, overwhelmed, and afraid to make mistakes and, thus, be "canceled" by their peers. They were also more likely to express that they just do not know where to start to make the changes in the world that they so desperately wanted. (Students who read this chapter as part of queer art nights, where they created art to work through this book's arguments, as I detail in the book's conclusion, agreed with this description.) This is not surprising. The political anxiety rippling through the country has seeped into our collective psyches, which, of course, informs how students engage in activism, classroom conversations, and their personal relationships.

I, too, am different, and therefore my relationships with my students are different. In 2011, I was a graduate student in my late twenties. Our play was not connected to a course and, because my role was more behind the scenes, I did not engage much with the student actors. Fast forward a decade: At the time of putting on the play at Middlebury College, I was a professor in my late thirties. I was teaching a class about reproductive justice through which I met with students four times weekly. Furthermore, I already had developed relationships with several of the students in the course prior to its inception. Seven students in the course had taken my Introduction to Queer Critique class, and a few had taken several additional courses with me. Other students registered for the class because their friends or teammates had recommended that they take a course with me. The affective ties and trust that we had built in other spaces meant that, even though most of the students had no prior engagement with academic feminist studies, we could have conversations that would have been otherwise impossible.

Considering this context, it is no surprise that students—especially those who had taken my Queer Critique class—began to express concern over certain aspects of the play. We returned to "the woman question" multiple times throughout the course of the class. Even the students most concerned with the erasure of trans men from the abortion conversation seemed to find comfort in the fact that the play is about activism that occurred in the 1960s and 1970s, when abortion was not only discussed as a *women's* issue but a women's *liberation* issue. Indeed, the demand for abortion rights emerged out of the women's liberation movement, and the play conveys this history well. No students wanted to erase or misrepresent this history, although they consistently drew from contemporary abortion discourses to raise concerns about it.

*My* concern was that we were getting far too wrapped up in terminology and were—like reproductive rights advocates wringing their hands over the issue of language use—losing sight of the bigger project. Jane did far more radical work than any of us critiquing them from the comfort of a fancy classroom at an elite liberal arts college ever had. Jane also did far more radical work than those contemporary advocates demanding so-called gender-inclusive language within reproductive justice organizing. Unless you are doing illegal shit in the service of social justice that could lead to being charged with murder, Jane was more radical than you, too. That the group was made up of women and that they served people who saw themselves as women should in no way make it difficult for us to recognize the radical and dangerous nature of their work or, even more importantly, to be able to learn crucial lessons from it. I was concerned that our repeated conversations about the language Jane used and their connecting abortion to women—a conundrum that would have been inconceivable in the moment in which Jane existed—were making it more difficult for us to reflect on the big questions the collective raises, as well as the insights they can offer activists today. In the end, my concerns were largely unrealized. With twelve hours a week together in class as well as several additional hours in rehearsals, we had enough time to address a plethora of reproductive justice issues, including "the woman question" and all of the affects and anxieties this question generated.

And I'm quite glad we did. On January 29 and 30, 2020, our class performed *Jane: Abortion and the Underground* to engaged audiences in two sold-out shows. And there, in the little black box theater on our elite New England campus, "the woman question" emerged yet again. We held talkbacks after both performances at which audience members could share their thoughts with and ask questions of the cast, director Taite Shomo, and me. Both nights, the very first question asked was about how the play ignored trans people and whether or not we discussed this erasure in our class. After several students responded by describing the depth with which we discussed this question and how the class came to terms with the play's focus on women through recognizing it as a period piece, the student who asked the question commented that they were just making sure our ignoring trans people was not a reflection of "TERFiness." (TERF is an acronym for trans-exclusionary radical feminist, or people who express their transphobia through deploying discourses of feminism.) That this question was the first question asked both nights says a great deal. Furthermore, one of the students asking this question referenced trans women in particular, without recognizing—much like Julián Castro—that trans women would not need abortions. Such questions and comments reflect broader concerns I have raised here regarding historical amnesia, an inability to recognize sexism and take it seriously, and the calling up of trans people as if doing so constitutes a critique in and of itself, even when such critiques belie a lack of understanding of the materiality of transness, particularly as it relates to reproduction.

As importantly, such questions—which position the student audience member as the critic and the original Jane activists, the *Jane* play, and the students and professor who put on the production as those in need of critique—make it difficult to recognize the lessons that both the original Jane activists as well as the play can teach us. Just as the Jane Collective was a remarkable and radical activist group, *Jane* is a unique piece of theater. Unlike most plays about abortion, *Jane* includes two abortion scenes on stage, such that audiences witness the procedure. That these scenes feel like some of the most intense in the play could encourage viewers to reflect on "the politics of depicting abortion."[68] What does it mean that we rarely see an abortion performed, even in theatrical performances about abortion? Why does witnessing an abortion feel so uncomfortable? How might registering the discomfort of engaging with the materiality of the procedure open up new political possibilities—and ones that are more queer, have greater relevance for the lives of LGBTQ+ people, and are more useful for countering antifeminist sentiment than what we have now? What, after all, is *Jane*'s queer potential?

## QUEERING *JANE*

Our desire to actualize *Jane*'s queer potential was central to our production. Such potential was thwarted far more by what was present than by what was not. Namely, my students and I were concerned with the ways in which the play reproduces heteronormativity. The final scene, for example, includes a voiceover of the playwright interviewing Judith, one of the Janes. The playwright asks: "What did you do after leaving the Service?" Judith responds: "I became a teacher, an author." The voiceover then asks, "And the rest of you?" The actors on stage respond in turn:

JODY: I was a national-champion dog trainer.

RUTH: A social worker.

ALICE: A teaching assistant.

HEATHER: Founder of Midwest Academy in Chicago, training leaders of social change organizations. . . . Today? The short version: A consultant to pro-democratic organizations and campaigns.

MICKI: Me, I was a state program administrator, then a community organizer. *(beat)* And a mother.

JUDITH: A mother.

JODY: A mother.

ALICE: A mother.

RUTH: A mother.

HEATHER: A mother.

To be frank, I hated the ending. So did the students—especially those who had taken Queer Critique with me and, like their professor, had been informed by Lee Edelman's *No Future*. Just as Edelman is concerned with the place that the Child has come to occupy within LGBTQ+ politics, and the deeply conservative impulses that become defensible when the Child is invoked, we, too, were concerned with what is lost when the defense of abortion justice hinges on the imagined future Child. None of us involved with the production wanted to use the figure of the sacred mother—and her need to control *when* she parents, not *if*—to justify the need for abortion.

As a class, we brainstormed and practiced alternative endings. After some doozies, we came up with something we were excited about:

JODY: I was a national-champion dog trainer.

RUTH: A social worker.

ALICE: A teaching assistant.

HEATHER: Founder of Midwest Academy in Chicago, training leaders of social change organizations. . . . Today? The short version: A consultant to pro-democratic organizations and campaigns.

MICKI: Me, I was a state program administrator, then a community organizer. *(beat)* And we are mothers.

JUDITH: Activists.

JODY: We give abortions.

ALICE: We receive abortions.

RUTH: We are feminists.

HEATHER: We are:

ALL: Jane.

Immediately after our class brainstorming session, Shomo and I emailed Kamen to ask for her permission to change the ending of her play, noting that our proposed changes better reflect the goals of the course performing her play. What follows is a largely unedited email exchange between Kamen, Shomo, and me, written as if the emails are themselves a part of the performance. In many ways, they were. In fact, these exchanges informed the final product as much as other crucial behind-the-scenes aspects of the performance, including marketing, lights, and sound.

INT. AT COMPUTERS—NIGHT—STATIONARY.

Three people—Paula Kamen, Taite Shomo, and Carly Thomsen—are sitting in front of three different computers. Kamen is a put-together, bubbly, and artsy fiftysomething playwright. Shomo is an articulate and motivated Gender, Sexuality, and Feminist Studies major and queer and feminist activist at a liberal arts college. Thomsen is an exhausted but excited Gender, Sexuality, and Feminist Studies professor in her late thirties. All are engaging in these exchanges with generosity and respect for one another.

KAMEN: My first gut response is for you to leave it as written since this is a different point being made here than I was making, that they are all mothers . . . [and] they were not anti-motherhood. It seems different from cuts you made before that don't create a new meaning. What is your reasoning . . . when you say it reflects your goals better? Would you feel more comfortable with the less gendered "parent" instead of "mother?" I know you're devoting a tremendous effort to this and want to make sure to be sensitive to your needs also!

SHOMO: When we were staging the final scene, we felt concerned that ending the play with the Janes describing themselves as mothers would somehow reinforce gendered expectations of women as mothers. As part of the class we're trying to think about undoing perceptions of women as solely or even primarily reproductive agents, and we thought that altering the final page might help acknowledge that. Additionally, our class is deeply informed by queer theory and critiques of the mainstreaming of gay politics. One text that we read by Lee Edelman suggests that one conservatizing force in progressive politics has been a centering of the normative nuclear family. Informed by queer politics, we are trying not to perpetuate the idea that abortion is important because it enables people to later plan their families, even if that was true for members of the Jane Collective. We appreciate your challenging of the idea that abortion-rights supporters are anti-motherhood, and we think that you do so beautifully throughout the play by showing how the Collective engaged in their work while pregnant and/or caring for their children. More than two-thirds of our class identifies as not-straight, and we are hoping that changing this aspect of the play will resonate more with members of the class and with LGBTQ youth today. Of course, we are also very cognizant of the fact that this is your intellectual and artistic work, and we do not want to take away from your labor. If you decide that we should not change the ending, we will absolutely respect that.

KAMEN: I can see your point about not making the mistake of glorifying motherhood on a pedestal as womankind's ultimate destiny. :) And also centering only on those identifying as women. Would you feel better using "parent" instead? Then the lines will still speak to a more narrow point I was making, not about motherhood as the be all and end all, and making it seem like women's defining trait, but that pro-choice people aren't against people having children. . . .

THOMSEN: Our play is sold out, our playlist is ready, and website is nearly done. (I'll send the website link once we finish it!) We're so close to being ready for opening night! . . . We have been struck by the ways students in the play are drawing from academic queer theory to think about the play. This is interesting because no one has written about The Jane Collective or your play in relation to LGBTQ+ issues—despite the fact that we are in a moment in which nearly everything, including abortion!—is discussed in relation to or through the lens of LGBTQ+ness. So, it isn't surprising that students' concerns about the play are largely related to the ways in which they see it as reproducing heteronormativity—epitomized by the play's ending focusing on mothers, as Taite mentioned in their email to you. I am really interested in thinking about how your play can be used in the contemporary moment in order to think through broader cultural narratives regarding LGBTQ+ness and abortion. How might Jane live on or reach new groups by thinking about it through the lens of LGBTQ+ness, for example? What are the benefits and limits of de-gendering the imagined abortion patient? We are drawing inspiration from Kelly O'Donnell's article about the ways in which narratives around Jane have centered different things in different historical moments.[69] I'll attach the article here. I'll also attach an article I cowrote about why we should think about abortion and queer justice in relation to each other in ways that go beyond reasons rooted in LGBTQ+ identity (that lesbians want babies and that trans men might need abortions, for ex). I hope to extend the arguments made in these articles by focusing on the Jane Collective and also your play.

I really appreciate your suggestion to swap "mother" for the ostensibly gender-neutral "parent"; however, this does not really fix the issues the students have articulated and that I agree with. In fact, while the more gender-neutral "parent" is in line with recent moves to de-gender abortion discourse ("pregnant people" instead of "women," for example), it does nothing at all to trouble the celebratory affects that get tethered to parenthood and reproduction. These attachments to the idea that people will and should parent are precisely the root of anti-abortion sentiment!! People should not have the rights and access to abortion because it will enable them to later have a family they want—which is what students feel the focus on mothers/parenting implies. People should have the rights and access to abortion because it allows people to live the kinds of lives they want to live—because, of course, abortion is a matter of liberation not just delayed parenting. Furthermore, it isn't transphobia that is leading to reduced access to abortion (transphobia is responsible for many other problems, but not this one) so using gender-neutral language doesn't address the problem; sexism and a continued belief that women should be mothers IS, however, the root of decreased access to abortion. So, it is the latter that I think abortion rights activists should challenge. And I think your play is particularly well suited to doing so!!—especially because your point that those who believe in abortion rights/access are not necessarily against having kids is very clear throughout your play, in that characters are mothers and/or pregnant while working in the Collective, and, as such, the final scene could make another point.

We practiced ending the play a lot of different ways, and students in the play agreed that ending with "We are . . . Jane." was really powerful, and further that it reinforced what seems to be a very important message of the play: that activism is never individual and is always collective. In this political moment, in which college students everywhere are expressing feeling daunted by the magnitude of the political problems facing them, I can imagine no more empowering lesson to end on. I hope you will consider our plea!:)

KAMEN: Thanks for such a thoughtful—and educational!—response. Through email, it's often hard to understand just how important a point is or what the tone of the person writing is. I see that this is a major issue for you and the students and see more why you would need changes beyond the surface level of just using "parent" instead of "mother." Yes, you can change what you have done according to the revised script Taite sent me.

It's been a confusing point for me to deal with. . . . But you especially got me with the point that the anti-choice side embraces the tyranny of the view that women should embrace motherhood. This is truly an interesting generational POV. This has never been brought up before, but this is the first post-Millennial group of students to produce the play. . . . Most directors of the play, that I know of, have been lesbians (that's true of the two Chicago productions and one Chicago reading so far). But no one has ever mentioned this point.

It's especially interesting because I just saw Lisa Loomer's *Roe*. She took pains to be sympathetic to all views, including that of Operation Rescue! For a big regional theater, having *anything* to do with abortion on the stage is pushing the envelope. And your students are going beyond that to question fundamental gender assumptions even by the pro-choice side.

[END SCENE]

While I do not want to belabor the points so clearly made in our email dialogue, a few points are worth emphasizing. That Kamen suggests swapping "mothers" for the ostensibly more gender-neutral "parents" speaks to the wide circulation by this time of the assumption that such shifts are progressive. Our exchange also makes clear that it is quite easy to explain why this shift is too superficial to unlock queer potential. Replacing "mothers" with "parents" does nothing to sever the celebratory affects associated with parenting, reproducing, and the nuclear family. And, as I noted in my email, it is precisely these affects that drive antiabortion sentiment. Disrupting the logics of antiabortion activism, then, requires that we do far more than swap out abortion rights supporters' use of overtly gendered terminology. It requires that we refuse the assumption that motherhood and parenthood are inevitable or desirable. And it requires that we approach abortion as a matter of liberation, not just delayed parenting. Actualizing such positions is far more difficult than utilizing so-called gender-inclusive language. Perhaps unlocking the queer potential of abortion and the theatrical stories about it requires us, to riff on Lee Edelman, to say "Fuck the Parent" and the collective terror perpetuated in their name.

Admittedly, the closing scene of our rendition of *Jane* did not exactly scream "Fuck the Parent." But we were able to create queer potential where it otherwise did not exist because of Paula Kamen's remarkable generosity. Her willingness to engage in queer theoretical conversations entirely new to her and to allow us to fundamentally change her art permitted us to queer *Jane*. In many ways, the primary beneficiaries of our efforts to queer *Jane* were those of us putting on the play. Through our in-class discussions of the limits of the final scene, we were able to discuss putting queer theory to work in the service of reproductive justice. And we practiced doing so through our conversations with Kamen and audience members at our post-performance talkbacks. During the show, the audience was not, of course, aware that we had made any changes to the script—though, to be frank, I doubt that most audience members, including those who raised questions regarding the play's ignoring of trans people who have abortions, would have taken issue with the original ending.

When students in the course responded to their fellow students' questions about transphobia in abortion discourse, they drew from our course conversations to describe the changes we made as a tactic for reducing heteronormativity and the necessity of eradicating heteronormativity for eliminating transphobia. They also told the audience that our changes to the final scene—in which all actors on stage spoke the last word, "Jane," in unison—were meant to make the point that sexual liberation requires collective effort. While this idea is, on the surface, quite simple, it also runs counter to the neoliberal impulses prominent in a great deal of contemporary liberal activism.[70] Our work to queer *Jane*, then, allowed us to articulate why queering reproductive justice requires more than including LGBTQ+ people in conversations about reproduction, and instead requires that we not only question the glorification of parenthood but demand that the conservative and domineering figure of the parent (of any gender!) be pushed to the margins of abortion discourse.

## UNIVERSALIZING, NUMBERS, AND THE MATTER OF RACE AND CLASS

I want to close by reflecting on the ramifications of producing a universal de-gendered abortion patient, including the ways in which this figure works in the service of post-raciality and classism—something I've gestured toward briefly a few times throughout this chapter, and now turn to more deliberately. Discussions of racism and classism, as well as women of color and poor women, are curiously absent in calls for "inclusive" or "gender-neutral" language. Caitlin Van Horn's article in *Allure* magazine speaks to this point:

> While cisgender people will never truly understand the difficulties that anyone who is trans or gender-nonconforming has in accessing abortion care, we can help make the conversation more inclusive. I do this by replacing the words "pregnant women" with "pregnant people," for example, in conversation—and most of the time, no one I'm talking to about abortion notices that I don't restrict the conversation to just women.
>
> Want some actual numbers? I'm a member of the board of directors for the New York Abortion Access Fund (NYAAF), a fund that helps people living in or traveling to New York state to pay for their abortion. NYAAF is committed to helping people get their abortions regardless of their gender—which is why we exclusively use gender-neutral language, having switched over in 2013. . . . It's clear from the increase that no one is confused about what we're doing, or put off by the fact that we serve a whole spectrum of genders.[71]

Let's leave aside the question of whether or not abortion conversations are becoming more inclusive if people having them are unaware of the shifts being made in the name of inclusivity. (Unlikely.) Let's also leave aside the assumption here that shifts in language use help anyone access actual care. (Also unlikely, as I suggested earlier.) Instead, I want to focus here on how this framing—as in others calling for "gender-neutral" language—fails to recognize the ongoing significance of race and class to reproductive outcomes. First, Van Horn's assertion that "cisgender people will never truly understand the difficulties that anyone who is trans or gender-nonconforming has in accessing abortion care" positions what she terms "cisgender people" as outside of difficulty. Such statements, which produce the abortion patient as upper-class and white, ignore the realities of the vast majority of abortion seekers, who are disproportionately poor, of color, and women. As such, it is likely that abortion seekers have faced obstacles due to classism, racism, and, yes, even sexism—both in relation to their abortion experience and far beyond.

Second, Van Horn connects the 100 percent increase in the number of caseloads managed by the New York Abortion Access Funds to their shift to gender-neutral language, rather than, say, to increased needs for abortion among those who cannot pay for the procedure on their own. We know who these people are. They are poor. They are women. They are Black and Latina. Ultimately, the one commonality among people who go through the hassle of contacting an abortion fund is that they cannot pay for the procedure themselves. Discussing an organization's caseload increase in relation to its use of gender-neutral language—rather than in terms of the reason people contact abortion funds—ignores the centrality of class and poverty to abortion decisions. I imagine that many people accessing the fund care far less about debates over gender-neutral language than they do about accessing funds to terminate their unwanted pregnancy.

To be clear, I'm not arguing for addressing the omission of race and class evident throughout calls for gender-neutral language by simply acknowledging that abortion seekers have a race and class. I'm suggesting something far more damning for advocates of gender-neutral language: That the underlying logics at play in demands for gender-inclusive language are *precisely* what make it difficult to address race and class. While centering one marginalized group (in this case, trans and gender-nonconforming people) need not preclude discussing other marginalized groups (poor women and women of color), that is the result of calls to avoid the term "woman." Put more directly, if we cannot talk about women, we cannot talk about low-income women or women of color. And if we cannot acknowledge these women—those most likely to get an abortion—we cannot acknowledge that racism and classism are social conditions that deeply inform who gets abortions. Even worse, we can't do anything about it. An advocate for gender-neutral language may correctly respond that we can talk about poor *people* and *people* of color. The discursive tools we have at our disposal, however, become dulled when we do so. This is precisely what Katha Pollitt referred to when she noted that "there are broader questions of political language" at stake. "One organization," Pollitt noted, "tweeted that one in three 'people' has had an abortion—actually, if we're talking about people, it's more like one in six."[72]

As it turns out, the question of numbers has been a point of contention in this debate over politicized language. In December 2020, I attended a Zoom event entitled "Illegal Abortion to Election 2020: What You Can Do to Advance Abortion Rights" organized by the Center for Women, Gender, and Sexuality at the University of Massachusetts, Dartmouth. The event featured three panelists: an original member of the Jane Collective, a staff member at a national reproductive justice organization, and a president of a law student group for reproductive justice. Considering the event's title as well as the event organizer's request that audience members watch the documentary *Jane: An Abortion Service* prior to attending, I expected that the event would draw specifically on the story of Jane to think through contemporary abortion issues. In fact, little was said about Jane. Early on in the conversation, however, the law student panelist pointed out that "there are *plenty* of trans men and nonbinary people getting abortions."

It is my contention that these two facts are linked. We could not discuss the lessons Jane can offer us because Jane was run by women for women, and this is a history that must be critiqued and moved beyond. More specifically, it was, as several activists in the collective have noted over the years, run by women primarily for women of color and poor women. Women with the financial capability to do so traveled to places where they could secure legal abortions or they used their cultural capital—including networks—to secure safe abortions via sympathetic doctors. Having access to the Jane Collective, with their sliding scale and feminist commitment to refuse to turn away people in need, even if they couldn't pay, was the only hope for many poor women, who were and continue to be disproportionately Black, Latina, and Native. Although Jane can offer lessons regarding the burdens the bodies of poor women and women of color bear when abortion is illegal or so inaccessible it might as well be, we did not hear these lessons. Instead, audience members were reminded that "plenty" of people other than women seek abortions.

In making such a claim, the law student utilized the draw of the quantitative, much like Van Horn did when she asked her readers if they "want some actual numbers?" In a similar vein, Katha Pollitt noted in her op-ed in *The Nation* that we don't know how many people get abortions who do not see themselves as women: "The primary sources of abortion data in the US—the CDC and the Guttmacher Institute—don't collect information on the gender identity of those who seek abortion." But, based on discussions with abortion providers, Pollitt surmised that "the number of transgender men who want to end a pregnancy is very low," claiming that "99.999 percent of those who get pregnant" are women.[73] Rye Young took issue with Pollitt's use of numbers: "She invented the statistic that TGNC people have only .001 percent of abortions, and uses testimony from clinic staff to further emphasize how few TGNC people need access to abortion services."[74]

Pollitt and Young were both mostly correct. In 2015, numbers were unavailable and so Pollitt had to have made hers up. Today, this is no longer the case. The currently available data suggests, again, that between .05 and .06 percent of people having abortions see their gender as other than woman. Pollitt's guesstimate wasn't too far off, it turns out. Further, if 2 percent of *transmasculine* people in one study and 4 percent of those in another study experienced abortion, then between 1 and 2 percent of trans *people* obtain abortions—or, actually fewer, considering that trans women make up a greater proportion of trans people than do trans men. These numbers raise interesting questions regarding the use of gendered language. We should be able to talk about the fact that not all trans *people* experience abortion, but we can't do that if we do not talk about gender. Saying 2 or 4 percent of trans *people* have abortions is inaccurate. But it is also more powerful than saying that somewhere between 1 and 2 percent of trans people have abortions. Alternatively, we can acknowledge gender—noting that between 2 and 4 percent of transmasculine and nonbinary people obtain abortions—and make an accurate and more compelling claim, although we should also take care to disaggregate nonbinary and trans in future studies. Here, the result of so-called gender-inclusive language (that is, refusing to acknowledge gender except in terms of transness, but crucially, nothing more specific than transness) is that transmasculine people stand in for all trans people, leaving trans women and their reproductive health concerns aside.

As I mentioned previously, I am not suggesting for even a second that the trans and gender-nonconforming people who have abortions do not matter. And healthcare institutions should take care to meet trans patients' needs. I am, however, unconvinced that shifting to gender-neutral language in our political advocacy does this work. A story on National Public Radio entitled "Getting an Abortion as a Trans Person is Hard—With or Without State Restrictions," speaks to this point. D, a person interviewed for the story, obtained an abortion at a clinic that had "gender-neutral intake forms, including boxes for legal name and chosen name." D then describes their experience in this clinic: "I put my name that I go by on my form. I put my pronouns. I put my gender identity. And I was called the wrong name and I was misgendered. And there was a trans flag hanging on the wall behind me. And I just, like, could not believe what was happening."[75] Discursive inclusion does not necessarily translate to a feeling of belonging, as this story highlights. In addition, I am concerned that in the rush to "inclusivity" or "gender neutrality" we have too easily ignored the structural issues, particularly those manifesting along racial, class, gender, and geographic lines, that inform the experiences of the vast majority of abortive subjects. Who and what is ignored in calls for language that is intentionally devoid of specificity?

Black Lives Matter, the most prominent social justice movement in the moment I wrote this chapter, offers lessons for thinking through this question—a point reproductive justice advocate Loretta Ross made in an interview Carrie Baker and I conducted for a *Ms. Magazine* article.[76] Black Lives Matter has made it common knowledge that police violence is a racial justice issue because this form of violence results in the disproportionate incarceration of, physical and psychological harm to, and death of Black people. When right-wing critics respond to Black Lives Matter arguments with "All Lives Matter" rhetoric, liberals and leftists rightly respond with outrage. Why? Because we understand this rhetorical move as a reflection of white supremacist desires to avoid acknowledging racism, and more specifically anti-Black racism. Critics of "All Lives Matter" accurately understand the retort as decidedly racist, or in the very least so steeped in post-raciality that it is largely indistinct from overt racism. What we have discussed less in relation to "All Lives Matter" is how its racism is spurred by the concept of a universal human.

Core to feminist, queer, trans, Black, and ethnic studies—and many related activist struggles—is the belief that the concept of a universal subject is not only ludicrous but dangerous. All people are not equally likely to own a boat, be raped, work jobs that pay a living wage, take vacations, own a home, die in police custody, or have an abortion. Our ability to access these things and our proximity to risks associated with these things are mediated by social factors. It is for this reason that scholars work against universalizing tendencies, suggesting that the differences between us are just as important as the similarities, which are themselves often exaggerated. Ignoring this fact is precisely what allows meritocracy and bootstrap ideology to persist—or the ideas that we are individually responsible for our successes as well as our challenges and failures.

Black Lives Matter has made it clear that the state informs not only who can be successful but who gets to live and breathe, able to move through their days free of state violence. State violence, perhaps most obvious as police violence, is a racial justice issue in part because Black people disproportionately experience it. According to the Mapping Police Violence project, in 2020 police killed 1,066 people. Of those murdered, 28 percent were Black. For reference, Black people make up 13 percent of the US population. As these numbers suggest, white people and non-Black people of color also experience police violence. And Black Lives Matter does not ignore this fact, so much as ask us to end violence that disproportionately impacts Black people and harms Black communities. But it isn't just the *ramifications* of police violence that Black Lives Matter has asked us to contend with; the movement has made clear that we must also address the historical *roots* of the problem. Many of the problems with contemporary policing can be traced back to "slave patrols," organized groups of armed men that sought to capture enslaved people who had escaped, terrorize them, and return them to their owners. In short, anti-Blackness is woven into policing, even if everybody who is targeted by and/or dies at the hands of police isn't Black.

Imagine knowing that 99.9 percent of people experiencing an issue fit into one demographic—and recognizing that subgroups within this demographic are disproportionately impacted—and ignoring this fact in favor of acting as if everybody, *every body*, is equally likely to face this issue. This is "All Lives Matter" logic, as Loretta Ross warns. We all matter. Sure. But we aren't all equally likely to die at the hands of police. We also aren't equally likely to have an abortion. Nearly one-quarter of women will experience abortion, while somewhere between 2 and 4 percent of transmasculine and nonbinary people will do the same.[77] Further, the percentage of pregnancies among transmasculine people that end in abortion is actually lower than the reported US abortion rate.[78] And regardless of the percentage of trans people having abortions, the current data suggest that 99.9 percent of people obtaining abortions experience the world as women. In 2014, 28 percent of these women were Black, the same percentage of people killed by police.[79] Just two years later, the Kaiser Family Foundation, a leading health policy organization, reported that 42 percent of abortion patients in 2016 were Black. We can recognize that some trans men and gender-nonconforming people will need abortions without producing an abortion patient as a universal subject, always already de-raced, de-classed, and de-gendered. In short, the demand for "gender neutrality" in abortion debates is the "All Lives Matter" corollary, but under the guise of inclusivity. As Ross so eloquently put it, "Using gender-neutral language around pregnancy, abortion, and sex discrimination is as damaging as using colorblind language around race discrimination because it fails to identify the targets, the victims, and the specificity of the oppression."[80]

Queer theorists have long been skeptical of notions of "inclusivity," highlighting both what gets excluded in the name of inclusion and the ways in which such notions rely on the production of an imagined universal subject. In general, queer theorists work against universalizing tendencies, focusing on the differences between and among people, LGBTQ+ and otherwise. Miranda Joseph, for example, argues that we should be wary of invocations of LGBTQ+ "community," as they tend to rely on simple assumptions about inclusivity that require flattening differences among LGBTQ+ people. Further, Joseph says that the role of sexual identity in the creation of shared community is overemphasized while the roles of production and consumption are underemphasized.[81] What might queer politics look like if we imagined the heterosexual janitors who clean the bathrooms at LGBTQ+ nonprofit organizations, the heterosexual staff at childcare facilities watching the children of lesbian couples, or the heterosexual food cart owners at Pride parades as if they were as central to queer community as the LGBTQ+ people their labors support?

The problems with imagining LGBTQ+ people as necessarily part of one big community are evident in a 2015 *Reuters* story. Reporting on an article published in the *American Journal of Public Health*, the headline reads, "Pregnancies More Common Among Lesbian, Gay, Bisexual Youths." Crucially, the original study *Reuters* referenced did not differentiate between different types of LGBTQ+ people. Reuters reported that the study's lead author cautioned that their findings "can't untangle nuances in pregnancy rates between subgroups, such as lesbians compared to bisexual women." Further complicating our ability to draw firm conclusions from the study is that researchers did not compare "all lesbian, gay and bisexual youths—only those who had sex with a person of the opposite sex." It seems clear that if inclusion into quantifiable LGBTQ+ness rests on engaging in heterosexual sex, the conclusions we can draw are quite limited. The more accurate story here is that a study concluded that people who have same-sex sexual relations *in addition to* heterosexual sexual relations are more likely to get pregnant than those who only have heterosexual sex—quite a different, and far less inflammatory, claim.[82] We can see here the results of the ubiquity of discourses of LGBTQ+ community that produce it as a monolith.

We need an approach that differs from the kinds of simplistic one-size-fits-all identity-driven politics common in 1997 when Cathy Cohen wrote "Punks, Bulldaggers, and Welfare Queens" and that remain hegemonic today. To make this point, Cohen quotes Barbara Smith's "Queer Politics: Where's the Revolution?": "Unlike the early lesbian and gay movement, which had both ideological and practical links to the left, black activism and feminism, today's 'queer' politicos seem to operate in an historical and ideological vacuum. 'Queer' activists focus on 'queer' issues, and racism, sexual oppression, and class exploitation do not qualify, despite the fact that the majority of 'queers' are people of color, female or working class."[83]

Following Cohen, Smith, and other Black feminist lesbians writing in this vein, I want to close by reflecting explicitly on what it means that LGBTQ+ rights and reproductive rights activists are now advocating for a universal abortive subject: pregnant people, callers, patients, everybody. This universal subject is, of course, "gender-neutral," something these activists celebrate. Let's leave aside the belief that gender neutrality can exist—very little is gender-neutral, because gender is not neutral—so that we can focus on the ramifications of calls for gender-neutral language. The experience of pregnancy and abortion is gendered. This does not mean it is universal or the same for everyone. But it is always already gendered, as it is, at once, a site for consolidating and challenging broader ideas about gender.

Our ability to talk about the gendered aspects of pregnancy and abortion are shrunk by demands for gender neutrality. As a result, we cannot talk about the centrality of gender to the trans man who became impregnated as a result of a gang rape through which the rapists were attempting to "correct" his transmasculine gender presentation. In this story, which was included in *GQ*'s article "Twelve Men Share Their Abortion Stories," pregnancy and abortion were intimately tied to the subject's gender. His gender was not neutral. Nor were his rape, pregnancy, or abortion. On the flip side is Julián Castro's aforementioned blunder, in which he positioned trans women as potential abortion patients. Caitlin Van Horn's *Allure* article similarly calls up the specter of the trans woman to argue for gender-neutral language. She notes that TERFS would "have us believe that trans women have no place in feminism or women-only spaces." Never again does Van Horn mention trans women or the reproductive issues they might face. She also mentions trans men just once. Throughout Van Horn's article, all people—trans and non-trans alike—are just people. We are universally one. One gender. One race. One class.

The celebratory affects that get attached to so-called gender-neutral language in abortion discourse do nothing for creating the kinds of radical coalitions for which Cohen calls. Further, those calling for such discursive shifts ignore the impacts of producing abortion as a gender-, race-, and class-neutral issue. Inspired by Cohen's critique of identity-based politics and the lack of racial, class, and gendered analysis in LGBTQ+ spaces, I want to assert that acknowledging that 99.9 percent of abortion patients are women—disproportionately poor, Black, and/or Latina and mostly heterosexual—need not be considered transphobic. Perhaps we need a new queer coalitional approach that expands upon Cohen's vision, one that includes another category of people marginalized by their heterosexuality: aborting women. We need coalitions where trans people are fighting for abortion rights alongside non-trans people fighting for increased access to gender-affirming health care for trans people *not* because either issue is likely to impact them *personally* but because both are crucial for gender and sexual liberation. While misogyny and sexism are the root of antiabortion activism, state-based legislative attempts to protect abortion access can and should be framed in such a way that they also protect gender-affirming care—both are, of course, about health care that allows for bodily autonomy. But we do not need to discursively disappear women in order to make this argument. Indeed, Cohen has shown us what a queer coalitional approach that centers those who do not benefit from heteronormativity looks like. It is time we add the abortive patient—in all of their materiality—to that coalition.

In this chapter, I have questioned activists' assumptions that the discursive exclusion of trans men from the abortion debate is the problem in need of being addressed, and further that "gender-neutral" language is the solution. The problems, which are much greater, include the antiabortion movement's successful work to limit abortion access and the systematic denial of health care (far beyond abortion) to trans people. The discursive shifts for which activists are calling do nothing to address these issues. Instead, these calls create additional harms, including producing abortion as outside of concerns related to racism, classism, and sexism. Again, we ought to more closely examine calls for "inclusivity" and "gender neutrality" and then move beyond this examining to actually do something about the lack of access to abortion. As it turns out, *doing* something is not the function of many of the deployments of trans and gender-nonconforming people in discussions of abortion. And if it were, we would be talking about who actually gets abortions and the possibilities and limits of abortion for creating collective liberation. Unlocking queer potential requires that we focus on how the needs associated with creating collective liberation may *differ* for different groups of people within our queer coalition and develop tools for rethinking that which has been produced as commonsensical, including the typical deployments of "parents" and trans men as abortion patients. We need a new approach to sexual liberation altogether—one that recognizes how social structures inform our material lives, asks earnest questions with good intentions, and avoids performative wokeness that masquerades as a solution.

# 4 Abortion as Gender Transgression

## REPRODUCTIVE JUSTICE, QUEER THEORY, AND ANTI–CRISIS PREGNANCY CENTER ACTIVISM

In 2012, End Fake Clinics, a student club at the University of California, Santa Barbara (UCSB), worked with our student government to make UCSB the first university in the country to ban crisis pregnancy centers from engaging in false advertising on campus. While this activist success makes End Fake Clinics a remarkable case, the group's core members did not consider it the most memorable aspect of our participation in the group. Instead, members cited the friendships we made with one another, the feeling of belonging to a collective built on shared political inquiry, and finding ways to put feminist and queer theory into practice as inspiring and sustaining our activism. In this chapter, which I originally coauthored with fellow End Fake Clinics activist Grace Tacherra Morrison and published in *Signs*, I expand on the limited feminist scholarship on crisis pregnancy centers and the little queer theoretical scholarship on reproduction by archiving and analyzing the activism of End Fake Clinics, a unique queer reproductive justice student group created to fight crisis pregnancy centers.[1]

Crisis pregnancy centers are religiously informed antiabortion nonprofits that claim to offer free services—including pregnancy tests, ultrasounds, counseling, and maternity and baby items—to those experiencing an unintended pregnancy. Crisis pregnancy centers target women they see as "abortion minded," often advertising on high school and college campuses. They deploy a range of deceptive tactics, including: opening crisis pregnancy centers near abortion clinics with the intention of confusing, and thus intercepting, those seeking abortion; obscuring their political and religious ideologies; implying that they offer abortions when they do not; and spreading false information regarding abortion, claiming incorrectly that abortion leads to breast cancer, mental health problems, and infertility.[2] In fact, a 2006 congressional investigation found that 87 percent of crisis pregnancy centers give out false medical information.[3] Crisis pregnancy centers' false claims are bolstered through their being "made to look and feel like doctor's offices," although they rarely staff medical professionals and are not subject to the governmental regulation of healthcare facilities.[4] In 2015, NARAL Pro-Choice California conducted an undercover investigation sampling approximately 25 percent of California crisis pregnancy centers.[5] While every center insisted that their client receive an ultrasound, not a single worker admitted that they could not detect a fetal heartbeat in investigators feigning pregnancy. One worker pointed to an investigator's IUD, calling it "her baby."[6] Such scenarios illustrate the potentially dangerous consequences of the lack of regulation of crisis pregnancy centers. Yet antiabortion advocates claim that legislation requiring crisis pregnancy centers to provide medically accurate information infringes on their constitutional rights to free speech and to conduct religious outreach, although they also argue that they need not disclose their religious ideology.[7]

At UCSB, students viewed crisis pregnancy centers as an impediment to reproductive justice, and End Fake Clinics was born in a process I describe below. That End Fake Clinics centered crisis pregnancy centers in our reproductive justice activism was unique, a fact that ought to be surprising, as such centers comprise the largest component of the antiabortion movement in the United States; more volunteers, volunteer hours, and resources are dedicated to crisis pregnancy centers than all other forms of antiabortion activism combined.[8] As such, one might assume that countering crisis pregnancy centers would be central to reproductive justice activism. In interviews with California-based organizers, however, we learned that this is not the case. Even for staff at reproductive rights organizations involved in crafting anti–crisis pregnancy center legislation, this advocacy comprised less than 10 percent of their work overall.

This is not to ignore the anti–crisis pregnancy center activism organizers have undertaken. In 2015, four reproductive justice groups in California came together to work with the state legislature to pass the Freedom, Accountability, Comprehensive Care, and Transparency (FACT) Act. This bill, struck down by the US Supreme Court in 2018, required crisis pregnancy centers to make clear when they were not licensed medical facilities and to inform clients about state programs that provide free or reduced-cost abortion, family planning services, and prenatal care. In the summer of 2017, a new coalition of reproductive justice groups launched the #ExposeFakeClinics campaign. However, just months later, the group seemed largely defunct.[9] Despite the recent increased focus on crisis pregnancy centers among those concerned with reproductive justice, crisis pregnancy centers have long been and remain much more central to the antiabortion movement than fighting them has been to reproductive justice activism.

End Fake Clinics is, then, in many ways an anomaly—and not only because this reproductive justice student group focused on crisis pregnancy centers. End Fake Clinics also made feminist and queer theory central to this activism. In this chapter, I use End Fake Clinics as a case study to outline the contours of what a queer reproductive justice politic might entail. Such a politic may appear paradoxical, in that queer theory has produced some of the most incisive critiques of identity politics and appeals to state protection, while reproductive rights and justice movements have long sutured politics to identity in demands for legal rights and state support. End Fake Clinics is a striking example of the activism that can emerge when ostensibly contradictory epistemologies collide. The creation of the group's politics was enabled, I argue, by members' collective belief that our activism would be best when informed by feminist and queer theory as well as by the deep affective connections developed through the group.

The depth of the relationships among group members was particularly remarkable when considering the group's diversity: students of color and white students; students with chronic illnesses and disabilities and those without; students from a range of class backgrounds; women, men, transgender, and genderqueer students; and LGBTQ+ and heterosexual students. End Fake Clinics' diversity was enabled because the group came together around shared feminist and queer political commitments rather than through a shared identity, experience, or embodiment. In many ways, End Fake Clinics epitomizes the kind of queer coalitional politics for which queer theorists have called. Cathy Cohen argues that queer politics will be most robust when they include those who have not benefited from heteronormativity (e.g., Black single mothers) as opposed to being limited to LGBTQ+-identified people.[10] Through End Fake Clinics, heterosexual students engaged in queer politics and queer students engaged in reproductive justice work that is often understood as outside the boundaries of queer struggle. That End Fake Clinics came to view itself as a queer reproductive justice group through focusing on crisis pregnancy centers—which are often conflated with abortion and thus imagined as a heterosexual "white feminist" concern, two troubling trends—has a great deal to teach us about the epistemological and political benefits of queering reproductive justice.

When we began to organize as End Fake Clinics in January 2011, we could not have predicted that the insights we would gain through our activism would be so relevant to feminist and queer knowledge production and politics in 2025, particularly because the group disbanded in June 2014 when its core members graduated. However, this discussion is particularly timely for several reasons. First, the number of crisis pregnancy centers is growing, while the number of abortion providers is shrinking; there are now approximately 2600 crisis pregnancy centers but just 765 facilities that provide abortion, numbers that were reversed in the 1980s. Second, the US Supreme Court heard *NIFLA v. Becerra* during the summer of 2018, a case through which antiabortion plaintiffs argued that California's FACT Act violated crisis pregnancy centers' First Amendment rights to free speech. While the Court's 5–4 decision to strike down the FACT Act was a huge blow to abortion justice, it also placed crisis pregnancy centers in the public sphere in new ways, creating opportunities for unique scholar-activist collaborations—the very dynamics that End Fake Clinics both emerged out of and enabled. Third, as reproductive justice activists and scholars have begun to use the phrase "queering reproductive justice" to refer to the reproductive concerns of LGBTQ+ people, and as increasing numbers of LGBTQ+ people engage in reproduction, we need more complicated ways to discuss what it might mean to queer reproduction beyond such an identitarian model.

In what follows, I review dominant narratives of reproductive justice, suggesting that both End Fake Clinics and crisis pregnancy centers trouble these narratives. I then outline the academic scholarship on crisis pregnancy centers, placing it in conversation with feminist and queer analyses of reproduction. Next, I describe our methods and provide a detailed account of End Fake Clinics' activism, focusing on our Queering Reproductive Justice workshop. I argue for reading abortion as gender transgression and suggest that approaching something as wildly ordinary as abortion—nearly one-quarter of US women obtain an abortion in their lifetime, after all—as transgressive encourages broadening queer conceptualizations of normativity and transgression, allowing us to recognize deeper connections between queer and reproductive issues and, further, to complicate this very distinction.[11] This position draws from and contributes to queer theoretical debates over normativity—what it means, its value, its harms, and its (lack of) place in our politics. I close by analyzing how affect and identity operated in End Fake Clinics, highlighting the value of epistemologically based and affectively bound activism.

## CRISIS PREGNANCY CENTERS AND END FAKE CLINICS: COMPLICATING REPRODUCTIVE JUSTICE NARRATIVES

Crisis pregnancy centers and End Fake Clinics alike complicate the typical narratives that advocates tell about reproductive justice, particularly those that frame reproductive rights and justice as distinct or that focus on the differences between the movements, as discussed in this book's Introduction.[12] This difference is often articulated in terms of how the two movements approach abortion. As the narrative goes, reproductive rights movements focus too much on the legal right to abortion, ignoring both access to abortion as well as other non-abortion reproductive issues.

But crisis pregnancy centers complicate the reproductive rights/justice dichotomy. Sure, crisis pregnancy centers' primary mission is to prevent abortion, but they aren't doing so primarily through legal channels, and they use approaches and engage in topics that ought to concern those dedicated to reproductive freedom more broadly. Crisis pregnancy centers use deceptive practices and circulate inaccurate information, which can negatively impact the health of those who end up at one; they insist that women are damaged by sex; and they implement abstinence-only sex education programs in schools. A recent Heartbeat International conference featured a "Sexual Integrity" workshop in which volunteers learned methods for countering comprehensive sex education, with the goal of challenging bans on abstinence-only education in schools.[13] Across their work, crisis pregnancy centers promulgate gender essentialism—suggesting that all women long to reproduce and thus that abortion harms women—and advance the very sexist ideologies that inform the broader issues reproductive justice advocates address. Just as crisis pregnancy centers trouble any dichotomous understandings of rights and justice, abortion and something more capacious than abortion, so too did End Fake Clinics. End Fake Clinics focused on abortion, was composed of more people of color than white people, addressed various reproductive issues as social justice matters, and used legislative channels as well as more creative activist approaches meant to shift campus culture. Following End Fake Clinics, I do not make a hard and fast distinction between reproductive rights and justice.

## CRISIS PREGNANCY CENTERS ARE EVERYWHERE—EXCEPT FEMINIST SCHOLARSHIP

Just as crisis pregnancy centers have not been a focus of reproductive justice activism, they have also been largely ignored by feminist scholars writing about reproductive politics—something apparent if you peruse feminist studies journals or books about reproductive justice. Two articles are notable exceptions. In "Beyond Pro-Choice Versus Pro-Life," Andrea Smith outlines the limits of the pro-choice framework for women of color.[14] Smith uses as evidence Planned Parenthood's eugenicist history as well as a crisis pregnancy center's claim that it has a "holistic" and "anti-racist perspective." Citing a *Christianity Today* article titled "Saving Black Babies," Smith relies on the North Baton Rouge Women's Help Center's stories about itself, noting that "it provides educational and vocational training, GED classes, literacy programs, primary health care and pregnancy services, and child placement services."[15] Smith then poignantly asks: "If we are truly committed to reproductive justice, why should we presume that we should necessarily work with Planned Parenthood and reject the Women's Help Center?"[16]

In asking this question, Smith equates Planned Parenthood, a national network, with a single crisis pregnancy center. (Smith mentions Planned Parenthood twenty-one times, while her discussion of the crisis pregnancy center is limited to one paragraph.) Examining crisis pregnancy centers as a network would render Smith's position impossible. The majority of centers are connected through two antiabortion organizations, Heartbeat International and Care Net, through which they receive staff training, pamphlets, consulting, assistance acquiring ultrasound machines, and legal guidance.[17] The problems with crisis pregnancy centers, then, cannot be understood in terms of the practices of individual centers. Furthermore, just 25 percent of crisis pregnancy centers even self-report that they provide supplies (such as maternity clothes and diapers) to clients, and yet all who enter receive antisex, antiabortion, and pro-(heterosexual)-marriage propaganda.[18]

The second academic article I know of, written by an author other than me, that discusses crisis pregnancy centers in an explicitly feminist publication is by Kimberly Kelly.[19] Kelly examines how conservative women volunteers at crisis pregnancy centers mobilize gender essentialism through their work. In contrast to many feminist and queer theorists wholly critical of biological essentialism because of the ways it undergirds and drives sexism, Kelly argues that "gender essentialism can be a unique resource that legitimates autonomous sex-segregated spaces, prompts gender identification across religious and political divides, and places explicit limits on men's power."[20] Kelly views crisis pregnancy centers as a space for evangelical women to negotiate power within the otherwise male-dominated antiabortion movement, suggesting that center volunteers use "woman-centered" approaches that are distinct from the "fetus-centered" focus of the broader antiabortion movement.[21] Kelly argues that activists' strategic framing of their work as "woman-centered" has allowed the number of centers to quadruple in the past two decades—without criticizing either the expansion of crisis pregnancy centers or the role of "woman-centered" discourses in this expansion.

Kelly's descriptions of crisis pregnancy centers as woman centered are not uncontestable. Laury Oaks examines the move by antiabortion activists to describe themselves as "woman centered" and even feminist because of their belief that they save women from the ostensible horrors of abortion or because they recognize that women need greater pregnancy and parenting resources.[22] Despite the claims made by crisis pregnancy center volunteers and self-described antiabortion feminists, however, most women report feeling relief after an abortion—not harmed or distraught—and furthermore, one can advocate for increased social supports without working to restrict access to legal abortion. Despite their claims to be "woman centered," self-proclaimed antiabortion feminists "fail to address some of the most critical sexual and reproductive issues for women."[23] We should see this approach as a cooptation of the feminist demand to center women for antifeminist purposes.

While little has been said about crisis pregnancy centers in feminist academic journals—and that which has been said is less critical of crisis pregnancy centers than I think is ethical—political scientists, legal scholars, and public health scholars have been writing about crisis pregnancy centers with increasing frequency, particularly since 2012.[24] Much of this scholarship is overtly critical of crisis pregnancy centers, framing them as "public health risks"[25] and as threats to informed decision-making.[26] An article published by medical doctors and public health scholars, for example, examines 254 crisis pregnancy center websites included in state resource directories, concluding that 80 percent include false or misleading information, most commonly by linking abortion to "mental health risks, preterm birth, breast cancer and future infertility."[27] Put more directly, the state is endorsing the false information peddled by crisis pregnancy centers. The authors conclude that "states should not list agencies that provide inaccurate information as resources in their directories."[28] Another scholar, in an article published in a law review, argues that "states are responsible for protecting vulnerable pregnant women from [crisis pregnancy centers'] deceptive practices" and "must enforce existing anti-deception statutes and enact legislation" to protect crisis pregnancy center clients.[29]

We might ask what to make of the fact that scholarship on crisis pregnancy centers is largely published outside of feminist studies journals, does not engage with feminist scholarship on reproduction more broadly, and is far more critical of crisis pregnancy centers than that published in feminist studies journals. We might also ask, as Jennifer Doyle does, why "connections between the pro-abortion position and the sex/gender radicalism at the heart of queer theory's central texts have been relatively unexamined."[30] This question is particularly illuminating in a moment in which scholarship on LGBTQ+ people and reproduction is growing. Such work focuses overwhelmingly on the use of reproductive technologies by LGBTQ+ people and, thus, on individuals who want to reproduce.[31] I follow Doyle in asking what it means that abortion has been so easily dismissed by queer theorists and, prior to the recent demands for gender-neutral language to include trans men in the abortion debate, imagined as outside of queer politics.

## MIXED AND AT TIMES UNCONVENTIONAL METHODS: OR, HOW WE CAME TO SEE END FAKE CLINICS AS A UNICORN

This mixed-methods approach draws from analysis of online databases of student organizations across California campuses, examinations of feminist and reproductive justice student groups' social media, and interviews with employees of three California-based reproductive justice organizations and also twelve core End Fake Clinics activists. Of the End Fake Clinics activists interviewed, eight identified as people of color (six as women of color, including Black, Chinese American, Filipina American, Latina, Middle Eastern American, and multiracial) and four as white. Six participants identified as queer, five as straight, and one as questioning. Nine participants identified as women and two as genderqueer.

Beyond these conventional research methods, I was deeply involved in End Fake Clinics, as was Grace Tacherra Morrison, who coauthored the original article out of which this chapter emerges. In the 2010–11 academic year, Morrison, then a first-year student at UCSB, enrolled in my Feminist Studies "Activisms" class, which I taught while a PhD student.

For her final course project, Morrison worked with a small group of classmates to conduct research on crisis pregnancy centers in the tricounty region surrounding Santa Barbara. End Fake Clinics grew out of this research. Over the next four years—the entire life of End Fake Clinics—both Morrison and I remained heavily involved. At the students' request, I served as the group's formal adviser, and for three years Morrison served as the group's cochair. Along with our fellow activists, we attended weekly meetings, planned events, and orchestrated campaigns and other creative projects.

In an effort to contextualize the work of End Fake Clinics within broader reproductive justice activism across California campuses, we searched the databases of registered student organizations at each of the University of California and California State University campuses. We used keywords such as "reproductive rights," "reproductive justice," "pro-choice," "pregnancy," "abortion," and "feminism" and located thirty-seven student organizations that engaged with feminist and reproductive justice issues. We then analyzed these groups' Facebook pages, Twitter accounts, and Tumblr pages, looking for any engagement with crisis pregnancy centers between 2011 (the year of End Fake Clinics' conception) and 2020 (the year our original article was published). Our research yielded zero results; it appeared that not one other California campus-based student group had engaged in a single event, project, or campaign addressing crisis pregnancy centers.

To confirm these findings, we reached out to California organizations engaged in reproductive justice, requesting interviews with people connected to campus activism or crisis pregnancy centers. In the summer of 2017, we interviewed employees of Black Women for Wellness, the Feminist Majority Foundation, and NARAL Pro-Choice California. We assumed that, as leaders in developing and organizing around the FACT Act, Black Women for Wellness and NARAL Pro-Choice California could provide additional information on anti–crisis pregnancy center activism. Similarly, we assumed that the Feminist Majority Foundation, which historically has had a developed campus outreach program, would have information on campus activism in California. However, none of the people we interviewed—those most connected to anti–crisis pregnancy center activism and campus-based activism—could recollect any overlap between the two.[32] Furthermore, activists mentioned that within their organizations and other reproductive justice groups in their broader coalitions, little time and few resources are dedicated to either campus organizing or crisis pregnancy centers. Our interviews with reproductive justice activists and our online scouring of databases of student organizations confirm that California campus-based organizing related to crisis pregnancy centers was nonexistent—with the exception of End Fake Clinics.

## BECOMING AND BEING END FAKE CLINICS

In January 2011, when Morrison and her classmates set out to learn about crisis pregnancy centers, virtually no academic work addressed the topic and very little related activism existed.[33] Eager to learn more, students designed an investigative project through which they visited seven crisis pregnancy centers in the Santa Barbara area, where they took pregnancy tests, collected promotional materials, and were "counseled" by volunteers on their supposed pregnancy options. Students were surprised to find the same pamphlets, life stories from volunteers, and incorrect information across the different crisis pregnancy centers they visited. They found these approaches—which scholars and activists have since argued are characteristic of crisis pregnancy centers—manipulative and deceptive.

This research spurred End Fake Clinics' first activist project: a photography campaign, the goal of which was to increase awareness about crisis pregnancy centers among UCSB students by countering the false information students received at crisis pregnancy centers. For many of the students involved, working on this campaign comprised their first engagement with activism. The emotions stirred by the project's success, along with the shocking nature of the lies students encountered in the crisis pregnancy centers, the intensity of their experiences conducting such research (especially at a time when no published academic scholarship could confirm the ubiquity of these approaches), and the bonds formed among group members spurred students to turn End Fake Clinics into a recognized student club. In fall 2011, students did precisely this, which allowed the group access to university resources, such as funding and space for events and meetings.

Campaign led by Grace Tacherra Morrison, with End Fake Clinics members and friends holding signs countering false information they received in local crisis pregnancy centers.

During this time, End Fake Clinics continued to engage in awareness-raising campaigns but decided—after realizing that local crisis pregnancy centers advertised in the campus newspaper and the coupon book given out at the university bookstore—that such approaches were not enough to counter the centers' effects on campus. End Fake Clinics then launched a campaign, initially spearheaded by just four students, to prevent crisis pregnancy centers from advertising on campus. To do so, we crafted a resolution with a member of the Associated Students Legislative Council and collected signatures in support of it from more than two thousand students, approximately 10 percent of the undergraduate student body. Students solicited signatures via classroom presentations, tabling in public areas, and at events we organized, including Reproductive Justice Awareness Week, academic talks, and a "Bust the Myth" breast- and chest-casting party at which we screened *12th and Delaware* (2010), a documentary about crisis pregnancy centers.

On January 25, 2012, armed with petitions and a PowerPoint presentation, End Fake Clinics presented its case to the Associated Students at an open, public meeting. Students discussed their research that led to founding End Fake Clinics, highlighting the inaccurate information they received at the crisis pregnancy center nearest campus and showing the center's two different websites, one that made clear its religious foundations and antiabortion politics, and one that did not. Immediately following the meeting, staff from the local crisis pregnancy center sent a detailed rebuttal to the Associated Students. Nonetheless, the elected board unanimously voted to prevent any boards, commissions, and committees under the purview of Associated Students from advertising for crisis pregnancy centers. And, in 2012, just a year after End Fake Clinics came into existence, UCSB became the first university to ban crisis pregnancy centers from advertising on campus.[34]

At the time, we were extremely proud of our activist successes. We had no idea then that this was just the beginning of what End Fake Clinics would become. In the two years that followed, End Fake Clinics continued to meet weekly, organize events, and produce creative projects. Members collaborated with fellow campus and community activists to bring scholars and activists, including Cecilia Fire Thunder, Judy Norsigian, and Kim Hall, to UCSB to give talks. Students presented about crisis pregnancy centers at UCSB's Women's Center and at the Women of Color Conference. End Fake Clinics activists also produced videos on the history of End Fake Clinics, published op-eds in the campus newspaper, created a weekly radio show called the "Reproductive Justice Power Hour" for UCSB's student station, co-organized a film series on reproductive issues, created a "Queering Reproductive Justice" zine, and produced a music video about crisis pregnancy centers.[35] Through completing these projects, End Fake Clinics activists put into practice the feminist and queer theory they were engaging in their classes, a process through which they came to view theory as crucial to activism.

## THE PRACTICE OF QUEERING REPRODUCTIVE JUSTICE

End Fake Clinics' mobilizing theory in the service of activism is perhaps most evident in a Queering Reproductive Justice workshop the group designed and facilitated for LGBTQ Pride Week. That End Fake Clinics was invited to participate in Pride evidences that the group was understood as queer—and not just because most members were LGBTQ+-identified. Being recognized as queer, however, did not necessarily translate into activists' ability to articulate what exactly was queer about End Fake Clinics. Therefore, we sought out resources linking queer and reproductive issues, looking specifically for reproductive justice groups framing themselves as queer; this yielded zero results. It appeared that, as of 2013, LGBTQ+ and reproductive justice activists had not articulated relationships between the movements.

This, of course, subsequently changed. The following year, in 2014, Unite for Reproductive and Gender Equity (URGE, formerly Choice-USA) added a "Queering Reproductive Justice" page to its website. In 2015, the University of Michigan organized "Queering Reproductive Justice: Opportunities and Challenges." In 2017, SisterSong held a "Queering Reproductive Justice 101" workshop and the National LGBTQ Task Force created "Queering Reproductive Justice: A Toolkit." The descriptions of these events, tool kit, and campaign link the movements through the "reproductive oppressions that trans and queer folks face" (SisterSong), right-wing opposition to LGBTQ+ and reproductive justice (National LGBTQ Task Force), and broad ideologies that undergird both movements, including desires for "agency, power, self-determination, autonomy, and dignity" (URGE).

As we brainstormed for our workshop, we, too, initially made similar links between reproductive and queer movements. Yet we ultimately felt dissatisfied with our ideas. None of these links captured the queerness of End Fake Clinics. Connecting the movements by claiming that reproductive issues impact LGBTQ+ people seemed insufficient politically and epistemologically. Further, because most social justice movements could claim to be connected through desires for agency and self-determination, as well as opposition from the right wing, neither seemed specific enough to articulate the relationship between queer and reproductive issues. Finally, it seemed obvious that trans men might want to give birth, LGBTQ+ parents might struggle to retain custody of their children, and LGBTQ+ people might experience difficulty adopting or accessing reproductive technologies—but all of these examples are built on what Lee Edelman calls "pronatalism" and "reproductive futurism," or the assumption that people want to reproduce and that this desire should be celebrated.[36]

Crafting a politic built on such examples also suggests that people ought to be concerned with issues impacting them personally—an approach that limits possibilities for coalitional work. We wanted to be able to articulate a queer approach to reproductive justice as epistemological. How else could we explain the involvement of all of us LGBTQ+ people in a reproductive justice group, especially at a time when there were no discourses in circulation attempting to link queerness and reproductive justice? Further, queer students did not join End Fake Clinics because they might need abortions or support in a custody battle for their (future) children. Could we craft a queer reproductive justice politic that did not focus primarily on children and families, that was relevant beyond individuals' immediate reproductive needs, and that understood "queering" beyond examining an issue in relation to LGBTQ+-identified people?

For those students who had not taken a queer theory course, these questions were perplexing and jarring. And the students who *had* taken queer theory were unable to articulate their ideas in a way that was intelligible to their peers. Furthermore, none of us could exactly answer the questions we posed—something we viewed as an opportunity rather than a problem. As a result, End Fake Clinics members participated in queer theory reading groups. In these intellectually exhilarating and exhausting meetings, we asked hard questions of one another, the authors, and our politics. How were we positioning feminist and queer knowledge in relation to each other, particularly feminist concerns with creating social supports for mothers and queer critiques of the place of the Child in our politics? Do we talk about women, or is that essentialist and even transantagonistic? How might we acknowledge that sexism drives reproductive injustices and thus that (people who experience the world as) women experience reproductive issues in ways that most (people who experience the world as) men do not—without reproducing a gender binary? At the same time, how can using ostensibly gender-neutral phrases such as "pregnant people" and "parent" operate in the service of sexism? As Laura Briggs argues, such gender-neutral language has undergirded conservatives' attempts to deny "protections against pregnancy discrimination in the workplace."[37] Considering these linkages, why was it so hard to articulate deeper connections between queer and reproductive justice issues in a way that didn't devolve into identity politics? Why were so many queer people involved in End Fake Clinics? What, after all, *was* queer about End Fake Clinics? Finally, we wondered, what would it mean to approach abortion as a form of gender transgression?

The latter question became the animating force of the Queering Reproductive Justice workshop. We argued that we cannot challenge dominant ideas about gender without taking reproductive norms seriously. We discussed how cultural ideas about reproduction shape how we experience and understand gender and sexuality more broadly and how broader ideas about gender and sexuality influence how we view reproduction. Because requirements for being considered a "good" woman are sutured to what it means to be a "good" mother, any work to upend gender norms requires critical engagement with ideas about reproduction—even for those of us who plan to avoid parenthood or do not have heterosexual sex. Perhaps, we suggested, aborting that which would turn one into a good woman could be read as a refusal of gendered expectations.

Put more directly, refusing motherhood constitutes a refusal of gendered expectations, and this refusal is even more pronounced when it is enabled by abortion. We might approach abortion, then, as enabling gender transgression and, indeed, as a moment of gender transgression. In making this argument, our workshop built on a long history of queer theorists who view refusals of heteronormativity and respectability politics—which may include avoiding parenting—as crucial to queer politics.[38] Simply put, queer theorists have long found refusing reproduction to be potentially generative for queer politics. Here, I extend these arguments to suggest that, perhaps, women who abort are not entirely distinct from pregnant (transgender) men, at least in terms of gender transgression.[39]

This position builds on Jennifer Denbow's discussion of abortion as "counter-conduct," "eccentricity," and "a challenge to cultural understandings of gender and reproduction." Following Denbow, "One way abortion might be understood is as a refusal to be compelled to bear children. It may be an act of autonomy that resists cultural understandings that identify women with reproductive capacity."[40] Lee Edelman also articulates a connection between abortive women and men who have sex with men; both, he says, are viewed by the political right as a threat to life.

Denbow, Edelman, and I are not suggesting, of course, that people obtain abortions *because* it enables gender transgression or counter-conduct. And yet, the public outrage in response to people using abortion to raise questions about gender, liberation, and in the case of Aliza Shvarts, transgressive feminist performance art, speaks to the political possibilities of our arguments. Shvarts, a Yale University fine arts student, inseminated herself monthly for nine months, took an abortifacient each month, and created an installation that included traces of her blood and images of her bleeding to prompt reflection on dominant gender ideologies. Her project, which Yale refused to include in the senior exhibition, was covered in the international press and led to moral outrage, expressed, for example, in anti-Shvarts Facebook pages.[41] Abortion, Jennifer Doyle argues, was not exactly the root of the moral panic surrounding Shvarts. Abortion is widely available to Yale students through campus health services, after all. Further, Shvarts never took a pregnancy test, so whether she was ever actually pregnant remains unknown. Doyle suggests that responses to Shvarts speak to "the difficulty of identifying with abortion itself . . . as a piece . . . [of] the practice of sexual freedom" and as deeply "ordinary."[42]

Abortion is, of course, both of these things: a simple medical procedure experienced by nearly one in four women and requisite for sexual freedom.[43] While some liberal discourse has prevented us from recognizing the ordinariness of abortion, as Doyle argues—including that abortion is a "difficult decision" and should be "safe, legal, and *rare*"—other liberal feminists have worked tirelessly to make abortion seem ordinary. Encouraging women to tell their abortion stories—much like gay rights groups' demands to come out about one's sexuality—has been one of the primary mechanisms for attempting to actualize this goal.[44] One can even purchase an "I Had an Abortion" tote bag or t-shirt. How can we understand abortion, then, as both wildly ordinary and a site of transgression, that which positions one outside the normal and normative? It is precisely this relationship between the ordinary and the extraordinary, between normativity and transgression—and, further, how abortion might complicate these very relationships—to which I now turn.

That abortion as a form of gender transgression became the focus of our workshop speaks to broader trends in queer theory: critiquing normativity and fetishizing antinormativity. In a special issue of *differences*, Robyn Wiegman and Elizabeth Wilson ask, "What might queer theory do if its allegiance to antinormativity was rendered less secure?"[45] In asking this question—and challenging a foundational tenet of queer thought and, incidentally, our workshop—Wiegman and Wilson seek to "show that norms are more dynamic and more politically engaging than queer critique has usually allowed."[46] Janet Jakobsen speaks to this point: "The regime of the normal . . . is . . . not a coherent thing; it is a matrix of multiple, contradictory norms."[47] For Jakobsen, the question of what constitutes a norm and how we operate in relation to norms has particular relevance for examining and enacting resistance. Social movements, Jakobsen says, "cannot successfully resist the forms of disciplinary power they face if they cannot analyze multiple, complexly interrelated, and even contradictory norms."[48]

Our workshop was guilty of ignoring the complexity of norms in precisely the ways these scholars describe. Doing so prevented us from examining multiple, interrelated, and contradictory reproductive norms. Even as abortion can create opportunities for gender transgression, it can also reflect broader racist, classist, and ableist ideologies. Dorothy Roberts argues, for example, that at the same time doctors refused white women's requests for sterilization, they sterilized Black women against their will and without their knowledge.[49] Today, three-quarters of women seeking abortions cite an inability to afford a child as a reason for their decision;[50] disability rights activists continue to push back against expectations of abortion in cases of fetal disability;[51] and Black women, followed by Latina women, consistently have the highest abortion rates.[52] People have abortions for many reasons; only one of them is a desire to not have a(nother) child. Does our argument apply to those who already have children, whose abortion decisions are often linked to the need to care for their existing kids? Can abortion be considered transgressive for those who have few other options or for those who have been told they should not reproduce? As these questions suggest, it is also crucial to articulate the limits of approaching abortion as gender transgression, to think through how challenging one set of norms can reaffirm others.

Creating the "Queering Reproductive Justice" workshop allowed us to articulate new links between queer and reproductive justice issues, and, as important, it allowed End Fake Clinics activists to spend time together. Interviews with group members encourage us to turn toward the affective attachments created through activism, to consider the role that feminist and queer theory can play in student organizing, and to appreciate the kinds of activism that can emerge when identity is not at its center. Let's turn to the End Fake Clinics activists now.

## AFFECT AND IDENTITY

End Fake Clinics viewed our successes—events, workshops, campaigns, and legislation—as important and as having left a mark on UCSB.[53] Yet members did not frame these forms of activism as the most significant elements of their participation. Instead, activists stressed the importance of the love, feelings, and feminist friendships that developed in the group and developed the group, as well as the opportunity to advance their own feminist and queer knowledge and put it into practice.

Most participants joined End Fake Clinics through connections they already had with active group members.[54] As Lauren, who identified as a Black woman questioning her sexuality, said, "A good friend of mine brought me to a meeting . . . I stayed involved . . . because I felt like I was learning a lot just from the meetings and talking with the people from the group."[55] Quinn, who identified as Chinese American and genderqueer, similarly said that attending weekly meetings was like being and talking with "all of the best students in all of your favorite Feminist Studies classes out of all of your time at UCSB." As Quinn and Lauren suggest, End Fake Clinics provided a space to intellectually engage with feminist and queer theory while building meaningful relationships with one another.

The affective attachments developed through End Fake Clinics cannot be disentangled from the group's intellectual and political work. Affect is, as Rosemary Hennessy argues, the matter upon and by which movements come together, the "glue" of activism.[56] When asked if End Fake Clinics had influenced members' time at UCSB, Hailey, who identified as a heterosexual white woman, said the group had made the difference between a "miserable" university experience without a meaningful community and a positive "life-changing experience" with "people, ideas, educational tracks, and activism" that had shifted her undergraduate experience. Reid, who identified as white and genderqueer, described meetings as "lifting [their] spirits" and as the only queer feminist space at UCSB that challenged members to think, discuss, and organize around such investments. For Anne, who identified as a heterosexual woman of color, joining End Fake Clinics was significant because it was the first time she felt part of a feminist community at UCSB and did not want to drop out.

When asked what they got out of participating in the group, Quinn said "So much knowledge! And community . . . it's sappy. I made friends. It's so nice." Maeby, who identified as a Black lesbian, stated, "The most enjoyable part of [End Fake Clinics] is that you get to meet different people and form new relationships and friendships all while working toward something that you believe in." Scout, who identified as a Middle Eastern American, queer woman of color, said, "I stayed involved because I loved going to meetings. I loved the people that went, and I respected them. And I loved the conversations that we would have. . . . honestly, when your friends are in the group and they're people that you look up to . . . you want to come back and you want to do well, and you want to bring good news to meetings, and you want to at least give your best." Group members' relationships deepened outside of End Fake Clinics' formal meetings and organizing. Meetings turned into potlucks, and retreats were followed by pizza and hanging out. On weekends, students congregated on each other's couches to complete Feminist Studies assignments, cook, and converse. When two members of the UCSB women's basketball team joined End Fake Clinics, the group began attending basketball games, cheering on and developing a relationship with the team.

The depth of students' relationships allowed forms of engagement that proved politically transformative for both individual activists and the direction of the group. The influence of students' affective connections on

End Fake Clinics' activism is perhaps best evidenced in the process of creating the poster pictured below. This poster, inspired by the Against Equality queer collective, resulted from hours of conversations at many meetings.[57] As students boiled down complicated ideas informed by academic texts, they taught one another, explicating why an articulation of an idea was too limited, vague, or politically or epistemologically problematic to add to the poster. At one point, End Fake Clinics activists discussed how to challenge cultural discourses of menstruation as disgusting. One student suggested adding "menstruation is natural." Reid pushed back, expressing that such sentiments function in the service of gender essentialism and, by extension, transphobia.

Reid reflected on this moment: "We were brainstorming about menstruation . . . then it veered a little close to 'menstruation reaffirms womanhood,' and I didn't feel that if we put this in that it would necessarily represent everyone who has a period. So that was an instance in which I felt my genderqueer identity was sort of important in contributing. It was great because End Fake Clinics is the kind of space where I feel like I can say those things. It's safe and even welcomed." Reid's comment was met with gratitude from those who had not considered the ramifications of producing menstruation as "natural" or tethered to "womanhood." This response was enabled by students' close relationships with one another; in a moment in which call-out culture is sutured to activism, it is worth noting that Reid was not calling anyone out.[58] Affective connections between group members enabled Reid's comment as well as the responses to it. Group members' relationships fostered intellectual growth and informed the direction of the project at hand.

This moment illustrates how End Fake Clinics' organizing around shared politics enabled the group's diversity. Coming together through shared epistemological commitments, rather than shared identity, offered members different benefits, visions, and forms of community. Had End Fake Clinics used an identity-based approach, several group members never would have joined. Members who identified as genderqueer, transgender, or uninterested in sex that might lead to pregnancy did not see typical reproductive justice activism as relevant to them in the ways that End Fake Clinics was.

ADOPTION IS NOT EASY.
POOR MOTHERS ARE NOT BAD MOTHERS.
TEENAGERS ARE NOT BAD PARENTS.
ABSTINENCE-ONLY EDUCATION IS NOT EDUCATION.
REPRODUCTIVE ISSUES ARE QUEER ISSUES.
ANTI-ABORTION IS ANTI-SEX.
REMEMBER THE HISTORY OF EUGENICS AND FORCED STERILIZATION.
HAVING A DISABLED CHILD IS AS MUCH OF A RIGHT AS CHOOSING NOT TO.
SEX WORK IS LABOR. PARENTING IS LABOR. WAGES FOR WORK.
SHACKLING INCARCERATED WOMEN GIVING BIRTH IS CRUEL.
DRUG TESTING WOMEN ON PUBLIC ASSISTANCE IS REPRODUCTIVE PROFILING.
BREASTFEEDING IS GOOD FOR YOU, THE BABY AND THE PLANET.
CHILDLESSNESS CAN BE LIBERATING. CHILDLESSNESS CAN BE PAINFUL.
LEGAL ABORTION MEANS NOTHING IF THERE IS NO ACCESS.
BIRTH CONTROL IS NOT A WOMAN'S RESPONSIBILITY.
ABORTION IS NOT A MORAL ISSUE.
CRISIS PREGNANCY CENTERS LIE TO WOMEN.
BIRTHING IS NOT FOR HOSPITAL PROFITEERING.
ORGASM DURING BIRTH. AND ALL THE TIME.
EVERYBODY DESERVES (REPRODUCTIVE) HEALTHCARE.
COMPLEX ISSUES CANNOT BE SUMMED UP IN A SENTENCE.
EQUALITY IS NOT JUSTICE.

PRODUCED BY END FAKE CLINICS
FOR MORE INFORMATION GO TO WWW.ENDFAKECLINICS.WIX.COM/EFC

Poster created collaboratively by End Fake Clinics members under the leadership of Sanaz Toosi.

This is not to downplay the role of identity in End Fake Clinics; all interviewees stated that identities were important in End Fake Clinics' activism. Reid felt their genderqueer identity informed their critique of the group's approach to menstruation. Dani, who identified as a queer Latina, stated that "people in [End Fake Clinics] have claimed different identities so there is more of a chance for different opinions and different ideas" to inform End Fake Clinics' activism. Scout said,

> We're not an identity group. And I think what's important to us is to always keep asking questions, and to always take that comprehensive approach knowing that when you're talking about abortion you're also talking about capitalism, and you're talking about race, you're talking about sex, and gender, and . . . it's important to be cognizant of that . . . so even though we don't take an identity-based approach, I think it's very interesting that out of [End Fake Clinics] I felt like I came away with a stronger identity. And I don't know if what I'm talking about is identity, I mean a stronger sense of myself and what is important to me. Because we're not like a group for women [laughs], at all.

As Scout states, students did not see End Fake Clinics as an identity group. Instead, members articulated their activism as organized around a set of shared political commitments. As such, many understood the group's treatment of identity to differ from other liberal and leftist organizing. "Feminist" was the one identification that activists claimed as central to End Fake Clinics, viewing it as a way to challenge and destabilize more essentialist deployments of identity common in activism. Anne responded to the question "What identities do you claim?" with "I identify as feminist. I think that's a big part of my activism . . . and just the way I look at the world in general." Scout answered similarly, stating: "Feminist. That's my first identity, or that's the one I love the most. It's how I think of the world. . . . I don't ever want to lose [feminism, asking questions]. That was my biggest fear graduating. . . . I don't ever want that to happen, and so that's my favorite identity."

"Feminist" functioned as a push to critique and to develop new tools and skills through which to better understand and organize against reproductive injustices. It was not a static identity; it was a practice. Hailey mused that a self-identified non-feminist could be in End Fake Clinics if they "valued a lot of feminist ideologies." Scout framed her feminist identity as something that could be lost by separating from her feminist community. For interviewees, "feminist" was a tool to critique operations of power and inspire "an openness to change" in one's thinking and politics—a way of doing and thinking rather than being. Thus, group members simultaneously claimed feminism as central to End Fake Clinics' organizing yet insisted that End Fake Clinics was not "an identity group." We had not come together as feminists but rather to organize around particular issues. None of us had a similar epistemologically based community in our lives outside of End Fake Clinics (though many of us participated in other activism). In many ways, the group actualized Cathy Cohen's call for activism that complicates and destabilizes how we think of identities and communities.[59] Drawing from Joshua Gamson, Cohen argues that queer activism complicates the "assumption that stable collective identities are necessary for collective action."[60] In the case of End Fake Clinics, students' recognition of individual identities as unstable and less relevant than political position enabled collective action. End Fake Clinics offers us an opportunity to reimagine how friendship, feminist and queer knowledge, and radical political organizing might inform one another.

End Fake Clinics engaged in forms of activism that are both typical and extraordinary, with both typical and extraordinary outcomes. As activists, we approached ourselves—our learning, political growth, and friendship-making—as a central project of our activism. Never did this approach *become* the political project or impede our political work; neoliberal self-craft was not the goal, after all. At the same time, End Fake Clinics suggests that friendships and a shared commitment to actualizing feminist and queer knowledge can drive the production of ourselves and our activism in beautiful ways. In fact, End Fake Clinics was the most active feminist or reproductive justice group at UCSB during its four-year existence because of the group's affective bonds and reliance on epistemological connections—which were, it turned out, mutually constitutive.

Put otherwise, we developed our friendships through struggling over epistemological and political questions, and we were committed to this struggle because of the friendships we developed, some of which live on today. End Fake Clinics offers a unique opportunity to think through the political rewards of friendship building and theory learning, to imagine what "absorb[ing] a radicalized position vis-à-vis abortion into discourse on queer sex politics" could look like.[61] Such imaginings allow us to approach crisis pregnancy centers not only as a threat to reproductive justice but also as a site that relies on the very gendered and sexual ideologies that feminist and queer theorists and activists have long worked to disrupt. We might think about, for example, how a focus on transgression—

rather than the widely critiqued centering of abortion rights—could allow for more complicated articulations of the relationship between reproductive rights and justice. Drawing from End Fake Clinics, scholars and activists might approach anti–crisis pregnancy center activism as a crucial site for expanding queer and reproductive justice politics as well as actualizing their connections.

# 5 Queer Feminist Parenting

As the phrase "queering reproductive justice" gains steam among activists and scholars alike, we are hearing more stories about those who are meant to benefit from this very "queering": gay men who use surrogates to enable their biological reproduction, trans men and nonbinary people who need abortions or give birth, and recipients of paid family leave who do not conform to the roles assumed by the language of maternity or paternity leave—all topics that this book takes up. In each of these cases, the imagined beneficiary of "queering" reproductive justice is an LGBTQ+ person, and, usually, a parent. Considering that 24 percent of women couples and 7.2 percent of men couples (the demographics of LGBTQ+ couples for whom there is available data) are parents, this imaginary is not terribly surprising.[1] It seems clear that parenting is an LGBTQ+ issue and that it transpires along gendered lines. Curiously underdeveloped in conversations that use the language of "queering" to describe reproductive justice, however, is a focus on the materiality of *parenting* (as opposed to, say, the process of getting pregnant, giving birth, or accessing parental leave). What does it mean to parent in queer ways? How do we talk about issues that LGBTQ+ parents experience without equating "queer" and LGBTQ+-identified? And how exactly does one do it?! This chapter takes up these questions through a roundtable discussion among parents who live their lives in feminist and queer ways.

This roundtable is not, of course, the first place that discussions about queer parenting have taken place. In fact, conversations about queer parenting are becoming increasingly widespread—even if the topic has been underexplored in relation to reproductive justice. In 2022, for instance, *Huffington Post* published an article entitled "The Best Books and Podcasts for Queer Parenting."[2] The article, subtitled "Don't miss out on these wonderful expert-backed resources for LGBTQ+ family planning," speaks to what is and is not taken up when "queer parenting" is invoked. First, the title suggests the article is concerned with "parenting," while the subtitle suggests its focus is on "family planning." While family planning might be a component of parenting, the two are not synonymous. Indeed, the "journey," to use a term that appears repeatedly in the article, to becoming a parent—adoption, surrogacy, fostering, and reproductive technologies—is the primary concern of the resources featured in the list. Even among the books and podcasts included on a list of resources related to "queer parenting," there is little discussion of how to parent queerly or any reflection on what it means to parent queerly.

But it is not just this article's conflation of parenting and family planning that should invite those interested in queer parenting to pause. It is also the slippage between "queer" and "LGBTQ+"—the former appearing in the article title and the latter in its subtitle. We are meant to understand that LGBTQ+ people who are parents are engaging in queer parenting. This issue is common in moments when the phrase "queer parenting" or "queer families" is deployed. In a recent *Gay Times* article entitled "What the World Needs to Know About Queer Parenting," the author notes that "while there is undoubtedly great pleasure in being a queer parent, 80% of the people *Gay Times* spoke to said that they felt it was difficult to meet other gay parents."[3] A post on the *Undefining Motherhood* blog similarly notes that "with [an] ever increasing number of gay or lesbian parents, the number of studies on queer families is increasing."[4] Even our algorithms make this slippage. When I googled "queer parenting," the search engine generated a Wikipedia sidebar entitled "LGBT Parenting," complete with photos of smiling lesbian moms with their cute babies.

Such conflations are not, of course, limited to conversations about parenting. "Queer" is often used as a stand-in, an "umbrella term," for

LGBTQ+. But queer theorists have long advocated against this slippage. Queer is a term with a history and a specific politicized meaning—one that asks us to question normativity and to push back against it. For many queer theorists, queerness refers to a political, rather than (solely) sexual, orientation. That is, one can be LGBT+ without being queer, and one need not be LGBT+ to be queer. Jack Halberstam describes queerness, for instance, as "an outcome of strange temporalities, imaginative life schedules, and eccentric economic practices."[5] Focusing on strange, imaginative, and eccentric practices informs the position that queerness "can never define an identity; it can only ever disturb one."[6]

Of course, all LGBTQ+-identified people do not live in such non-normative, strange, and disruptive ways. Queer theorist Lisa Duggan coined the term "homonormative" to describe "a politics that does not contest dominant heteronormative assumptions and institutions, but upholds and sustains them, while promising the possibility of a demobilized gay constituency and a privatized, depoliticized gay culture anchored in domesticity and consumption."[7] In many ways, the images of LGBTQ+ parents that circulate widely—those that appear as the face of campaigns for expanded surrogacy laws, for instance—can be described as homonormative. It is for precisely this reason, I suspect, that queer theory has been largely uninterested in developing an understanding of queer parenting. Lee Edelman notes that "queerness names the side of those *not* 'fighting for the children,'" further arguing that the increasingly common move within LGBTQ+ movements to argue for rights through invoking children is evidence that focusing on "the future"—rather than present political concerns—is responsible for watering down these movements.[8] Advocating for marriage, adoption, and raising kids has superseded prior demands for liberation, sexual and otherwise. Gone are the days of centering diverse sexual pleasures, of living in ways that challenge heteronormativity. Instead, we have "gaybies," lesbians hosting gender reveal parties, and gay men hiring surrogates. The queer, as Edelman says, has been sacrificed in the name of "The Child."

A decade before Edelman's polemic hit the shelves, Michael Warner offered another formulation of the centrality of reproduction to the dominant social order. Warner suggests that LGBTQ+ folks' widespread and disparaging use of the term "breeders" to describe heterosexuals suggests that what is at stake for those who operate queerly is not limited to sexuality.[9] It is, instead, a world order. Warner describes those who fit into this world order as suffering from "reprosexuality," a mode of being in which "heterosexuality, biological reproduction, cultural reproduction, and personal identity" become intertwined.[10] Reprosexuality, Warner says, "involves more than reproducing, more even than compulsory heterosexuality; it involves a relation to self that finds its proper temporality and fulfillment in generational transmission."[11] Reprosexuals are, in short, those whose sense of self is tied to their reproduction, and they are, at least for Warner, Edelman, and perhaps the many queer theorists who have avoided reproductive politics, anti-queer.

Informed by these critiques, Shelly Park begins with a simple question: "Is Queer Parenting Possible?" Park sees asking this question as "ironic" precisely because "'queer' is frequently defined in opposition to institutions of family and reproduction."[12] To answer her question, Park says, we need to ask other questions, including "whether parenting is the sort of activity that can be practiced outside the bounds of the normal. . . . To what extent does parenting perpetuate normalization?"[13] While parenting often operates in the service of normalization, Park argues that there are other ways to parent. Queer parenting, Park says, *is* possible.

Central to Park's imagination of queer parenting is that there are multiple homes. In her case, these homes include the main family home where the kids stay and which their divorced parents rotate in and out of, the beach home the divorced parents rent and stay at on their weeks off from the kids, the parents' girlfriends' apartments, and so on. For Park, having multiple homes can inspire "other ways of living in and thinking about domestic space and familial time than those privileged by traditional bourgeois families."[14] It seems obvious that this conceptualization is limited in that many people—those who cannot afford to own one home, let alone own or rent multiple homes simultaneously—could never access it. An additional key component of Park's vision of queer families includes the presence of multiple parents. In Park's case, these parents include her current girlfriend as well as her ex-husband and his girlfriend. Zena Sharman, another queer parent, concurs. In her article entitled "With Queer Co-Parenting, the More Is Definitely the Merrier," Sharman describes her queer family as one that emerged out of a platonic friendship between two queer people (one femme and one nonbinary person) who wanted children and decided to take the leap together.[15] Although both friends ultimately partnered with other people, they retain the title of "lead" parents. Their partners are the child's "vice-parents." In many ways, what Park and Sharman describe as queer parenting and queer family formations are not so unlike the familial structures of children whose heterosexual parents have divorced and repartnered.

Following Cheshire Calhoun's analysis of postmodern families, we ought to ask if adding more parents—or homes—and stirring necessarily results in a queerer family formation.[16] And, if not, what exactly will result in queerer families? A queerer world? What roles do families and parenting play in creating that world? Recently, parents of babies and young children have turned to what they describe as "gender-open," "gender-neutral," or "gender-creative" parenting as a solution to the troubles of the gender binary. Key to this approach, advocates say, is using so-called "gender-neutral" pronouns, such as they/them, to refer to the child until they decide on their own gender.[17] To illustrate this point, Sharman tells a story about a stranger asking if their child was a girl or a boy. When Sharman responded, "They're a baby!," the "nosy" stranger "stalk[ed] off with a harrumph." For Sharman, whose parenting includes refusal of gendered pronouns for their child until the child tells them otherwise, this encounter inspired both rage and "feeling fiercely protective of [their] family."

A *Time* article written by Kyl Myers, author of *Raising Them: Our Adventure in Gender Creative Parenting*, also focuses on pronouns.

> We weren't going to assign a gender or disclose their reproductive anatomy to people who didn't need to know, and we were going to use the gender-neutral personal pronouns *they, them* and *their*. We imagined it could be years before our child would tell us, in their own way, if they were a boy, a girl, nonbinary or if another gender identity fit them best. Until then, we were committed to raising our child without the expectations or restrictions of the gender binary.[18]

For both Sharman and Myers, so-called "gender-neutral" pronouns are required for "gender-creative" and "gender-open" parenting. This conflation of one's pronouns with one's gender—and, more specifically, the conflation of the refusal to assign pronouns with the refusal of dominant approaches to gender—is increasingly common among liberals and leftists. These assumptions make sense, given the messages all around us that knowing people's pronouns is crucial, from their inclusion in email signature lines, to their centrality to personal introductions, to DEI workshops dedicated to proper pronoun usage. It's not surprising that these broader cultural imperatives are informing what it means to parent today.

But what, perhaps, might be surprising to those who are interested in queer parenting but haven't spent all that much time with feminist and queer theory, is that these dominant ways of talking about gender have been challenged by feminist, queer, and trans studies scholars. More specifically, scholars have expressed concerns with the ways that pronouns are now used to stand in for understandings and experiences of gender. Jen Manion addresses precisely this issue.[19] Manion, a gender-nonconforming butch lesbian, considers how the pronoun go-round (or the expectation that everyone in a space articulates their gender pronouns as part of introducing themselves) has become synonymous with transgender inclusion. The pronoun exercise isn't, Manion says, really about pronouns. Instead, it is meant to reveal something crucial about the gender of the person in question: Are you cis or are you trans?

For Manion, and many people commenting on her article, the pronoun question can inspire anxiety because it reduces a complex question to something simple. That is, it suggests that one's gender can be summed up in a word. Despite her butchness, her masculinity, her gender nonconformity, Manion is perfectly comfortable with the pronoun "she." What she finds uncomfortable is that using pronouns consistent with one's assigned sex is now read as a sign of being cis, as a sign of gender conformity. Once, after Manion answered the pronoun question with "she," a student called her "cisgender," a descriptor that shocked her: "How could anyone—even just by looking at me—ever come to the conclusion that I was cisgender? I have always been a gender warrior and a gender outlaw." Her history of gender nonconformity and her current nonconforming gender presentation were written over because of her use of a particular pronoun. But Manion's comfort with using the gendered pronoun "she" is rooted in her "feeling that [the term] has no bearing on [her] gender." As Manion says, "My gender—a lifetime of non-conformity, masculinity, butchness, and transness—is neither validated nor undone by a one syllable word."

Manion makes clear that the cultural ramifications of these slippages are profound, and include the production of "a new gender binary," as Manion calls it, created in the name of dismantling the gender binary: One is now either "cis" or "trans." "Rituals of transgender inclusion," Manion says "have amplified binary thinking unwittingly by centering on pronouns." In this new gender binary,

> Cisgender advances the notion that gender for everyone else is fixed, knowable, and normative. By using cisgender as a normative category, we deny the permeability, temporality, and messiness of gender for everyone. Asserting the idea that only trans people are on a gender journey and only trans people face gender struggles is the implication of the category cisgender. It divorces our gender struggle from those of other gendered beings. By doing so, we are losing the war against the gender binary.[20]

Ultimately, Manion asks us to see that gender is complicated—for everyone—and that advancing gender justice requires far more than so-called gender-neutral pronouns. "Rituals of transgender inclusion" must, Manion argues, "move away from pronouns," which Manion views as a performative utterance that makes people "feel good while doing little to actually advance the cause of transgender rights." (Manion's argument is similar in many ways to the critiques I launch in chapter 3 of reproductive justice advocates' demands to use "gender-neutral" language to describe those seeking abortions, experiencing pregnancy, or giving birth—demands that "make people feel good while doing little" to address the actual health care needs of gender-nonconforming, nonbinary, and trans folks.)

So, where does this position leave those committed to parenting queerly? If multiple homes, multiple parents, and gender-neutral pronouns aren't the keys to parenting queerly, what are? We can return to Shelly Park to begin to answer this question. Park sees providing children with "encounters with otherness" and "abandoning images of the Child as pure, innocent, and vulnerable to contamination from impure sources" as central to queer parenting.[21] Taking seriously Edelman's critique of the future-oriented nature of gay rights activism, Park suggests that queer parenting might include a commitment to living in the present—both as a parent and for your child. Expanding upon Shannon Winnubst's assertion that queer liberation requires "having no fixed idea of who or what you are or might become and finding this pleasurable,"[22] Park suggests that a "truly queer parent might celebrate this freedom for her child as for herself."[23] A truly queer parent, Park makes clear, need not be LGBTQ+-identified themselves. Like other queer theorists, Park sees "queer" as a verb or adverb, rather than an adjective or noun, a descriptor of the act of parenting, rather than of the parent.

But, in a quotidian sense, what exactly does this look like? Jane Ward's article "Queer Parenting for Heteros (And Anyone Else Who Wants to Teach Kids That Being Queer is Awesome)" offers some suggestions.[24] Ward engages queer theory to move beyond the tendency to equate "queer parenting with LGBT people raising children." Ward's alternative conceptualization of queer parenting as "a way of relating to children" centers on "de-linking 'mother' and 'father' subjectivity from female and male bodies" and also "cultivating children's genderqueerness." In relation to the former point, Ward suggests that "cross-gendering the adult/child relationship (such as a child being raised by a female dad) demonstrates to children the social constructedness of gender in practical terms, introducing them to a broader range of relational options for both female- and male-bodied people." Ward continues:

> A queer approach to parenting recognizes differences that have long been associated with biological sex and detaches them from male and female bodies (some parents like to handle the sit-down emotional stuff, others prefer engaging kids in a series of physical activities; some want to parent full-time, others find part-time parenting more enjoyable). So, while our ultimate goal may be to imagine parenting models that transcend the mother/father binary altogether, until we have achieved this total gender revolution, a queer approach recognizes that parenting, like all of our relationships, is gendered, and that we need not throw gender out of the picture in order to create just and fulfilling relationships with children. Instead, we need to be clear about what, specifically, we imagine are the unique contributions that femininity and masculinity bring to parenting, and then make those parenting styles available to all people (regardless of biological sex).[25]

For Ward, cross-gendering the parent/child relationship can be a tool for cultivating children's genderqueerness, which she says will necessarily involve refraining from imposing gender onto children. For Ward, this has little to do with pronouns and everything to do with how we talk about behaviors, characteristics, activities, items, and bodies as gendered. (Refraining from describing aggressive behavior as a reflection of a boy being a "boy's boy," not letting your choice of clothing for your child be determined by a certain ("boys'" or "girls'") section of a store, incorporating stories about love and moments of intimacy when playing with dolls of the same gender, and so on.)

But Ward also makes clear that refraining from imposing gender onto children requires more than waiting around for them to tell you what pronouns to use: "Because heteronormativity and the gender binary structure all aspects of children's lives (their toys, their books, their peers, their schools, their extended family), waiting to see how children unfold is basically defaulting to heteronormativity. This means that adults need to actively place queerness in their children's paths—at least enough to equal the amount that children will encounter heterosexuality and gender normativity (which is A LOT!)"[26] Queer parenting, Ward says, "is about passionately and unrelentingly introducing children to queer ways of life, to the beauty and fun of gender exploration, and to the diverse possibilities of romantic and sexual partnership."

With this focus on gender, exploration, and diversity—all words that circulate in relation to feminism, as well as queerness—we might ask how exactly queer parenting is different from feminist parenting. Unfortunately, we're sort of on our own out here. I have not found a single moment where the insights regarding the relationship between feminist and queer analyses—and between gender and sexuality—have been applied to the topic of parenting. This isn't an easy topic to think through, in part because the pairing of feminist and queer theory "has been rendered both inevitable and impossible."[27] In their contribution to *Feminism Meets Queer Theory*, Judith Butler reflects on what it means that their work was taken as a queer departure from feminist studies—rather than as providing the basis for an alliance between feminist studies and lesbian/gay studies, as they had intended. This breakdown, Butler asserts, speaks to the heterosexism of 1990s feminism. At the same time, Butler says that "a set of paradoxes has emerged within recent debates in feminist and queer theory that complicates any effort to stage a simple standoff between the two domains."[28] My goal here is certainly not to create any strict delineations between feminist and queer thought vis-a-vis feminist and queer parenting. But I also have no desire to flatten the differences between feminist and queer approaches or to suggest that the two are always in alignment.

Considering conversations about feminist parenting in relation to those on queer parenting gestures toward their overlaps and divergences. An article on *Everyday Feminism* notes that while feminists have discussed at length the various issues mothers face, less information circulates on "feminist parenting." The author, Paige Lucas-Stannard, notes that by "feminist parenting" she does not mean "'I'm a feminist and a parent,' but more in the actionable, skill-based philosophy of parenting through feminism."[29] This position is remarkably similar to those articulated by both Shelly Park and Jane Ward on queer parenting: feminist and queer parenting as something one *does*, rather than something one is. Lucas-Stannard lists four goals of feminist parenting: cultivating in one's kid(s) respect for self (including bodily autonomy, feelings, and choices); respect for others; respect for diversity; and life tools (critical thinking, nonviolent communication, and acts of happiness). A 2015 *Bustle* article provides a similar checklist outlining

> nine things feminist parents do differently, including 1.) Maintaining an equal respectful relationship with their partner (if they have one); 2.) Assigning chores equally; 3.) Letting kids make decisions about their own bodies; 4.) Never considering toys gender specific; 5.) Never considering activities gender specific; 6.) Teaching kids to embrace diversity; 7.) Teaching kids to ask for what they deserve; 8.) Communicating openly with kids about sex; and 9.) Being body positive.[30]

Lucas-Stannard asks what readers' parenting styles would look like if "every decision you make about raising your child was seen through the lens of feminism? What if you didn't use domination and power over your children but instead shared power with your children?"

I admit that I find these questions, as well as the feminist parenting prescriptions, fantastical, just as I find skeptical the assumption that refraining from using gendered pronouns to refer to kids will have the revolutionary consequences some parents believe it will. These deployments of feminism traffic in the most basic and widespread ideas about what feminism is—fighting for so-called equality, seeing power as negative, seeing body positivity as, well, necessarily positive. Feminist Studies scholars have long worked to disrupt precisely this version of feminism. How, we should ask, does the assertion that a feminist parent maintain an equal and respectful relationship with their partner extend heteronormative beliefs in the value of the couple and nuclear family formation? What does it mean to assign chores equally—especially in cases where partners do not or cannot work equal numbers of hours outside the home? Indeed, as Aren Aizura argues in his discussion of being a transmasculine parent partnered with another transmasculine person, "care is never '50/50' because care isn't quantifiable."[31] And, further, the idea that one could make "every decision" about parenting "through the lens of feminism," or that parents never use power over their child(ren), seems pretty delusional—even to someone who is child-free!

I've spent enough time with people I love who have kids (who I also love!), to know that kids will do things that can challenge even the most patient of parents. They will refuse to eat foods that were their favorites yesterday, they manage to stay alive without sleep, and they willfully do things you have taught them not to do. When I was recently talking to a dear friend about her spirited, assertive, opinionated, and self-assured (and, this auntie asserts, PERFECT) two-year-old daughter, I commented that she was lucky to have a child with these characteristics. She responded, "The feminist in me loves it. The mother in me hates it." I think that assertion sums up the paradox of trying to parent in feminist and queer ways—and it is a paradox that is rarely addressed in the feminist and queer literature on parenting, which, for the most part, celebrates parenting in feminist and queer ways. It's one thing to write a blog post about feminist or queer parenting. But let's be real. Often, it is remarkably difficult to live our feminist and queer principles precisely because we do not live in a feminist or queer world. And most of us don't live our feminist or queer principles 100 percent of the time. So, how, in a material quotidian way, do people practicing feminist or queer parenting do it? How do they deal with the challenges of trying to create the kinds of humans our world is not set up to create? How do parents cut themselves some slack when they make decisions that don't neatly align with their philosophies? And how can we talk about feminist or queer parenting without contributing to heteronormativity, reproductive futurism, and reprosexuality? The following roundtable is helpful for thinking through these questions—and more.

ROUNDTABLE CONTRIBUTORS

*Philip Brown, Erin Durban, Laurie Essig, Maryam Griffin, Hemangini Gupta, David Miranda-Hardy, Rosemary Hennessy, Miranda Joseph, Natasha Ngaiza, Jennifer D. Ortegren, Kelly Sharron, Myrna Perez Sheldon, Abraham Weil*

*You were invited to this roundtable because you have kids (ranging in age, at the time you engaged here, from two months old into their forties), you live in feminist and/or queer ways, and you are my friends. Please tell us about yourself and who makes up your family/crew of care-givers and care-receivers.*

LAURIE ESSIG: I am a professor, activist, mother, and friend, among other things. I have two amazing daughters who are twenty-three and twenty-six. One of them identified as my son when they were in second grade. I had a partner when they were born, but she was not anxious to be a parent and dipped out. Not that I blame her. Parenting is ridiculously difficult, but I was thrilled to be a single mom in a network of queer and feminist friends and lovers. I raised them in all sorts of ways and was often an abject failure as a feminist, a queer, and, most sadly, as a parent. But one way I succeeded was by giving them a deep understanding of what it means to be queer and feminist in the world. I think they would agree that queer and feminist politics were a far more regular part of their lives than family dinners or clean clothes.

I raised them to be devout atheists and cultural Jews. We have rollicking Passover Seders where the plagues are patriarchy, white supremacy, and GOP leaders. I instilled the obligation of Tikhun into them as the only thing they need to know about being Jewish: they must leave the world a better place than they found it. I raised them to be activists. Demonstrations were planned in our living room, where they engaged with the connections among being anti-war, feminist, and queer. Of course, there were the more obvious protests too: the ones in front of abortion clinics or against trans- and homophobia. I dragged them to DC and NYC and downtown Burlington (where we live) far more than I took them to soccer practice. I didn't give them a choice. In some ways, feminist/queer activism was our religion. It is how I instilled my values into their lives and gave them,

I hope, a sense that we work for a better world even when we don't know if change is possible.

PHILIP BROWN (he/they): I'm a small business owner and the managing partner of a law firm. I'm the parent of nine-year-old twins, Ahni and Jude, born through surrogacy in India. I identified as bisexual for most of my life until I met Carly, who introduced me to the word "queer," which felt so much better to me. I always felt like "bisexual" was too clinical a word, something you told your doctor rather than your friends. For the first year and a half or so of the kids' lives, I was a single parent, and although I never encouraged it, my kids called me Mom, and still do at home. Now they are embarrassed to call me that in front of their friends, so they call me Phil or Phil Phil. I'm mostly partnered in an open relationship with a heterosexual woman who has a sixteen-year-old, Maya. The kids regularly see me in gender-nonconforming clothing, including skirts and makeup. I'm pretty sure one of the twins will eventually identify as nonbinary, but who knows.

ERIN L. DURBAN: Because my family never expected for me to have kids of my own, I was expected to take on a significant role for my sister's kids, who were born when I was in college. (Don't get me wrong, I loved and enjoyed the undertaking! And both niblings turned out to be queer!) My oldest nibling, Aurelia, feels in many ways like my first kid, though I couldn't continue to play an intimate role in day-to-day life once my sister and I lived in separate states. I came into parenting when I started a relationship with my ex Gayle, who had two teenage sons from a previous lesbian relationship. The younger one, Dashiell, lived with us for most of our ten-year relationship. I was careful about entering into an already-established family and tried to create the kind of environment that I would have liked to have had growing up with divorced parents. Six years later, I decided that I wanted to try to get pregnant, and luckily—because I have endometriosis and for so many other reasons (including the difficulty of finding a cooperative known donor)—it worked! I gave birth to Fen who is now nine years old. Gayle and I are divorced and live in different states, so I primarily coparent with my partner Miranda.

MIRANDA JOSEPH: I am a professor of Gender, Women's, and Sexuality Studies at the University of Minnesota. I'm old to have a nine-year-old kid. Fen came into my life with Erin when she was almost four. Fen and I "got used to each other"—a phrase that started as a description of the process between Fen and Chuch (our trans* cat). Fen adopted me as a parent, with Erin's encouragement. And likewise, with Erin's encouragement, I've grown into being a parent, "Papa," to Fen. While our life together with cats makes us lesbian, being queer, genderqueer, and just weird, each of us in our way, is what we encourage and love about each other.

ROSEMARY HENNESSY: I have two daughters, Molly and Kate, who I birthed and raised with their dad. We were married for fourteen years. It was a queer marriage for its time, given that Fred was clear about his attraction to men and wrestled with that during and after our marriage. I had unfinished history with the lesbian feminism of the early '70s. When I fell in love with Chrys in the 1980s, Fred and I separated and later divorced. We shared caring for the kids and Chrys took on a major role that had no name. The girls lived with us and stayed with their dad on alternate weekends and summers. Together we saw these two girls through their teens. Chrys moved out at year seven but she continued to maintain her relationship with the girls. Recently their closeness has been rekindled after she was diagnosed with cancer. In 1999, I met Martha and we have been together since, for nine of those years managing the distance between upstate New York and south Texas. She has a goddaughter who is like a daughter to her, Ashley, and another goddaughter, Cynthia. From age six, Ashley was with us in the summer, sometimes with her sister as well. Cynthia and her husband lived with us for a time. These daughters are now grown up. Molly and Kate are in their forties, Ashley is twenty-nine. Cynthia in her late thirties. Frida (eleven) and Lucy (eight) HF Bostelmann, Jakob (twelve) and Jaden (eight) Faz, and Steven (ten) and Caleb (seven) Aboites are the next generation in this queer family. I have found a loving relationship with Chrys again since her illness; we talk often and visit when we can.

MYRNA PEREZ SHELDON: I am a professor and live in southeastern Ohio with my two children Indigo (four) and Garnet (twenty months) and my husband Seth. We bought our home with my mother Terrie, and have remodeled it to have two independent but connected living spaces. My brother Bren also lives on our property in a "tiny home" that he and Seth built. I'm second generation in the Filipino diaspora, my mother and husband are both white, and because of this our family conversations often circulate around the fluidity of racial identity alongside gender and sexuality. Our children go to a Montessori daycare/preschool. During the pandemic we had long stretches of time without outside childcare and those times represented some of the most physically and spiritually challenging experiences of my life.

MARYAM GRIFFIN: I'm a university professor who recently became a first-time mother. My baby is eight months old, so thinking of myself as a parent—of any kind!—is still really new and even strange to me. My baby's hands-on childcare team includes me, my husband, my parents (who live in another state but travel to us frequently), a dear babysitter who helped us for a few months while I recovered from postpartum anxiety, and the caregivers at daycare. I also consider my cousins, close friends, in-laws, therapist, and online academic mothers group as part of this childcare team because of the advice and support they offer, especially during hard times.

KELLY SHARRON: I am a very new parent to a two-month-old, Langston, with my partner, Abraham Weil. I consider our caregiving team to be expansive, including a community of friends, family, and loved ones who have been present and supportive for his early days. I've been immensely grateful for those relationships which have deepened through his existence, and the ways that when people love and respect him, I also feel loved and respected. We are in the so-called "fourth trimester," and feel very much psychically and physically connected in ways that I have found beautiful and enriching. Parenthood has also made me feel intense, yet flickering, bonds with folks, including our labor and delivery nurse who did everything she could to keep doctors and the medical industrial complex at bay in a hospital birth (no easy feat!). She feels intimately connected to his birth story, and yet she is someone with whom I will likely never again interact. I never imagined myself as a parent until very recently, and am continually surprising myself with my decisions and desires around pregnancy, labor, and now raising him. In this sense, it has already felt like a very queer journey, one I never intended to take and one where I find myself on different paths than I had imagined. I look forward to the other queer turns it offers.

JENN ORTEGREN: I am a professor of Religion at Middlebury College, and I have a willful and adorable 2.5-year-old daughter, Zahina, who I parent with my husband, Ajay, in our one-bedroom faculty house because we cannot compete in the current housing market. My daughter was three months old when the pandemic hit. We spent the first summer living with my in-laws who helped care for her, then had a nanny share with a lesbian couple and their daughter for a year, then spent the next summer with our in-laws again because we couldn't get childcare in Vermont, and she now has part-time childcare in a daycare and a part-time nanny. But we don't have strong networks with other parents with kids Zahi's age in part, I think, because we're all so busy and burned out and, and in part because we didn't develop those networks early on and it feels really exhausting to do it now. It's incredibly difficult and stressful to parent in the pandemic, especially when vaccines have not yet been approved for kids her age. My strongest parenting networks are really with friends who live elsewhere and offer emotional and intellectual support through texting.

ABRAHAM WEIL: My parents divorced before my mother knew she was pregnant with me. My father is aggressively charming, smart, and abusive, and my mother is a dexterous, creative, and unfolding person, for whom relationships to men have been complicated and painful throughout her life. I have siblings on both sides, and we all grew up scattered across Los Angeles, CA. I've had several parents because of my mother's and father's bumpy and bumptious affairs—some profoundly loving and long-lasting, some venomous and cruel—and have learned a great deal from each of them. I share this because scenes of violence, abuse, abandonment, and escape were formative in my arrival to feminism and to gender studies. At seventeen, like so many before me and to come, I entered the classroom in search of a way to heal. I found it there, and elsewhere, and continue to uncover the deep and relentless pursuit of joy that I know myself capable of feeling (Lorde). The violence that can be edited out in one generation has been put into sharp relief by the birth of my first child, Langston Brookes. His arrival has been a cosmic invitation to think on the water, in the wake, through the delta, and from the hood about the impossibility of *me* having become a parent. It is a profound futurity brought about by profound survival. It has been a transformative experience which has emerged through the immense healing that has resulted from my partnership with Kelly Sharron. We are both professors of Women's, Gender, and Sexuality Studies, and having met at our graduate orientation ten years ago, I would suggest that our feminist and queer approaches to kinship have been conforming ever since. Langston was born on Valentine's Day (2022) in Long Beach, CA, and soon, we will move to Lawrence, KS. This parenting journey is also the result of queer, Black, trans, and feminist love. I'm honored to collaborate on this roundtable with you all, many of whom have parented and loved me in moments of need and celebrated and held me in moments of joy.

HEMANGINI GUPTA: I currently live and work in Vermont, a place I like to think I chose to come to, after having lived in Maine and Montreal and feeling, when I left, that I somehow wasn't done with this part of the world yet. My son, Nikhil, was born in Montreal, in the bitter cold of mid-January, and turned five recently. I had moved to Montreal for the year because my partner, Moyukh, whom I am married to and live with, was at McGill on a postdoc and I was determined that I should give birth in Canada not only for the citizenship it would grant my son but because the healthcare would allow me to have the doulas and birth ritual that I wanted. My journey as a parent began—like others have said—in an unexpected way; I was not particularly keen to be a parent but was very keen to try to achieve some of the stability and family that I had lacked growing up amidst my parents' tumultuous marriage. We had few friends in Montreal having just moved there, and our experience of the birth was taking an Uber to the hospital and then one back in less than forty-eight hours since we were eager to escape the medicalized hospital routines. Since then, Nikhil has been raised by us, by my mother, and very many beloved friends who have sprung up around us. We have been precarious and ever-moving, changing eight houses and three countries in these past five years. We found a wonderful group of friends in Vermont and I feel that raising him here, so far from anything that feels remotely like home in India, has profoundly shifted who and what I think of as home and who and what he would consider as family. Holidays—Christmas, Easter, the New Year, Thanksgiving—have all been with friends we made here and I have never felt the power of found kin as strongly as now.

DAVID MIRANDA-HARDY: I'm a Chilean media professor and filmmaker living in Vermont. I grew up in Spain as a political refugee after my family fled from Pinochet's regime. My parents had all the discourses of the 1970s left but—as usual—discourse rarely became practice. My dad described himself as a feminist because he "helped" in the house. We returned from Spain to a broken Chile and my parents' marriage also broke, in great part because of gendered expectations around domestic life. What Hemangini said about her parents resonated with me, too. A sense of precariousness in my childhood pushed me to have a strong desire for stability, in the most conventional ways: owning my home, finding a life partner, having kids. Moving to the US facilitated my encounter with Natasha, the love of my life and someone I met when I was trying to build relationships out of love and joy and not fear or anxiety. Together, we coparent three girls, born in Philadelphia, Santiago, and Vermont. While our oldest has lived in seven different homes, the youngest was born in the beginning of our most stable time as a family. I don't think we describe ourselves as actively engaging in queer parenting, but many of the ideals of queer and feminist dreams resonate with me. I identify as Latino in the US, but I was raised where ethnic identity was fairly homogenous, so it has been an adaptation for me. My wife is Black, and I'm constantly learning how to engage with my daughters' biraciality amidst the whiteness of Vermont.

NATASHA NGAIZA: I'm a Black Tanzanian-American mother, wife, film professor and filmmaker raising three wonderful daughters ages 10, 8, and 4 with my Chilean husband in Vermont. My parents, who recently celebrated their fortieth wedding anniversary, provided my first glimpse of what queer or feminist parenting might look like. Although my father has always been the primary breadwinner, and my mother the primary caregiver and house manager, they carved out small but impactful spaces to disrupt the traditional gender roles they inherited from their Catholic, socially conservative African upbringing. When I was two years old my father was a stay-at-home dad so that my mother could pursue her PhD. My father cooked, cleaned, and braided my and my sisters' hair when my mother traveled for work. My mother was the first person to teach me about feminism and both parents regularly engaged my sisters and brother, over family dinners, about the importance of fighting patriarchy. I see my relationship with my husband David as a reflection and expansion of the values and dreams my parents instilled in me. I think it's important for our daughters to witness the equitable nature of our marriage. We're always talking and reading books about equality and diversity, but I think it's our shared routines and daily habits that will have the biggest impact.

*What aspects of you or your life most inform your approaches to parenting? That is, if you pause and think about why you do much of what you do as a parent, what factors have had the most influence, explicit or otherwise? How have these factors shaped or come into contact with your feminist or queer principles?*

ROSEMARY HENNESSY: In thinking about these wonderful provocations for reflection, I have struggled with the verb "parenting," unsure what it means. That may sound odd, but something about "parenting" as an ongoing action performed on someone does not ring true to my experience of being a parent. Maybe there isn't a verb that works for the relation. I was and am a mother, a feminist, and a lesbian. As for their combined effect on my daughters. . . . When they were little, there were times I felt like a fugitive from something or some time I was simultaneously fiercely bound to. The "something" was never my girls; they are sealed into my being, my life, and all that I am.

The public intellectual, single mother, and lover of women, Muriel Rukeyser, touches on that "some time" when she comments that another time arrives "in the long rearrangement of life that predictably will come to women who write, after the birth of their children." Was I looking for an exit from that other time? I remember in the 1980s when I was still married and living with Fred and the girls in Syracuse, I decided I would take up jogging. It didn't last long, but when I ran I imagined I was running away. If you had asked me then what I was running from or to, I would not have been able to tell you. By the end of that decade, however, the long rearrangement of my life had irrevocably changed.

I was a child of the 1950s and 1960s, and the contradictions and upheavals of those times in the US imprinted who I was and would be. The second of seven girls, I grew up in an intensely Catholic family. We lived in Philadelphia with my mother's mother, a house full of women and my dad. When I went away to college in 1968, the world was shifting on its axis in a time of widespread rebellion against imperial conquest, racism, and patriarchy. Four years later, I was a committed feminist. One by one, the women in my consciousness-raising group were coming out as lesbians, some calling themselves "political lesbians" or "women identified women." These notions questioned not only heteronorms but the straightjacket of identity. For me, they suggested the possibility of something wildly other.

Nonetheless, I married Fred in the heady times of the early 1970s when recasting the institution of marriage and affirming an ample sexuality were in the air of our queer marriage. Once our girls were born (through the feminist inflected "natural childbirth" prep so different from my mother's) and my wildness tamed, I promoted the "Free to Be You and Me" values of feminist parenting while pursuing a PhD in English. Unlike my mother, I was busy with a life outside of home, and I wanted the girls to see that. Nonetheless, I often felt like a distracted and divided mom. I argued with Fred about the gender politics of domestic labor from my emerging Marxist feminist standpoint. I still don't know if the kids heard or absorbed those conflicts. I was keenly aware at the time that many of my reflexes as a mother were shaped by my mother's ways, even if in tension with my feminist values. I worked to fill the girls' lives with options I never had (sports and girl power) while reiterating patterns from my own childhood as taskmaster with chores, gifts of dresses and dolls, even finally giving in to Barbie.

My "fugitive" parenting erupted when they were ten and twelve and Chrys entered my life. She was a sociology grad student, also in her late thirties. We met in the first feminist theory course at Syracuse. Our relationship was an enormous leap for both of us: me into being lesbian, her into a family with children. We were very feminist about all of it (deliberate, thoughtful, in counseling). The girls, we hoped, witnessed parents who were learning to love one another and them, too, in more ample ways. One of the pleasures for them was having in their lives a super loving cool adult who wasn't Mom, who brought laughter, crystals, being vegetarian and countless other resources. Through Chrys and me, they came to know a wider world of options for living and loving. Gay Pride, Provincetown, *Dykes to Watch Out For*, and new family friends were huge additions to their lives. Fred, meanwhile, was figuring out if he was gay, bi, straight or just Fred. For me, and Chrys too, the queerness was much bigger than gay; it was attached to the systemic politics we were figuring out and writing and it flavored those years.

My fugitive leap into loving Chrys and embracing lesbian life had a profound impact on the girls not because we set out to reinvent a model of parenting, and yet, of course, that is precisely what we were doing. The impact followed from our flight from an institution and also from other fugitive actions, Marxism for one, that followed. Once we moved to Albany where I got a job, the girls met other kids who had lesbian moms, but few of them were in their middle and junior high classes. High school was harder for Molly and Kate than I knew at the time. They only talked later about their struggles to navigate the fear and silence around their queer family life. When Chrys eventually left her relationship with me, the pain of those silences was a large part of what she could not reckon.

The rearrangement into a family that went against many grains was painful for everyone. And yet . . . Molly found her kindred spirit at Harvard, a friend who identified as lesbian and was thrilled to have a friend whose mom was lesbian. She also pursued ways to be out, loud, and proud as a queer advocate. Kate also found her queer cohort at Brown among the co-op crowd who all thought she was as queer as the rest. Fred married a woman (named Chris) and they foster-parented more than a dozen kids, ultimately adopting three siblings—Dorthy, Michael, and Tanika—who they saw into adulthood. The queer family grew. The Tylers and Chris's son, Nathan, became stepsiblings for Molly and Kate.

Martha came into my life when Molly and Kate were in college, and she stretched the impact of a fugitive family even farther geographically and politically. As Mexican and a labor organizer, she has deeply affected these adult children, bringing to their feminism and queer affiliations her history, wisdom, courage and warmth.

My flight from heterosexual marriage and my "salto mortal" into a relationship with Martha provoked dramatic "rearrangements of life." They shaped my writing and teaching and imprinted my children with the aspirations and contradictions of my time and theirs. These changes weren't easy. The fact is they were deeply painful for the girls at the time and not at all welcome by them at first. Reflecting on these years now, I think the most powerful queer and feminist effects of this strange verb "parenting" are as diffuse as the air we breathe. They register in what children absorb of their caregivers' fugitive acts. Those acts take place in the time of ongoing process, a time of small affirmations when daring to rearrange the bonds and care of life-making find their way again and again toward the possibility of imagining and making more ample relations and more just worlds and the knowledge that rebellion, like love, is rooted there.

LAURIE ESSIG: Rosemary, I love what you say here about parenting not being a verb, something you do unto others, but perhaps an inner practice? Like meditation? I think that makes total sense. So much of parenting felt like just the discipline of not running away (my own version of jogging is I would fantasize that I lived in a starkly empty studio apartment with nothing in it but three library books and a vase with a single flower). I love how much love there was and is between you and all your life partners. That's really beautiful and feminist and queer. I also appreciate that you acknowledge how difficult it was for your daughters to have lesbian parents. I think I often dismissed that when my children were young and I'm trying really hard to listen now to the pain that living inside a queer family—and perhaps especially a queer political family—caused them.

KELLY SHARRON: I'm struck by Rosemary's questioning of "parenting" as an ongoing verb, as well. We can take from "queer" that the question of part of speech is an important one: Are queer and parent actions or identities? Can you move in and out of doing and being? Ultimately, as Rosemary describes, I think both are about "life-making," and the culmination of acts. I find both parenting and queerness to be ongoing engagements with critique and possibility that condense into a particular outcome—a child and a familial relationship and a queer politic.

PHILIP BROWN: My parents have definitely had the greatest impact on my parenting style. They are Jamaican immigrants and had an approach that was much more hands-off than the parents of my peers. The household was always loving and stable, which is something I didn't always appreciate growing up. They were married for forty-nine years before my mother passed. We always had jobs from a very young age and they forced us to be independent and make our own money. I'm sure it influenced my decision to have kids even though I was single. I knew I could do it and just had to figure out how.

Interestingly, my parents knew little about American-style racism when we were children, which, in hindsight, is something that was good. It was something my siblings and I had to point out to them. They were in the Jamaican upper class and expected no less from us. They were super progressive, other than my father's homophobia, which was as much a reflex for him from his upbringing as an internalized prejudice.

One thing I always think about is whether I made the right decision to have girls instead of boys or just leaving it to chance. I went through a surrogacy company in India, and I was able to select girls for an extra fee. At the time, I didn't think that I wanted to bring a Black boy with a queer "father" into the United States. I thought it would be too much to ask of that child. Now I sometimes wonder.

Tucson is a fairly progressive island in Arizona. The city has had housing and job protections for gender identity and sexual orientation since the '70s (I clerked for the equal opportunity office during law school). It is an atmosphere that has allowed lots of freedoms with the kids. Their school is fairly progressive, and I often pick them up in a skirt and nobody seems to care. We often discuss moving to Mexico for a couple of years, and I'm not sure I can do that in most places in Mexico.

As I write this I am moving into a new relationship with my partner. I purchased a home down the street a few years ago, and I've used that home to see other people. Now I'm moving into that home, and we are trying to navigate how that will look with the kids. We have been trying to explain that our relationship ebbs and flows and this is the direction that it is flowing in right now, but that doesn't mean it can't flow in different directions in the future. I think the kids understand but I'm not sure. I do hope that because our family has always operated a little differently and the kids have already spent so much time at the house I'm moving into, it may not be as stressful for them when they start to spend more nights there. I'm thankful that we have the flexibility to ease that transition.

KELLY SHARRON: I remember telling my parents that I had no intention of having children, and my mother's response was, "What did we do so wrong?" That question stuck with me, both because I had no response and because I found it to be so oddly personalized.

The truth is, they really didn't do anything wrong, which seems surprising. I often find myself on an island when I tell friends that I have a close, loving, and supportive relationship with my parents. They have always supported and continue to support my decisions and autonomy. Critical thinking and education were the largest values in our home, values which are tied to my own feminist and queer perspectives. When COVID was raging, and taking a serious toll on my dad's industry (movie theaters), my mom was recounting other economic traumas of 2008, and said, "You know, I think we're working class," followed by an exasperated discussion of the difficulties of getting ahead, or even maintaining a life. This is something that, as a Marxist, I've defined very differently than they have, and always known, but this class identity has been critical in forging our familial relationship of mutual aid and trust. It's also something I intend to foreground as a parent—denying personal autonomy, responsibility, and boundedness in favor of the collective.

The question of having children was one I logically rebuffed—it had nothing to do with my own relationship to family as my mother had accused, but rather because we know that parenting is difficult, generally unsupported and invisible, and nearly impossible to do if you also value a career and personal enrichment. And so, to make that decision thoughtfully is not a straightforward one. And for me, that decision came from a place of queer, feminist love, for wanting to extend and expand that love in such a radical way as to grow it from within.

I originally expressed a desire to have a child to my partner in the summer of 2020 in Minneapolis. Amidst the atmosphere of uprising, revolt, and upheaval, I felt hopeful that the world was cracking anew in my hometown. This futurity and desire influenced my decision in ways I still don't think I can quite grasp, but that felt immediately obvious at the time. I want to hold that moment and energy, in parenting, and proceed in ways that are guided by queer feminist principles, grounded in my own instincts.

ERIN DURBAN: Until recently, I probably identified as a feminist, queer, anti-racist, and leftist parent in terms of how I foregrounded my politics in my parenting practices with the young people in my life. But during the past several years, the intensification of my chronic illnesses has shaped the relationships in our family, and I/we have been learning together from disability justice activists about care, collaboration, interdependence, and sustainability. As a crip parent, I am more attentive to the reciprocity of our relationships, especially during the pandemic when we have all had to take care of each other in ways that were more apparent on the surface.

HEMANGINI GUPTA: My parenting is most influenced by my feminism and how I came to it. When I was growing up, my mother often took me to feminist protests where—in the early '90s—I saw how feminists agitate, protest, and appear publicly in ways that challenge normative ideas of gendered and classed behavior. This made feminist spaces appealing to me, and as I grew, I was attracted to spaces of activism and movement work. I tended to surround myself with other feminists, queers, activists, and artists. I now have a PhD in gender studies and teach in a gender studies department. Nikhil, my child, has always interacted with my queer friends and queer students and is gently introduced by them to the ways they move through the world. Nikhil has always loved glitter and rainbows and dresses, once even dragging me to Target to find the perfect nightgown, but recently, at age four, has become circumspect about loving dresses and in the last few months has abandoned a pink rainbow mask, reminding me that rainbows and unicorns are "for girls." Nikhil would like a Paw Patrol mask instead. I feel sad at the way Nikhil's play—and world—are diminishing with age but also hopeful that my friends and students will always remind Nikhil of how many possible ways there are to exist in this world, and I see my role as facilitating Nikhil's capacity to imagine all kinds of ways to be.

ABRAHAM WEIL: I went walking on the beach with Langston as I thought through this question and Rosemary's stunning detailing of the multiplicity of ways that queer families become and become connected. It's a reminder of the guidance that she has offered me throughout the years, parenting me, as so many of you have. The etymology of 'parent' marks a 'bringing forth' that feels more useful to emphasize than my own embodied differences, although those differences most certainly choreograph my standpoint. What has informed my approach to *bringing forth*?

A first attempt at an answer: people and places, violence, difference, feminism and pleasure. As we were walking the shoreline, I had this nagging memory of an old mentor who would paraphrase this Ani DiFranco lyric as she moved around the call center where I volunteered, singing "*every move that I make is a feminist movement.*" I haven't really thought of Ani in years, and I was trying to come up with a different way to say this, but when I came back to write I saw that Phil referred to Ani DiFranco [in a later response] and I realized that, indeed, this is the way I want to enter this provocation. The nagging memory emerged as a resistance to Carly's suggestion in the initial framing: "Most of us don't live our feminist or queer principles 100 percent of the time." I want to suggest that I do live them all of the time because I am so formed by these registers—queerness and Blackness in particular—that I cannot disarticulate myself from them in any meaningful way.

During my senior year of high school, I began volunteering at a rape crisis hotline. A space of refuge for some, my work often consisted of men calling to say they'd been assaulted, so that they could masturbate. The other calls were harder and more familiar to me. It was an incredibly difficult job but remains a key moment in how I came to think about feminist labor, care, and reproduction (an absorbent and resilient project that asks us to witness with abandon). It was also a key moment because it was the first time that I encountered a scholar in women's studies. The evening shift manager and Ani DiFranco expert was truly remarkable. She taught me a little bit each day—from the beats of Le Tigre to what I would come to understand and inherit in my following years as Marxist feminism—offering me a new way to think about identity. By the next fall I was a first-year student in women's studies. In those rooms, I found others wanting to think like me, wanting to solve different problems than our desires. Even so, I was Black, butch, and bold, which made for a target in my predominantly white institution. There was a lot of violence there too, but also spaces to explore my own political commitments and ways of indexing myself in Black feminist, queer, and trans theory.

After college I moved to San Francisco and found myself saturated in my partner's lesbian community; mothers, sisters, aunties, and friends helped me rethink kinship. After a year, I left California for graduate school at Rutgers. My first year of graduate school impressed upon me the importance of theoretical precision and slow-thinking, both ideals that have shaped how I approach parenting. I still return to my notes from Elizabeth Grosz's seminars where I felt captivated by the mastery of her lectures that make careful, nuanced, and creative connections between philosophy and feminism. Grosz's influence on my own intellectual trajectory is a sensual one. As I began to transition, I thought through the ways that Grosz foreclosed transgender in Darwinian selection processes and wondered why these theories were incompatible. At the same time, her masterful weaving of feminist theory with the philosophies of Lacan, Spinoza, Deleuze, Nietzsche, Bergson, and Irigaray was blowing my mind; she was bringing me forth. In a seminar with Jasbir Puar, she asked that we take seriously the provocations of Gayatri Spivak's seminal essay "Can the Subaltern Speak?" We spent an entire semester working through the essay, struggling with each passage with generosity and conviction. Her demand for a philosophy that attended to the body and the body's capacities set the groundwork for my thinking since. Working through the essay provided a backdrop for Drucilla Cornell's seminar on Derrida, where we worked through deconstruction to the drumbeats of Occupy Wall Street. We held seminars inside the protest as we sweated through Derrida's embodied philosophy. It was a really important time for how I think about *how to live a feminist life.* It is when I met Carly, who has brought me forth with care, kindness, laughter, and trust. These memories feel deeply parental and they are instructive to how I will parent.

My time at Rutgers was a relatively violence-free couple of years, full of good friends, love affairs, and unforgettable moments. But, my time ended there after I was attacked at a bar. Surrounded by my people, dancing, and joyful, there it was again, that violence that permeates at the surface of my skin. Memory fails from there as I was hit in the face with a barstool. My friend and I were laid out on the floor: Black, queer, and bleeding. The time spent with the police and in the hospital was trauma-filled; I try not to think of it when I can manage, which is less these days. A few days after I returned home from the hospital, Black feminist theorist and activist Cheryl Clarke came to my apartment and sat at the foot of my bed. She brought food, poetry, and an envelope full of cash collected by the gender studies department to cover my rent, bills, and impending move to the University of Arizona. My parents did not come, but I was parented by partners, friends, and colleagues.

That experience shaped the next few years. I would come to find several key mentors at University of Arizona, most notably Susan Stryker and Eva Hayward. Working with them was life-saving and it helped me to reimagine the ways I had been thinking through this deeply embodied experience. I'd also come to know queer parents in this time. The births of Fenniver, Arden, Seth, and Elouise were all instructive, all parts of the story that would lead me to Langston.

Following the murder of George Floyd, Kelly and I drove to Minneapolis (her hometown). There, after a long and beautiful walk, she told me that she thought she might want to have a kid. As if I had known the answer for generations, I gave an enthusiastic yes. It felt momentous and was shaped by the acute moment of racial reckoning happening around us and in the wake of my own experiences. So many things changed about my life that night and I have been in awe of and humbled by the whole experience and the folks that lead me to it continue to shape my approach.

DAVID MIRANDA-HARDY: Because my father was more intellectually than homemaking oriented, it's important to me that our daughters see me as a nurturing presence in their lives, someone that comforts them emotionally, feeds them home-made meals, does their hair, gives them baths, puts them to bed. I always wanted to be "in the mud" of parenting.

My model to be a father is actually my mother, the one who did the above for me, without much "thesis" about it.

I come from an assembled family, but I was raised as an only child. As a result, I was too dependent on the world of the adults, privy to their conflicts and tribulations. With Natasha we want our daughters to stay children for as long as they feel like it, introducing them gradually to the adults' problems and concerns. I've always hoped that our daughters can create a world of their own, without us (to a degree), and present themselves "in opposition" to us. I believe family is a good place to learn solidarity and companionship, but also to advocate for oneself and your peers. I try to create spaces for them to solve their conflicts without my intervention.

I've read some parenting books, but it's hard to know whether they ended up influencing the reality of our home. I've paid attention to the girls' attachments to and bonds with us. I believe in the concept of the "good enough mother" (or father); Bowlby's and Winnicott's attachment theory still makes sense to me.

Natasha has been a fantastic role model for me, with the funny, firm, and gentle hand she uses to help the girls navigate the world. It is very important for us that the girls believe in being kind, respectful of everybody's dignity, and appreciative of the many ways humans present themselves. Hopefully, we're teaching them that by example, starting with the way we appreciate them in their amazing differences. We hope that they can create without restriction, that imagination always feels unlimited. And that they feel not only intensely loved but heard and seen as they are.

NATASHA NGAIZA: Ditto to what David said! But really, my husband David has probably been the biggest influence on my parenting. In a very practical sense, I would not be the kind of parent I am if I didn't have his consistent partnership; his emotional, psychological and physical support. David has always been fully present and fully invested in his daughters' care and upbringing from the mundane and dirty (explosive newborn diapers at 3:00 a.m.) to the fun and immediately rewarding (riding bikes and tickle fights). If I hadn't been able to regularly take naps or sleep in like I do, be taken care of when sick and healthy, how could I dedicate myself to the more reflective parts of parenting? Years ago, I remember reading how common it is for fathers to become jealous of their newborn children because of the attention they require from mothers. If that had been my experience, I would be a completely different parent.

When I was pregnant with our first daughter, David found a free parenting book in a box left on the street. *Children: The Challenge* is an old book with some outdated examples, but the essence—*treat your children with respect and show them through action*—was revolutionary for me. It was the first time I saw someone frame parenting and discipline as positive, straightforward, and democratic. It was the first time I had seen parenting connected to social justice. Growing up in an African household, the idea that children should be treated with as much respect as their parents/elders was completely outside my worldview. But the idea resonated with me deeply and I still consult the book on a regular basis, even a decade into parenting.

DAVID MIRANDA-HARDY (it's me again, in response to Natasha): With Natasha, we've always been in conversation about our own upbringings. My parents were on the opposite side of the spectrum. Coming from the Latin American left, they believed in treating me as an equal, at least in terms of respect and opinion. Sometimes that was daunting. I think missing some of the common boundaries imposed by parents was responsible for a high dose of anxiety growing up. With Natasha, I try to get a balance between respecting/hearing our daughters without relinquishing our roles as their guides and—yes, loaded word—authority.

MYRNA PEREZ SHELDON: I have come to describe my racial identity in terms of diaspora, because although it's on my face and skin, my race is not grounded in culture, language, or even family ties. Because of violence, my relationship with my Filipino family is almost entirely cut off, although moving between that world and my mother's Anglo-Protestant one was part of the intuitive structure of my childhood. On the most basic level, I realize that my parenting is directed at making a childhood for Indigo and Garnet that I wanted for myself—a childhood where they feel safe but also free.

My deep embrace of feminism came late in life—I learned it from Carly and Rosemary while doing a postdoc, and after finishing a PhD in the history of science. During my PhD I had drifted from the religious and ethical convictions that brought me to scholarship in the first place; learning from radical feminism and queer theory brought me back home to my spiritual life, but in a way that was more liberatory and compassionate than the way I had been religious in my youth. To me, a queer and feminist worldview is not a set of disciplines or a series of affirmed beliefs. It is a posture of true humility that is life-giving.

So how does this shape my day-to-day relationship with my children? They are so young; my relationship with them is still about basic caregiving, especially for Garnet. But my hope is that what I have learned from queer and feminist voices helps me to parent them both not for what they should or might become, or how they may or may not reflect on me in some imagined future moment. I try not to envision them at the beginning of a script that I am preparing them for, or urging them along. I try to relate to them for this moment, for this present; realizing that it also may be all we have in an uncertain world. And I hope that helps me to be kinder, more patient, or more honest with them in this moment, right here, because I am not pressing them on to a future I am trying to control.

JENN ORTEGREN: There are a few moments from my childhood that stand out to me with regards to my mother's attitude toward/encouragement of me to be an independent person. Most of the moments revolve around her reminding me that I begged to play with my older brothers and therefore could not get too upset when they let me play, but didn't take it easy on me. These moments were inevitably followed by her yelling at my brothers to take it easier on me. Looking back, I appreciate this dual messaging—that I needed to be strong and not expect special treatment at the same time that my brothers needed to be gentle (including with each other) and recognize when to recalibrate. I don't think about that element of my upbringing explicitly in my own parenting, but it's clear to me that I, and my family, are much less risk averse about my daughter, Zahi, than my husband and his family. For example, I'm happy to let her go up the stairs by herself while I stand at the bottom instead of following behind her every step. This may seem minor, but it's a way of instilling confidence in her—and resisting suggestions that she should be afraid (even when my husband claims I coddle her too much in terms of disciplining her). I see this as a feminist act and it aligns with how my mother raised me.

But I think the biggest influence for me has been my sister-in-law and watching her parent the two children she has with my brother, long before I had my own child. I don't know what her influences were, or how explicitly she thinks about her parenting as feminist, but I have marveled at her intuitions and ability to balance kindness and discipline, authority and generosity, and I have tried to follow her model. Her approach to parenting is the most explicitly feminist/queer I've encountered. Over Christmas this past year, their eldest child—my nibling, Parker—came out as nonbinary. It has not only been beautiful to watch them, and my brother and sister-in-law, grow into new roles and relationships with each other and us, but it's also been an interesting challenge to live up to my own feminist principles. My sister-in-law explained that Parker was apparently scared to share their nonbinary identity with me because they know I'm "a big feminist." This was surprising to me because it is precisely my feminist commitments (combined with my love of them) that would push me to support them in this transition, but I think the assumption that my feminist politics would create a problem are related to the fact that they are a huge Harry Potter fan, and have been navigating the author's TERF politics. This pushed me to think about how I frame my feminist politics for my daughter.

Equally interesting to me has been thinking about how I use pronouns and how to frame Parker's name and pronoun shift for Zahi. On the one hand, while Zahi still instinctively refers to Parker by the name by which she has known them until now, she also has no problem just calling them something else! Gender and gender conformity is not already set for Zahi and when we remind her that Parker goes by Parker now, she just says, "Oh, I forgot" and carries on. It's a great model and reminder for how to approach this. But on the other hand, this shift is coming *right* as my daughter is exploding into language and I'm realizing—in ways that I'm not sure I would have had I not started using new pronouns for Parker—how much what I think of as teaching my daughter "proper grammar" is also molding her into particular gendered assumptions about the world. I find myself reflexively correcting her pronoun usages to be consistent within sentences when she talks about her stuffed animals, for example. I then immediately think that it doesn't matter how she genders—and wildly switches between gendered pronouns for—her stuffed animals and that, in fact, letting and encouraging her to do so is excellent practice for having queer and feminist orientations later in life. So, I'm learning all the time and my family, including my in-laws, are critical in this.

*How has your parenting been informed by your child/children (e.g., their personalities, needs, social location vis-a-vis race, gender, class, sexuality, ability, geography and so on)?*

PHILIP BROWN: Ahni Zula was named after characters in two books. Ahni (pronounced like Ani DiFranco) is a goddess in *Who Fears Death* by Nnedi Okorafor, and Zula is the protagonist in *Reamde* by Neil Stephenson. Together they make for a very powerful name, and she is a powerful child. For example, she hated for me to comb her hair so I gave her a choice between combing it or cutting it short. She said, "cut it off" and we did. The last time I put her in a dress (as part of her school uniform) she took scissors to it in class. She hasn't worn one since. She has embraced her "theyness" and we are, I think, doing a good job of letting that flow. Ahni has taught me so much about myself. She is neurodivergent. She strikes me as more intelligent and insightful than a lot of kids, but she struggles with writing and keeping it between the lines. What I love most about her is her strong will. She's not going to be told what to do without understanding why she's doing it.

Jude is sensitive about the color of her skin, and she wants to be a "normal" girl with a "normal" family. She is often annoyed that I'm different than her friends' fathers. I try to point out all the different families around us, but being Black and Indian, there is nobody around who looks like her. When we went to Costa Rica, she was so happy to have lots of brown people around, so that is part of the reason I want to live elsewhere. I'd like for her to experience looking like other kids. Recently, I spoke with Jude about the changes our family was going through (my partner and I moving into different homes but staying together, nonmonogamously). She asked me insightful questions about whether I would be dating other people. I finally "came out" to her and said that I've been dating other people the entire time with my partner's consent. I mentioned my friend Ralph who I go see and who spent a weekend with us, and my other friend Jane who lived with us for a little while at the beginning of the pandemic. I think it calmed her fears to know I've been dating people other than Michelle throughout her entire life. That isn't something I had told her before, but I think she was ready.

JENN ORTEGREN: This is an interesting question for me because my husband is of Indian descent and our daughter, Zahina, is biracial, but I have no idea how her race is read by others and she has not articulated any understanding of it. Yet, as an upper-middle-class white girl from Midwestern suburbs that literally had no people of color, I am hyperaware of her race and the need to think critically about how her experiences will be different from mine. Or maybe they won't and I'll be more concerned about it than she is! I'm unsure how much to introduce race as an issue/topic and how much to let her do it. I'm also not sure how prepared I am for when it will come up or how much the reading I do can prepare me when I don't have my own experiences to draw on. And being married to a Brown man in the whitest state in the US has cued me into the subtle racism of my own being and I'm trying to be aware of not doing the same with her (i.e., casually dismissing a sense that an encounter has racist undertones). But in some ways, we've already started the work. If you ask my daughter, "How do we feel about the police?" she will reply, in a very chipper and incredibly endearing toddler lilt, "We don't trust the police!" This performance upset my parents quite a bit—my mother especially—but I know I have to prepare her to be a woman and woman of color in the world.

DAVID MIRANDA-HARDY: I can relate to what Jenn was saying on the issue of racism. One of the constant concerns we share about raising our multiracial daughters is the trade-off between the many opportunities they have in rural Vermont—like access to good public schools, contact with nature, the feeling of community inherent to small towns—and the lack of diversity that many times signals them as "different." The universal struggle against the failures of representation (in books, films, tv, and media in general) gets reinforced by what they see around them here. We engage in an ongoing effort to improve the diversity of media they consume and to relate to it from positions of joy and celebration rather than deficit and discrimination. Nonetheless, we feel we need to do more to improve the girls' connections to more diverse communities. Racially, but also in terms of gender expressions, sexual orientation, etc. I, in particular, sometimes struggle to be more present when discussing "Blackness" and how it's perceived in the US, because I often defer to Natasha's experience and expertise.

ABRAHAM WEIL: For me, becoming a man has not been without the acute and inborn knowledge of once being a woman. As Kelly and I discussed what having a child might be(come), we thought about how gender has inflected our lives and how our kid's gender would be auto-enrolled into a system that neither of us care much for, but also one that we often participate in. We both thought it might be easier to relate to a *girl*, since we have both suffered at the hands of *men*.

In the essay "Man Child" Audre Lorde taps on the *why* of this feeling: "Our daughters have us, for measure or rebellion or outline or dream; but the sons of lesbians have to make their own definitions of self as men. This is both power and vulnerability. The sons of lesbians have the advantage of our blueprints for survival, but they must take what we know and transpose it into their own maleness."[32] My relationship to men and masculinity is always unfolding; transitioning remains one of the most interesting things I have done (or, that I continue to do). It has taught me a great deal, to use Lorde's terms, about *self-definition and letting go*. The move from Black dyke to Black man is a powerful phenomenological bend in our contemporary political landscape and it brings about a porous space for thinking about how to raise our Black son.

"Raising Black children," Lorde says, "in the mouth of a racist, sexist, suicidal dragon is perilous and chancy. If they cannot love and resist at the same time, they will probably not survive. And in order to survive they must let go."[33] I see a connection between my social location and Langston's, even at the tender age of zero. The archival footprint of slavery imprints our Blackness. My curated masculinity charts a potential roadmap for him to do his own emotional work with mindful vulnerability. Following Lorde: "I wish to raise a Black man who will not be destroyed by, nor settle for, those corruptions called power by the white fathers who mean his destruction as surely as they mean mine. I wish to raise a Black man who will recognize that the legitimate objects of his hostility are not women, but the particulars of a structure that programs him to fear and despise women as well as his own Black self."[34] This will mean several things, but is most certainly tied to his social location, geography, and ways of knowing.

As I make my early parenting choices, I take solace in the fact that identity is undergoing rapid changes in how it is deployed. My greatest hope is that I too can shift as he emerges into new ways of being that have not yet been realized.

*How has your feminist-ness or queer-ness informed your experience of parenting and/or the process of becoming a parent? Do you see your approach to parenting as feminist or queer? What does it mean to you to parent in feminist or queer ways?*

LAURIE ESSIG: I was on the initial cusp of lesbian families formed through sperm banks (as opposed to lesbian families that started in heterosexual relationships). My kids were born in the mid-'90s. And I remember feeling as a lesbian mom that I had to be perfect, but as a feminist mom, that "blaming the mother" for all that went wrong was a patriarchal trap. At some point when my kids were little, I decided to embrace the bad mother trope despite the stares from other parents. My kids participated in my politics on a daily basis, learning how to be drag queens and kings, come up with political actions, and sit around the table long past dinner for political discussions. There was a lot of joy in these queer and feminist communities, built around caring for one another even as we did the work of imagining a different world. But the truth is, I didn't do all those "good mother" things—I rarely went to sporting events or volunteered at the school, and I never made friends with other parents unless they were feminist queer parents. As teenagers, my children rejected everything I taught them and decided to go to prom. Unlike "good mothers," I was not excited. I refused to pay for anything and when the other parents asked me to join in some super straight pre-prom photo taking event, I puked a little in my mouth. Sometimes I wonder if I was doing the right thing—being so different from the other mothers, even including the more homonormative lesbian moms (and I was single . . . which did not look good to those nice married lesbians). But in the end, I stayed true to my feminist and queer principles and my daughters criticize me for letting them go to prom. "How could you let me participate in that?" they ask. How indeed. The negotiation between structure and agency is always a dilemma.

MARYAM GRIFFIN: When I pursued support for postpartum anxiety, I heard a similar refrain from so many sources; as if to anticipate guilt I was feeling about doing anything for myself, I was reassured that it's important to "put on your own oxygen mask," as in, a mother needs to take care of herself so that she can be well enough to care for her child. This was messaging I received even though I was not saying I felt guilty about seeking help. I felt like I was running from the judgment that a woman who wanted to feel better during the early days of the transition into parenthood just because she deserves to feel better is a woman who is not a good mother, maybe not yet a mother at all. So this is one place I have felt my feminism—and indeed my feminist parenting—kick in. Knowing that women are inherently worthy of care and that such worthiness is not conditional on any other relationship seems a clear feminist principle. But I am also starting to see this as a feminist parenting principle in that it is necessary (though not sufficient!) to the full and just participation of women in the project of parenting.

KELLY SHARRON: I have found parenting and the process of becoming a parent to be one of the few parts of my life which I've not begun from the outset with an overarching paradigm or framework. A piece of early advice I received as I was trying to set criteria for when I'd be ready for children was, "You'll never be ready." I took that to heart and started seeking out options immediately. I've continued that kind of impromptu, instinctual approach to parenting. My birth plan was written the day before labor; I have no desire to pump a freezer full of breastmilk; and I've generally eschewed things like sleep training, instead trusting that my son and I will both cross various stages and milestones as we are ready.

When I was speaking with my partner, Abe, about this question he remarked that he was also more or less moving day by day, but that feminist and queer politics are so ingrained in our worldviews such that our instincts in conceiving, birthing, and raising him are necessarily feminist and queer.

In Carly's writing to set up this roundtable, this tension plays out in the literature—what is the difference between feminist and queer parenting and feminist and queer parents? As Carly notes, how authors writing about feminist and queer parenting often do so suggests there is a difference. But Abe and I are unable to articulate such a distinction. For us, we find our identification as feminist and queer to be interwoven into feminist and queer actions and worldviews. It feels impossible to disentangle those identities from our ways of parenting. Sure, as Jane Ward suggests, that involves being thrust into queer culture and aesthetics and being familiar with queer and feminist people and families. But thus far it has not involved such gender play as being a female dad and a male mom. Instead, we intend to try to model attention to gender and the ways that it shapes and forms our world, rather than a model of play and interchangeability. For instance, when talking about raising a boy with friends prior to his arrival, I remarked that it's very important to me that he both not experience harm *and* not commit harm. Both are noble goals regardless of gender, but the latter part for me is more important because of his body and identity than it might be otherwise. We've engaged in queer feminist parenting by virtue of taking seriously our own feminist and queer identities and developing them politically.

I also want to comment on Maryam's point about the "oxygen mask"—a philosophy my mother insisted upon and which presumes a different option, or that a woman caring for herself is a radical departure from the norms of motherhood. The medical system exacerbates this with little to no attention to the birthing person in the hospital or in postpartum appointments. At the hospital the only after-birth care I received was half-hearted lactation consulting and pressing my uterus to examine the bleeding. In my postpartum appointment I was asked to do a Kegel and given an unnecessary prescription for birth control. I've yet to have a medical professional ask about my mental health. This is demonstrative of the larger societal expectations of parenting, and mothering specifically, that do require foregoing personal needs.

*Can you share an example of a parenting moment when life made it difficult to parent in feminist queer ways? Considering that "living a feminist life," as Sara Ahmed says, in an overwhelmingly nonfeminist and non-queer world is itself challenging, I imagine that attempting to parent in feminist and queer ways involves its own hardships. What makes it hard to parent in feminist queer ways and how have you dealt with these challenges?*

LAURIE ESSIG: Every day was a failure. I never ended a day and thought "great job practicing feminist queer parenting." I never even ended a day and said "great job parenting." I would say "everyone is still alive" but also berate myself for my many failures as a parent committed to feminist and queer values. I said messed up things to my usually female-identified kids—like "you're so beautiful" rather than "you're so strong." I worked out obsessively when they were younger in a way that showed my own unease with my body and, truthfully, gender. I was struck by their ease with femininity (compared to my own unease) and I attempted to embrace the feminine more fully in part because of the presence of my two daughters. I suspected that I—like nearly anyone raised in a patriarchal culture—had a conflicted relationship with femininity because of my own internalized misogyny. So I did what any good parent would do and began to write about and hang out with a bunch of burlesque performers at Coney Island. I liked the pasties and false eyelashes that felt hilariously wrong on my then carefully cultivated androgynous body and the burlesque performers' raunchy heterosexuality felt like a queer revelation to me. I would drag my small children to Coney Island on a regular basis. One time at the Mermaid Parade, my youngest daughter was hit in the head by a flying alcoholic beverage. It left a mark. That moment made me feel like a failure as a parent, but also as a mother—because I was so not comfortable with that highly feminized role even as I recognized my discomfort as misogynist. My kids didn't call me mom because I told them to call me by my name. I think my inability to help them navigate the gender assigned to them—and the one they have so far mostly landed in—felt like a failure as a parent. A week after the flying beverage incident, I returned to Coney Island and got a big Mother tattoo on my arm. It didn't make me any less conflicted about the abjection of femininity, but I did increasingly try to model a different sort of relationship to "being a woman" (performing as a woman) after that. I tried to exhibit ease with femininity for myself and whatever gender they decided or will decide is theirs. I wish I'd navigated some of that before I had two daughters. I felt like I was learning how to be a feminist/queer parent and a mother by failing at it in front of them all the time. Weirdly, as adults they remain at ease with gender as both innately theirs and also socially constructed and imposed. They do not struggle as I did, perhaps because they have less internalized misogyny or at least more tools for speaking about how patriarchy fucks us all up. Would I do it differently now? Yes, every single day. But am I just in awe of these two amazing humans who happened to live with me for a couple of decades? Yes, every single day.

MARYAM GRIFFIN: This question really resonates with me and stirs up a lot, which is funny because my child's life is just shy of eight months long so far, but it's already manifestly difficult to pursue feminist and queer parenting. I do much more of the childcare than my male partner even though I have a demanding full-time job. I have let myself feel bad about relying on daycare or feeling overwhelmed even though I have my baby in daycare. Above, Rosemary evocatively writes about having felt like a fugitive in the early days of parenthood. This struck me as a perfect way of describing how I feel: like a fugitive. Feeling like I'm on the run, wondering about my own culpability, and suspecting that the judgment is both unjust and inescapable. I get the sense that it's common for new parents, especially those perceived as women, to feel targeted by an onslaught of "information" whose sum total effect is to convince them of their inadequacy. So perhaps I've already been primed to integrate everything into that framework, but indeed my own aspirations to parent in feminist and/or queer ways within a nonfeminist and nonqueer (in fact, *anti*feminist and *anti*queer) world have often felt like yet another rubric by which to assess my own failures. The main way I have dealt with this challenge is by calling in more queer and feminist politics, mainly in the form of friends reminding me that these difficulties are not entirely of my own making and that I am in the struggle, the wide, deep, vibrant, relentless, and collective struggle.

MYRNA PEREZ SHELDON: This might be a strange analogy: My husband assesses climate impacts of technologies, but he isn't necessarily the poster child for the personal habits we often associate with environmentalism. I'm often more drawn to these kinds of personal practices—especially zero waste ones—and will get drawn into the question of how to minimize the plastic content of my shampoo bottles. (Which he will roll his eyes about and point me to some decidedly less sexy task like reading our utility bills in my quest to be environmentally sound). A lot of the models he builds are based in life-cycle analysis, which essentially demonstrates how impossible it is to make truly ethical (however defined) choices. Well, that's not true, he always jokes that the least impactful choice is not to do something—the least impactful food is the kind you don't grow or eat. The least impactful car is the kind you don't make or drive. I think he is less drawn to these sorts of personal practices because he spends his working life dealing with the true complexity of impacts on the environment, and so these individualized choices feel less meaningful.

I bring this up to try to describe my wariness with purity ethics that focus on individual behavior as the center of any political ideology: We take a canvas bag to the grocery store to escape the taint of plastic or we buy from sustainable clothing brands to free ourselves from the violence of the global fashion industry. These practices are important—but I think of them almost as something closer in kind to prayer and/or meditation. They can and should be about orienting ourselves into the work we must do every day, but they should never make us believe that we are not complicit in the violence of the structures we benefit from.

Perhaps the analogy I want to make to queer and/or feminist parenting is going to be apparent now. We can become overly focused on a "pure" way of doing these things—the proper language or dress, the right books and movies. Of course, I think these daily and intimate actions matter. But I am wary of the potential to fall into self-righteousness as I police these kinds of actions in myself or in my children.

I am most grateful to queer and feminist lives and doings because they have helped me to imagine love in a way that nothing else has (or I think could). I also think they teach us that our desire for mastery—whether of social or epistemological power—is a source of suffering. And because of this, I don't especially believe that I could master being a good feminist. Not trying to do that is actually the point.

*While Sara Ahmed has demonstrated the power of the figure of the feminist killjoy, I've recently been thinking more about feminist joy, minus the kill. Don't get me wrong: I love killjoy sensibilities and regularly experience the joy of being the killjoy![35] I'm wondering here, however, if you might share an example of a parenting moment that reflects your feminist or queer principles and to which you attach joy, pride, pleasure, happiness or other affects that we don't tend to associate with the killjoy.*

ROSEMARY HENNESSY: I am so moved by Myrna's reflection on feminism teaching her love and how that translates into not trying to be good or the best at it. That helps me wrestle with my sense of my limits as a parent. Myrna, you remind me that compassion is hard to hold close and to practice with oneself. For my daughters, my decision to run away from heteronormativity was certainly killjoy material. Their nostalgia for the imagined and actual joys of their former family package became something like a phantom limb for them, a wound that opened in times of crisis. I'm not sure that the many joys of queer family life ever made that lost limb go away, even though the queerness allowed something wild and appealing and free for them, too.

I remember the first time Chrys and I took them (at ages thirteen and eleven?) to the all-women "lesbian beach" on Cape Cod. They were initially resistant, intrigued, and a little freaked out. It was the (officially prohibited) custom then that bathing suit tops at Herring Cove were optional. By the end of our first day, Molly was delighted to be an outlaw and discreetly took hers off, too. They both still love to tell stories of the crowd's solidarity when shouts of "Ranger! Ranger!" rolled down the beach, warning the topless to suit up and how Leah Deloria (before she became famous) in full butch form used the occasion as a raucous rehearsal for her stand-up routine. As we wandered through the streets of Provincetown at night and mingled with drag queens, other lesbians, men holding hands, Chrys and I saw these kids' pleasure in being part of the queer scene.

As a parent of adult children now, I read what Kelly and Abe, Philip, Myrna, David and Natasha, Maryam, Hemangani, Erin and Miranda, and Jenn write as parents of little ones and I want to warn them: everything you say and do will have a tremendous influence on your children, more than you ever imagined or wanted. At the same time, it comes with no guarantees. As Laurie writes, "The negotiation between structure and agency is always a dilemma." And maybe that's a gift. Kids absorb feminist and queer lessons and weave them into the contradictions they grow up with, and you never know where that will go. The license to be different that they thrillingly join imprints their desires and even perversely their resistance. Molly converted to Catholicism at fourteen and became a courageous outspoken feminist in high school; she still embraces the glitter and glitz of drag style. Kate helped organize an anti-racism effort in those years and was elated to go to her senior prom with two girlfriends. Both of my daughters married men. As a journalist, Molly has reported on trans migrants from Mexico, women in Afghanistan, Egypt, and Syria, Black victims of police shootings, and women's struggle for reproductive freedom. Kate teaches high school social studies to newcomers to the US. They model being feminists and are, in their own ways, quite queer. That gives them and me a lot of joy.

MYRNA PEREZ SHELDON: What Rosemary shared here reminds me of a conversation we had (at a conference!) after Indigo was born, but before I had Garnet. I described to her my decision not to baptize my children although I am a deeply religious person, because I don't want them to think that it matters to me whether they are religious or not. I want them to feel free to explore life and its existential questions on their own terms, and to not worry that I will love them less for the ideologies they adopt. And then Rosemary described to me Molly's conversion to Catholicism and Molly's desire for a clearer overarching and authoritative worldview. And I still think about that conversation. It helped me see that while I thought I found a way out of disappointing or damaging my children, it is impossible to know all the ways I will do both. If I'm honest, there are moments when this realization has been paralyzing! But it also has helped me to see the limits of my own attempts at control of the family/parenting narrative, and I hope it opens me more fully to letting go of that control.

ROSEMARY HENNESSY: I remember that time, Myrna! I think you put your finger on the dialectic at the heart of all parenting—children need the control that is a parent's protection and they need the parent who lets go.

I want to think that our feminist and queer values help us navigate that dialectic with wise minds. Friends are helpful, too!

I want to thank Carly for making this conversation happen. It has been so rewarding and affirming for me to hear your stories and to learn more about you all as parents. As you say, Myrna, these conversations stay with us, and in that sense, they are profound guides. I didn't realize how much I needed to hear from you all on this topic. Thank you for sharing your stories!

CARLY THOMSEN: My dear friends! Thank you, thank you, thank you for sharing your beautiful insights about feminism and queerness and parenting here. They are a crucial companion to a belief that I repeat often: In a world in which LGBTQ+ people are increasingly reproducing, and in which 86 percent of US women have children, it seems fundamentally queer and feminist to *not* reproduce. I certainly see my decision to avoid reproduction and parenting as queer. I also think that parenting can be a site for the development and enactment of feminism and queerness. And I'm grateful for the time and care you invested here to articulate what feminist and queer parenting can look and feel like, that is, how these epistemologies shape your parenting and are shaped by your parenting.

I'm also grateful that you share your kids and their lives and your lives together with me! I will always be the auntie who, upon hearing from another room that your kid is requesting a gummy from my kitchen shelf, runs quickly screaming, "NOT THOSE GUMMIES!!!!" [Yes, this happened. Yes, pot is legal where I lived at the time. No, the kid did not eat any inappropriate gummies. In fact, the gummies the kid could see were vitamins. All other gummies remain out of the reach of children.] I will always be the auntie who gives your kids as many cookies as they want. And I will always be the auntie who is in awe of you and the humans you are molding. Differences in life stages and geographic distances mean that I have interacted with some of your kids far more than others. I have shared lovely meals with Rosemary's and Laurie's adult children, and, through listening to their stories and watching how they interact with their moms as adults, I gained new insights about my friends. In other cases, I've gotten to know another side of my friends through watching them parent—either through photos and stories you share from afar or through witnessing you and your kids in action on a regular basis. Just a few days after Maryam gave birth, when she was experiencing the postpartum anxiety she mentioned in one of her responses to this roundtable, I received a voicemail from her. I cried in my car while listening to it, and knew I needed to get to Seattle as soon as possible. When I arrived and witnessed everything she was dealing with to keep her newborn alive, fed, clean, and sleeping mostly on her own (while her husband was working long hours in a new job), I found myself completely floored by her resilience. I felt similarly when her husband needed to return to Palestine to support his family because his brother was detained by the Israeli state and she was left alone again. Through her experience parenting, I witnessed firsthand the far-reaching, maddening, and devastating consequences of the occupation of Palestine. I also was able to experience the joys of Jenn's and Kelly's changing pregnant bodies alongside them, as we were living nearby one another at the times of their pregnancies. I was the very first person that Langston, Kelly's and Abe's baby, shit on. In the early stages of the pandemic, my weekly Saturday morning hikes with Hemangini, Moyukh, and Nikhil were life-giving, something I looked forward to all week. I learned to see birds and trees through the eyes of a four-year-old, and was reminded to slow down and enjoy it all. A few months ago, Zahina, Jenn's three-year-old, called me on Facetime because she wanted me to watch her eat a pickle. She ate her pickle, said nothing, and then hung up. It was epic. Recently, I was at the gym with David's and Natasha's daughter, who asked if I would show her how to use the machines. We were struggling to figure out appropriate weights (she is just eight years old!) and, so, I asked her how much she weighed so that I could adjust the machine accordingly. She looked at me and sternly replied, "That's a rude question." I responded that yes she's right, this question can be rude but whether or not that is the case depends on context. I explained that I was only asking her so that we could figure out how she could effectively play on the machine. I also mentioned as another example that a doctor might ask how much you weigh to decide how much medicine you can take if you're sick. And in these kinds of cases, I said, the question isn't rude. But I left feeling totally unsure about my answer. Did my response glorify a medical system that I should be encouraging this small human to think critically about? At what point does one do so? I couldn't stop thinking about my response, so I asked my friend David, her Papa, about it. And his take was totally different: Isn't it incredible, he said, that this little girl will look you in the eye and feel both safe and empowered enough to tell you how she is feeling about something you said that she felt was wrong?! He was right, of course. Another dear friend, J Finley, a Black butch lesbian whose birthing experience I was in the room for, along with her wife, holding a leg and watching her pelvic bones shift back and forth while she pushed, asked me afterward, "Do you think this experience will change how you teach Politics of Reproduction?!" Without hesitation, I said, "Yes. How could it not? It changed my life." Rarely do we get to be a part of things that are both quotidian and miraculous, full of such intense pain alongside pleasure, joy, wonder, and hope. I can't tell you how often I think about the moments I shared here. Thank you for being the feminist and queer parents at the heart of them. You and your sweet, smart, creative, loud, hilarious, germy children bring such deep pleasure, joy, wonder, and hope to my life.

# Conclusion

## PLAYING WITH QUEER THEORY: THE QUEER POTENTIAL OF ART

This book argues that reproductive justice and queer theory are better together, though one wouldn't know this from surveying either queer theory or reproductive justice activism. This is because queer theory has largely avoided "traditional" feminist reproductive issues, such as abortion and birth control, an irony considering the field's commitment to sexual liberation. It is also because the perspectives of reproductive justice supporters, who increasingly use discourses of queerness, often run counter to those of queer theory. It is my hope that this book will spur queer theorists to approach reproductive issues as worthy of analysis and reproductive justice supporters to engage more deeply and critically with their deployments of queerness vis-a-vis queer theory.

Such engagement could allow us to develop approaches to reproductive justice that are actually queer. As I've argued throughout this book, queering reproductive justice requires something far greater than simply deploying the term "queer," banning the word "woman," or centering gay and trans men in discussions of reproduction. These shifts alone will not lead to necessary research on trans healthcare or increase the numbers of medical professionals equipped to provide trans-specific care. They will not force us to grapple with the racist and classist roots of surrogacy and its ongoing racialized and classed implications, including how the deeply unregulated practice impacts the lives of surrogates. These shifts will not help us defeat the misogyny driving the antiabortion movement, which successfully passed 561 abortion restrictions in forty-seven states in 2021 alone—more than any other year in US history.[1] And they will not ensure that the many forms of social reproduction outside of hetero- and homonormative childbearing are recognized and remunerated—all issues *Reproductive Justice, Queerly* takes up.

It is the contention of this book that current approaches to queering reproductive justice *impede* our ability to approach reproduction queerly and to develop queer socialities. But, as students often ask of the theory we read in class, what, exactly, do we *do* with these arguments? How might we craft cultural interventions that disrupt taken-for-granted assumptions about what it means to approach reproductive justice queerly?

To answer these questions, I worked with my thoughtful, creative, and talented research assistants to develop a Queer Artists' Collective. The student-led group was responsible for two things: 1.) Organizing queer art nights at which participants discussed chapters of this book and subsequently created art and 2.) Creating a playable game, which resulted in a Cards Against Humanity–inspired game entitled Cards for Queering Reproductive Justice. Both were meant to translate ideas from this book into an alternative medium and to encourage the circulation of these arguments. Our method was informed by a pedagogical approach I use across my classes, where students "translate" an academic article into a playable board game.[2] Each of my research assistants had previously completed "translation" assignments in my courses, so our method was familiar to everyone. Our approach was also informed by recent scholarship that suggests that people respond differently to what they hear spoken versus what they read, even if the words themselves are exactly the same.[3] In short, people are less likely to dismiss another person's ideas if they hear, versus read, them. This finding suggests that actualizing queer reproductive justice requires something beyond the written word. Perhaps, we thought, we could develop spaces where people could craft new ways to communicate with one another about what it means to queer reproductive justice.

And that is exactly what we did. Our ability to create these spaces was enabled by what Rosemary Hennessy calls "affect-cultures," or those emotional ties that bind "people to a common cause and to one another."[4] Just as the affect-cultures that enabled the labor organizing about which Hennessy writes were not always necessarily positive or negative, and were, at times, "inchoate, even unnamable," so, too, were the affects that circulated throughout the art nights. Sometimes participants just weren't quite sure what they were doing or why they were doing it, although they also weren't exactly confused. In other moments, the affects swirling were easily nameable. At one queer art night, which brought together students who had participated in the play *Jane: Abortion and the Underground* a year earlier (see chapter 3), attendees described the experience as "super fun," "thoroughly enjoyable," and "special." People were smiling and laughing and talking over one another. It was clear that we were enjoying each other and having fun. In short, the affects generated through this set of encounters were enabled by broader affective networks at the small liberal arts college where we all coexisted. Put more colloquially, queer art night participants typically attended because one of their friends invited them.

But, importantly, it wasn't just our affective ties that led people to show up. Also at play were what I think of as *queer knowledge-cultures*. Many of the student participants joined because they had taken my Queer Critique course and were already familiar with the possibilities of queer theory in motion. Just as the activism of End Fake Clinics (see chapter 4) was "epistemologically bound and affectively oriented," so too was the work of the Queer Artists' Collective. There are, however, key differences between the groups. While I attended nearly every weekly meeting of End Fake Clinics over the course of its four-year existence, I did not attend the majority of the queer art nights and offered little direction to the collective. The entire enterprise was decidedly student-led. There were two exceptions. Dr. Hemangini Gupta, my friend and colleague (a true "frolleague!"), incorporated a chapter into her Gender, Technology, and the Future course, and I attended this class along with two student members of the collective. I also attended the art night with students from my class that had put on the *Jane* play. Both of these examples speak to the impossibility of a distinction between knowledge-cultures and affect-cultures, as the affects that connect me to my frolleague and students developed in the space of knowledge-sharing and production. At the same time, I did not know everyone who attended art nights or created art for this project. Some participating artists were part of my research assistants' kinship networks and attended purely out of a desire to support their friends and without much interest in academic queer theory. But considering that all of my research assistants have taken my courses and were working on a project on queering reproductive justice, queer theoretical knowledge was at play even when affective—rather than epistemological—connections drove their friends' participation. In the case of the Queer Artists' Collective, queer knowledge-cultures and affect-cultures fed one another.

Affects and anxieties swirled within our research team too. At some point in the semester, students began to question the efficacy of the queer art nights and their ability to advance this project, primarily because most participants were not exactly artists and the quality of the art produced reflects this—although my research assistants didn't share these concerns with me until much later, mostly, I suspect, because they were getting paid to talk about queer theory with their friends and produce wacky art together, and they didn't want that to end. (When a collective member read a penultimate draft of this chapter, she commented "cute" on the prior sentence. I responded to ask if she was being sarcastic and if she found my analysis offensive. She commented "nooo I'm being very serious! I think you are right!") But at the same time, and as this later exchange suggests, we had created a relationship such that research team members wanted what was best for the advancement of this project.

By contrast, I was elated by my research assistants' weekly updates, their sharing of artwork created at the latest workshop, reading aloud a newly uploaded artist's statement, or reporting on their work to organize the next workshop. I could see that they were having a good time talking queer theory and creating visual art with fellow students. I trusted, based on the stories that they were sharing with me, that the queer art nights and game nights were functioning just as we had intended: a space for playing with queering reproductive justice. And not just for those people who found themselves at a queer art night—for my research assistants and for me too. This playing functioned as practice, which elevated my research assistants' contributions to this project. It allowed them to see which arguments were resonating with others. It also reminded them—and, by extension, me—that ideas that had become old news to us were still cutting-edge and provocative to others. In the weeks after students gathered at queer art nights, my assistants came to our team meetings far more excited about the research. My belief in this queer method was informed by Patricia Zavella, who argues that the multidimensional "culture shift work" of reproductive justice organizations includes four prongs: cultivating leaders capable of articulating what a reproductive justice approach entails, conducting research, collaborating with artists and storytellers, and using traditional and social media.[5] In our case, all four prongs were one and the same. My research assistants became culture shift leaders on campus through doing research while creating art and media—something enabled because I cared less about the actual art being produced than the conversations transpiring, conversations that circled back to me and informed the shape of this book.

But, unlike those students most involved with organizing through the Queer Artists' Collective, I am not exactly an artist. I'm a scholar who has been informed by the insights of scholars of cultural studies, feminist theory, and queer theory, who have written about the power in thinking alongside the minor, the trivial, the everyday, the inconsequential. Culture with a small "c." In the 1980s, renowned cultural studies scholar Stuart Hall argued for the value of taking seriously the kinds of cultural formations too often viewed as beneath scholarly analysis. But Hall's concern was not simply culture itself. For Hall and his contemporaries, culture can operate as a "critical site of social action and intervention, where power relations are both established and potentially unsettled."[6] Informed by the work of Antonio Gramsci, Hall worked to upend what he famously termed the "high theory/low culture" formulation. Forty years later, queer theorist Jack Halberstam adapted Hall's work to develop what he termed "low theory."[7] Halberstam articulates the contours of "low theory" through compiling an eccentric archive of things largely considered frivolous and analyzing them through forms of thinking largely considered serious. Focusing, for example, on animated children's films, Halberstam demonstrates how that which is associated with silliness can be a profound site for upending hegemonic ideas about failure and success. "Low theory," then, is both a "mode of accessibility" and also a call to fail, especially because success is often measured in terms of capitalist accumulation and heteronormative ideals.[8] Failing can create possibilities for rethinking hegemonic ideologies and also open up possibilities for enacting alternative desires. In developing low theory, Halberstam, who prioritizes "getting lost over finding our way," demonstrates how we might approach less-than-serious (but still super high budget!) visual texts as containing serious queer life lessons and possibilities for analysis.[9]

What is less obvious is how *we* might produce our own (and very low budget!) images in order to move around the kinds of feminist and queer theory with which Halberstam is concerned and that are explored in this book—which is exactly what the Queer Artists' Collective set out to do. Over the course of three academic years (2020–23), the collective organized nine art nights and six game nights. Approximately 140 people attended the game nights, where they played the Cards for Queering Reproductive Justice game that my research assistants and I created as well as games that students had made in my Politics of Reproduction and Queer Critique courses. The art nights were attended by 60 students, approximately one-third of whom attended and made art at more than one of our events. It is not surprising that more people attended the game nights than the art nights, as the latter demanded far more from participants. Prior to the art nights, student organizers circulated drafts of chapters of this book. Participants then read the chapter and came prepared to discuss it in a reading-group-like environment. After the discussion, students created art together, initially primarily on Zoom, and as pandemic-related restrictions loosened, in person. The events typically lasted 1.5 hours, with about half of the time dedicated to discussing the text and the other half to making art. Again, the "quality" of the art produced at the queer art nights was not the point. The process of creating the Cards for Queering Reproductive Justice game was quite different; my research team made it on our own. In this case, it was in playing the game—not in cocreating it—that participants engaged with queering reproductive justice.

In what follows, I first share a small sampling of the artwork created at queer art nights as well as one piece of art made by a Queer Artists' Collective organizer that references creating the Cards for Queering Reproductive Justice game. For members of the Queer Artists' Collective, the process of creating visual imagery and an intentionally irreverent game meant to put into circulation queer theoretical ideas raised questions about the relationships among art, use, affect, failure, and transgression. As a way to think through these questions, which animated our weekly research team meetings, the Queer Artists' Collective organizers and I began reading texts and meeting to chat about them—a reading group within a reading group. During these conversations, we took notes in what became an increasingly messy Google doc. Eventually, Rayn Bumstead and Cat La Roche, two Queer Artists' Collective organizers, and I transformed our scribbles into a roundtable discussion. In the concluding part of this chapter, we reflect on our conversations, further develop the ideas in this chapter's introductory section, and share the queer insights we gained through playing with queer theory.

A final anecdote before moving onto the queer art exhibition: Prior to our last meeting of the semester, I sent a draft of this chapter to my research assistants, noting that we'd spend meeting time reflecting on it. My students—my interlocutors and collaborators—were far more excited than I anticipated. "It was SO fun to read the chapter and to see your thinking about what we were doing!" one exclaimed. Another joked, "Who knew that what we were doing was so cool?!" We all laughed before I earnestly expressed confusion. At that point, we had been working together on this project for at least a year, so, of course we all knew that what we were doing was cool! Right?! Not exactly. It was at this moment that the students confessed their prior doubts regarding whether our weird queer approach could advance this book—all of which, they noted, were eradicated through stepping back and looking at the project through the lens of the queer theory this chapter uses to reflect on our work. There we were, more than a year into a project that argues for the necessity of queer theory for reproductive justice, being reminded of the value of theory, and not just for upending common ideas about what queering reproductive justice entails, but also for how we see ourselves, enact queer methods, and actualize queer potential through our affective connections. Queering, we were reminded, requires practice, and it is best done collectively. The visual art made at queer art nights—which demonstrate the possibility of queer critique in motion—reflects our belief in engaging in the exercise that is the collective practice of queering.

But before we reflect further on queer artmaking, let's look at some student-made art.

A Scene from *Jane: Abortion and the Underground,* illustration by Allegra Molkenthin.

### A Scene from *Jane: Abortion and the Underground,* Allegra Molkenthin

In *Jane: Abortion and the Underground,* I played Dr. C, who performed four onstage abortions and taught members of the Jane Collective how to conduct the simple procedure. As a class and cast member, I was able to process what it means to perform an abortion and the related stigma/controversy in the context of our discussions about the politics of reproduction and specifically, the Jane Collective. In this piece of art, I drew Dr. C overseeing an abortion being performed by a Jane member, with the patient lying down and another member consoling her. I also included the outline of an audience to show that the scene is being observed. Reading this chapter, I reconsidered the impact these scenes may have had on our audience and the feelings, reactions, and questions they may have elicited, and I wanted to highlight that perspective here.

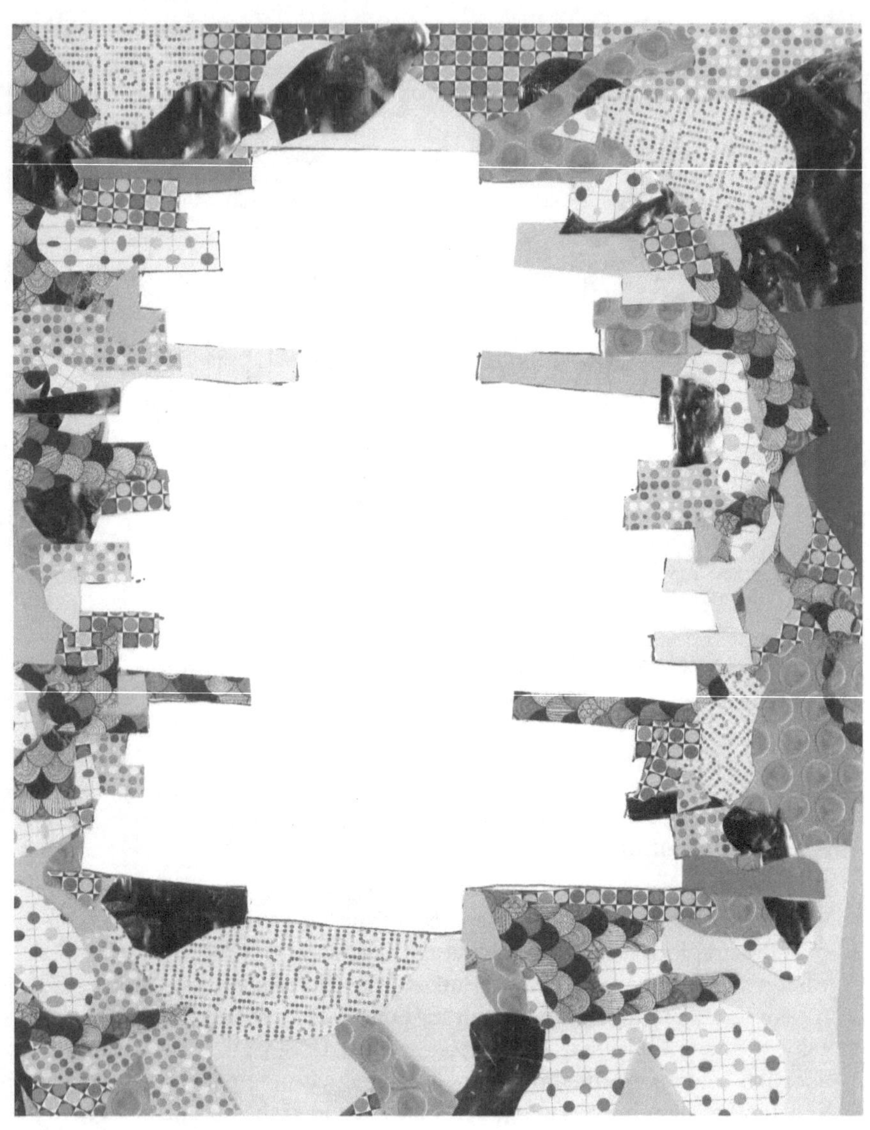

*The Things Left Out*, collage on paper by Sophie Hochman.

*The Things Left Out,* Sophie Hochman

This collage is a response to the poster created by End Fake Clinics. Our queer art night group chatted about how even though it took EFC hours to negotiate the sentences about reproductive justice making up each line of the poster, we still found ourselves wanting to add a caveat to each. While we discussed the feasibility of making a version of that poster ourselves, we eventually determined that the process of reconstructing each statement to better represent the complexity of reproductive justice would be to miss the point of the poster itself: as it says, "complex issues cannot be summed up in a sentence." In response to this discussion, I made a piece of art that wasn't about revising the sentences, but instead sought to explore the potential value of a poster like this one in the first place. As such, my art replicates the shape of the text on the initial poster, but instead fills in the negative space outside of the text in collage, leaving the space meant for text blank. The abstract origami paper shapes represent what can emerge when we unpack what is left unsaid.

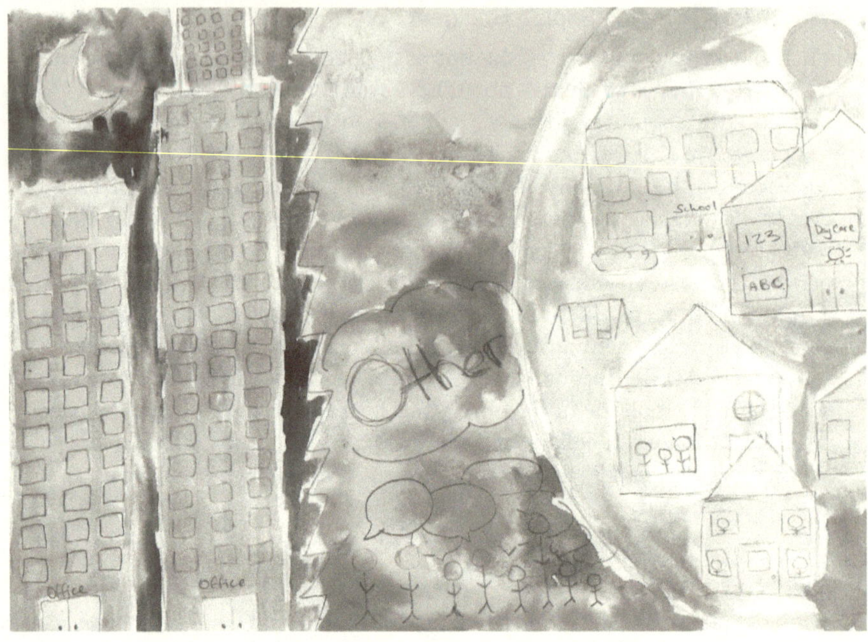


*In the Policy Gap,* watercolor on paper by Sarah Le.

*In the Policy Gap,* Sarah Le

My artwork was inspired by the quote, "We need [care] especially when our lives fall in the gaps between institutions and conventional familial structures." I center such gaps between institutions and conventional structures, which are represented by office buildings, day cares, and schools. In the middle, I show the "other"—those who fall between or outside of such structures. As the chapter on paid family leave demonstrates, policies regarding social reproduction create strict categories designed to exclude certain people from support and aid, such as those who fall outside the heterosexual order. I want my art to encourage thinking about how we can support people that policies fail to support and how care and aid can and do expand beyond the family or beyond the office.

*The Strange Verb,* watercolor on paper by Emily Ribeiro.

*The Strange Verb,* Emily Ribeiro

I was inspired by the quote "The most powerful queer and feminist effects of the strange verb 'parenting' are as diffuse as the air we breathe." This roundtable made me question my ingrained ideas regarding parenting and explore key aspects of queer and feminist parenting, highlighting the significance of "queering" parenting, in the sense that it offers different perspectives and approaches that break "normal" barriers. The heteronormative, patriarchal, stereotypical family is outdated, as are the parenting styles associated with it.

*Fuck the Child,* watercolor on paper by Kayla Richards.

*Fuck the Child,* Kayla Richards

My art was inspired by a quote from the chapter on social reproduction in which Dr. Thomsen outlines "a queer critique of paid family leave, ultimately proposing another path: the utopian, aspirational model of 'Fuck the Child' as a new way to interrogate and move beyond the public/private split and familialism that haunts discussions of care." I came up with the idea of using the philosophy of "Fuck the Child" to plant the seed of the future we want to see, a queer futurity in direct opposition to reproductive futurism. Hence, the image of "Fuck the Child" sprouting from the ground amongst blades of grass. I wanted to capture the feeling of aspiration mentioned and also the renewal and new growth associated with life and the future.

*Affective Map of an Affective Attachment*, watercolor and mixed media on paper by Cat La Roche.

*Affective Map of an Affective Attachment*, Cat La Roche

I was thinking a lot about the affective attachments that tied together End Fake Clinics, and affective attachments turned out to be the theme of the art night discussion. When I made this piece, I was thinking about what an affective map of an affective attachment would look like and how beautiful it would be for all of its layers and dimension. You can get a sense of someone when you first meet them, but as the experiences with this person accumulate and pull your relationship in all sorts of directions, your sense of them is deepened and heightened. I tried to represent this idea with the different patterns and the ripped and reattached parts of this piece.

*I Guess You're a Terf*, cartoon by Ivy Geilker.

*I Guess You're a Terf*, Ivy Geilker

I feel nervous speaking about gender today. And I'm a gender non-conforming person who majored in Sociology and has read a lot of feminist and queer theory. It seems we have suddenly decided our language is insufficient. But hasn't it always been? Theory is not imagined, it is built from evidence, an accumulation of real occurrences. Different viewers might look at this cartoon and walk away with totally different interpretations, but that's not a glitch, it is how I know the sketch represents something real. When it comes to the ever present "woman issue" in feminist and queer theory, no interpersonal interaction is too small to investigate. I don't think my drawing necessarily has a protagonist. There is a question mark in one of the speech bubbles for a reason! Aren't we all wondering if we are allowed to say that? Whatever "that" is in a given moment.

Some additional thoughts from Ivy, pulled from an email exchange we had regarding this very artist's statement:

> In some ways it pains me to say "I'm a gender non-conforming person." It's true, I know, but it feels like another modern-day box people created to make sense of something that already made sense: people are multifaceted. It reminds me what a sham gender is. I guess what I'm saying is . . . if I were choosing between survey boxes that said "cis-woman" and "transgender" or "non-binary" I would choose cis-woman. But when people see me on the street, they might label me "woman" but they also might (and often do) label me "man" and surely some think "trans???" I believe other people decide my gender. My gender is what others can perceive. That does not mean I am what others perceive . . . In those moments where strangers choose ma'am or sir, I'm honestly shocked either way every time. That is, it's just as surprising that they can read me as female as that they can read me as male. When strangers think I'm male it does not bother me. In fact, it makes me chuckle. In those moments I think, well, I guess I am socially a man/boy right now. I don't feel like I'm not a woman, but I wear a wide spectrum of clothing (and have varied mannerisms and hobbies), and that means that strangers call me "sir" nearly as often as "ma'am." I suppose that is the definition of gender-nonconforming? Because conforming is an action—and I am not doing it. It is interesting to me that pronouns are an attempt for individuals to define their own genders, regardless of how they may appear/act. But is gender not just a mix of how we appear/act?? I think trying to prove oneself as any gender is a losing battle. You will be read as what society knows how to read. And if we are truly non-conforming—AKA queer—we don't worry about being legible, do we? Perhaps this comes down to me believing that we can never have (and shouldn't want) our exteriors to reflect our interiors. I like that about being human.

*Melting the Matrix*, collage on paper by Celia Gottlieb.

*Melting the Matrix,* Celia Gottlieb

My art is meant to exhibit the public/private split that Thomsen argues we must move past through an aspirational model of "Fuck the Child." The images I selected—the house gone awry, skateboard, college banner, spilled water—represent the reimagined domestic, the child, a place of work and a social location, and unseen domestic labor. Through this piece, I am imagining a melting of the system that adheres the care agenda to the heterosexual matrix.

*Berry Bortion*, drawing on paper by Lu Mila.

*Berry Bortion*, Lu Mila

The chapter on surrogacy makes clear that many ways people attempt to queer reproductive justice pander to the heterosexual nuclear family structure. Gay men are centered in discussions of surrogacy—something presented as "progress," even though we should think of obsessions with biology as conservative. We should view attempts to produce surrogacy as queer as absurd. What, I wondered, would a representation of abortion look like that was equally absurd? Absurdity and absurd aesthetics have long been a part of queer and trans subcultures and I wanted to draw from this history to create an absurd, queer approach to abortion. The result: a baggie of fetus gummies.

*Beyond the Nuclear Family,* watercolor on paper by Kamari Williams.

*Beyond the Nuclear Family,* Kamari Williams

Dr. Thomsen's reflections on paid parental leave, including the image and concept of the family, reminded me of my first encounter with the term "nuclear family." Often, when people reference immediate families, they mean parents and children living in one house. But I have always lived with extended family. When I was asked to describe my family to classmates in elementary school, I responded by listing my cousins and grandparents. I was quickly corrected, an experience that was extremely jarring for me. In response to this chapter, which calls into question the positive affects that "stick" to "the family," I decided to illustrate this experience by painting a nuclear family in a colorful house. In the periphery, I painted other relatives, friends, and an entire world that lives outside the bounds of the normative "family" concept. When we begin to reimagine what care looks like and what family means, we can discover a bigger and brighter world.

*Surrolove*, watercolor on paper by Isabel Perez-Martin.

*Surrolove,* Isabel Perez-Martin

This piece explores the relationships between surrogates and people hiring them. Here, a heterosexual couple, informed by dominant ideas about love, hired a surrogate. The man is seeping into the silhouette of a woman, the surrogate. Her body is full of question marks. Who is this reproductive vessel? Why did you choose her? This work focuses on the humanization and characterization of the surrogate in relationship to dominant ideas of family.

*Little Freaks*, cartoon by Rayn Bumstead.

*Little Freaks,* Rayn Bumstead

In this cartoon, I reflect on the project as a whole and the making of the companion game (Cards for Queering Reproductive Justice). My fellow research assistants and I were trying to write a text blurb about the game for the project website and included the phrase "it is unlike any other game." This is, of course, untrue as we based the game on Cards Against Humanity. So, this cartoon shares a funny behind-the-scenes moment that went into making the game and gives insight into what it meant to be part of this amazing research team. (Do not fear: we were never called creepy or freaks! But that we can joke like this speaks to our meaningful connections.)

*Anatomy of a Queer Art Night*, cartoon by Rayn Bumstead.

*Anatomy of a Queer Art Night*, Rayn Bumstead

I wanted to make a cartoon about the experience of hosting and attending these queer art nights. These art nights were, notoriously, a little bit awkward and, at times, it was apparent that participants were confused about what the point actually was. At the same time, participants described the events as generative, contemplative, and fun—a paradox we reflect on in the roundtable that follows.

## ON MAKING ART, QUEERLY

*Use, Friendship, Transgression*

A CONVERSATION WITH QUEER ARTISTS' COLLECTIVE ORGANIZERS RAYN BUMSTEAD AND CAT LA ROCHE

CARLY: Rayn and Cat, you spent your senior year of college working on this weird queer project. By way of getting us started, I'm wondering if you can share **how you talked about it in your day-to-day life? How did you discuss your work with your friends? Did you "come out" to your parents regarding your queer research position?**

CAT: Truth time: I haven't told my parents about my work on this project! If I were going to, I would say that our research team holds a Zoom meeting every month or so in which we discuss chapter drafts of this book and make art based on it with our friends. Maybe I would skip describing the art nights as "queer," but if I did, I would note that the art nights aren't queer because they necessarily have to do with LGBTQ+ people, but rather that they're queer as in "strange."

When I describe the art nights to friends I'm inviting, I skip a description and say something like, "I have stuff for collaging if you feel like reading this academic text beforehand" or "Are you free tonight, and if so, do you have about an hour and a half to two hours to read this book chapter that calls into question the assumption that using phrasing like 'pregnant people' helps trans people in health settings?" Real friends don't need a description, really, they just trust the process.

RAYN: When I tell my father about the work I do at college I make it sound serious and intense. My dad is a house painter and I know he thinks academic work is fake and oh so elitist. So, I have avoided telling him about the queer art nights project. Not because I think the work is fake, elitist, or unimportant (that I feel the opposite will, I hope, become apparent). But because I find it difficult to tell someone who has been outside painting in the sun all day that I feel exhausted after organizing a queer art night. If I did tell him, I would probably avoid calling it "work" and maybe refer to it as "a project."

Cat is really good at tricking people into doing things. I think you, Cat, have this ability because people really love and care about you and it results in them going to things they wouldn't otherwise attend. Art nights have been no exception. When I have described this work to friends it has been different every time. To my gender studies or sociology friends, I described it more casually. I know they already believe in the value of this type of work. But when I described the project to physics or computer science majors I would go full serious hard-o, focusing on notions of translation and communicability that underlie the ethos of the project. In these moments it felt important to convince those in other disciplines that queer and feminist theory are also academically rigorous. And that just because we have carved out an approach to knowledge production that is, at times, experimental does not undermine the validity of the work.

CARLY: My first thought is that having this conversation in writing is going to be so fun! My second thought was a joke: Good thing we know queer critiques of "coming out" or we'd all be failures! My third thought is more serious: the degree to which your relationships with your interlocutors inform your approach to (not) discussing what you're up to. You both describe your approach to inviting your friends as casual and low-key, although Rayn, you also noted that your friends' academic interests informed how you framed your invitations. And Cat, you note that, essentially, you expect your friends to attend because they are your friends and you are asking them to. I get that. Friends show up for each other. I'm wondering how your friends' attendance impacts your feelings about the art nights? A couple of questions to this effect: **How did the art nights feel? How did it feel to participate/chat/make art that extended queer theoretical ideas? Did the events feel like a failure or a success?**

RAYN: To conceptualize these art nights in terms of success or not success is an interesting thing. Do I think we were successful? Well, if our goal was to simply have a collection of images at the end of this endeavor, then, yes, I might say we were successful. Over the course of these art nights, I found myself constantly reassessing and reconceptualizing what the point of them really was. At the beginning, when we first considered the project, Dr. Thomsen was interested in the potential of art to circulate queer theoretical ideas. In looking at the images produced, I cannot really imagine them circulating en masse. Perhaps, this is a failure. Yet, when I look at them, I cannot help but feel a profound fondness and deep admiration as these images are representative of important experiences and people in my life. In this regard, I would consider these art nights extremely successful. The success of the art nights feels most apparent when I consider them in relation to the things they produced that are non-material. I think about this often in relation to my own artistic practice and even my academic work. This environment prioritizes the *thing* which is produced. In conversations with my art professors, they often bemoan students' hyperfixation on product over process. They say that students' preoccupation with a "good," an "A-worthy," final project often leads to avoiding taking artistic risks. Their bigger concern, it seems, is students' aversion to failure.

There is a tendency to believe that the art object can be entirely representative of the process. The belief that the object can capture one's alleged learning. However, this is often not the case. More often than not, the final product obscures much of the process behind the thing. An outsider cannot, of course, see the conversations and moments of bonding that exist behind the scenes of the art produced during art nights. Maybe this is a shame. That you all can never really see what I see in this work. But this fact, I hope, will urge you to try it out for yourselves. You say you're not an artist? Well, I'd make the argument, after this experience, that an artist is just someone who cares enough to endure and engage in the artistic process. Who cares what you produce. . . . Go on and fail a little bit.

CAT: I agree with you, Rayn, that there are certain criteria by which the art nights can be considered a roaring success. For example, based on what you wrote on low theory, Dr. Thomsen, I agree that our art can be considered a successful answer to a Halberstamian call to fail, in that we didn't, like, make a Mona Lisa or monetize this idea and make a million dollars. The art nights were kind of bad in that they didn't produce anything groundbreaking. That being said, I will happily accept queer theory's offer to see the art nights as successful! What definition of success wouldn't include "most people had a fun time?" I certainly had fun. I think one of the best parts of the art nights, something I also felt when we made the game, was that we made topics that are serious silly without making fun of them. We twisted ideas until they were goofy, lighthearted, and tongue-in-cheek but also completely text-informed. The art adds an unexpected dimension to the text. I'm thinking of "In Defense of the Poor Image," in which Hito Steyerl suggests that poor images are pirated and reproduced and changed a little bit by everyone who touches them.[10] Our art pieces were perhaps just poor images of the original text, but each one includes someone's personal touch, making a new thing.

People also made very beautiful pieces that were not silly at all, and that, too, fed into our success. People created things that made you look back at the text and go "huh," such as Sophie's "What's Left Unsaid" collage that recreates End Fake Clinics' poster. Other pieces provided clear visual interpretations of the text. I think any art at all is a sweeter treat than no art. So, I'm inclined to say that the fact that art was created makes this a success.

CARLY: Your beautiful reflections remind me why I love working with students and also suggest that, perhaps, my original questions were themselves a failure—but a queer one in that they generated thoughts that encouraged me to reflect on why I thought success or failure might be useful analytics for thinking through the queer art nights and their queer products. I'm realizing that my questions likely say more about my engagement with queer theory, and how deeply it has informed my life, than anything else. I have found inspiration in Jack Halberstam's *The Queer Art of Failure* since it was published more than a decade ago.[11] It has helped me to think through the usefulness of *In Plain Sight*, an unconventional (and, at times, even aesthetically displeasing) film I produced in conjunction with publishing my first book, *Visibility Interrupted: Rural Queer Life and the Politics of Unbecoming*. It has encouraged me to implement new epistemological approaches for which there isn't a manual. I don't know, for instance, of another book that came to exist quite like this one, where students read chapters, gave feedback, and produced art alongside it being written. It has also inspired me to be bolder pedagogically. I stopped assigning final research papers in most of my classes, and instead, as you both know, students in my courses now create board games that translate arguments into a playable format. When we aren't trying to achieve conventional forms of success and aren't afraid to fail, Jack Halberstam argues, new possibilities for imagining how to live our lives can open up. We can fail our way into feminist and queer existence and I have tried to do that, in part, through teaching and research.

In many ways, the queer art nights and the art produced therein are interesting sites for thinking about queer failure and success. Your answers raise questions regarding the relationships among success, scale, and quality. If, you both suggest, the scale of the circulation of the queer theoretical ideas you discussed was not grand or if the art produced was not groundbreaking, then the events were, perhaps, a failure. I think otherwise. I think the art nights were a success because they inspired people to engage queer theory and apply it to commonsensical ideas about reproductive justice. Those people were you and me and people in our networks! If this approach were to grow, if in other words, you two were facilitating art nights with people who you did not know, they likely would have been decidedly less fun and you would feel less admiration and fondness for the art produced. Perhaps this would have been a failure? So, rest assured, you were queerly successful, or queer failures, whatever you prefer. ;)

I wonder how your answers to my questions about how the art nights felt would have differed if I had not asked about success and failure. How would you answer the first two questions I asked: **How did the art nights feel? How did it feel to participate/chat/make art? And I want to add another one: What adjectives would you use to describe the art nights, the art, and/or the game?**

CAT: Some adjectives I would use to describe the art nights: goofy, relaxed, charmingly awkward, and self-reflective.

In looking for inspiration to help me answer this question, I turned to Ursula Le Guin's essay "The Carrier Bag Theory of Fiction," which Rayn sent to us because she thought it would be useful for thinking about the art nights. Le Guin writes about how bags and sacks are a very human accessory; she says that there is something distinctly human about putting something you like into a bag or sack or bit of rolled bark for later, when you can take it out, share it, or enjoy it yourself. Le Guin compares her own science fiction novels to bags, writing that they are: "Full of beginnings without ends, of initiations, of losses, of transformations and translations, and far more tricks than conflicts, far fewer triumphs than snares and delusions; full of space ships that get stuck, missions that fail, and people who don't understand."[12] Where Le Guin's novels are bags full of messy plots and storylines, our Google Drive folder is like a bag full of bags that is a companion to a bag of ideas (this book)—a messy archive, if you will—a bag holding mismatched academic language, bendy arms, squiggly lines, collages, watercolors, redrawn ink, little bits of writing. And then, if you zoom out to all the work we do as a research team, there are so many bags there, too. Talk about beginnings without ends! We have so many ideas, some that don't go anywhere. The Queer Artists' Collective was a bag that we opened up and managed to fill. So a fifth adjective might be "bag-ish" or "sack-like."

I just read Octavia Butler's short story "Bloodchild," and one of the little blurbs on the back cover describes the story as "set forth in calm, lucid prose with never a word wasted."[13] It stuck out to me because that was my impression, too: every sentence carefully in service of plot development. In contrast to this characterization of Butler's writing, I notice, is the bag of things that Le Guin describes. I think our art nights are more akin to Le Guin's "bag" than Butler's "never a word wasted." If I wanted to really follow this line of thinking, I would even say that we were waste*ful*, decadent, with our extravagant squiggles and overall conceit—who ever heard of students creating art to accompany an academic text! But maybe calling the art nights "wasteful" would be pushing it. They were mostly very sweet!

RAYN: Cat, I am glad the Le Guin reading resonated with you. A studio art professor assigned it and it changed the way I think about what it means to be an artist or a producer. According to Le Guin, the notion of being a creator is wrapped up in narratives of the heroic. A narrative that, of course, is very linear and concerned with product. This narrative is so pervasive, inescapable really, that I often find myself assessing my own work in terms of success and failure—even when I don't want to.

I also think success and failure, in relation to the art nights, map onto questions of use and transgression. That is to say, through the process I found myself assessing the work we were doing in terms of its potential political usefulness via transgression. And it becomes quite difficult to separate those feelings from my memory of the art nights. This is often the case when I am dealing with a subject that is serious or has implications outside of the immediacy of my little universe. In these situations, I want my work to be doing something, to be going somewhere. If I am being honest, I want it to be going forward. I want it to be linear, progressing towards something. In these moments I am confronted with the fact that my relationship to work and art is in opposition to my politics. I want to take seriously the value of not taking things so seriously. I want to treat things more like bags. To use Cat's new adjective, I want my work to be more bag-ish. I think these art nights helped me feel like I am getting closer to achieving that.

CARLY: Rayn, you mentioned transgression and use, and that one of the transgressive or useful potentials of the art nights may have been in their asking you to not take things so seriously. I'm struck that the adjectives Cat connected to the art nights, aside from self-reflective, are decidedly anti-serious: goofy, awkward, sacks full of squiggles. But at the same time, my approach to working with students is rooted in taking seriously your ideas and what you bring to the table that I simply do not. Doing so is actually pretty transgressive, at least in terms of how academic scholarship is typically produced and circulated. I'm struck here by our differential relationships to the relationship between seriousness and transgression. The long history of drag, camp, and kitsch within queer subcultures makes clear that transgression can be enabled by not taking things so seriously. But queer theorists also make the case that taking seriously that which typically isn't can also open up possibilities. I'm interested in thinking through this paradox with you!

CAT: I like the idea of taking the wrong thing seriously. It reminds me of a line from this reality show *Vanderpump Rules*, in which one character,

Ariana, feels slighted by another character's appearance in a video sketch, and retorts, to snickers from other characters, that she "[takes] sketch comedy very seriously."[14] My equivalent would be that I took creating Cards for Queering Reproductive Justice very seriously; though it is a ridiculous game, I wanted it to be really fun and clever. I'll also say that it feels good to toe this line between seriousness and silliness, and it feels good to be taken seriously about something silly and to laugh about something serious. I, too, wonder about the transgression question, though. The more I think about transgression the less I can parse what it is—I feel like I'm better at declaring things *not* transgressive. Rayn, what do you think?

RAYN: Laura Kipnis discusses the paradoxes in how we think of transgression today, noting that in the avant garde art world, where transgression was more embraced than in other areas of life, acts considered transgressive have long had institutional backing. For instance, the Salon Des Refuses, which translates to "exhibition of rejects," was an exhibition of art rejected by the jury of the official Paris Salon. Sounds cool and transgressive, right? Well, let's not forget that this exhibition was sponsored and sanctioned by Emperor Napoleon III himself. Hmmm, state sanctioned transgression . . . isn't that an oxymoron? Kipnis concludes that "there's always a certain complicity between the transgressive and the covertly permitted."[15] This is a fact I am often hung up on. Can anything I do at a small liberal arts college be truly transgressive? I mean, outside of dropping out, can you really think of anything? But this thought hinges on an absolute definition of transgression. The idea that something is either transgressive or not. I find Transgression, as a concept, is more helpful as a metric for assessing the ways our actions are simultaneously transgressive and not transgressive and what this reveals about transgression as an act that is spatially and temporally constituted. Rules aren't applied uniformly and therefore what constitutes transgression isn't either. Can you know transgression as you are doing it? Or better yet, if you do transgression and no one sees it, is it even transgression? What does this reveal about the relationship between transgression, art, and visibility?

CARLY: This is a great series of questions, Rayn! I would love to hear your responses to yourself. I also love that you pull in Kipnis here because it points to another piece of our process. [Reminder to reader: An incredibly generative component of writing this book included reading texts alongside some of my research assistants, with whom I then discussed the ideas of the text in question and its relationship to the arguments in this book. A queer classroom, if you will. Laura Kipnis's essay on transgression was one text we read and discussed.] In her telling of the contemporary history of transgression, Kipnis laments transgression's death on the political left. Kipnis argues that liberals and leftists have increasingly moved toward political correctness, respectability politics, and claiming injury. Today, transgression, Kipnis says, is happening on the political right. (Yes, you read that right.)

> These days it's the *transgressed-upon* who are the protagonists of the moment: the *offended*, people who are *very upset* by things. . . . And the mainstream cultural institutions are, on the whole, deferring, offering solace and apologias, posting warning signs and caveats to what might cause aesthetic injury. Aesthetic injuries flourish nonetheless. Sure, there have always been offended people, but those people used to be conservatives. Who cared if they were offended, that was the point. What has changed is the social composition of the offended groups. At some point offendability moved its offices to the hip side of town. The offended people say they're progressives! Which requires some rethinking for those of us shaped by the politics of the previous ethos.[16]

If transgression—characterized by crass rebuking of rigidity that could allow for the disruption of both the social order and one's own sensibilities—is dead, can we possibly hold onto its potentials for leftist queer politics? Kipnis says no. "Transgression has been replaced by trauma as the cultural concept of the hour: making rules rather than breaking them has become the signature aesthetic move, that's just how it is, there's no going back. New historical actors have taken up places on the social stage and made their bids for cultural hegemony, having sent the old ones to re-education camp."[17] It is precisely Kipnis's refusal to give a shit about whether she is seen as someone who needs to be sent to re-education camp that I find so refreshing. So transgressive even. Perhaps ironically, Kipnis's analyses remind me of the "wonderful political optimism" that can emerge when we believe in "the possibility of smashing everything, [our] own boundaries included."[18]

Kipnis's insights inspire some additional questions through which to consider the art nights and conversations and art that emerged through them: **Did creating queer-theory-informed art or discussing queer-theory-in-progress with your friends feel transgressive? Was there any element of smashing anything involved?**

RAYN: To feel so bound and obligated to adhere to notions of transgression feels a little *untransgressive*. I believe, as Cat mentioned earlier, there is merit in letting go and figuring out what it all means after the fact. An image is nothing without its context anyway. So here we are giving it context.

When we were having these art nights, I cannot recall feeling that we were doing something transgressive. The joke of the art night was often that we were changing the world by translating queer theory into bad art that maybe no one outside of the Collective would ever see. The scale of the events also made it hard to feel that the work we were doing was transgressive in a way that was significant. In re-reading what I had to say about the success of these art nights above, it now feels apparent to me that there is a relationship here between success and transgression. In my discussion of success, I was arguing for the merits of process and the inevitability of failure in terms of product. I think this is interesting to consider in relation to transgression. What would it mean to consider transgression in relation to *process*? To consider transgression not as a singular point or product but as something that is processual?

As Dr. Thomsen noted, for Kipnis, another characteristic of transgressive acts is that they imply a degree of offensiveness and discomfort on the part of the viewer or those present. I cannot say that we made anyone uncomfortable. And, as is characteristic of the ultra-woke liberal arts students we are, we tried very hard not to offend anyone. But as participants noted, there is a degree of discomfort in putting oneself out there. Most of the art night participants don't consider themselves artists and the prospect of making art in a group was intimidating. I want to push back on Kipnis's argument slightly and argue for the value of making people comfortable. Or at least to expand upon her argument by making a case that transgression can be created out of comfort.

Outside my work with Dr. Thomsen and the Queer Artists' Collective, I also am the general manager at the college radio station and serve on the organizing board for the college's student-run arts festival. Both organizations are marked historically by an aesthetic code that denotes insiderness or outsiderness (like punks but more establishment, more college-sanctioned transgression). Much of the work within these groups has been centered on dissolving those, let's say, identity-based lines of division and working towards finding people who are genuinely interested in and excited by the groups' projects. Across lines of "difference" there is a deep engagement in a collective project. And this has been achieved by making people comfortable, by *not* offending. Yes, perhaps I wish we were not all offended so easily, but alas this, as Kipnis points out, is the cultural moment in which we find ourselves. And while we can wish for a time when offensive art and humor was king, it seems more helpful to consider how transgression is possible within this cultural moment?

CAT: In reading Rayn's thoughts about Kipnis's reflections on transgression and its requisite making people uncomfortable, I find myself thinking "I really don't want to do that!" I don't want anyone to feel uncomfortable, even though I know that this is an impossible ideal to uphold. At the very least, I don't want people with me in a warm and intimate setting to feel uncomfortable. I want, say, Republicans to feel uncomfortable, of course, but I'm not at queer art night with them, and probably if I was, I'd be nice to them because I'm wimpy.

My ideal level of transgression is like, slight impishness. I agree with you, Rayn, that there are few things one can do at a liberal arts college that are genuinely transgressive, but I do think there is plenty of opportunity for mischief. While I'm not sure that the art nights were transgressive, they were very mischievous—a bunch of research assistants and their friends slipping onto Zoom under the cover of darkness to discuss queer theory and make paintings, collages, and pastel pieces. And getting paid by the college to do so! Getting paid for our conversations and our gossip, while we create. I don't think that we can, in good faith, give ourselves a cookie for subverting all norms and shocking the world with our queer art, *but* I will give us a little cookie for mischief.

CARLY: Cookies for you, and your friends too! In fact, your friends and friendships come up in many of your reflections on transgression, affect, use, and process. I'm wondering if you have reflected on the Queer Art Nights with your friends? **What do you think your friends and fellow participants got out of the art nights?**

CAT: Something I learned from my friends through these art nights is a heightened willingness to show up for random stuff. I've said this in so many ways throughout this roundtable, but sometimes just being with your friend makes the night a success. Another thing I got out of these art nights is a renewal of my desire to make art. It's also sweet to think of these art nights as a little treat to the attendee, especially those who commented that they would make more art if they had the time.

RAYN: Cat's reflections on what she learned from the art nights feel true for me too, and I would imagine for other participants. I like the idea of the art nights teaching a "heightened willingness to show up for random stuff." And as Cat mentioned, I also think the art nights illuminated the communicative potentials of art—particularly to those who didn't consider themselves artists. Perhaps especially for activism. Most of my peers have one vision of what activism looks like: protesting. This sensibility strikes me as rigid and ignores the potential for other forms of activism that involve creative practice.

Recently I have been thinking about the way people talk about the political Instagram graphics that took off during the Black Lives Matter protests. Now, at demonstrations and protests speakers feel the need to say "we need to do more than share graphics on social media." I have no interest in commenting on the efficacy of Instagram graphics as an activist tool. But the common critique among my peers of this kind of political engagement is that social media overly aestheticizes "serious issues." There are many reasons to be critical of digital activism, but I find this fear of the power of aesthetics misses the mark and ignores the powerful ways in which social movements have used art throughout history . . . they're called political cartoons for a reason! So, I hope these art nights showed participants that aesthetics are integral to activism, or any social movement for that matter. But I am just assuming. . . . So why don't we just ask them?! We did just that, and asked participants to reflect on why they decided to come to the art nights. Their responses to this question were a little bit snarky and really boiled down to "because you asked me to." This has less to do with what they learned, but it is exciting to reflect on as an organizer: People will show up to things just because you asked them to. There is hope!

We also asked participants: "How did you feel during the art nights? After?" Almost all of the respondents commented on the awkwardness of the virtual art nights. I am trying not to feel offended. I am trying to reconfigure the awkward as productive. However, my favorite participant reflection came from Chris: "I was a little confused what the point of it was." This tickled me because *during* the art nights I too found myself in a state of "what's the point?" or "why does it matter?" In the moment it can be hard to see the forest and easy to hyper-focus on the tree. However, after the fact when we zoom out it becomes much easier to see why this all matters. And feel, as Chris did, "glad that I was part of a community that organized things like this." Allegra, too, reflected on feeling gratitude for getting "to be part of a community that values pushing each other, patience as we all learn in different ways, laughing, and creating (whether ideas or art)." Allegra graduated a year before attending the art night and, as a soon-to-be graduate myself, I was interested in her responses from the outside. Allegra reflected on how she missed getting to read and discuss articles like she did in the classroom, which made me consider what it would be like to start a queer art group once I graduate.

Reading participants' responses brought me back to the first art nights, when we discussed the End Fake Clinics chapter. During these art nights our conversations centered around affective attachments and our own queer kinship networks. Similarly, many of the participants commented on the way the art nights reaffirmed bonds among participants.

CAT: Rayn, I too laughed when I read Chris's note that he was "a little confused what the point of it was." What a great sentence that reflects perfectly what we've been thinking through in this roundtable, about queer failure and use. While we have reflected primarily on the awkwardness of the art nights, many people genuinely enjoyed the experience. Adjectives attendees used were "joyful," "contemplative," "fun," "energizing," "experimental," "open," "silly," "relaxed," "comical," and "generative." Haegen said that they "learned more about reproductive justice through conversation." Sophie said that she learned that she is "more capable of conceptualizing queer theory in artistic terms than [she] had imagined!" Allegra reflected on her experience: "I was engaged, had fun, loved reflecting on my time in the play and in our class . . . it was useful in that it allowed me to re-emerge into the discussion and put on my 'analysis hat' that I am trying to wear more in my everyday life." Zach said it "felt like a valuable experience to think through visualizing arguments that are at times confusing and overly intellectual." Ultimately, everyone had something kind to say.

I loved reading people's reflections on the art nights. As a voyeuristic snoop, it's such a treat to get to know what someone is thinking under the guise of "collecting responses for the concluding chapter of *Reproductive Justice, Queerly*." It's a two-way window, though, as revealed by Haegan: "I think the nights were useful to me. I got to see what my friends were working on, because they often bring up this work in conversation." It's now occurring to me that it's lovely to bring people into our little subworlds—our Dr. Thomsen research assistant world—so that they can see what we're up to firsthand. And like Rayn touched on, people feel closer to each other once they've come across one another in different settings. Like, you can go to ballet class with the same person for ten years, but there's only so much you can find out within the context of a ballet class, if that's the only place you've encountered each other. Each new place you meet someone opens up a new facet. I suppose I'm saying that I think people know the members of the research team a little better having witnessed us in this odd context, and that's something!

RAYN: Cat, that has to be the corniest way you could have possibly ended that response. So on the note of corny endings, there is one last thing I want to share in what feels like the closing of this chapter. I just want to say how fucking cool it is to have had the opportunity to work on this project. In this conversation, we have reflected on the queer nature of this book in terms of the art nights as a site of queer knowledge production, but we gave hardly any airtime to the fact that the ideas of undergrads are being taken seriously in an academic text. Don't get me wrong, I think my fellow research assistants and I are amazing and brilliant and deserve to be taken seriously. But I did want to thank Dr. Thomsen, and perhaps hear her reflect on the matter, for continually taking our ideas seriously. I would also be interested to hear from Cat on her feelings about what it has been like to contribute to this book.

CAT: Raynie, don't get too sentimental! I agree, though, of course. I wasn't there for the conception of the art night idea, but it has been the treat of all treats to ride this idea out. Not to add another question, but I'd love to hear the story of how you came up with the idea of the art nights.

CARLY: As we wrap up these reflections on the place of art in queering reproductive justice, I love that Cat is asking us to reach back to the beginning, to think about conception, and that Rayn is asking for deeper reflections on possibilities for queering knowledge production! How fitting. In many ways, taking seriously students' skills and ideas was central to the project's conception and birth (okay, I'll stop with the reproductive metaphors now). It was the summer of 2020. I had just finished my first book and I was heading into sabbatical when I received the invitation to write this book. As I worked to conceptualize the book's contours, I knew I wanted it to be as queer in form as it is in content, to play with the extent to which queering form can result in queering knowledge.

As you both know, I have some experience doing so in other settings. In addition to making the film to accompany my first book, I also use game-making to teach feminist and queer theory. In fact, both of you have made games in my courses. And Rayn was a key member of the research team that developed The Games Project website. I have witnessed the benefits of playing—quite literally—with theory, both for students in my classes as well as their friends who come to our class game nights where we play students' games. So, I had a template from which I could draw in terms of thinking about possibilities for creating a game to accompany this book. But, beyond that, I really wasn't sure how to queerly create something academic and in such a way that its final form reflects, at least to some degree, this queerness. So, I brought this vague idea to my summer 2020 research team, to which Rayn was key. We brainstormed collectively. And developing a student-led artists' collective, through which students could make art and talk queer theory on their own terms, emerged as the winning idea. What's not to take seriously about your students banishing you from your own project?!

All jokes aside, I'm a professor because I enjoy working with students and I believe in the power of feminist and queer ideas for changing the social order, or at the very least, our relationship to it. Working with students as collaborators seems like the logical outgrowth of both. But I want to make clear that I don't take every student's ideas seriously, and I don't take all ideas that students have seriously. And I refuse to act like I do. I'm not interested in occupying the kind of maternal subject position that women professors are still too often expected to occupy, wherein we must perform concern for our students' *feelings*, one part of which is acting as if all of their ideas are good ones. They are not. The dark side of acting as if all ideas are good ideas or that all feelings are legitimate is that those ideas and feelings are rarely questioned, rarely poked and prodded, especially if they appear to be rooted in vulnerability. This approach renders students' feelings more important than disrupting their bad—read: dangerous—ideas. All ideas and all feelings are not worthy of engagement. But the even darker side is this: Professors' discomfort with pushing back on students' ideas and students' discomfort with critique makes true collaboration between students and faculty impossible. It is precisely my refusal to view students as incapable of hearing critique, of being pushed, that enables our collaboration. Our work together involves asking critical questions of one another. That's part of the fun. Beyond this, taking your ideas seriously—as worthy of critique—is another way through which I refuse to occupy a maternal subject position.

This is a very different approach to thinking about how faculty ought to work with students than we typically get in academic settings, which frame students as vulnerable and fragile, always at risk, in danger, in need of care. I refuse these ideas, which effectively position students as children and faculty as parental figures. The irony here is that I am a feminist and queer theorist who swears a lot, loves scotch, and seeks to sever the maternal from the positive affects that circulate around it. I work against the gendered ideologies that animate assumptions about who ought to care and how. My job is not to protect you. My job is to support you as you take intellectual risks, to encourage you to do so to the degree that you dream and fail bigger than you could have without the feminist and queer theory we engage together, and to help you craft a sturdy toolbox for taking feminist and queer theory into a world that is less hospitable to it than the worlds we live in together while you are a student. I don't take your ideas seriously out of some paternalistic neoliberal imperative to make you feel good. Far from it. I take your ideas seriously because—and when—they are full of joy and wonder and power. I take your ideas seriously because—and when—they inspire and excite me. I take your ideas seriously because—and when—they transform my own into something that is otherwise impossible.

There is a mutuality here that reminds me of how acclaimed feminist artist and cultural critic Carmen Winant talks about her photographic installations. Winant's exhibition, *the last safe abortion*, displayed at the Whitney Biennial, features nearly three thousand photos of abortion clinics across the United States, most of which came from the archives of clinics and some of which are Winant's original photos. Fellow photographer Alice Zoo reflects on this piece of work in relation to Winant's oeuvre, noting that her "feminist vision of photography" makes clear that the medium can be "an act of care, of maintenance, of guardianship and partnership. The act of taking these photographs, the act of keeping and preserving them by the clinics, Winant's own warm and careful stewarding and curation—all of these are undertakings grounded in generous mutuality."[19] I see this same "generous mutuality" in the queer art nights as well as our reflections on them here.

Further, I see the queer art nights, and to a lesser degree, game nights as evidence for what can emerge when we approach knowledge production queerly. That is, the ideas that we came up with in conversation *together* led to the project taking this wacky queer form. On this point, I draw inspiration from Laura Perez, who notes, "Form is not mere surface to me. . . . Form is a language in and of itself. It is the walk of the talk."[20] I want to close by thanking you both for reflecting here with me on the language of this project, the potentials we actualized, and the fun we had. Thank you for working with me to create the walk to this book's talk. Above all, thank you for helping me hold onto the belief that animates *Reproductive Justice, Queerly*: Other reproductive horizons are possible and playing with queer theory can help us imagine and actualize them.

# Epilogue

## ONWARD, QUEERLY: ART EXHIBITIONS AND MINI GOLF

I've been thinking a lot lately about what resistance *looks like*, especially in this moment. I mean this question quite literally. What would our resistance look like if we thought more about aesthetics? What new kinds of resistance might emerge if aesthetics were central to our very conceptualization of reproductive resistance? While scholars have talked at length about reproductive health, rights, and justice in terms of ethics, literature, politics, religion, public health, media, and history, very little work on reproduction focuses specifically on aesthetics. What can happen to our art, our politics, and our feminism when the creation of cultural texts becomes our way of *doing something* politically? What are the aesthetics that make our *doing* reproductive justice sing? These questions are in many ways inspired by a question that feminist artist Carmen Winant asks in *Notes on Fundamental Joy*: Does hope have an aesthetic?[1]

I admit that I desperately want to end on a hopeful note, to feel hope. In this moment, hopefulness is unlikely to come to us through policy or the courts, at least on a federal level. But I see reasons to be hopeful all around us. Activists connected to abortion funds continue to raise money to financially support those needing abortions, despite the increased difficulty of this task as travel distances, and therefore costs, continue to increase. Activists continue to send abortion pills across state and national lines, ensuring that people in ban states and countries can get abortions.[2] Activists are working to regulate crisis pregnancy centers to a degree that has never existed before. Activists are working to ensure that the resources crisis pregnancy centers claim to provide, such as free ultrasounds, maternity clothes, and necessities for babies, are available at places where clients won't be subject to antiabortion propaganda. Activists are making all kinds of art about all kinds of reproductive issues that pushes back against dominant ways of thinking about gender and reproduction. There are so many reasons to be hopeful.

By way of wrapping up, I want to share two different public humanities projects that emerged out of my desire to approach reproductive justice queerly, both of which, I think, suggest that the answer to Carmen Winant's aforementioned question is a resounding YES.

In 2022 and 2023, I facilitated two Public Feminism Labs, which generated art for reproductive justice exhibitions, and I led the creation of a mini golf course where creators and players learned about reproductive justice. These projects took place at three different moments in what, I imagine, we will remember as the single most tumultuous year in the history of abortion rights. One Public Feminism Lab, at the Gender Institute for Teaching and Advocacy at Metropolitan State University in Denver, took place when we were anticipating the overturning of *Roe*. The second Public Feminism Lab, at Middlebury College, transpired at exactly the same moment as the Supreme Court's *Dobbs* decision was made public. And Reproductive Justice Mini Golf debuted less than a year into this new post-*Roe* reality. Central to these projects, the groundwork for which I had developed over the course of a few years prior to the *Dobbs* decision, was the premise that abortion justice activism should be joyful, pleasurable, and fun. As such, my collaborators and I spent a great deal of time discussing how art can be a vehicle for generating these feelings. Through the anger, desperation, rage, and mourning we felt in the moment that *Roe* was overturned and after, we kept showing up, talking, and making art. Through this process, we came to believe the new post-*Roe* political landscape actually requires that we take *more seriously* the political potential of feminist art as well as the joyful affects it can generate.

These reflections are deeply inspired by J Finley, whose work on Black women's deployments of sass demonstrates the degree to which comedy can be a site through which Black women assert their humanity, resist dehumanization, and challenge power structures.[3] Just as generating humor can serve as a vital site of liberation, pleasure, and political critique, so, too, can the collective creation of art and the curating of related public exhibitions. In what follows, I first describe the contours of the Public Feminism Labs, focusing on the lab at Middlebury College, and then turn to the mini golf course.

## PUBLIC FEMINISM LABS

The Public Feminism Lab consisted primarily of three things: reading texts helpful for thinking about crisis pregnancy centers and reproductive justice; meeting to discuss those texts; and translating our conversations into art. The idea for this approach grew out of the queer art nights discussed in this book's Conclusion. What, I wondered, would happen to our art and conversations about reproductive justice if the creation and discussion occurred in more sustained ways? To begin to answer this question, I secured funding, created a call for student applicants, sent it out, and worked with colleagues to review applications and select fellows. All fellows were Middlebury College students, who collectively occupied a diverse range of social locations: Black, Brown, and white students; women, transgender, and nonbinary students; students with disabilities and chronic health issues and those without; LGBTQ+ and heterosexual students; and students who grew up in various geographic locations and classed situations. Fellows, who were paid stipends through the gender studies department, had varying degrees of experience with both the academic field of gender studies and also creating art; some were feminist-identified art majors who had little prior involvement with gender studies, while others were gender studies majors who did not consider themselves artists. The group's diversity in terms of life experiences and intellectual and artistic training informed our conversations, as well as the art that emerged out of them.

One especially generative aspect of the lab was that our discussion of academic work on reproductive justice was never separate from our production of art about reproductive justice. In fact, our readings gave us precise language to discuss fellows' art in progress. Meetings began with students presenting art they had created since our last gathering and engaging their peers' responses to it, a process that allowed each artist to strengthen and transform their art. Ultimately, the fellows produced more than fifty original pieces of art, spanning a variety of mediums: sculpture, acrylic paint on canvas, photography, collage, embroidery, 3D installations, film, AI-generated imagery, watercolor, and graphic design. All art was accompanied by a developed artist's statement that included ideas about reproductive justice, abortion, and crisis pregnancy centers we had addressed throughout the lab. Our desire was to create an exhibition that could speak to people who are unsure how they feel about abortion as well as those who see themselves as ardent supporters of reproductive justice. As it turns out, neither group is likely to know much about crisis pregnancy centers.

To our great surprise, more than 250 people—at this small liberal arts college with a student body of approximately 2,500—showed up for the opening event of "Visualizing Reproductive Justice: A Call to End Fake Clinics," a number that far exceeds attendance at the vast majority of campus events, including the various events focused on reproductive justice that took place right around the same time as the exhibit opening. The success of our exhibit speaks to the galvanizing nature of art, and therefore, its usefulness for reproductive justice activism. The exhibit did more to create buzz about crisis pregnancy centers on campus and in the broader community than many of the things my students and I had done over the course of my eight years at Middlebury College—including teaching about crisis pregnancy centers in my classes, publishing my research on crisis pregnancy centers (including in some high profile venues such as the *New York Times*), writing op-eds in the campus newspaper, and protesting the local crisis pregnancy center's involvement at an annual student activities fair. The director of the nearby crisis pregnancy center attended the exhibit's opening event and later penned an op-ed in the local paper declaring that the exhibit misrepresented their work. Someone stole a piece of art in the exhibit, and after a fellow used the YikYak app to ask for information about the missing art, the art was anonymously returned, creating quite a stir. The student newspaper covered the exhibit's opening event. Several professors across various departments brought their classes to the opening exhibit event and related academic talk on the world-building power of feminist and queer aesthetics. In the weeks leading up to the exhibit opening, I gave a public presentation on campus about crisis pregnancy centers, two student fellows and I gave a guest lecture on the topic in a public health class, and fellows tabled multiple times. One fellow led the most well-coordinated, well-attended, and well-covered student protest of the local crisis pregnancy center at the campus student activities fair to date. Energy, excitement, and interest was high. And the calls and emails I received from the campus communications office and members of the college administration suggest that so, too, was anxiety.

I see the exhibit's success as enabled by past anti–crisis pregnancy center organizing on campus and as enabling future action. To ensure that our exhibit was a means rather than an end, so to speak, we took several steps: We created a digital version of the exhibit, which is housed on the Center for Public Feminism website.[4] We worked with the Archives of Dissent, a digital archive of campus-based feminist activism, to archive anti–crisis pregnancy center organizing on campus. During her participation in the lab, one fellow founded a coalition to work across New England liberal arts colleges to ban crisis pregnancy centers from campuses. Perhaps most notably, we invited Ruth Hardy, a Vermont state representative, to the exhibit opening, and she not only attended but expressed her commitment to introducing legislation to regulate crisis pregnancy centers in Vermont. She also followed through. Just a few months later, in February 2023, I testified in support of legislation that would both protect gender-affirming care and regulate crisis pregnancy centers in Vermont.

There are many possible takeaways from this brief description of the Public Feminism Lab and our related public humanities installation, but we don't need to get fancy here. Suffice it to say that an art exhibition is rarely just an art exhibition.

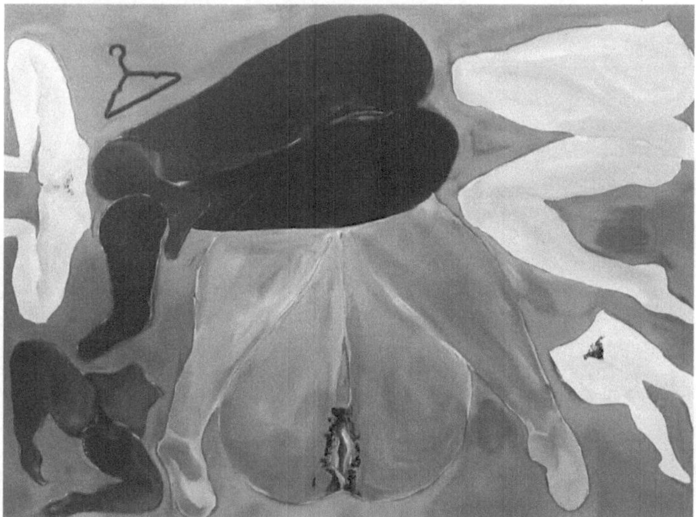

*Positions*, art by Isabel Perez-Martin.

*Positions*, Isabel Perez-Martin

"Positions" explores the link between safety and abortion. CPCs exaggerate the risks of legal abortion and fabricate nonexistent dangers. At the same time, making abortion illegal makes the procedure riskier. First, when abortion is illegal, people are more likely to travel for the procedure, something that increases its costs and, therefore, pushes people who need to raise funds to cover these costs further into their pregnancies, leading to later-term—and riskier—abortions. Second, making abortion illegal means that people are more likely to be pushed to self-abort or use other unsafe methods, including physical exertion, incorrect pills, special herbs, and foreign objects. These approaches can cause extreme pain and discomfort, represented here by the abortive patients' legs in different positions and the red bloody background.

*To Be Seen as a Woman*, art by Alexis Welch.

*To Be Seen as a Woman,* Alexis Welch

While learning about CPCs, I began feeling alien in my own skin—unsure who had the capacity to make decisions on behalf of my body and others'. The rhetoric used by CPCs is scary, guilt-inducing, and deceiving. It is also absurd. In this work, I wanted to reclaim that alien feeling, something I do through illustrating the absurd ways that CPCs approach women's bodies.

*Regulated or Unregulated?*, art by Emily Ribeiro.

*Regulated or Unregulated?*, Emily Ribeiro

How should we think about the role of the state in our lives, especially when trigger laws—which outlawed abortion in any state that had one once *Roe* was overturned—are going into effect left and right? As I processed, grieved, and acted in the wake of *Roe v. Wade*'s reversal, I thought about the hypocrisy of regulation. CPCs are completely unregulated, which is part of what makes them so dangerous. On the other hand, abortion clinics are highly regulated, and these regulations harm hundreds of thousands of women annually. We live in a country where women's bodies are more regulated than guns. In this quadriptych, I highlight the absurdity of current abortion regulations. The CPC and gun industries both cause danger to those who come into contact with them, are primarily funded by wealthy white men, and benefit from regulatory loopholes that make restricting their harms difficult. I represented the CPC and the abortion clinic with the same image because CPCs disguise themselves as abortion clinics on the outside, so visitors are unaware of what they are walking into. The color of the clinic is inspired by the Pink House in Mississippi, the last clinic open in the state before *Roe v. Wade* was overturned.

## QUEERING MINI GOLF

The following semester, spring 2023, I built, quite literally, on the model we crafted through the Public Feminism Labs as I developed a one-of-a-kind and, I think, very queer approach to reproductive justice: the world's first and only feminist reproductive justice mini golf course. Housed in a hockey rink unused during the summer months, Reproductive Justice Mini Golf consisted of eleven holes. Each focused on a different topic and was built to gesture to where the issues associated with that topic play out in the real world. Topics included: history of science and medicine (a hospital); contraception (a church); care work (a kitchen); surrogacy (a baby's nursery and living room); sex education (a classroom); crisis pregnancy centers and abortion (a crisis pregnancy center and abortion clinic); transportation (a series of intersections on a map); environmental concerns (a court house); foster care (a bedroom of a child in the foster care system); incarceration (a prison); and reproductive justice organizing and activism (a bar). Players reported that this approach helped them to see how reproductive injustices occur in everyday spaces.

At each hole, players were greeted by a feminist pin-up style dinosaur holding a placard with text about the topic that hole explored. To create opportunities to engage with additional content, each hole included five QR codes, which took players to a website with additional information.[5] Throughout the golf course, there were approximately sixty-five distinct QR codes. Through this approach, we were able to incorporate fifty single-spaced pages of educational content into the exhibit. Breaking this material up into 250-word bits made it more digestible and less overwhelming, leading people to actually engage with it; the website has been viewed 3,200 times by 2,100 unique visitors. Additionally, each hole included related artwork and artists' statements. Much of the content of the art and the text alike is serious, heavy, and depressing—terms we didn't necessarily want to be the first associated with our installation. The dinosaurs who appeared throughout many aspects of the project's branding provided some levity and connected our exhibition to the quirkiness associated with mini golf.

A project of this magnitude was enabled by deep collaboration rooted in trust and admiration—feelings that develop over time. Indeed, I had worked with the project's two most key collaborators, Colin Boyd and Rayn Bumstead, on prior projects, including the crisis pregnancy center exhibit. Put frankly, the project would have been impossible without both Boyd, a talented sculptor, the manager of the campus arts building, and the project's Director of Operations, and Bumstead, an impressive graphic artist and the project's Director of Design. Boyd and I codesigned and cotaught Feminist Building, through which nine students contributed, to wildly varying degrees, to building the physical course with extensive support from a local master carpenter, Boyd and me (the faculty co-teaching the class), and student workers from the Makerspace. Bumstead, by that time a Middlebury alum working in the arts in New York City, managed the project's physical and digital design. The twenty-seven students in my Politics of Reproduction course contributed artwork and website content.

The collaborations that made the project a success don't end there. David Miranda-Hardy's Film and Media Studies class created films featured at several holes. Kelly Sharron produced a related trivia game, which debuted at the grand opening event, and is featured on the Trivia Time podcast, allowing our project a wider reach. I also worked with faculty and students at Hamilton College (Stina Soderling), Providence College (Virginia Thomas), and Metropolitan State University, Denver (Anahi Russo Garrido) to generate material for the project. MSU Denver students, for instance, designed and constructed a hole to display at the Gender Institute for Teaching and Advocacy, both as a piece of public art and also to connect their work to the broader mini golf project. A replica of their hole was then built by women in the Trailblazers apprenticeship program at Vermont Works for Women, an organization dedicated to supporting women in the trades, and included in the mini golf course in Middlebury. We also worked closely with Erin Quinn, the Director of the Middlebury College Athletics Program. In short, constructing the physical mini golf course represents a fraction of the work of this project; securing grants, creating the content for the website, the art, and trivia game, managing people, monitoring budgets, and writing final reports was far more time-consuming than the construction itself.

Then, after more than two years of work, it was finally—finally!—game time! On May 12, 2023, Reproductive Justice Mini Golf debuted at a vibrant opening event that approximately 450 people attended. The course then officially reopened to the public on June 1 and was open until July 15 for three hours every Thursday, Friday, and Saturday.

To give a better sense of what you would have experienced at Reproductive Justice Mini Golf, I'll walk you through a single hole. The tenth hole highlighted reproductive justice issues that emerge in and adjacent to the prison. Our dinosaur mascot welcomed players with the following text: "The story of incarceration is one of violence: forced separation from children, being shackled while giving birth, loss of parental rights, forced sterilization, criminalization of Black mothers, immigrant detention, complete rejection of bodily autonomy. You are about to enter a replica of a 6' x 9' solitary confinement cell, where many of these forms of state violence play out." A QR code took players to a longer introduction to the topic:

> Little reproductive justice activism focuses on the concerns of incarcerated people and, similarly, the U.S. penal system tends to ignore reproductive health issues. These oversights have serious consequences. Scholars estimate that 5–10% of women entering prison are pregnant, and others become pregnant while there. With little access to abortion while incarcerated, many of these women will become mothers. Further, 80% of women in jails and 58% of women in U.S. state and federal prisons were mothers when they were sentenced. Black women are imprisoned at 1.6 times and Latinx women at 1.3 times the rate for white women. Here, we focus on shackling during birth, forced sterilization, drug testing, and immigrant detention—all of which allow us to think through a key question that historian Rickie Solinger asks: Who gets to be a legitimate mother?[6]

Prior to putting, players were forced to answer a question: "Do you consent to being sterilized?" If the player went the "Yes" route, they would be better set up for their next shot. The QR code next to the question explained why:

> Do you consent to sterilization in exchange for a reduced prison sentence? This might feel like an impossible question to answer, but it is one the state sometimes asks of individuals prior to sentencing. In Tennessee, for example, inmates were offered the choice of sterilization or increased jail time. In California, prison doctors recommended that inmates undergo the removal of reproductive organs as a treatment for cervical cancer. The problem: the patients didn't have cancer. The doctors lied. Inmates have also been victims

of non-consensual hysterectomies after giving birth. Between 2004 and 2013, nearly 150 incarcerated women underwent tubal ligations—a procedure in which fallopian tubes are cut, tied, or blocked to permanently prevent pregnancy. Only in 2014 did California pass a bill to ban sterilization for birth control purposes among incarcerated people. We should see controlling incarcerated people's capacities to reproduce as modern-day eugenics.[7]

After deciding between forced sterilization or a longer prison sentence, players moved to a cell the size of those used for solitary confinement. Inside, players found letters, cards, and drawings that children and parents had sent to one another decorating the cell walls. After leaving the cell, players encountered a stunning wall plastered with prison abolition posters. One QR code placed on the wall included information about shackling during birth.

Incarcerated people often are shackled while giving birth—despite laws in at least 37 states meant to limit the practice. A 2018 study found that 82.9% of hospital nurses shackled incarcerated patients during pregnancy or the postpartum period. Supporters of shackling during birth often argue that the practice is necessary for the safety of others. This position reflects inaccurate stereotypes of incarcerated people, including that they are violent or flight risks. In reality, women are typically non-violent offenders and those who are pregnant, in labor, or recovering from labor pose especially low risks.[8]

Another poster on the mural wall, which included a link to an ACLU petition players could sign in support of banning shackling, focused on the racism of the prison system. Content at the QR code included:

More than 1/4 of people arrested in the U.S. are Black, approximately double the percentage of Black people in the U.S. population. Further, Black women comprise 1/3 of women serving life sentences. Clearly, anti-Black racism informs who is arrested, who is incarcerated, and the length of their sentences. The so-called "crack baby" epidemic in the 1980s and 1990s—during which babies were born to mothers who had used crack cocaine during pregnancy—speaks to the differential treatment of Black mothers. In 1989, Jennifer Clarise Johnson, a 23-year-old Black woman, was convicted for transferring cocaine to her child during the short 60 seconds between the birth and when the umbilical cord was cut. She was sentenced to drug

> treatment and fourteen years' probation. If Johnson violated any of her probation terms, she faced incarceration. Johnson's story isn't unique. In 1992, more than 160 pregnant women faced charges for alleged drug use, 3/4 of whom were people of color. But a 1991 study by the South Carolina State Council on Maternal Infant and Child Health revealed that "high percentages of pregnant women were abusing marijuana, barbiturates, and opiates—drugs primarily used by white women." Few of these white women faced charges. The disproportionate prosecution of Black mothers, therefore, was not exclusively motivated by desires to protect fetuses from drug use. If that were the case, white women would have suffered equal rates of prosecution. This disparity is why legal scholar Dorothy Roberts argues that drug tests are a way to punish Black women for having children.[9]

Students transformed the same posters that comprised the mural wall into protest signs, which lined the metal prison yard fence that surrounded the hole. A QR code explained the scene:

> U.S. immigrant detention is a form of incarceration, although immigrant detention has even less oversight than state and federal prisons and jails. This lack of oversight exacerbates possibilities for violations. With the five-fold increase in the number of immigrant detainees in the past two decades, these abuses have become even more commonplace. In fact, immigration detention facilities have been subject to numerous civil and human rights violation complaints. These include: allegations of substandard medical care, sexual and physical abuse, and exploitative labor practices. The horrors of these injustices are observable in Georgia's Irwin County Detention Center. In 2020, approximately 40 women were subject to unnecessary invasive gynecological procedures by a doctor, known as the "uterus collector," who commonly performed unnecessary hysterectomies and other procedures. As another example, pregnant detainees who want an abortion have constricted or no access to the procedure. Fighting effectively for reproductive justice requires recognizing the overlaps between the issues incarcerated and detained people experience, as well as the specificity of the oppressions undocumented people face. To learn more about reproductive justice in immigrant detention, check out the National Latina Institute for Reproductive Justice.[10]

On the outside of the prison wall, but inside the prison fence, students created a visitation booth. There, players could pick up phones, like those used in visitation booths, to listen to stories shared by a student in my Politics of Reproduction class as well as her mother, whose lives were

Birds-eye view of Reproductive Justice Mini Golf.

impacted by the mother's incarceration when her child, my student, was 10 years old. Their stories are devastating, brave, and beautiful. One last QR code provided additional context for their stories:

> Mass incarceration in the U.S. and the penal system's differential application of laws begs the question: Who gets to be a legitimate mother in the United States? Rickie Solinger raises this question in an exhibition that features art created by incarcerated mothers, as well as letters, photographs, and legal documents shared by current and former prisoners. The exhibition marks the first time a major exhibition opened in a prison. The installation then traveled to various college campuses, museums, and institutes. In the related article Solinger wrote about the exhibition, she comments on the rules governing visits by children. They are, Solinger says, "hard to read and impossible to avoid. They are, in totality, often contradictory and illogical. For incarcerated women, however, they are The Rules; they must be memorized and treated as watchwords." "Violations of any visiting rule outlined in this policy may result in the termination of the visit, disciplinary action against the inmate, and restriction of any future visiting privilege." The Rules restrict, for instance, "how many hugs and kisses a mother can give her child, who is not allowed, in any case, to sit on her mother's lap."[11]

Student playing the prison hole at Reproductive Justice Mini Golf.

Prison abolition wall at Reproductive Justice Mini Golf.

Approximately 1,800 people visited Reproductive Justice Mini Golf during its installation. Visitors included people of all genders, races, sexual orientations, abilities, and socioeconomic classes. We were delighted by the number of families with children of all ages who showed up to play mini golf and learn about reproductive justice. The significant local press coverage we received meant that people from all over the state learned about the installation, and many people reported that they had driven two or more hours to visit the exhibit. Many visitors also brought out of state guests. One alum, who graduated more than thirty years ago, shared that he had never been as proud to be a Middlebury graduate as he was when he learned about the mini golf course, a sentiment that became more pronounced when he made the trip to the installation.

This overwhelmingly positive reception should not suggest that the construction process was smooth sailing. Of course, the process for getting to the finish line—like that of so much activism—was full of aggravations, inequitable distribution of work due to certain contributors not, well, contributing and others being forced to pick up their slack, bureaucratic red tape, personalities you'd rather not deal with, unforeseeable setbacks, and far, far too many hours of unpaid labor. But my belief in the power of this kind of queer, public-facing project was confirmed time and time again by players excitedly sharing how much they learned and by reflections from those students who invested most seriously in bringing the public-facing projects I shared here to fruition. In many ways, then, I see these projects as victories that reflect the power of both feminist and queer theory-informed art and art-infused activism. Figuring out how to play with academic feminist and queer theory is no easy task. But when we do, our activism is better and so is our thinking.

Throughout the Public Feminism Lab, we had a running Google doc where fellows could input quotes from readings that spoke to them, reflections on our seminar conversations, ideas about feminist and queer art, and so on. Emily Ribeiro, one of the fellows, commented on the transformative power of the lab, noting

> This experience has aided my belief that art is an incredibly powerful tool for activism, both for the creator and the viewer. The opportunity to create art regarding reproductive rights in a time where my rights, and the rights

> of other women, are being taken away every day, has provided me with some hope and made me feel deeply, actively involved in the movement. Protesting, donating, and voting are all important for protecting our reproductive freedoms, but the space this fellowship provided for me to educate myself and others is what made me feel most powerful.

These affects were reiterated by other fellows, who, in our same Google doc, responded to my question regarding how they would describe the process of making art: inspiring, provocative, educated, pensive, soothing, fun, proud, empowered, badass, iconic, enlightening, creative, messy, killjoy (emphasis on the joy), provocative, cathartic, freeing, confusing. When I asked what words they would use to describe the conversations we had, they said: supported, powerful, active, thoughtful, kind, educational, community oriented, hopeful, encouraging, empowering, understanding, inspiring, gritty, exciting, badass, validating. Contrast this with the words they connected to the process of learning about crisis pregnancy centers: terrifying, horrifying, enraging, small, belittling, disrespected, mournful, shocking, baffling, angry, headachy, frustrating, disappointing.

These lists illustrate what feminist killjoys, to use Sara Ahmed's formulation, have long known: We can find joy, pleasure, and fun in things that are enraging, headachy, horrifying, and shocking—and we can use feminist and queer knowledge production and artistic production in order to do so. In fact, the greatest lesson we can learn from these public-facing attempts to queer reproductive justice is that we absolutely have to. Grab your putter, paintbrush, or pen. Your megaphone. Your jokes, your facts, and your stories. Whatever tools and sources of inspiration you've got. Bring along your friends, your neighbors, and even strangers. And don't forget your joy and laughter. We've got work to do.

# Acknowledgments

Writing this book has indebted me to many people. I am thankful for my colleagues, friends, family, mentors, and students who have generously allowed my debts to grow into something unwieldy. The list of those to whom I am indebted is long, and only in part because I wrote this book while I was employed at two different institutions: Middlebury College in Vermont and Rice University in Houston, Texas.

The most challenging and rewarding parts of completing this book had little to do with the actual book itself. The queer outputs inspired by this book—queer art nights, games, art exhibitions, and, most spectacularly, Reproductive Justice Mini Golf, all of which I reflect on in the conclusion and epilogue—are, in many ways, the heart of this project. Creating these outputs was an incredibly rewarding, generative, and beautiful part of the process and reminded me time and again of the value of approaching reproductive justice queerly. Two collaborators were particularly crucial to completing the "Visualizing Reproductive Justice: A Call to End Fake Clinics" exhibition and Reproductive Justice Mini Golf: Rayn Bumstead and Colin Boyd. Neither project would exist without these two dreamboat collaborators. They are the two most generous, brilliant, hardworking, and wildly talented collaborators with whom I've ever worked. With projects the size of the mini golf course, in particular, one expects that interpersonal aggravations may float to the surface at some point. We experienced many frustrations along the way, but never once were my aggravations with the two people most key to the project. Completing the mini golf course required that all three of us invested

500 percent of typical human capacities for an extended period of time. What an incredible treat it is to work with people whose commitments to a project's success match yours, whose talents and ideas blow your mind every day, whose ideas improve your own, and who you genuinely look forward to seeing and working with every single day. I see the mini golf course as my greatest professional achievement (a sentence I certainly didn't have on my professional bingo card!) and I'm endlessly grateful to Rayn and Colin for the many things they did to bring our wacky ideas to fruition and to make them more beautiful and bolder than they could have been otherwise.

Many others contributed in deep and meaningful ways to Reproductive Justice Mini Golf, as well. David Miranda-Hardy produced an original soundscape and students in his Film and Media Studies class created films featured at several holes. Kelly Sharron developed a related trivia game, which debuted at the grand opening event, and is featured on the Trivia Time podcast. The students of Stina Soderling (Hamilton College) and Virginia Thomas (Providence College) created art featured throughout the exhibition, while students at the Gender Institute for Teaching and Advocacy (GITA) at Metropolitan State University, Denver, directed by Anahi Russo Garrido, designed and constructed a hole to display at GITA, both as a piece of public art and also to connect their work to the broader mini golf project. A replica of their hole was then built by women in the Trailblazers apprenticeship program at Vermont Works for Women, an organization dedicated to supporting women in the trades. We also worked closely with Erin Quinn, the Director of the Middlebury College Athletics Program, who generously donated the physical space. Mark Jensen, a local master carpenter, contributed heartily by mentoring student builders, most of whom had few if any construction skills prior to taking the Feminist Building course I cotaught with Colin Boyd. In Feminist Building, Eliot Nebolsine and Lindsey Lessing stood out for their dedication, consistent hard work throughout the semester, and production of especially thoughtful and well-constructed holes. I was lucky to have an incredible group of students in my spring 2023 Politics of Reproduction course, and many students contributed by producing content and art related to their assigned mini golf hole. Even out of this remarkable bunch of dedicated students, a few stand out as exceptions. Special thanks to El Fahey and Katherine Lantzy, who picked up many pieces when they fell by the wayside. Extra special thanks to Eliot Nebolsine, the only student in both Politics of Reproduction and Feminist Building. Eliot went above and beyond all semester, modeling for fellow students how to be a teammate and a leader simultaneously.

I am grateful for the substantial private foundation grant that funded the mini golf course, as well as funding from Middlebury College departments, programs, and administrators, most significantly former college president Laurie Patton, the Gensler Family Fund managed by the Gender, Sexuality, and Feminist Studies department, and the Center for Community Engagement. Jenn Ortegren has given me sharp and generous feedback—and typically with very little notice!—on nearly every grant I've ever received, for the mini golf course and more broadly, and I'm endlessly grateful for the dynamism she brings to my life.

I'm thankful to my undergraduate student research assistants, whose imprint is all over this book, as well as its queer outputs. At Middlebury, I worked with many brilliant, creative, and hardworking student research assistants: Rayn Bumstead, Kayla Richards, Isabel Perez-Martin, Lu Mila, Eliot Nebolsine, Kamari Williams, El Fahey, Emily Ribeiro, Joan Vera, Chris Gernon, Zach Levitt, Penelope Spencer, Rebecca Wishnie, Sophie Hochman, Cat LaRoche, Tate Serletti, Georgia Crosby, Rose Evans, Arthur Romero da Veiga Martins, Luna Gizzi, and Amelia Pollard. At Rice, I have again been blessed to work with energetic, dedicated, and brilliant student members of my research team: Imogen Brown, Miranda Xing, Annika Bhananker, Lajward Zahra, and Abbie Proell. Thank you, all, for reminding me consistently of the pleasures of doing cross-generational intellectual work that sets out to be useful in the world. Thanks, too, to Middlebury College and Rice University for the institutional funds necessary to hire and pay student workers. I am also thankful to Erik Bleich and Maurits van der Veen, who developed the methodology behind the quantitative figures that appear throughout this book. Bleich and van der Veen also mentored my research assistant Amelia Pollard as she learned how to use their methodology to answer the questions that led to these figures. And Rayn Bumstead's imprint on this book extends far beyond her work as a student research assistant, and even beyond her post-graduation work with the mini golf course and art exhibition. She designed the book's cover, dealt with the formatting of images, and has given me feedback on all of the ideas in this book. Rayn and I are consistently cooking up ways to continue to think and create alongside one another and my life is richer because of it.

Thanks, too, to the dedicated students in the "Representing Reproduction" course through which we put on Paula Kamen's play *Jane: Abortion and the Underground*, which I reflect on in chapter 3. Even among the exceptional students in this class, several stand out: Lucy Weiss, Allegra Molkenthin, Ivy Geilker, Rebecca Wishnie, and Kira Waldman. Extra special shout out to Taite Shomo, who served as the student director of the play, and whose role in the course and production far exceeded that task. Shomo is a force to be reckoned with, and I count myself lucky to be one of their co-conspirators. Special thanks to Paula Kamen for engaging with our questions around the play and for modeling feminist generosity. Thanks also to the student activists in End Fake Clinics, and especially to Grace Tacherra Morrison, with whom I coauthored an earlier iteration of what is published as chapter 4 here.

To my dear friends who shared their beautiful insights in the queer feminist parenting roundtable, thank you, thank you, thank you. I appreciate the many things each of you, and your children, bring to my life: Philip Brown, Erin Durban, Laurie Essig, Maryam Griffin, Hemangini Gupta, Rosemary Hennessy,

Miranda Joseph, David Miranda-Hardy, Natasha Ngaiza, Jenn Ortegren, Kelly Sharron, Myrna Perez Sheldon, Abraham Weil.

Many friends, mentors, colleagues, and collaborators have supported me as I've written this book and completed these various wacky outputs, support that looks a lot of different ways: feeding me when I am in a work hole, sharing meals while talking through arguments I make here, giving feedback on chapter drafts, attending the art exhibition and mini golf installation and sharing reflections after, sending along articles useful for my thinking, and being a co-conspirator in the kind of mischief-finding that takes one's mind off of work. Those thoughts and affects form the backbone of this book. I had eight great years in Middlebury, Vermont. These rockstar folks, both at Middlebury College and beyond, can almost make you forget how unrelenting the winters are: Laurie Essig, Mark Jensen, Erin Eggleston, Rebecca Tiger, Natasha Ngaiza, Ajay Verghese, Scott Barkdoll, Pam Berenbaum, Mark Lewis, Caitlyn Myers, Andy Hooper, Catherine Nichols, Robert Borden, Nikolina Dobreva, Enrique Garcia, Patricia Saldarriaga, Aaron Brown, Ellery Foutch, Zoe Kaslow, Nial Rele, Catharine Wright, Kristy Bright, Karin Hanta, Marion Wells, Laura Thomas, Andy Dosmann, and Karin Gottshall. Jenn Ortegren, Matt Lawrence, David Miranda-Hardy, Kemi Fuentes-George, J Finley, Toni Cook, and Daniel Rodriguez Navas are the friends with whom I spent most of my Vermont life: completing home renovation tasks, lifting weights, hiking, playing Monopoly Deal, sharing countless meals and drinks, playing squash, watching the Green Bay Packers and *Wheel of Fortune*, going on adventures, celebrating holidays and birthdays together, and loving and supporting one another. You all have so profoundly shaped my life. I loved my time in Vermont because of you.

Although I have been at Rice University for just under two years, I have found the Department of English and Creative Writing as well as the Center for the Study of Women, Gender, and Sexuality to be enriching, lively, and supportive spaces. Special thanks to those at Rice who have made this an incredible intellectual home so quickly: Lacy Johnson, Michael Dango, José Aranda, Cameron Dezen Hammon, Kiese Laymon, Benjamin Parris, Krista Comer, Rosemary Hennessy, Matthew Schneider-Mayerson, Nandi Theunissen, Brandon Levin, Brian Riedel, Eve Dunbar, Helena Michie, Susan Lurie, Ian Schimmel, Sarah Ellenzweig, Matthias Staisch, Margarita Castroman Soto, Linda Evans, Anne Smith, Jennifer Luu, Emily Houlik-Ritchey, Lora Wildenthal, Alexander Regier, Thomas Morin, Nicole Waligora-Davis, Zach Neville, and Cymene Howe. I'm especially grateful for the fun, fierceness, and brilliance that Ragini Tharoor Srinivasan and Khadene Harris bring to my life. How lucky to find your people so soon after landing in a new place. I'm also deeply grateful to my Houston friends who remind me repeatedly that there is so much beautiful life beyond the academy: Paola Tello, Pablo Morales, Jeff Senison, Kat Robinson, and William Shoemaker.

My life is deeply enriched by friendships and collaborations that extend far beyond Rice and Middlebury. Many of you have engaged me in conversations about this book, and equally importantly, in activities that allowed my brain a break from work. Thank you to Ilene Resnick, Daniel Weiss, Debbie Rogow, James Carter, Zach Carter, Alyson Patsavas, Sarah Jane Pinkerton, CJ Jones, Ayisha Ashley Al-Sayyad, Heather Fukunaga, Laura Briggs, Loretta Ross, Carrie Baker, Yousef Crownhead, Jae Basiliere, Stina Soderling, Elizabeth Riccio, and Matt Riccio. I continue to benefit from the mentorship, support, and wisdom of Leila Rupp and Eileen Boris, both of whom were on my dissertation committee more than a decade ago and now are cherished friends.

The arguments I present here benefited from insightful feedback from audiences at National Women's Studies Association conferences, American Studies Association conferences, the University of Texas Medical Branch's Reproductive Ethics conference, and UCSB's Center for Feminist Futures. I also benefited from feedback on pieces of this manuscript that were published previously. A version of chapter 4, which I coauthored with Grace Tacherra Morrison, was published in *Signs*. One part of the epilogue was published in Krystale Littlejohn's and Rickie Solinger's *Fighting Mad: Resisting the End of Roe v. Wade*, and another part of the epilogue was published in *ASAP/Review*, a journal by the Association for the Study of the Arts of the Present. Thanks to these publishers for granting permission to reproduce this material here. I also co-authored an earlier version of the chapter on paid parental leave with Eileen Boris. Although that article remains unpublished, our time working on it dramatically impacted my thinking and writing on the topic here.

Many thanks to my editor, Naomi Schneider, and the University of California Press team, who have been incredibly supportive throughout the long process of finishing this book. One member of this team deserves a special shoutout. Rickie Solinger is so much more than the head editor for the UC Press Reproductive Justice series. She is a true friend, an indefatigable cheerleader, an incredible mentor, and someone who manages to inspire and push me every time I speak to her. Thanks, also, to the reviewers whose insightful feedback substantially improved the book, and especially to Carmen Winant and Laura Harrison, who allowed the press to release their names to me. Their overwhelmingly positive responses kept my commitment to this project alive and their critiques pushed me to make it better.

I didn't know any academics before I went to college. Somehow, my sister, Danielle Thomsen, and I both ended up on this path. She is a brilliant and inspiring scholar, and she is also a lot of fun. I'm grateful for her and the richness she brings to my life, which includes her husband, Mohammad Mojdehi, and new baby, Max. What a joy to witness those you love transition into a new life phase. When I started writing this book, I had lived in a tiny, two-hundred-square-foot apartment with a mini fridge and two-burner stove for a couple of years, including during part of the pandemic. (Warning to students considering an academic life: It is not one of luxury, especially when you are an untenured professor!) Over the course of the five years I wrote this book, I got tenure, I spent two different stints in Santa Barbara, California, doing research, I bought an 1890s farmhouse in Vermont that was in disrepair, I renovated that house while living there, and I got a new job and moved to Houston, where I bought a 1970s townhome in disrepair, moved in, and started home reno 2.0. That's a lot of cross-country drives, days covered in grout and sawdust, and general upheaval. My parents, Kent and Rita Thomsen, have shown up for me in ways that remind me every day how lucky I am to have hit the parent jackpot. These hard-working Midwesterners drove from South Dakota to Vermont to help me move into my new house and to begin the long process of making that house home. Together, we cleaned, painted, killed mice (ok, that one was just my Dad), cut down dead trees and cleared out the overgrown yard, and scraped and sanded a century of paint off of beautiful old wood. And we had a good time doing it! I drafted much of this book in that drafty, glorious, quirky house, and I'm grateful to my parents for supporting me on that home-making journey—even when I suspect they found my decision to take on that project questionable. What a blessing it is to have people in your life who support you as you make decisions that they would never make themselves. Anahi Russo Garrido also did far more than she signed up to do at the farmhouse—painting walls, sealing floors, sanding ceilings, gardening, trying to calm me down while I swore profusely at wallpaper, listening to my endless design chatter, and the list goes on and on. But this description doesn't even begin to scratch the surface of Anahi's influence on my life or investments in this book. She has been near me every step of the way, reading chapter drafts, talking through ideas, picking me up when things weren't going well, and, perhaps most importantly, insisting that we celebrate every little victory along the way. More than anyone else in my life, she has championed me and reminded me again and again of the need for this book. Her commitment to joy, peace, and happiness, and her ability to locate these affects in the most quotidian things, inspire me and make the world a better place.

I ended the acknowledgements in my last book with the sentence "I have so much to be grateful for"—something that feels truer every day. What a gift to share life with you all.

APPENDIX

# Methods for Quantitative Analysis

Chapters 1, 2, and 3 include graphs that represent quantitative data analysis. My research assistant Amelia Pollard and I assembled three different corpuses of articles, with significant support from Dr. Erik Bleich and Dr. Maurits van der Veen, who developed this methodology.[1] All articles were published during a ten-year period (January 1, 2010 to December 31, 2019) in one of the four US newspapers with the widest national circulation: *The New York Times*, *The Washington Post*, *The Wall Street Journal*, and *USA Today*. The graphs in the surrogacy chapter represent findings from considering 532 articles that include the terms "surrogacy" or "surrogate." The graphs in the maternity leave chapter represent findings from analyzing 4,117 articles that include the terms "maternity leave," "parental leave," "paternity leave," "paid leave," or "medical leave." The graphs in the chapter on gender-inclusive language in abortion debates represent findings from examining 18,787 articles that mention the term "abortion" or "abortions." Through this quantitative analysis, we created a list of "features" for each corpus. This approach enabled us to identify articles that contain one or more of the words associated with each feature and to track the evolution of certain words or phrases over time. For the feature words associated with our corpuses, see below; an * indicates a search for words with any letters following the root, so a search for "feminis*" would return "feminist," "feminists," "feminism," and so on.

Surrogacy

- *Surrogate*: surrogate
- *Feminism*: feminis*
- *LGBTQ*: LGBT*, gay*, queer*, lesbian*, homosexual*, same-sex
- *Couple*: couple*
- *Family*: famil*

Maternity Leave

- *Maternity Leave*: maternity leave*
- *Parental Leave: parental leave**
- *Paid Leave: paid leave**
- *Paternity Leave: paternity leave**
- *Medical Leave*: medical leave*
- *LGBTQ*: LGBT*, gay, queer, lesbian*, homosexual*, same-sex

Pregnant People

- *Patient*: patient*
- *Women*: woman, women, female*
- *Pregnant Person*: pregnant person, pregnant people
- *Pregnant Patient*: pregnant patient*
- *Pregnant Woman*: pregnant woman, pregnant women
- *Trans*: transgender, trans man, trans woman, trans men, trans women, trans person, trans people, trans individual*, trans activist*, trans movement*, trans folk*, trans community, trans patient*

We used the presence of positive, neutral, and negative words (such as "attack" or "beautiful") to gauge the tone of individual articles. Negative articles contain more negative than positive words, and vice versa. To clearly communicate our measure of article tone, we broke it into blocks of significance. Any score between 0.1 and -0.1 is close enough to 0 that it is essentially neutral. If it is between -0.1 and -0.3, it is modestly negative; between -0.3 and -0.5, clearly negative; and less than -0.5, strongly negative.

# Notes

## ON THE TASK AT HAND. A PROLOGUE

1. A. Kheyfets, S. Dhaurali, P. Feyock, F. Khan, A. Lockley, B. Miller, and N. Amutah-Onukagha, "The Impact of Hostile Abortion Legislation on the United States Maternal Mortality Crisis: A Call for Increased Abortion Education," *Frontiers in Public Health* (December 2023): https://pmc.ncbi.nlm.nih.gov/articles/PMC10728320.

2. "State Bans on Abortion Throughout Pregnancy," Guttmacher Institute, March 26, 2025, https://www.guttmacher.org/state-policy/explore/state-policies-abortion-bans.

3. Jessica Valenti, *Abortion: Our Bodies, Their Lies, and the Truths We Use to Win* (New York: Penguin Random House, 2025); Carly Thomsen, "Abortion Affects," *Signs: Journal of Women in Culture and Society* (2025), https://signsjournal.org/jessica-valentis-abortion.

## REPRODUCTIVE JUSTICE, QUEERLY. AN INTRODUCTION

1. Michelle Peng, "How Employers Can Stand with Their LGBTQ+ Employees Post-Roe," *Time*, June 30, 2022, https://time.com/charter/6192358/lgbtq-post-roe.

2. Holly Corbett, "Representation Matters: The Impact of Overturning Roe v. Wade on LGBTQ Rights," *Forbes*, June 29, 2022, https://www.forbes.com/sites

/hollycorbett/2022/06/28/representation-matters-the-impact-of-overturning-roe-v-wade-on-lgbtq-rights; Aden Choate and Isabelle Guis, "Post-'*Roe*,' Transgender People Fear for the Future," *The American Prospect*, August 1, 2022, https://prospect.org/health/post-roe-transgender-people-fear-for-the-future; Silvia Foster-Frau, "LGBTQ Community Braces for Rollback of Rights After Abortion Ruling," *The Washington Post*, June 28, 2022, https://www.washingtonpost.com/nation/2022/06/24/abortion-fears-lgbtq-gay-rights; Julie Moreau, "How Will *Roe v. Wade* Reversal Affect LGBTQ Rights? Experts, Advocates Weigh In," NBCNews.com, June 24, 2022, https://www.nbcnews.com/nbc-out/out-news/will-roe-v-wade-reversal-affect-lgbtq-rights-experts-advocates-weigh-rcna35284; Jasmina Kelemen and Dina Bass, "What's Next After Roe v Wade? LGBTQ Americans Worry for Their Rights After *Roe* Reversal," Bloomberg.com, June 27, 2022, https://www.bloomberg.com/news/articles/2022-06-27/whats-next-after-roe-v-wade-lgbtq-americans-worry-their-rights-at-risk.

3. For a queer critique of the place *Lawrence v. Texas* came to occupy in LGBTQ+ rights circles, the sanitization of the details of the case that centering required, and what this reveals about both the racialization of intimacy and the depoliticization inherent to mainstream contemporary LGBTQ+ rights activism, see David Eng, *The Feeling of Kinship: Queer Liberalism and the Racialization of Intimacy* (Durham: Duke University Press, 2010).

4. Laurie Essig, "U.S. Culture is So Deeply Patriarchal, We Can't Even Admit Overturning Roe is About Women," *Ms. Magazine*, May 9, 2022, https://msmagazine.com/2022/05/09/roe-v-wade-women-patriarchy-misogyny.

5. Jenna Jerman, Rachel K. Jones and Tsuyoshi Onda, "Characteristics of U.S. Abortion Patients in 2014 and Changes Since 2008," Guttmacher Institute, August 24, 2022, https://www.guttmacher.org/report/characteristics-us-abortion-patients-2014.

6. Susan A. Cohen, "Abortion and Women of Color: The Bigger Picture," Guttmacher Institute, August 6, 2008, https://www.guttmacher.org/gpr/2008/08/abortion-and-women-color-bigger-picture.

7. Carly Thomsen, Zach Levitt, Christopher Gernon, and Penelope Spencer, "Presence and Absence: Crisis Pregnancy Centers and Abortion Facilities in the Contemporary Reproductive Justice Landscape," *Human Geography* 16, no. 1 (2022): 64–74.

8. Alize Miranda Ollstein, Josh Gerstein, and Alex Thompson, "Texas Ban Spotlights Democrats' Generational Divide on Abortion and Trans Issues," *Politico*, September 10, 2021, https://www.politico.com/news/2021/09/10/texas-democrats-abortion-trans-issues-511078.

9. Helen Lewis, "The Abortion Debate Is Suddenly About 'People,' Not 'Women,'" *The Atlantic*, June 2, 2022, https://www.theatlantic.com/ideas/archive/2022/05/abortion-rights-debate-women-gender-neutral-language/629863; Helen Lewis,

"Why I'll Keep Saying 'Pregnant Women,'" *The Atlantic*, October 26, 2021, https://www.theatlantic.com/ideas/archive/2021/10/pregnant-women-people-feminism-language/620468.

10. Brendan O'Neill, "Rescuing Women's Rights from the Trap of Identity Politics," *Spiked*, May 7, 2022, https://www.spiked-online.com/2022/05/07/rescuing-womens-rights-from-the-trap-of-identity-politics. Emphasis and brackets in original.

11. A. C. Facci, "Why We Use Inclusive Language to Talk About Abortion," American Civil Liberties Union, July 12, 2022, https://www.aclu.org/news/reproductive-freedom/why-we-use-inclusive-language-to-talk-about-abortion.

12. Women's Health Protection Act of 2021, H.R. 3755, 117th Cong. (2021).

13. "Style Guide," Trans Journalists Association, December 11, 2020, https://transjournalists.org/style-guide.

14. Jack Qu'emi, "4 Ways to Be Gender Inclusive When Discussing Abortion," *Everyday Feminism*, August 13, 2020, https://everydayfeminism.com/2014/08/gender-inclusive-discussing-abortion.

15. "Guidelines for Promoting an Anti-Bias and Inclusive Curriculum," Columbia University Vagelos College of Physicians and Surgeons, May 19, 2021, https://www.vagelos.columbia.edu/education/academic-programs/md-program/curriculum/guidelines-promoting-anti-bias-and-inclusive-curriculum.

16. Shelly DeBiasse, "POV: Who Is Forgotten in Our Discussion of Abortion?," Boston University, September 11, 2021, https://www.bu.edu/sargent/pov-who-is-forgotten-in-our-discussion-of-abortion.

17. "The Abortion Course," Innovating Education in Reproductive Health, accessed February 11, 2022, https://www.innovating-education.org/course/the-abortion-course.

18. Sara Ahmed, *The Cultural Politics of Emotion*, 2nd ed. (Edinburgh: Edinburgh University Press, 2004).

19. For examples of the vast queer theoretical scholarship on these topics, see Eng, *The Feeling of Kinship*; Teagan Bradway and Elizabeth Freeman, eds., *Queer Kinship: Race, Sex, Belonging, Form* (Durham: Duke University Press, 2022); Marty Fink, *Forget Burial: HIV Kinship, Disability, and Queer/Trans Narratives of Care* (New Brunswick: Rutgers University Press, 2020); Lauren Jae Gutterman, Martin Manalansan IV, and Stephen Vider, eds., "Queering the Domestic," *GLQ* 30, no. 4 (2024).

20. Jennifer Doyle, "Blind Spots and Failed Performance," *Qui Parle* 18, no. 1 (2009): 25–52.

21. Laura Mamo, Queering Reproduction: Achieving Pregnancy in the Age of Technoscience (Durham: Duke University Press, 2007).

22. Marcin Smietana, Charis Thompson, and France Winddance Twine, "Making and Breaking Families—Reading Queer Reproductions, Stratified

Reproduction and Reproductive Justice Together," *Reproductive Biomedicine and Society Online* 7 (2018): 112–30.

23. Lauren J. Silver, "Queering Reproductive Justice: Memories, Mistakes, and Motivations to Transform Kinship," *Feminist Anthropology* 1, no. 2 (2020): 217–30; see Zakiya Luna, "Black Celebrities, Reproductive Justice and Queering Family: An Exploration," *Reproductive Biomedicine and Society Online* 7 (2018): 91–100.

24. Natalie Fixmer-Oraiz and Shui-yin Sharon Yam, "Queer(ing) Reproductive Justice," *The Oxford Research Encyclopedia of Communication*, November 29, 2021.

25. Marie-Amelie George, "Queering Reproductive Justice," *University of Richmond Law Review* 54 (2020): 672.

26. Kimala Price, "Queering Reproductive Justice in the Trump Era: A Note on Political Intersectionality," *Politics & Gender* 14 (2018): 584.

27. Lee Edelman, *No Future: Queer Theory and the Death Drive* (Durham: Duke University Press, 2004).

28. Doyle, "Blind Spots."

29. Chris Barcelos made this claim by citing an unpublished conference paper I presented on a panel that Barcelos did not attend. See *Youth Organizing for Reproductive Justice: A Guide for Liberation* (Oakland: University of California Press, 2025), 143.

30. "Fact Sheet: LGBTQ+ People & *Roe v. Wade*," Human Rights Campaign Foundation, June 2, 2022, https://www.hrc.org/press-releases/human-rights-campaign-fact-sheet-lesbian-bisexual-queer-women-who-have-been-pregnant-are-more-likely-to-need-abortion-services-demonstrates-impact-roe-reversal-would-have-on-lgbtq-people.

31. Paisley Currah, "Disappearing Women," March 13, 2005, https://www.paisleycurrah.com/2015/03/13/disappearing-women.

32. Paisley Currah, "Feminism, Gender Pluralism, and Gender Neutrality: Maybe it's Time to Bring Back the Binary," April 26, 2016, https://www.paisleycurrah.com/2016/04/26/feminism-gender-pluralism-and-gender-neutrality-maybe-its-time-to-bring-back-the-binary. See also Paisley Currah, *Sex is as Sex Does: Governing Transgender Identity* (New York: NYU Press, 2022).

33. L. Abern, S. Nippita, and K. Maguire, "Contraceptive Use and Abortion Views Among Transgender and Gender-Nonconforming Individuals Assigned Female at Birth," *Contraception* 98, no. 4 (2018): 337; Alexis Light, Lin-Fan Wang, Alexander Zeymo, and Veronica Gomez-Lobo, "Family Planning and Contraception Use in Transgender Men," *Contraception* 98, no. 4 (2018): 266–69; Heidi Moseson, Laura Fix, Sachiko Ragosta, Hannah Forsberg, Jen Hastings, Ari Stoeffler, et al., "Abortion Experiences and Preferences of Transgender, Nonbinary, and Gender-Expansive People in the United States," *American Journal of Obstetrics and Gynecology* 224, no. 4 (2021): 376.e1–11.

34. Joshua D. Safer, Eli Coleman, Jaime Feldman, Robert Garofalo, Wylie Hembree, Asa Radix, et al., "Barriers to Healthcare for Transgender Individuals," *Current Opinion in Endocrinology, Diabetes & Obesity* 23, no. 2 (2016): 168–71.

35. Deirdre A. Shires and Kim D. Jaffee, "Factors Associated with Health Care Discrimination Experiences Among a National Sample of Female-to-Male Transgender Individuals," *Health & Social Work* 40, no. 2 (2015): 134–41.

36. Deirdre A. Shires, Daphna Stroumsa, Kim D. Jaffee, and Michael R. Woodford, "Primary Care Clinicians' Willingness to Care for Transgender Patients," *The Annals of Family Medicine* 16, no. 6 (2018): 555–58.

37. N. Dubin, Ian T. Nolan, Carl G. Streed Jr., Richard E. Greene, Asa E. Radix, and Shane D. Morrison, "Transgender Health Care: Improving Medical Students' and Residents' Training and Awareness," *Advances in Medical Education and Practice* 9 (2018): 377–91.

38. Olivia H. Chang, Miriam J. Haviland, Emily Von Bargen, Yvonne Gomez-Carrion, Michele R. Hacker, and Janet Li, "Female Pelvic Medicine and Reconstructive Surgery Fellows' Exposure to Transgender Health," *American Journal of Obstetrics & Gynecology* 219, no. 6 (2018): 625–26.

39. Hayley Braun, Rebecca Nash, Vin Tangpricha, Janice Brockman, Kevin Ward, and Michael Goodman, "Cancer in Transgender People: Evidence and Methodological Considerations," *Epidemiology Review* 39, no. 1 (2017): 93–107.

40. Judith Butler, "Performative Acts and Gender Constitution: An Essay in Phenomenology and Feminist Theory," *Theatre Journal* 40, no. 4 (1988): 519.

41. Mairead Sullivan, "Lesbian Feminism and the Challenge of Community," *Introduction to Feminist Studies: Notes from the Field* (London: Routledge, 2025).

42. Paisley Currah, "Expecting Bodies: The Pregnant Man and Transgender Exclusion from the Employment Non-Discrimination Act," *Women's Studies Quarterly* 36 (2008): 330–36.

43. Loretta Ross and Rickie Solinger, *Reproductive Justice: An Introduction* (Oakland: UC Press, 2017).

44. Zakiya Luna and Kristin Luker, "Reproductive Justice," *Annual Review of Law and Science* 9 (2013): 328.

45. As quoted in Patricia Zavella, *The Movement for Reproductive Justice* (New York: New York University Press, 2020), 11.

46. Carly Thomsen, "The Politics of Narrative, Narrative as Politic: Rethinking Reproductive Justice Frameworks Through the South Dakota Abortion Story," *Feminist Formations* 27 no. 2 (2015): 1–26.

47. Kimala Price, "What Is Reproductive Justice? How Women of Color Activists Are Redefining the Pro-Choice Paradigm," *Meridians* 10, no. 2 (2010): 42.

48. Thomsen, "Politics of Narrative," 19.

49. See Jennifer Nelson, *Women of Color and the Reproductive Rights Movement* (New York: New York University Press, 2003); Zakiya Luna, *Reproductive*

*Rights as Human Rights* (New York: New York University Press, 2020); Loretta Ross, Lynn Roberts, Erika Derkas, Whitney Peoples, and Pamela Bridgewater Toure, *Radical Reproductive Justice: Foundation, Theory, Practice, Critique* (New York City: The Feminist Press at CUNY, 2017); Barbara Gurr, *Reproductive Justice: The Politics of Healthcare for Native American Women* (New Brunswick: Rutgers University Press, 2014); Jael Silliman, Marlene Gerber Fried, Loretta Ross, and Elena Gutiérrez, *Undivided Rights: Women of Color Organizing for Reproductive Justice* (Chicago: Haymarket Books, 2016); Patricia Zavella, *The Movement for Reproductive Justice: Empowering Women of Color Through Social Activism* (New York: New York University Press, 2020).

50. Clare Hemmings, Why Stories Matter: The Political Grammar of Feminist Theory (Durham: Duke University Press, 2011), 13.

51. Briggs, "Activisms and Epistemologies."

52. Loretta Ross, Calling In: How to Start Making Change with Those You'd Rather Cancel (New York: Simon and Schuster, 2025).

53. Torrey Peters, *Detransition, Baby* (London: Serpent's Tail, 2021).

54. Abraham Weil, "Psychoanalysis and Trans*versatility," *Transgender Studies Quarterly* 4, no. 3–4 (2017): 639–46.

55. Currah, "Disappearing Women."

56. Cathy J. Cohen, "Punks, Bulldaggers, and Welfare Queens: The Radical Potential of Queer Politics?," *GLQ: A Journal of Lesbian and Gay Studies* 3, no. 4 (1997): 441.

57. Cohen, "Punks, Bulldaggers," 457.

58. Cohen, "Punks, Bulldaggers," 458.

59. Cohen, "Punks, Bulldaggers," 453 and passim.

60. Edelman, *No Future*, 2.

61. Edelman, *No Future*, 4.

62. Edelman, *No Future*, 3.

63. José Esteban Muñoz, *Cruising Utopia: The Then and There of Queer Futurity* (New York: New York University Press, 2009), 95.

64. Gayatri Gopinath, "The Utopian in the Everyday," Social Text blog, June 25, 2010, https://socialtextjournal.org/periscope_article/the_utopian_in_the_everyday_a_response_to_jose_esteban_munozs_cruising_utopia_the_there_and_then_of.

65. José Esteban Muñoz, "Response," *Social Text* blog, June 19, 2010, https://socialtextjournal.org/periscope_article/response.

66. Doyle, "Blind Spots," 27–28.

67. Jennifer Nash, *Birthing Black Mothers* (Durham: Duke University Press, 2021).

68. Martin Manalansan IV, "The 'Stuff' of Archives: Mess, Migration, and Queer Lives," *Radical History Review* 120 (2014): 94–107.

69. Kelli Auerbach, "Opinion: Surrogacy Is About Bodily Autonomy. Feminists Should Embrace It," *Buzzfeed News*, July 17, 2019, https://www.buzzfeednews.com/article/kelliauerbach/surrogacy-bodily-autonomy-feminists-embrace.

## CHAPTER 1. SURROGACY WITHOUT SURROGATES

1. Molly Horton Booth, "LGBTQ+ Celebrities & Surrogacy: Why Representation Matters," Gay Parents To Be, July 13, 2021. This article appears, as of 2025, to have been removed from the site.

2. Martha Ertman, "What's Wrong with a Parenthood Market? A New and Improved Theory of Commodification," *North Carolina Law Review* 82, no. 1 (2003): 1–60; Sophie Lewis, *Full Surrogacy Now: Feminism Against Family* (London: Verso Books, 2019); Dorothy Roberts, "Race and the New Reproduction," *Hastings Law Journal* 47, no. 4 (1996): 935–49.

3. Sydney Page, "They Were Gay and Wanted a Baby. She Loved Being Pregnant. They Made a Deal," *Washington Post*, September 8, 2018, https://www.washingtonpost.com/national/health-science/they-were-gay-and-wanted-a-baby-she-loved-being-pregnant-they-made-a-deal/2018/09/07/a001f19c-9014-11e8-bcd5-9d911c784c38_story.html.

4. Leslie Morgan Steiner, "Who Becomes a Surrogate?," *The Atlantic*, November 25, 2013, https://www.theatlantic.com/health/archive/2013/11/who-becomes-a-surrogate/281596.

5. Heather Jacobson, "A Limited Market: the Recruitment of Gay Men as Surrogacy Clients by the Infertility Industry in the USA," *Reproductive Biomedicine & Society Online* 7 (2018): 16.

6. For reflections on the place of gay marriage in LGBTQ+ movements, see Ryan Conrad, *Against Equality: Queer Revolution, Not Mere Inclusion* (Edinburgh: AK Press, 2014); George Chauncey, *Why Marriage: The History Shaping Today's Debate Over Gay Equality* (Cambridge: Basic Books, 2004); Mary Bernstein and Verta Taylor, *The Marrying Kind: Debating Same-Sex Marriage Within the Lesbian and Gay Movement* (Minneapolis: University of Minnesota Press, 2013).

7. Laura Briggs, *How All Politics Became Reproductive Politics: From Welfare Reform to Foreclosure to Trump* (Oakland: University of California Press, 2018), 149.

8. Lisa Duggan, *The Twilight of Equality? Neoliberalism, Cultural Politics, and the Attack on Democracy* (Boston: Beacon Press, 2003).

9. In this chapter, people with disabilities are not the focus of my analysis precisely because surrogacy campaigns and conversations have prioritized and centered gay men.

10. "ART and Gestational Carriers," Centers for Disease Control and Prevention, August 5, 2016, https://www.cdc.gov/art/key-findings/gestational-carriers.html.

11. "ART and Gestational Carriers."

12. Raywat Deonandan, "Recent Trends in Reproductive Tourism and International Surrogacy: Ethical Considerations and Challenges for Policy," *Risk Management and Healthcare Policy* 8 (2015): 112.

13. Deonandan, "Recent Trends," 111.

14. Laura Harrison, *Brown Bodies, White Babies: The Politics of Cross-Racial Surrogacy* (New York: New York University Press, 2016).

15. Roberts, "Race and the New Reproduction," 937, 939–41.

16. Roberts, "Race and the New Reproduction," 941, 937, 942–43.

17. Dorothy Roberts, *Killing the Black Body: Race, Reproduction, and the Meaning of Liberty* (New York: Vintage, 1998), 246–93.

18. Dorothy Roberts, "Race, Gender, and Genetic Technologies: A New Reproductive Dystopia," *Signs* 24, no. 4 (2009): 783–804. See also Dorothy Roberts, "Privatization and Punishment in the New Age of Reprogenetics," *Emory Law Journal* 54 (2005): 1343–60.

19. Harrison, *Brown Bodies, White Babies*, 1–2 and passim.

20. Amrita Pande, "Surrogacy," in *The Wiley Blackwell Encyclopedia of Gender and Sexuality Studies*, ed. Nancy Naples, Renee Hoogland, Maithree Wickramasinghe, and Wai Ching Angela Wong (Hoboken: Wiley Blackwell, 2016).

21. Alys Eve Weinbaum, *The Afterlife of Reproductive Slavery: Biocapitalism and Black Feminism's Philosophy of History* (Durham: Duke University Press, 2019), 7.

22. Weinbaum, *The Afterlife of Reproductive Slavery*, 2.

23. Weinbaum, *The Afterlife of Reproductive Slavery*, 5.

24. April L. Cherry, "Nurturing in the Service of White Culture: Racial Subordination, Gestational Surrogacy, and the Ideology of Motherhood," *Texas Journal of Women and the Law* 10, no. 2 (2001): 83–128, quote at 87.

25. For scholarship linking surrogacy and sex work see Jean M. Sera, "Surrogacy and Prostitution: A Comparative Analysis," *Journal of Gender & the Law* 5, (1997): 315–42; Tatiana Patrone, "Is Paid Surrogacy a Form of Reproductive Prostitution? A Kantian Perspective," *Cambridge Quarterly of Healthcare Ethics* 27, no. 1 (2018): 109–22.

26. Lauren Mello, "Surrogate Timeline: How Long is the Surrogacy Process for Surrogates?" Reproductive Possibilities blog, May 28, 2020, https://reproductivepossibilities.com/blog/surrogacy-timeline-surrogate-mothers.

27. Mello, "Surrogate Timeline."

28. "What A Surrogate Can Expect From An Embryo Transfer," Extraordinary Conceptions, accessed August 11, 2022, https://www.extraconceptions.com/surrogate-can-expect-embryo-transfer.

29. Kate Swanson, Nina K. Ayala, Randall B. Barnes, Nidhi Desai, Marcy Miller, and Lynn M. Yee, "Understanding Gestational Surrogacy in the United States: a Primer for Obstetricians and Gynecologists," *American Journal of Obstetrics and Gynecology* 222, no. 4 (2020): 333.

30. "Do Surrogates Get Paid for Failed Transfers?," American Surrogacy blog, June 1, 2019, https://www.americansurrogacy.com/blog/do-surrogates-get-paid-for-failed-transfers.

31. For scholarship on commercial surrogacy in India, see Amrita Pande, *Wombs in Labor: Transnational Commercial Surrogacy in India* (New York: Columbia University Press, 2014); Anindita Majumdar, *Transnational Commercial Surrogacy and the (Un)Making of Kin in India* (Delhi: Oxford Academic, 2018).

32. Sara Ainsworth, "Bearing Children, Bearing Risks: Feminist Leadership for Progressive Regulation of Compensated Surrogacy in the United States," *Washington Law Review* 89 (2014): 1077–1123, at 1087.

33. Vidhi Doshi, "'We Pray that this Clinic Stays Open': India's Surrogates Fear Hardship from Embryo Ban," *The Guardian* (London), January 2, 2016.

34. Fariyal Ross-Sheriff, "Transnational Cross-Racial Surrogacy: Issues and Concerns," *Affilia* 27, no. 2 (2012): 126.

35. Serene J. Khader, "Intersectionality and the Ethics of Transnational Commercial Surrogacy," *International Journal of Feminist Approaches to Bioethics* 6, no. 1 (2013): 70.

36. Khader, "Intersectionality," 77.

37. Heather Jacobson, "Cross-Border Reproductive Care in the USA: Who Comes, Why Do They Come, What Do They Purchase?," *Reproductive Biomedicine & Society Online* 11 (2020): 42–47, at 44.

38. "About Hatch Fertility," accessed January 8, 2024, https://www.hatch.us/why-hatch.

39. "Explore the Best U.S. States for Surrogacy in 2023," Hatch Fertility, April 26, 2023, https://www.hatch.us/en/blog/best-states-for-surrogacy-2023.

40. Ertman, "What's Wrong with a Parenthood Market?," 12.

41. Ertman, "What's Wrong with a Parenthood Market?," 12. Ertman notes that by 1995, nineteen states had passed laws banning commercial surrogacy or refusing to honor surrogacy contracts.

42. "The United States Surrogacy Law Map," Creative Family Connections, accessed August 11, 2022, https://www.creativefamilyconnections.com/us-surrogacy-law-map.

43. Ertman, "What's Wrong with a Parenthood Market?," 4.

44. Ertman, "What's Wrong with a Parenthood Market?," 8.

45. Khiara Bridges, "*Windsor*, Surrogacy, and Race," *Washington Law Review* 89, no. 4 (2014): 1126.

46. Bridges, "*Windsor*," 1127.

47. Bridges, "*Windsor*," 1127.

48. Judith Stacey, "Queer Reproductive Justice?," *Reproductive Biomedicine & Society Online* 7 (2018): 6.

49. Marcin Smietana and France Winddance Twine, "Queer Decisions: Racial Matching Among Gay Male Intended Parents," *International Journal of Comparative Sociology* (2022): 1.

50. Pablo Pérez Navarro, "Surrogacy Wars: Notes for a Radical Theory of the Politics of Reproduction," *Journal of Homosexuality* 5, no. 67 (2020): 577–99.

51. Jacobson, "A Limited Market," 16; Laura Mamo and Eli Alston-Stepnitz, "Queer Intimacies and Structural Inequalities: New Directions in Stratified Reproduction," *Journal of Family Issues* 36, no. 4 (2015): 519–40.

52. Kristen E. Cheney, "Discordant Expectations of Global Intimacy: Desire and Inequality in Commercial Surrogacy," *Sociological Research Online* 27, no. 1 (2022): 46–59.

53. Erika L. Fuchs and Abbey B. Berenson, "Outcomes for Gestational Carriers Versus Traditional Surrogates in the United States," *Journal of Women's Health* 27, no. 5 (2018): 640–45.

54. Steiner, "Who Becomes a Surrogate?"

55. Harrison, *Brown Bodies, White Babies.*

56. A. Kaing, E. W. Scibetta, S. L. Gaw, R. Rao, Y. Afshar, C. S. Han, et al., "Gestational Carriers: The Demographics Behind a Frequently Overlooked Population," *Fertility and Sterility* 108, no. 3 (2017).

57. Kaing et al., "Gestational Carriers."

58. Fuchs and Berenson, "Outcomes for Gestational Carriers."

59. Harrison, *Brown Bodies, White Babies.*

60. Harrison, *Brown Bodies, White Babies*, 5.

61. Steiner, "Who Becomes a Surrogate?"

62. Steiner, "Who Becomes a Surrogate?"

63. Swanson et al., "Understanding Gestational Surrogacy," 332.

64. Kiran M. Perkins, Sheree L. Boulet, Denise J. Jamieson, Dmitry M. Kissin, and National Assisted Reproductive Technology Surveillance System (NASS) Group, "Trends and Outcomes of Gestational Surrogacy in the United States," *Fertility and Sterility* 106, no. 2 (2016): 435–42.

65. Swanson et al., "Understanding Gestational Surrogacy," 333.

66. Xavier Symons, "More Gay Couples Using Surrogates in US," BioEdge, November 26, 2016, https://bioedge.org/uncategorized/more-gay-couples-using-surrogates-in-us.

67. Steiner, "Who Becomes a Surrogate?"

68. Samantha Yee and Clifford L. Librach, "Analysis of Gestational Surrogates' Birthing Experiences and Relationships with Intended Parents During Pregnancy and Post-Birth," *Birth* 46, no. 4 (2019): 628–37.

69. Camisha Russell, "Rights-Holders or Refugees? Do Gay Men Need Reproductive Justice?," *Reproductive Biomedicine & Society Online* 7 (2018): 131–40.

70. Symons, "More Gay Couples Using Surrogates."

71. Brian Glassman, "Same-Sex Married Couples Have Higher Income Than Opposite-Sex Married Couples," United States Census Bureau, September 17, 2020.

72. For scholarly analysis of surrogacy legislation in New York, which preceded this recent campaign, see Susan Markens, *Surrogate Motherhood and the Politics of Reproduction* (Oakland: University of California Press, 2007).

73. "New York 'Love Makes A Family' Campaign Fights for Legalized Surrogacy, LGBTQ Rights," *CBS* 6 (Albany, NY), February 11, 2020.

74. "New York 'Love Makes A Family' Campaign."

75. "New York 'Love Makes A Family' Campaign."

76. "New York 'Love Makes A Family' Campaign."

77. David Kaufman, "The Fight for Fertility Equality," *New York Times*, July 22, 2020, https://www.nytimes.com/2020/07/22/style/lgbtq-fertility-surrogacy-coverage.html.

78. Kaufman, "The Fight for Fertility Equality."

79. Kaufman, "The Fight for Fertility Equality."

80. Amy Paulin, "Surrogate Parenting Contracts," New York State Assembly, March 3, 2014, video, 1:16, https://nyassembly.gov/mem/Amy-Paulin/video/3999.

81. "Governor Cuomo Launches 'Love Makes A Family' Campaign to Legalize Gestational Surrogacy," New York State Press Release, February 11, 2020, https://fertilitylaw.wbny.com/siteFiles/34270/governors-press-release_love_makes_a_family_2020-feb-11.pdf.

82. "The Child-Parent Security Act: Gestational Surrogacy," New York State Department of Health, accessed August 2, 2022, https://health.ny.gov/community/pregnancy/surrogacy.

83. "The Child-Parent Security Act."

84. "The Child-Parent Security Act."

85. "The Child-Parent Security Act."

86. John Burger, "Gloria Steinem Comes Out Against Bill That Would Legalize Paid Surrogacy," *Aleteia*, June 14, 2019, https://aleteia.org/2019/06/14/gloria-steinem-comes-out-against-bill-that-would-legalize-paid-surrogacy.

87. Vivian Wang, "Surrogate Pregnancy Battle Pits Progressives Against Feminists," *The New York Times*, June 12, 2019, https://www.nytimes.com/2019/06/12/nyregion/surrogate-pregnancy-law-ny.html.

88. "About MHB," Men Having Babies, accessed August 2, 2022, https://menhavingbabies.org/about.

89. "Surrogacy for Gay Men: Grants and Overcoming Financial Obstacles," Daddy Squared: The Gay Dads Podcast, July 9, 2020, https://daddysqr.com/gay-surrogacy-grants-2020/.

90. "Surrogacy for Gay Men."

91. "About MHB."

92. "The Gay Parenting Assistance Program (GPAP) of Men Having Babies," Men Having Babies, accessed August 2, 2022, https://menhavingbabies.org/assistance.

93. Latoya Hill, Samantha Artiga, and Usha Ranji, "Racial Disparities in Maternal and Infant Health: An Overview," Kaiser Family Foundation, November 10, 2020, https://www.kff.org/report-section/racial-disparities-in-maternal-and-infant-health-an-overview-issue-brief.

94. Michele Goodwin, "The New Jane Crow: Women's Mass Incarceration," Just Security, July 20, 2020, https://www.justsecurity.org/71509/the-new-jane-crow-womens-mass-incarceration; Dorothy Roberts, "How the Child Welfare System Polices Black Mothers," *Scholar & Feminist Online* (2019), https://sfonline.barnard.edu/unraveling-criminalizing-webs-building-police-free-futures/how-the-child-welfare-system-polices-black-mothers.

95. "Framework for Ethical Surrogacy: Principles, Protocols, and Best Practices," Men Having Babies, September 6, 2016, https://menhavingbabies.org/get-involved/advocacy/ethical-surrogacy.

96. "Framework for Ethical Surrogacy."

97. "Framework for Ethical Surrogacy."

98. "Framework for Ethical Surrogacy."

99. "Framework for Ethical Surrogacy."

100. "Framework for Ethical Surrogacy."

101. Kaufman, "The Fight for Fertility Equality."

102. Christopher S. Carpenter and Samuel T. Eppink, "Does It Get Better? Recent Estimates of Sexual Orientation and Earnings in the United States," *Southern Economic Journal* 84, no. 2 (2017): 426–41.

103. National Committee on Pay Equity website, accessed August 3, 2022, https://www.pay-equity.org/index.html.

104. Jacobson, "A Limited Market."

105. "GWK Academy: The First Stop on Your Journey to Fatherhood," Gays with Kids, accessed August 3, 2022, https://www.gayswithkids.com/gwk-academy.

106. "LGBTQ+ Family Building Grants," Family Equality, accessed August 3, 2022, https://www.familyequality.org/resources/lgbtq-family-building-grants.

107. "Gay Parenting Assistance Program."

108. Page, "They Were Gay and Wanted a Baby."

109. Steiner, "Who Becomes a Surrogate?"

110. Steiner, "Who Becomes a Surrogate?"

111. Men Having Babies (@menhavingbabies), "It's sage advice time! Luis and Ron are fathers to their baby Preston and they would like to think that they are semi experienced . . ." Instagram, March 10, 2017, https://www.instagram.com/p/CMPhkzDMgC8.

112. Kaufman, "The Fight for Fertility Equality."

113. Kaufman, "The Fight for Fertility Equality."

114. Medusaisdone (@medusaisdone), Twitter, July 22, 2020, 2:14 AM, https://twitter.com/medusaisdone/status/1292705973979746304.

115. WEP Women's Sex-Based Rights Caucus (@WepWomen), Twitter, August 10, 2020, 5:33 AM, https://twitter.com/WepWomen/status/1292755997027598337.

116. ARRR Morgan (@grumpwitch), Twitter, July 22, 2020, 4:20 AM, https://twitter.com/grumpwitch/status/1292737482149289985.

117. Isa Elfers, "Alienation, Commodification, and Commercialization: A Feminist Critique of Commercial Surrogacy Agreements Through the Lens of Labor Exploitation and U.S. Organ Donation Law," *Hastings Journal on Gender and the Law* 33, no. 2 (2022): 183.

118. David Dodge, "Meet the Women Who Become Surrogates," *New York Times*, February 15, 2021, https://www.nytimes.com/2021/02/15/parenting/fertility/surrogates-new-york.html.

119. Dodge, "Meet the Women."

120. Kaing et al., "Gestational Carriers."

121. Men Having Babies (@menhavingbabies), Instagram, Profile, https://www.instagram.com/menhavingbabies. These data include the two hundred most recent posts as of August 2, 2022. To come up with our figures, my research assistants and I read the race of the people in the photos as white or non-white in ways that are in line with what we see as typical reading practices—that is, most members of the general public viewing these posts would read the races of the people in question similarly. Clearly, this approach is not methodologically robust. In providing these numbers, the goal is simply to highlight that the site is overwhelmingly white.

122. Brad Spencer, "Tips for Successful Surrogate Match Meeting," Men Having Babies, accessed August 3, 2022, https://menhavingbabies.org/surrogacy-resources/ask-the-expert/user-view/post.php?permalink=surrogate-matching.

123. "Does Race Matter When Choosing a Surrogate?," American Surrogacy blog, June 15, 2020, https://www.americansurrogacy.com/blog/does-race-matter-when-choosing-a-surrogate.

124. Steiner, "Who Becomes a Surrogate?"

125. A. Rochaun Meadows-Fernandez, "For Black Women, Reproductive Justice Is About More Than High-Risk Pregnancies," *Yes Magazine*, April 2, 2019, https://www.yesmagazine.org/social-justice/2019/04/02/black-women-fertility-reproductive-justice.

126. Wonder World, "World's First Black Woman to Give Birth to Two White Babies," June 7, 2019, 4:26, https://www.youtube.com/watch?v=MzOEXiUtHuQ; Helen Weathers, "I'm a White Woman but I've Become a Surrogate Mother for an Asian Couple," *Daily Mail*, March 1, 2008, https://www.dailymail.co.uk/femail/article-522670/Im-white-woman-Ive-surrogate-mother-Asian-couple.html.

127. Sarah-Kate Templeton, "White Surrogate Mother Breaks Silence on Bearing Asian Baby," *The Times*, February 24, 2008, https://www.thetimes.co.uk/article/white-surrogate-mother-breaks-silence-on-bearing-asian-baby-ndv3qcdmkp2.

128. Sylvia Wynter, "Race and Our Biocentric Belief System: An Interview with Sylvia Wynter," in *Black Education, A Transformative Research and Action Agenda for the New Century*, ed. Joyce E. King (Washington, DC: American Educational Research Association, 2005): 361.

129. Wynter, "Race and Our Biocentric Belief System," 361.

130. Wynter, "Race and Our Biocentric Belief System," 364.

131. Weathers, "I'm a White Woman."

132. For an extended discussion of this methodology, see Appendix A.

133. Smietana and Twine, "Queer Decisions."

134. Laura Mamo, Queering Reproduction: Achieving Pregnancy in the Age of Technoscience (Durham: Duke University Press, 2007).

135. Mamo, "Queering the Fertility Clinic," *Journal of Medical Humanities* 34, no. 2 (2019): 227–39, at 231.

136. Mamo, "Queering the Fertility Clinic," 230.

137. Stacey, "Queer Reproductive Justice?," 4.

138. Stacey, "Queer Reproductive Justice?," 6.

139. Mary Gray, *Out in the Country: Youth, Media, and Queer Visibility in Rural America* (New York: New York University Press, 2009); Carly Thomsen, *Visibility Interrupted: Rural Queer Life and the Politics of Unbecoming* (Minneapolis: University of Minnesota Press, 2021).

140. For additional discussion of this point, see Lauren Berlant, *The Queen of America Goes to Washington City* (Durham: Duke University Press, 1997); Dorothy Roberts, "Race and the New Reproduction," *The Reproductive Rights Reader: Law, Medicine, and the Construction of Motherhood*, ed. Nancy Ehrenreich (New York: New York University Press, 2008).

## CHAPTER 2. THE HETERONORMATIVITY OF PAID PARENTAL LEAVE

1. Erin Hill, "Meghan Markle and Prince Harry Share First Photo of Baby Lilibet Diana—on Their Holiday Card!," *Yahoo! News*, December 23, 2021, https://news.yahoo.com/meghan-markle-prince-harry-share-135937081.html.

2. Meghan Markle, "Letter from Meghan, The Duchess of Sussex," Paid Leave for All, October 20, 2021, https://paidleaveforall.org/theduchessofsussex.

3. Jen Juneau and Lindsay Kimble, "Serena Williams 'Can't Imagine' Taking Just Two Weeks of Maternity Leave: 'It's Impossible,'" *People*, August 26,

2019, https://people.com/parents/serena-williams-maternity-leave-two-weeks-impossible-exclusive.

4. Anne Hathaway, "Paid Parental Leave is About Creating Freedom to Define Roles," speech, UN Women (New York, NY), March 8, 2017, https://www.unwomen.org/en/news/stories/2017/3/speech-anne-hathaway-iwd-2017.

5. Gretchen Livingston and Deja Thomas, "Among 41 Countries, Only U.S. Lacks Paid Parental Leave," Pew Research Center, December 16, 2019, https://www.pewresearch.org/fact-tank/2019/12/16/u-s-lacks-mandated-paid-parental-leave.

6. "Paid Family & Medical Leave," Moms Rising, accessed July 1, 2022. https://www.momsrising.org/campaigns/paid-family-medical-leave.

7. Pamela Joshi, Maura Baldiga, and Rebecca Huber, "Unequal Access to FMLA Leave Persists," Diversity Data Kids, January 16, 2020, https://www.diversitydatakids.org/research-library/data-visualization/unequal-access-fmla-leave-persists.

8. Ann Bartel, Soohyun Kim, Jaehyun Nam, Maya Rossin-Slater, Christopher Ruhm, and Jane Waldfogel, "Racial and Ethnic Disparities in Access to and Use of Paid Family and Medical Leave: Evidence from Four Nationally Representative Datasets," *Monthly Labor Review*, January 1, 2019, https://www.bls.gov/opub/mlr/2019/article/racial-and-ethnic-disparities-in-access-to-and-use-of-paid-family-and-medical-leave.htm.

9. Bartel et al., "Racial and Ethnic Disparities."

10. Bartel et al., "Racial and Ethnic Disparities."

11. Julia M. Goodman, Connor Williams, and William H. Dow, "Racial/Ethnic Inequities in Paid Parental Leave Access," *Health Equity* 5, no. 1 (2021): 743, https://www.ncbi.nlm.nih.gov/pmc/articles/PMC8665807.

12. Jocelyn Frye, *The Missing Conversation About Work and Family: Unique Challenges Facing Women of Color* (Washington, DC: Center for American Progress, 2016), https://www.americanprogress.org/article/the-missing-conversation-about-work-and-family.

13. Jeremy Hull, "Potential Barriers to Aboriginal Teenaged Mothers' Access to Maternal and Parental Benefits," *International Indigenous Policy Journal* 4, no. 1 (2013).

14. Jamila Taylor, Cristina Novoa, Katie Hamm, and Shilpa Phadke, *Eliminating Racial Disparities in Maternal and Infant Mortality A Comprehensive Policy Blueprint* (Washington, DC: Center for American Progress, 2019), https://www.americanprogress.org/article/eliminating-racial-disparities-maternal-infant-mortality.

15. Vicki Shabo, "Polling Summary: In Build Back Better, Paid Family and Medical Leave Is One of the Most Popular Policies," Better Life Lab, *New America* (blog), November 10, 2021, https://www.newamerica.org/better-life-

lab/blog/polling-summary-paid-family-and-medical-leave-is-one-of-the-most-popular-planks-in-the-build-back-better-agenda.

16. Dawn Motsiff, "Ditch Maternity Leave for Parental Leave—Here's Why," *Insperity* (blog), accessed July 5, 2022, https://www.insperity.com/blog/parental-leave.

17. Silvia Federici, *Reproduction at Point Zero: Housework, Reproduction, and Feminist Struggle* (Oakland: PM Press, 2012).

18. Kathi Weeks, *The Problem with Work: Feminism, Marxism, Antiwork Politics, and Postwork Imaginaries* (Durham: Duke University Press, 2011).

19. Heather Berg, "An Honest Day's Wage for a Dishonest Day's Work: (Re)Productivism and Refusal," *Women's Studies Quarterly* 42, no. 1/2 (2014): 161–77.

20. José Esteban Muñoz, *Cruising Utopia: The Then and There of Queer Futurity* (New York: New York University Press, 2009).

21. Lee Edelman, *No Future: Queer Theory and the Death Drive* (Durham: Duke University Press, 2004).

22. John D'Emilio, "Capitalism and Gay Identity," in *Powers of Desire: The Politics of Sexuality*, ed. Ann Snitow, Christine Stansell, and Sharon Thompson (New York: NYU Press, 1983), 100–14; Peter Drucker, *Warped: Gay Normality and Queer Anti-Capitalism* (Leiden: Brill, 2015); Kevin Floyd, *The Reification of Desire: Toward a Queer Marxism* (Minneapolis: University of Minnesota Press, 2009); Rosemary Hennessy, *Profit and Pleasure: Sexual Identities in Late Capitalism* (New York: Routledge, 2000); Rosemary Hennessy, *Fires on the Border: The Passionate Politics of Labor Organizing on the Mexican Frontera* (Minneapolis: University of Minnesota Press, 2013); Grace Kyungwon Hong, "Existentially Surplus: Women of Color Feminism and the New Crises of Capitalism," *GLQ* 18, no. 1 (2012); Miranda Joseph, *Against the Romance of Community* (Minneapolis: University of Minnesota Press, 2002); Miranda Joseph, *Debt to Society: Accounting for Life Under Capitalism* (Minneapolis: University of Minnesota Press, 2014); Alan Sears, "Queer Anti-Capitalism: What's Left of Lesbian and Gay Liberation?," *Science & Society* 69, no. 1 (2005): 92–112; Jordy Rosenberg and Amy Villarejo, "Queer Studies and the Crisis of Capitalism," *GLQ* 18, no. 1 (2012); Weeks, *The Problem with Work;* Meg Wesling, "Queer Value," *GLQ* 18, no. 1 (2012): 107–25; Carly Thomsen, "Queer Labors," in *Visibility Interrupted: Rural Queer Life and the Politics of Unbecoming* (Minneapolis: University of Minnesota Press, 2021).

23. Cathy J. Cohen, "Punks, Bulldaggers, and Welfare Queens: The Radical Potential of Queer Politics?," *GLQ: A Journal of Lesbian and Gay Studies* 3, no. 4 (1997).

24. Martha Albertson Fineman, Jack E. Jackson, and Adam Romero, *Feminist and Queer Legal Theory: Intimate Encounters, Uncomfortable Conversations* (London: Routledge, 2009); Annamarie Jagose, "Feminism's Queer Theory," *Feminism & Psychology* 19, no. 2 (2009): 157–74; Biddy Martin, "Sexualities Without Gender and Other Queer Utopias," *Diacritics* 24, no. 2/3

(1994): 104–21; Amber Jamilla Musser, "Gender and Queer Theory," in *A Companion to Critical and Cultural Theory*, ed. Imre Szeman, Sarah Blacker, and Justin Sully (Oxford: Wiley, 2017), 243–54; Elizabeth Weed and Naomi Schor, *Feminism Meets Queer Theory* (Bloomington: Indiana University Press, 1997).

25. Kathy Spiller, "House Passes the Historic Build Back Better Act: 'A Giant Step Forward,'" *Ms.*, November 19, 2021, https://msmagazine.com/2021/11/19/build-back-better-house.

26. Lorie Konish, "Senate Majority Leader Chuck Schumer Calls Paid Leave 'One of the Most Important Planks' in Build Back Better," *CNBC*, December 9, 2021, https://www.cnbc.com/2021/12/09/sen-chuck-schumer-says-paid-leave-is-so-vital-to-build-back-better.html.

27. Brenda L. Lawrence, "Building Back Better for Women and Families," *Ms. Magazine*, October 29, 2021, https://msmagazine.com/2021/10/29/build-back-better-women-families-biden-harris; Carrie N. Baker, "Build Back Better Would Achieve Feminists' Long-Deferred Dream of Affordable Childcare," *Ms. Magazine*, November 2, 2021, https://msmagazine.com/2021/11/02/childcare-build-back-better-biden; Nina Perez and Julie Kashen, "The U.S. Is in Urgent Need of Childcare Solutions. Build Back Better Would Be a Game-Changer," *Ms. Magazine*, January 6, 2022, https://msmagazine.com/2022/01/06/build-back-better-childcare-parents-moms.

28. Mary Babic, "Why Is the Senate Failing To Build Back Better? Blame Sexism," *Ms. Magazine*, January 14, 2022, https://msmagazine.com/2022/01/14/build-back-better-women-senate-sexism-families-infrastructure; Katie Fleischer, "Build Back Better Is in Peril. Low-Income Families Can't Afford To Lose It," *Ms. Magazine*, December 20, 2021, https://msmagazine.com/2021/12/20/build-back-better-low-income-families-guaranteed-income-magnolia-mothers-trust-mental-health-holiday-stress; Jhumpa Bhattacharya and Saadia McConville, "Death of Build Back Better Will Hurt Women and Kids the Most," *Ms. Magazine*, March 28, 2022, https://msmagazine.com/2022/03/28/build-back-better-women-children-child-tax-credit-universal-pre-k-paid-leave.

29. Hathaway, "Paid Parental Leave."

30. Alexis Ohanian, "Paternity Leave Was Crucial After the Birth of My Child, and Every Father Deserves It," *New York Times*, April 15, 2020, https://www.nytimes.com/2020/04/15/parenting/alexis-ohanian-paternity-leave.html.

31. For an extended discussion of our methodology, please see Appendix A.

32. Motsiff, "Ditch Maternity Leave."

33. Motsiff, "Ditch Maternity Leave."

34. Megan Brenan, "Women Still Handle Main Household Tasks in U.S.," Gallup, January 29, 2020, https://news.gallup.com/poll/283979/women-handle-main-household-tasks.aspx.

35. Carla A. Pfeffer, "'Women's Work'? Women Partners of Transgender Men Doing Housework and Emotion Work," *Journal of Family and Marriage* 72, no. 1

(2010); Jane Ward, "Gender Labor: Transmen, Femmes, and Collective Work of Transgression," *Sexualities* 13, no. 2 (April 2010): 236–54.

36. Leigh Cuen, "Here's Why Paternity Leave Is a Huge Feminist Issue," *Mic*, June 17, 2016, https://www.mic.com/articles/146313/here-s-why-paternity-leave-is-a-huge-feminist-issue.

37. Kylie Gilbert, "The Fight for Paternity Leave Is a Feminist One," *Instyle*, November 23, 2020, https://www.instyle.com/politics-social-issues/paternity-leave-is-feminist.

38. Gilbert, "The Fight for Paternity Leave."

39. Cuen, "Here's Why Paternity Leave Is a Huge Feminist Issue."

40. Jennifer E. Karr, "Where's My Dad? A Feminist Approach to Incentivized Paternity Leave," *Hastings Women's Law Journal* 28, no. 2 (Summer 2017): 225.

41. Gilbert, "The Fight for Paternity Leave."

42. Gillian B. White, "Paid Leave for Dads: A Feminist Issue," *The Atlantic*, November 29, 2015, https://www.theatlantic.com/business/archive/2015/11/both-moms-and-dads-need-paid-leave/417708.

43. Gilbert, "The Fight for Paternity Leave."

44. Cuen, "Here's Why Paternity Leave Is a Huge Feminist Issue."

45. IWPR, "Build Back Better Framework Outlined by President Biden is a Down Payment on Fairer, More Equitable Economy that Works for Everyone," press release, October 28, 2021, https://iwpr.org/media/press-releases/build-back-better-framework-outlined-by-president-biden-is-a-down-payment-on-fairer-more-equitable-economy-that-works-for-everyone.

46. Melissa Boteach, "Tell Congress: It's Time to Solve Child Care," National Women's Law Center, October 14, 2021, email to author.

47. Brenda Lawrence, "Building Back Better for Women and Families," *Ms. Magazine*, October 29, 2021, https://msmagazine.com/2021/10/29/build-back-better-women-families-biden-harris.

48. "Marshall Plan for Moms," Marshall Plan for Moms, accessed July 13, 2022, https://marshallplanformoms.com/; The NY Women's Foundation (@nywomensfdn) Instagram, December 7, 2021, https://www.instagram.com/p/CXMjvbbFq43.

49. Raena Joy (@theworkingmomtras), Instagram, December 6, 2021, https://www.instagram.com/p/CXJc67Mr9cH.

50. Hathaway, "Paid Parental Leave."

51. Cuen, "Here's Why Paternity Leave Is a Huge Feminist Issue."

52. Motsiff, "Ditch Maternity Leave."

53. David Dodge, "The Fight for Paid Parental Leave is a Fight for Queer Rights," Opinion, *Newsweek*, November 22, 2021, https://www.newsweek.com/fight-paid-parental-leave-fight-queer-rights-opinion-1650999.

54. Eileen Boris and Allison Elias, "Workplace Discrimination, Equal Pay, and Sexual Harassment: An Intersectional Approach," in *The Oxford Handbook of*

*U.S. Women's Social Movement Activism*, ed. Holly J. McCammon, Verta Taylor, Jo Reger, and Rachel L. Einwohner (New York: Oxford University Press, 2017).

55. Daisuke Wakabayashi and Sheera Frenkel, "Parents Got More Time Off. Then the Backlash Started," *New York Times*, July 28, 2021, https://www.nytimes.com/2020/09/05/technology/parents-time-off-backlash.html.

56. Wakabayashi and Frenkel, "Parents Got More Time Off."

57. Sara Ahmed, *Complaint!* (Durham: Duke University Press, 2021).

58. Hathaway, "Paid Parental Leave."

59. Hathaway, "Paid Parental Leave."

60. Anna Davies, "I Want All the Perks of Maternity Leave—Without Having Any Kids," *New York Post*, April 28, 2016, https://nypost.com/2016/04/28/i-want-all-the-perks-of-maternity-leave-without-having-any-kids.

61. Davies, "I Want All the Perks."

62. Mary Elizabeth Williams, "Don't Call it Maternity Leave: Non-Parents Could Use Time Off Work, Too—But it's Not the Same," *Salon*, April 28, 2016, https://www.salon.com/2016/04/28/yes_non_parents_deserve_maternity_leave_we_could_all_use_a_break_for_self_reflection.

63. Kyle Smith, "Parents Should Be Worshipped by their Childless Co-Workers," *New York Post*, April 28, 2016, https://nypost.com/2016/04/28/parents-should-be-worshipped-by-their-childless-co-workers.

64. Smith, "Parents Should Be Worshipped."

65. Smith, "Parents Should Be Worshipped."

66. Sydney Bucksbaum, "'*Unbreakable Kimmy Schmidt*'s Feminism Is Strong As Hell," *Bustle*, May 19, 2017, https://www.bustle.com/p/unbreakable-kimmy-schmidt-season-3s-feminism-is-strong-as-hell-58946; Sabrina Schnabel, "The Radical Feminism of Downton Abbey," *Mantle*, September 26, 2019, https://www.mantlemagazine.com/index.php/2019/09/26/the-radical-feminism-of-downton-abbey; Jack Persico, "The Women of Downton Abbey vs. Women of the Super Bowl," *Philadelphia*, February 1, 2013, https://www.phillymag.com/news/2013/02/01/women-downton-abbey-vs-women-super-bowl.

67. Virginie Boone, "Top Wine Terms Defined," *Wine Enthusiast*, November 26, 2014, https://www.winemag.com/2014/11/26/top-wine-terms-defined.

68. Smith, "Parents Should Be Worshipped."

69. Saba Mughal, Yusra Azhar, and Waquar Siddiqui, *Perinatal Depression* (StatPearls Publishing, 2021), https://www.ncbi.nlm.nih.gov/books/NBK519070.

70. Kate Johanns, "What You Need to Know When Covering for Someone on Maternity/Paternity Leave," *Washington Post*, January 16, 2020, https://jobs.washingtonpost.com/article/what-you-need-to-know-when-covering-for-someone-on-maternity-paternity-leave.

71. Tayelor Valerio, Rose M. Kreider and Wan He, "No Kids, No Care? Childlessness Among Older Americans," US Census Bureau, December 14, 2021,

https://www.census.gov/library/stories/2021/12/no-kids-no-care-childlessness-among-older-americans.html.

72. Anna Brown, "Growing Share of Childless Adults in U.S. Don't Expect to Ever Have Children," Pew Research Center, November 19, 2021, https://www.pewresearch.org/fact-tank/2021/11/19/growing-share-of-childless-adults-in-u-s-dont-expect-to-ever-have-children.

73. Gretchen Livingston and D'Vera Cohn, "Childlessness Up Among All Women; Down Among Women with Advanced Degrees," Pew Research Center, June25,2010,https://www.pewresearch.org/social-trends/2010/06/25/childlessness-up-among-all-women-down-among-women-with-advanced-degrees.

74. "Percentage of Same-Sex Couples in the United States in 2019, Sorted by Children in the Household," US Census Bureau, data visualization by Statsita, accessed March 1, 2022, https://www.statista.com/statistics/325083/same-sex-couples-in-the-us-by-children-in-the-household.

75. Diego Lasio, Jessica Lampis, Roberta Spiga, and Francesco Serria, "Lesbian and Gay Individual Parenting Desires in Heteronormative Contexts," *Europe's Journal of Psychology* 16, no. 2 (2020): 210–28.

76. Maddy Savage, "How to Say No at Work When You Don't Have Kids," Worklife, *BBC*, August 15th, 2017, https://www.bbc.com/worklife/article/20170814-how-to-say-no-at-work-when-you-dont-have-kids; Kathryn Nawrockyi, Laura Swiszczowski, Rachael Saunders and Thomas Colquhoun-Alberts, *Opportunity Now*, Project 28–40: The Report (London: Business in the Community, 2014), https://pwc.blogs.com/files/project28-40_finalreport_010414.pdf.

77. Marc Goulden and Robert Drago, "Balancing Work & Family for Faculty," University of Washington, July 28, 2005, https://advance.washington.edu/resource-admin/file/yMYer06bOB.

78. Goulden and Drago, "Balancing Work & Family."

79. Jamilah Lemieux, "Am I Selfish for Forcing Vegetables on My Meat-and-Carbs Family?," Care and Feeding, *Slate*, January 22, 2021, https://slate.com/human-interest/2021/01/cooking-selfishness-vegetables-care-and-feeding.html.

80. Lemieux, "Am I Selfish."

81. Doyin Richards, "My MIL Has Gross Misconceptions About How We Plan to Raise Our Daughter," Care and Feeding, *Slate*, July 5, 2022, https://slate.com/human-interest/2022/07/in-laws-views-religion.html.

82. Richards, "My MIL Has Gross Misconceptions."

83. Doyin Richards, "My In-Laws Want My Son to Call Them Names I Despise," Care and Feeding, *Slate*, May 4, 2021, https://slate.com/human-interest/2021/05/hate-name-family-wants-child-call-them-care-and-feeding.html.

84. Richards, "My In-Laws."

85. Richards, "My In-Laws."

86. Carvell Wallace, "Stop Losing Your Coat!!," Care and Feeding, *Slate*, April 17, 2019, https://slate.com/human-interest/2019/04/kids-losing-coats-care-and-feeding.html.

87. Wallace, "Stop Losing Your Coat!!"

88. Andrea Reupert, Shulamith Lala Straussner, Bente Weimand, and Darryl Maybery, "It Takes a Village to Raise a Child: Understanding and Expanding the Concept of the 'Village,'" *Frontiers in Public Health* 10 (March 2022).

89. Maxine Baca Zinn, "Feminism and Family Studies for a New Century," *The Annals of the American Academy of Political and Social Science* 571 (2000): 45.

90. Baca Zinn, "Feminism and Family," 45.

91. Baca Zinn, "Feminism and Family," 47.

92. Baca Zinn, "Feminism and Family," 47.

93. Bonnie Thornton Dill, "Fictive Kin, Paper Sons, and Compadrazgo: Women of Color and the Struggle for Family Survival," in *Women of Color in U.S. Society*, ed. Maxine Baca Zinn and Bonnie Thornton Dill (Philadelphia: Temple University Press, 1994), 149–70.

94. Johanna Brenner and Barbara Laslett, "Gender, Social Reproduction, and Women's Self-Organization: Considering the U.S. Welfare State," *Gender & Society* 5, no. 3 (1991): 314.

95. Tithi Bhattacharya, *Social Reproduction Theory: Remapping Class, Recentering Oppression*. (London: Pluto Press, 2017), 2.

96. Bhattacharya, *Social Reproduction Theory*, 2.

97. Bhattacharya, *Social Reproduction Theory*, 3.

98. Kathi Weeks, "Feminism and the Refusal of Work," interview by George Souvlis, Verso, September 19, 2017, https://www.versobooks.com/blogs/3400-feminism-and-the-refusal-of-work-an-interview-with-kathi-weeks.

99. Michelle Barrett and Mary McIntosh, *The Anti-Social Family* (London: Verso, 1982); Heidi Hartman, "The Unhappy Marriage of Marxism and Feminism: Towards a More Progressive Union," *Capital & Class* 3, no.1 (1979): 1–33.

100. Mariarosa Dalla Costa and Selma James, *The Power of Women and the Subversion of the Community* (Brooklyn, NY: Petroleuse Press, 1972).

101. Dalla Costa and James, *Power of Women*.

102. Bhattacharya, *Social Reproduction Theory*, 13.

103. Bhattacharya, *Social Reproduction Theory*, 1.

104. Bhattacharya, *Social Reproduction Theory*, 2.

105. Dalla Costa and James, *Power of Women*.

106. Weeks, "Feminism and the Refusal."

107. Mary Gray, *Out in the Country: Youth, Media, and Queer Visibility in Rural America* (New York: New York University Press, 2009); Thomsen, *Visibility Interrupted*.

108. Thomsen, *Visibility Interrupted.*

109. Bhattacharya, *Social Reproduction Theory*, 2.

110. Nina Jackson Levin, Shanna K. Kattari, Emily K. Piellusch, and Erica Watson, "'We Just Take Care of Each Other': Navigating 'Chosen Family' in the Context of Health, Illness, and the Mutual Provision of Care Amongst Queer and Transgender Young Adults," *International Journal of Environmental Research and Public Health* (2020).

111. Lindsay Mahowald and Diana Boesch, "Making the Case for Chosen Family in Paid Family and Medical Leave Policies," *Center for American Progress* (blog), February 16, 2021, https://www.americanprogress.org/article/making-case-chosen-family-paid-family-medical-leave-policies.

112. Mahowald and Boesch, "Making the Case."

113. Mahowald and Boesch, "Making the Case."

114. Julie Compton, "'Chosen Families' Ruptured: How Covid-19 Hit an LGBTQ Lifeline," *NBC*, December 20, 2020, https://www.nbcnews.com/feature/nbc-out/chosen-families-ruptured-how-covid-19-hit-lgbtq-lifeline-n1251849; Sandy Allen, "Between the Binary: On the Gratitude I Feel to My Chosen Family," *them*, April 3, 2020, https://www.them.us/story/gratitude-for-chosen-family-during-coronavirus; Matthew Wade, "How My Queer Chosen Family Got Me Through COVID," *JUNKEE*, March 4, 2021, https://junkee.com/queer-chosen-family/289152.

115. "COVID-19 Response," Funders for LGBT Issues, accessed July 13, 2020 https://lgbtfunders.org/covid-19-response.

116. "LGBT Older People & COVID-19: Addressing Higher Risk, Social Isolation, and Discrimination," LGBT Map, May 2020, https://www.lgbtmap.org/file/2020%20LGBTQ%20Older%20Adults%20COVID.pdf.

117. Hil Malatino, *Trans Care* (Minneapolis: University of Minnesota Press, 2020), 3.

118. Malatino, *Trans Care*, 6.

119. Malatino, *Trans Care*, 6.

120. Malatino, *Trans Care*, 42; Martin Manalansan, "Queering the Chain of Care Paradigm," *The Scholar and Feminist Online* 6, no. 3 (2008).

121. Malatino, *Trans Care*, 2.

122. Aren Aizura, "Reproduction," in *Keywords for Gender and Sexuality Studies*, ed. Keywords Feminist Editorial Collective (New York: New York University Press, 2021), 192.

123. Aizura, "Reproduction," 192; Talia Lewis, "Disability Justice in the Age of Mass Incarceration: Perspectives on Race, Disability, Law and Accountability," lecture, Syracuse College of Law, Syracuse, NY, March 29, 2018.

124. Edelman, *No Future.*

125. Lauren Berlant, *Cruel Optimism* (Durham: Duke University Press, 2011).

126. "Queering Communities of Care," Duke Department of Gender, Sexuality Feminist Studies, accessed July 12, 2022, https://gendersexualityfeminist.duke.edu/events/queering-communities-care.

127. Lisa Nagele-Piazza, "Trump Approves Paid Parental Leave for Federal Workers," December 20, 2019, SHRM, https://www.shrm.org/resourcesandtools/legal-and-compliance/employment-law/pages/trump-approves-paid-parental-leave-for-federal-workers.aspx.

## CHAPTER 3. THE WOMAN QUESTION, THE TRANS QUESTION

1. Rayka Zehtabchi, dirl, *Ours to Tell,* video created for Planned Parenthood and We Testify, launched January 21, 2020, https://www.plannedparenthoodaction.org/rightfully-ours/ours-to-tell.

2. "Fact Sheet: LGBTQ+ People & Roe v. Wade," Human Rights Campaign Foundation, June 2, 2022, https://www.hrc.org/press-releases/human-rights-campaign-fact-sheet-lesbian-bisexual-queer-women-who-have-been-pregnant-are-more-likely-to-need-abortion-services-demonstrates-impact-roe-reversal-would-have-on-lgbtq-people.

3. L. Abern, S. Nippita, and K. Maguire, "Contraceptive Use and Abortion Views Among Transgender and Gender-Nonconforming Individuals Assigned Female at Birth," *Contraception* 98, no. 4 (2018): 337.

4. Alexis Light, Lin-Fan Wang, Alexander Zeymo, and Veronica Gomez-Lobo, "Family Planning and Contraception Use in Transgender Men," *Contraception* 98, no. 4 (2018): 266–69.

5. Heidi Moseson, Laura Fix, Sachiko Ragosta, Hannah Forsberg, Jen Hastings, Ari Stoeffler, Mitchell R. Lunn, Annesa Flentje, Matthew R. Capriotti, Micah Lubensky, Juno Obedin-Maliver, "Abortion Experiences and Preferences of Transgender, Nonbinary, and Gender-Expansive People in the United States," *American Journal of Obstetrics and Gynecology* 224, no. 4 (2021).

6. The Williams Institute, "How Many Adults and Youth Identify as Transgender in the United States?" September 27, 2022, https://williamsinstitute.law.ucla.edu/publications/trans-adults-united-states.

7. Heidi Moseson, Laura Fix, Sachiko Ragosta, Hannah Forsberg, Jen Hastings, Ari Stoeffler, et al., "Abortion Experiences and Preferences of Transgender, Nonbinary, and Gender-Expansive People in the United States," *American Journal of Obstetrics & Gynecology* 224, no. 4 (2021).

8. Finn Enke, "The Education of Little Cis: Cisgender and the Discipline of Opposing Bodies," in *Transfeminist Perspectives: In and Beyond Transgender and Gender Studies,* ed. Finn Enke (Philadelphia: Temple University Press, 2012): 60–77.

9. Kadji Amin, "We Are All Nonbinary: A Brief History of Accidents," *Representations* 158 (2022): 109.

10. Amin, "We Are All Nonbinary," 113.

11. Amin, "We Are All Nonbinary," 114.

12. Amin, "We Are All Nonbinary," 114.

13. Amin, "We Are All Nonbinary," 116–17.

14. Amin, "We Are All Nonbinary," 111.

15. For an extended discussion of the methodology, please see Appendix A.

16. Linda Greenhouse, "Heavy Lifting," *The New York Times*, December 10, 2014, https://www.nytimes.com/2014/12/11/opinion/the-supreme-court-and-rights-for-pregnant-workers.html.

17. Veronica Bayetti Flores, "We Make the Road by Walking: Trans-Inclusive Language and Reproductive Justice," *URGE*, June 12, 2013.

18. Glosswitch, "The Problem with Talking About 'Pregnant People,'" *The New Statesman*, 29 September 2015, https://www.newstatesman.com/politics/feminism/2015/09/what-s-matter-talking-about-pregnant-people.

19. Katha Pollitt, "Who Has Abortions?," *The Nation*, March 13, 2015, https://www.thenation.com/article/archive/who-has-abortions.

20. Elinor Burkett, "What Makes a Woman?," *The New York Times*, June 6, 2015, https://www.nytimes.com/2015/06/07/opinion/sunday/what-makes-a-woman.html.

21. Burkett, "What Makes a Woman?"; Glosswitch, "The Problem"; Pollitt, "Who Has Abortions?"

22. Glosswitch, "The Problem."

23. Pollitt, "Who Has Abortions?"

24. Alicia Johnson, Katha Pollitt, and Rye Young, "Does Talking About 'Women' Exclude Transgender People From the Fight for Abortion Rights?," *The Nation*, April 22, 2015, https://www.thenation.com/article/archive/letters-505.

25. Johnson, Pollitt, and Young, "Does Talking About 'Women' Exclude Transgender People?"

26. Barbara Gurr, *Reproductive Justice: The Politics of Healthcare for Native American Women* (New Brunswick: Rutgers University Press, 2014); Zakiya Luna, *Reproductive Rights as Human Rights* (New York: New York University Press, 2020); Jennifer Nelson, *Women of Color and the Reproductive Rights Movement* (New York: New York University Press, 2003); Faith Pennick, dir., *Silent Choices* (Newburgh, New York: New Day Films, 2007); Jael Silliman, Marlene Gerber Fried, Loretta Ross, and Elena Gutiérrez, *Undivided Rights: Women of Color Organizing for Reproductive Justice* (Chicago: Haymarket Books, 2016); Patricia Zavella, *The Movement for Reproductive Justice: Empowering Women of Color Through Social Activism* (New York: New York University Press, 2020).

27. Clare Hemmings, *Why Stories Matter: The Political Grammar of Feminist Theory* (Durham: Duke University Press, 2011), 57.

28. Hemmings, *Why Stories Matter*, 13.

29. Dawn Ennis, "Abortion Is an Issue for Transgender Bodies, Too," *Forbes*, May 20, 2019, https://www.forbes.com/sites/dawnstaceyennis/2019/05/20/from-africa-to-alabama-men-seek-to-control-womens-bodies; Rebecca Nelson, "12 Men Share Their Abortion Stories," *GQ*, October 21, 2019, https://www.gq.com/story/gq-glamour-men-abortion-stories; Isabelle Kohn and Calvin Kasulke, "The Trans Men Who Get Abortions," *MEL Magazine*, 2019, https://melmagazine.com/en-us/story/the-trans-men-who-get-abortions; Caitlin Van Horn, "Trans and Nonbinary People Get Abortions, Too," *Allure*, July 30, 2019, https://www.allure.com/story/abortion-gender-neutral-language-transgender-men-nonbinary.

30. Van Horn, "Trans and Nonbinary People."

31. Samantha Schmidt, "At First Debate, Transgender Issues Were Raised Like Never Before—and the Community Noticed," *The Washington Post*, June 27, 2019, https://www.washingtonpost.com/dc-md-va/2019/06/27/first-debate-transgender-issues-came-up-like-never-before.

32. Julian Castro (@juliancastro), Twitter, June 26, 2019, https://twitter.com/JulianCastro/status/1144055853093462016.

33. Schmidt, "At First Debate"; Jason Le Miere, "Julián Castro Earns Acclaim for Including Trans Community in Impassioned Call for Reproductive Justice," *Newsweek*, June 26, 2019, https://www.newsweek.com/julian-castro-trans-debate-reproductive-justice-1446182; Antonia Blumberg, "Julián Castro Gives Nod To Trans Community While Sharing His Abortion Views," *Huffington Post*, June 27, 2019, https://www.huffpost.com/entry/julian-castro-democratic-debate-reproductive-justice_n_5d141d98e4b0e455603742aa.

34. Blumberg, "Julián Castro Gives Nod"; Le Miere, "Julián Castro Earns Acclaim."

35. The archive on Planned Parenthood's website suggests that the organization first engaged publicly with the topic of trans men and abortion in 2019.

36. Madhuri Sathish, "NARAL President Ilyse Hogue Says Young Activists Are Key To Reproductive Freedom—EXCLUSIVE," *Elite Daily*, January 22, 2020, https://www.elitedaily.com/p/naral-president-ilyse-hogue-says-young-activists-are-key-to-reproductive-freedom-exclusive-21532946.

37. Sathish, "NARAL President."

38. Sathish, "NARAL President."

39. Paisley Currah, "Expecting Bodies: The Pregnant Man and Transgender Exclusion from the Employment Non-Discrimination Act," *Women's Studies Quarterly* 36 (2008): 330–36.

40. Mary Gray, *Out in the Country: Youth, Media, and Queer Visibility in Rural America* (New York: New York University Press, 2009); Carly Thomsen,

"The Post-Raciality and Post-Spatiality of Calls for LGBTQ and Disability Visibility," *Hypatia* 30, no. 1 (2015): 149–166; Carly Thomsen, "In Plain(s) Sight: Rural LGBTQ Women and the Politics of Visibility," in *Queering the Countryside: New Frontiers in Rural Queer Studies*, ed. Mary L. Gray, Colin R. Johnson, and Brian J. Gilley (New York: New York University Press, 2016); Carly Thomsen, *Visibility Interrupted: Rural Queer Life and the Politics of Unbecoming* (Minneapolis: University of Minnesota Press, 2021).

41. Thomsen, *Visibility Interrupted.*

42. Joshua D. Safer, Eli Coleman, Jamie Feldman, Robert Garofalo, Wylie Hembree, Asa Radix, et al., "Barriers to Healthcare for Transgender Individuals," *Current Opinion in Endocrinology, Diabetes and Obesity* 23, no. 2 (2016): 168–71.

43. Deirdre Shires and Kim Jaffee, "Factors Associated with Health Care Discrimination Experiences Among a National Sample of Female-to-Male Transgender Individuals," *Health and Social Work* 40 no. 2 (2015): 134–41.

44. Deirdre Shires, Daphna Stroumsa, Kim D. Jaffee, and Michael R. Woodford, "Primary Care Clinicians' Willingness to Care for Transgender Patients," *The Annals of Family Medicine* 6 (2018): 555–58.

45. Samuel N. Dubin, Ian T. Nolan, Carl G. Streed Jr., Richard E. Greene, Asa E. Radix, and Shane D. Morrison, "Transgender Health Care: Improving Medical Students' and Residents' Training and Awareness," *Advances in Medical Education and Practice* 9 (2018): 377-91.

46. Olivia H. Chang, Miriam J. Haviland, Emily Von Bargen, Yvonne Gomez-Carrion, Michele R. Hacker, and Janet Li, "Female Pelvic Medicine and Reconstructive Surgery Fellows' Exposure to Transgender Health Care," *American Journal of Obstetrics and Gynecology* 219, no. 6 (2018): 625–26.

47. Haley Braun, Rebecca Nash, Vin Tangpricha, Janice Brockman, Kevin Ward, and Michael Goodman,"Cancer in Transgender People: Evidence and Methodological Considerations," *Epidemiology Review* 39, no. 1 (2017): 93–107.

48. Ana Maria Lopez, Lauren Hudson, Nathan L. Vanderford, Robin Vanderpool, Jennifer Griggs, and Mara Schonberg, "Epidemiology and Implementation of Cancer Prevention in Disparate Populations and Settings," *American Society of Clinical Oncology Education* 39 (2019): 50–60.

49. Alec W. Gibson, Asa E. Radix, Shail Maingi, and Shilpen Patel, "Cancer Care in Lesbian, Gay, Bisexual, Transgender and Queer Populations," *Future Oncology* 13, no. 15 (2017): 1333–44.

50. John David Fernandez and Lisa R. Tannock, "Metabolic Effects of Hormone Therapy in Transgender Patients," *Endocrine Practice* 22, no. 4 (2017): 383–88; Darios Getahun, Rebecca Nash, W. Dana Flanders, Tisha C. Baird, Tracy A. Becerra-Culqui, Lee Cromwell, et al., "Cross-Sex Hormones and Acute Cardiovascular Events in Transgender Persons," *Annals of Internal Medicine* 169, no. 4 (2018): 205; Wylie C. Hembree, Peggy Cohen-Kettenis, Henriette A.

Delemarre-van de Waal, Louis J. Gooren, Walter J. Meyer, Norman P. Spack, et al., "Endocrine Treatment of Transsexual Persons: An Endocrine Society Clinical Practice Guideline," *The Journal of Clinical Endocrinology & Metabolism* 94, no. 9 (2009): 3132–54; Kate Steinle, "Hormonal Management of the Female-to-Male Transgender Patient," *Journal of Midwifery and Women's Health* 56 (2011): 293–302; Carl G. Streed, Omar Harfouch, Francoise Marvel, Roger S. Blumenthal, Seth S. Martin, and Monica Mukherjee, "Cardiovascular Disease Among Transgender Adults Receiving Hormone Therapy: A Narrative Review," *Annals of Internal Medicine* 167 (2017): 256–67.

51. Hembree, et al., "Endocrine Treatment," 3132.

52. Juno Obedin-Maliver, "Pelvic Pain and Persistent Menses in Transgender Men," *UCSF Transgender Care*, June 17, 2016, https://transcare.ucsf.edu/guidelines/pain-transmen.

53. Obedin-Maliver, "Pelvic Pain"; "Pelvic Floor PT & the Transgender Experience," *Body Connect Health and Wellness*, https://bodyconnecthw.com/pelvic-floor-pt-the-transgender-experience.

54. Lopez et al., "Epidemiology and Implementation of Cancer Prevention."

55. Lindsey M. Hutchison, Francis P. Boscoe, and Beth J. Feingold, "Cancers Disproportionately Affecting the New York State Transgender Population, 1979–2016," *AJPH* 108, no. 9 (2018): 1260–62.

56. Frances W. Grimstad, Kylie G. Fowler, Erika P. New, Cecile A. Ferrando, Robert R. Pollard, Graham Chapman, et al., "Uterine Pathology in Transmasculine Persons on Testosterone: A Retrospective Multicenter Case Series," *American Journal of Obstetrics and Gynecology* 220, no. 3 (2019): 257.

57. Michelle Louie and Janelle Moulder, "Hysterectomy for the Transgender Man," *Current Obstetrics and Gynecology Reports* 6 (2017): 126.

58. Louie and Moulder, "Hysterectomy," 126.

59. "Committee Opinion no. 512: Health Care for Transgender Individuals," *Obstetrics and Gynecology* 118, no. 6 (2011): 1454–58.

60. R. Joint, "Breast and Reproductive Cancers in Transgender Population: a Systemic Review," *BJOG* 125 (2018): 1505–12.

61. Christel de Blok, "Breast Cancer Risk in Transgender People Receiving Hormone Treatment: Nationwide Cohort Study in the Netherlands," *BJM* 365 (2019): 1652.

62. Breast Cancer Now, "Transgender Women Have an Increased Risk of Breast Cancer," *Breast Cancer Now*, June 25, 2019, https://breastcancernow.org/about-us/news-personal-stories/transgender-women-have-increased-risk-breast-cancer; Robert Preidt, "Trans Women on Hormones Have More Breast Cancer," *WebMD*, May 15, 2019, https://www.webmd.com/breast-cancer/news/20190515/trans-women-on-hormones-have-more-breast-cancer.

63. Planned Parenthood, "Breast Cancer," https://www.plannedparenthood.org/learn/cancer/breast-cancer.

64. This quotation was previously on the New York State Department of Health website, but has since been removed.

65. Juno Obedin-Maliver and Harvey J. Makadon, "Transgender Men and Pregnancy," *Obstetrics Medicine* 9, no. 1 (2016): 4–8.

66. Light et al., "Family Planning."

67. Laura Kaplan, *The Story of Jane: The Legendary Underground Feminist Abortion Service* (Chicago: University of Chicago Press, 1997).

68. Gretchen Sisson and Katrina Kimport, "Facts and Fictions: Characters Seeking Abortion on American Television, 2005–2014," *Contraception* 93, no. 5 (2016): 450.

69. Kelly Suzanne O'Donnell, "Reproducing Jane: Abortion Stories and Women's Political Histories," *Signs: Journal of Women in Culture and Society* 43, no. 1 (2017): 77–96.

70. Lisa Duggan, *The Twilight of Equality? Neoliberalism, Cultural Politics, and the Attack on Democracy* (Boston: Beacon Press, 2003).

71. Van Horn, "Trans and Nonbinary People."

72. Pollitt, "Who Has Abortions?"

73. Pollitt, "Who Has Abortions?"

74. Johnson, Pollitt, and Young, "Does Talking About 'Women' Exclude Transgender People?"

75. Brianna Scott, "Getting an Abortion as a Trans Person Is Hard—With or Without State Restrictions," NPR, October 18, 2022, https://www.npr.org/2022/10/18/1129736018/getting-an-abortion-as-a-trans-person-is-hard-with-or-without-state-restrictions.

76. Carrie N. Baker and Carly Thomsen, "The Importance of Talking About Women in the Fight Against Abortion Bans," *Ms. Magazine*, June 23, 2022, https://msmagazine.com/2022/06/23/women-abortion-bans-inclusive-language-pregnant-people.

77. Rebecca Wind, "Abortion Is a Common Experience for U.S. Women, Despite Dramatic Declines in Rates," Guttmacher Institute, October 19, 2017, https://www.guttmacher.org/news-release/2017/abortion-common-experience-us-women-despite-dramatic-declines-rates.

78. Light et al., "Family Planning."

79. Jenna Jerman, Rachel K. Jones and Tsuyoshi Onda, "Characteristics of U.S. Abortion Patients in 2014 and Changes Since 2008," Guttmacher Institute, August 24, 2022, https://www.guttmacher.org/report/characteristics-us-abortion-patients-2014.

80. Baker and Thomsen, "Importance of Talking About Women."

81. Miranda Joseph, *Against the Romance of Community* (Minneapolis: University of Minnesota Press, 2002).

82. Andrew M. Seaman, "Pregnancies More Common Among Lesbian, Gay, Bisexual Youths," *Reuters*, May 14, 2015, https://www.reuters.com/article/business

/healthcare-pharmaceuticals/pregnancies-more-common-among-lesbian-gay-bisexual-youths-idUSKBN0NZ2AS.

83. Cathy J. Cohen, "Punks, Bulldaggers, and Welfare Queens: The Radical Potential of Queer Politics?," *GLQ: A Journal of Lesbian and Gay Studies* 3, no. 4 (1997): 451. See original quote in Barbara Smith, "Queer Politics: Where's the Revolution?" *The Nation*, July 5, 1993, https://www.thenation.com/article/activism/wheres-revolution.

## CHAPTER 4. ABORTION AS GENDER TRANSGRESSION

1. Carly Thomsen and Grace Tacherra Morrison, "Abortion as Gender Transgression: Reproductive Justice, Queer Theory, and Anti-Crisis Pregnancy Center Activism," *Signs: Journal of Women in Culture and Society* 45, no. 3 (2020): 703–30.

2. For scholarship on CPCs that makes these points, see Alice X. Chen, "Crisis Pregnancy Centers: Impeding the Right to Informed Decision Making," *Cardozo Journal of Law and Gender* 19, no. 1 (2013): 933–60; Amy G. Bryant, Subasri Narasimhan, and Katelyn Bryant-Comstock, "Crisis Pregnancy Center Websites: Information, Misinformation and Disinformation," *Contraception* 90, no. 6 (2014): 601–5; Carly Thomsen, "Animating and Sustaining Outrage: The Place of Crisis Pregnancy Centers in Abortion Justice," *Human Geography* 15, no. 3 (2022): 300–6; Carly Thomsen, Zach Levitt, Christopher Gernon, and Penelope Spencer, "Anti-Abortion Ideology on the Move: Mobile Crisis Pregnancy Centers as Unruly, Unmappable, Ungovernable," *Political Geography* 92 (2021): 1–10; Carly Thomsen, "Feminist Art as Feminist Activism: An Anti-Crisis Pregnancy Center Exhibition in the Post-*Roe* Landscape," in *Fighting Mad: Resisting the End of* Roe v. Wade, ed. Krystale E. Littlejohn and Rickie Solinger (Oakland: University of California Press, 2024): 151–59.

3. Henry A. Waxman, "False and Misleading Health Information Provided by Federally Funded Pregnancy Resource Centers," United States House of Representatives Committee on Government Reform (2006). The original report has been removed from Waxman's congressional website, but it is available at https://www.motherjones.com/wp-content/uploads/waxman2.pdf.

4. Chen, "Crisis Pregnancy Centers," 934.

5. "Unmasking Fake Clinics: An Investigation into California's Crisis Pregnancy Centers," National Abortion and Reproductive Rights Action League (NARAL) Pro-Choice California, 2015, available at https://reproductivefreedomforall.org/wp-content/uploads/2018/03/NARAL-Pro-Choice-CA-Unmasking-Fake-Clinics-2015.pdf.

6. "Unmasking Fake Clinics."

7. Chen, "Crisis Pregnancy Centers"; Aziza Ahmed, "Informed Decision Making and Abortion: Crisis Pregnancy Centers, Informed Consent, and

the First Amendment," *Journal of Law, Medicine, and Ethics* 43, no. 1 (2015): 51–58.

8. Ziad W. Munson, *The Making of Pro-Life Activists: How Social Movement Mobilization Works* (Chicago: University of Chicago Press, 2008), 157.

9. Morrison and I contacted #ExposeFakeClinics five times between August 23 and November 3, 2017, via their website, Facebook page, and email. We received no response.

10. Cathy J. Cohen, "Punks, Bulldaggers, and Welfare Queens: The Radical Potential of Queer Politics?," *GLQ: A Journal of Lesbian and Gay Studies* 3, no. 4 (1997).

11. Rachel Jones, Elizabeth Witwer, and Jenna Jerman, "Abortion Incidence and Service Availability in the United States, 2017," Guttmacher Institute, September 2019, https://www.guttmacher.org/report/abortion-incidence-service-availability-us-2017.

12. Carly Thomsen, "The Politics of Narrative, Narrative as Politic: Rethinking Reproductive Justice Frameworks through the South Dakota Abortion Story," *Feminist Formations* 27, no. 2 (2015): 1–26.

13. "Heartbeat International Conference 2018," Heartbeat International, 2018, https://www.heartbeatinternational.org/training/conference#emotional-branding.

14. Andrea Smith, "Beyond Pro-Choice Versus Pro-Life: Women of Color and Reproductive Justice," *NWSA Journal* 17, no. 1 (2005): 119–40.

15. Smith, "Beyond Pro-Choice," 133.

16. Smith, "Beyond Pro-Choice," 133.

17. Margaret H. Hartshorn, *Foot Soldiers Armed with Love: Heartbeat International's First Forty Years* (Virginia Beach: Donning, 2011); Kimberly Kelly, "In the Name of the Mother: Renegotiating Conservative Women's Authority in the Crisis Pregnancy Center Movement," *Signs: Journal of Women in Culture and Society* 38, no. 1 (2012).

18. Ziad Munson and Christopher Scheitle, "Crisis Pregnancy Centers" (unpublished manuscript, 2009).

19. Kelly, "In the Name of the Mother," 214.

20. Kelly, "In the Name of the Mother," 204.

21. Kelly, "In the Name of the Mother," 214.

22. Laury Oaks, "What Are Pro-Life Feminists Doing on Campus?," *NWSA Journal* 21, no. 1 (2009): 178.

23. Oaks, "What Are Pro-Life Feminists Doing," 197.

24. In 2007 and 2008, respectively, political scientist Alesha Doan and sociologist Ziad Munson published monographs on the antiabortion movement, both of which include brief discussions of crisis pregnancy centers. However, neither book appears in a search for information on crisis pregnancy centers, as these are not their focus. See also Laura S. Hussey, "Crisis Pregnancy Centers,

Poverty, and the Expanding Frontiers of American Abortion Politics," *Politics and Policy* 41 no. 6 (2013): 985–1011; Chen, "Crisis Pregnancy Centers"; Jessie B. Hill, "Casey Meets the Crisis Pregnancy Centers," *Journal of Law, Medicine, and Ethics* 43, no. 1 (2015): 59–71; Amy G. Bryant and Erika E. Levi, "Abortion Misinformation from Crisis Pregnancy Centers in North Carolina," *Contraception* 86, no. 6 (2012): 752–56; Bryant et al., "Crisis Pregnancy Center Websites."

25. Joanne D. Rosen, "The Public Health Risks of Crisis Pregnancy Centers," *Perspectives on Sexual and Reproductive Health* 44, no. 3 (2012): 201–5.

26. Bryant and Levi, "Abortion Misinformation"; Chen, "Crisis Pregnancy Centers"; Bryant et al., "Crisis Pregnancy Center Websites."

27. Bryant et al., "Crisis Pregnancy Center Websites," 603.

28. Bryant et al., "Crisis Pregnancy Center Websites," 604.

29. Chen, "Crisis Pregnancy Centers," 934–35.

30. Jennifer Doyle, "Blind Spots and Failed Performance," *Qui Parle* 18, no. 1 (2009): 47.

31. See the Introduction for expanded discussion of this point.

32. The single exception: NARAL Pro-Choice CA supported a group of gender studies students at San Diego State University who engaged in a one-semester class research project on CPCs in San Diego, which culminated in a meeting with the San Diego City Council.

33. Resources that came up in a search for information on CPCs in 2011 include the film *12th and Delaware* (HBO Films, 2010) and a toolkit on Feminist Majority Foundation's website.

34. Previously, I claimed that UCSB was the second US university to pass such legislation, citing an email Feminist Majority Foundation received from University of Maryland students regarding their work to pass similar legislation. However, Feminist Majority Foundation never heard from these students again, and I have been unable to locate any information to confirm this claim. See Carly Thomsen, "From Refusing Stigmatization Toward Celebration: New Directions for Reproductive Justice Activism," *Feminist Studies* 39, no. 1 (2013): 154.

35. Class Leadership, "Music Video: Let's Learn about Crisis Pregnancy Centers,"YouTube,June4,2013,https://www.youtube.com/watch?vpG14RZDpGfCQ.

36. Lee Edelman, *No Future: Queer Theory and the Death Drive* (Durham: Duke University Press, 2004).

37. Laura Briggs, *How All Politics Became Reproductive Politics: From Welfare Reform to Foreclosure to Trump* (Oakland: University of California Press, 2018), 5.

38. Michael Warner, *The Trouble with Normal: Sex, Politics, and the Ethics of Queer Life* (Cambridge, MA: Harvard University Press, 1999); Ryan Conrad, *Against Equality: Queer Critiques of Gay Marriage* (Lewiston, ME: Against Equality, 2010); Suzanna Danuta Walters, *The Tolerance Trap: How God, Genes, and Good Intentions Are Sabotaging Gay Equality* (New York: New York University Press, 2016).

39. Paisley Currah, "Expecting Bodies: The Pregnant Man and Transgender Exclusion from the Employment Non-Discrimination Act," *WSQ: Women's Studies Quarterly* 36, no. 3–4 (2008): 330–36.

40. Jennifer Denbow, *Governed Through Choice: Autonomy, Technology, and the Politics of Reproduction* (New York: New York University Press, 2015).

41. Doyle, "Blind Spots."

42. Doyle, "Blind Spots," 41.

43. Jones et al., "Abortion Incidence and Service."

44. For examples of activism encouraging women to tell their abortion stories, see Jennifer Baumgardner and Gillian Aldrich, dirs., *I Had an Abortion* (2005) and the 1 in 3 campaign, http://www.1in3campaign.org.

45. Robyn Wiegman and Elizabeth A. Wilson, "Introduction: Antinormativity's Queer Conventions," *differences* 26, no. 1 (2015): 1.

46. Wiegman and Wilson, "Introduction," 2.

47. Janet R. Jakobsen, "Queer Is? Queer Does? Normativity and the Problem of Resistance," *GLQ* 4, no. 4 (1998): 513.

48. Jakobsen, "Queer Is?," 522.

49. Dorothy Roberts, *Killing the Black Body: Race, Reproduction, and the Meaning of Liberty* (New York: Vintage, 1997).

50. Lawrence B. Finer, Lori F. Frohwirth, Lindsay A. Dauphinee, Susheela Singh, and Ann M. Moore, "Reasons U.S. Women Have Abortions: Quantitative and Qualitative Perspectives," *Perspectives on Sexual and Reproductive Health* 37 no. 3 (2005): 110–18.

51. Marsha Saxton, "Disability Rights and Selective Abortion," in *The Disability Studies Reader*, ed. Lennard J. Davis (New York: Routledge, 2006), 105–17.

52. Cohen, "Abortion and Women of Color."

53. Other scholars at UCSB during End Fake Clinics' tenure reference our passage of legislation prohibiting the advertising of CPCs, which speaks to the group's presence on campus. See Laury Oaks, *Giving Up Baby: Safe Haven Laws, Motherhood, and Reproductive Justice* (New York: New York University Press, 2015), 227; Alison Dahl Crossley, *Finding Feminism: Millennial Activists and the Unfinished Gender Revolution* (New York: New York University Press, 2017), 106.

54. This point mirrors social movement scholars' analyses of political mobilization: That activists become involved when invited by someone they know through existing social networks. See Doug McAdam, *Freedom Summer* (Oxford: Oxford University Press, 1988).

55. Since these interviews were conducted in 2014, several additional group members have come to identify as queer, not straight, and/or trans. As such, we use the past tense to describe interviewees' identities as they were at the time of the interviews.

56. Rosemary Hennessy, *Fires on the Border: The Passionate Politics of Labor Organizing on the Mexican Frontera* (Minneapolis: University of Minnesota Press, 2013), 68.

57. Against Equality describes itself as a queer collective dedicated to challenging mainstream gay and lesbian politics, particularly those that request inclusion in oppressive institutions such as the military, marriage, and, via hate crimes legislation, the prison system. For more information, visit https://www.againstequality.org.

58. Loretta Ross, *Calling In: How to Start Making Change with Those You'd Rather Cancel* (New York: Simon and Schuster, 2025).

59. Cohen, "Punks," 459.

60. Cohen, "Punks," 439. See Joshua Gamson, "Must Identity Groups Self-Destruct? A Queer Dilemma," *Social Problems* 42, no. 3 (1995): 390–407.

61. Doyle, "Blind Spots," 27.

## CHAPTER 5. QUEER FEMINIST PARENTING

1. "Percentage of Same-Sex Couples in the United States in 2019, Sorted by Children in the Household," US Census Bureau, data visualization by Statista, accessed March 1, 2022, https://www.statista.com/statistics/325083/same-sex-couples-in-the-us-by-children-in-the-household.

2. Lourdes Avila Uribe, "The Best Books and Podcasts for Queer Parenting," *Huffington Post*, January 20, 2022, https://www.huffpost.com/entry/best-queer-parenting-books-podcasts_l_61e71b43e4b0a864b078df32.

3. Alim Kheraj, "What the World Needs to Know About Queer Parenting," *Gay Times*, December 16, 2021, https://www.gaytimes.co.uk/in-partnership-with/what-the-world-needs-to-know-about-queer-parenting.

4. Katy Huie Harrison, "Stigma Leads to LGBT Parenting Issues: Hilary's Story of Raising a Daughter with 2 Moms," Undefining Motherhood, February 4, 2020, https://undefiningmotherhood.com/lgbt-parenting-advice.

5. Jack Halberstam, *In a Queer Time and Place* (New York: New York University Press, 2005), 1.

6. Lee Edelman, *No Future: Queer Theory and the Death Drive* (Durham: Duke University Press, 2004), 17.

7. Lisa Duggan, *The Twilight of Equality? Neoliberalism, Cultural Politics, and the Attack on Democracy* (Boston: Beacon Press, 2003).

8. Edelman, *No Future*, 50.

9. Michael Warner, *Fear of a Queer Planet: Queer Politics and Social Theory* (Minneapolis: University of Minnesota Press, 1993). Warner is referring to heterosexual people who uncritically decide to reproduce, rather than the system

that forced enslaved people to reproduce and is often referred to as a "breeding industry."

10. Warner, *Fear of a Queer Planet*, 3.

11. Warner, *Fear of a Queer Planet*, 9.

12. Shelley Park, "Is Queer Parenting Possible," in *Who's Your Daddy? And Other Writings on Queer Parenting*, ed. Rachel Epstein (Toronto: Three O'Clock Press, 2009), 319.

13. Park, "Is Queer Parenting Possible," 317.

14. Park, "Is Queer Parenting Possible," 326.

15. Zena Sharman, "With Queer Co-Parenting, the More is Definitely the Merrier,"*Xtra*,April21,2021,https://xtramagazine.com/love-sex/queer-co-parenting-198978.

16. Cheshire Calhoun, "Family's Outlaw: Rethinking the Connections Between Feminism, Lesbianism, and the Family," *Philosophical Studies: An International Journal for Philosophy in the Analytic Tradition* 85, no. 2 (1997): 181–93.

17. Sharman, "With Queer Co-Parenting."

18. Kyl Myers, "I Let My Child Create Their Own Gender Identity. The Experience Has Been a Gift for Us Both," *TIME Magazine*, September 3, 2020, https://time.com/5885697/gender-creative-parenting.

19. Jen Manion, "The Performance of Transgender Inclusion," Public Seminar, November 27, 2018, https://publicseminar.org/essays/the-performance-of-transgender-inclusion.

20. Manion, "The Performance."

21. Park, "Is Queer Parenting Possible," 326.

22. Shannon Winnubst, *Queering Freedom* (Bloomington, Indiana University Press, 2006).Park, "Is Queer Parenting Possible," 199.

23. Park, "Is Queer Parenting Possible," 326.

24. Jane Ward, "Queer Parenting for Heteros (And Anyone Else Who Wants to Teach Kids that Being Queer is Awesome," *Offbeat Home & Life*, September 17, 2012, https://offbeathome.com/queer-parenting.

25. Ward, "Queer Parenting."

26. Ward, "Queer Parenting."

27. Elizabeth Weed and Naomi Schor, eds., *Feminism Meets Queer Theory* (Bloomington: Indiana University Press, 1997).

28. Judith Butler, "Against Proper Objects," in Weed and Schor, *Feminism Meets Queer Theory*, 3.

29. Paige Lucas-Stannard, "Want to be a Feminist Parent?: 4 Goals to Consider," *Everyday Feminism*, April 19, 2013, https://everydayfeminism.com/2013/04/feminist-parenting.

30. Elizabeth Enochs, "9 Things Feminist Parents Do Differently," *Bustle*, August 18, 2015, https://www.bustle.com/articles/104356-9-things-feminist

-parents-do-differently-because-raising-the-next-generation-of-badasses-is-no-small.

31. Aren Aizura, "Communizing Care in the Left Hand of Darkness," *Ada: A Journal of Gender, New Media, and Technology* 12 (2017).

32. Audre Lorde, "Man Child: A Black Lesbian Feminist's Response," in *Sister Outsider* (Feasterville Trevose, PA: Crossing Press, 1982), 73.

33. Lorde, "Man Child," 74.

34. Lorde, "Man Child," 74.

35. Sara Ahmed, *The Feminist Killjoy Handbook: The Radical Potential of Getting in the Way* (New York: Basic Books, 2023).

## CONCLUSION. PLAYING WITH QUEER THEORY

1. Elizabeth Nash and Lauren Cross, "2021 Is on Track to Become the Most Devastating Antiabortion State Legislative Session in Decades," Guttmacher Institute, April 30, 2021, https://www.guttmacher.org/article/2021/04/2021-track-become-most-devastating-antiabortion-state-legislative-session-decades.

2. The Games Project, https://www.thegamesproject.org.

3. Juliana Schroeder, Michael Kardas, and Nicholas Epley, "The Humanizing Voice: Speech Reveals, and Text Conceals, a More Thoughtful Mind in the Midst of Disagreement," *Psychological Science* 28 (2017): 1745–62.

4. Rosemary Hennessy, *Fires on the Border: The Passionate Politics of Labor Organizing on the Mexican Frontera* (Minneapolis: University of Minnesota Press, 2013), xii.

5. Patricia Zavella, *The Movement for Reproductive Justice* (New York: New York University Press, 2020).

6. James Procter, *Stuart Hall* (London: Routledge, 2004), 2.

7. Jack Halberstam, *The Queer Art of Failure* (Durham: Duke University Press, 2011).

8. Halberstam, *Queer Art*, 16.

9. Halberstam, *Queer Art*, 15.

10. Hito Steyerl, "In Defense of the Poor Image," *e-flux Journal* 10 (November 2009).

11. Halberstam, *Queer Art*.

12. Ursula Le Guin, "The Carrier Bag Theory of Fiction," in *The Ecocriticism Reader: Landmarks in Literary Ecology*, ed. Cheryll Glotfelty and Harold Fromm (Athens: University of Georgia Press, 1996), 153.

13. Octavia Butler, *Bloodchild and Other Stories* (New York: Four Walls Eight Windows, 1995).

14. Vanderpump Rules, 2016, Season 4 Episode 17, "Beach, Please," aired February 22, 2016 on Bravo (34:28).

15. Laura Kipnis, "Transgression, An Elegy," *Liberties* 1 (Fall 2020): 27.

16. Kipnis, "Transgression," 28.

17. Kipnis, "Transgression," 28.

18. Kipnis, "Transgression," 31.

19. Alice Zoo, "A Conversation with Carmen Winant," *Interloper*, May 1, 2024, https://interloper.substack.com/p/a-conversation-with-carmen-winant.

20. Laura Perez, *Eros Ideologies: Writings on Art, Spirituality, and the Decolonial* (Durham: Duke University Press, 2019).

## EPILOGUE. ONWARD, QUEERLY

1. Carmen Winant, *Notes on Fundamental Joy: Seeking the Elimination of Oppression Through the Social and Political Transformation of the Patriarchy That Otherwise Threatens to Bury Us* (New York: Printed Matter, 2019).

2. Carrie Baker, *Abortion Pills: US History and Politics* (Amherst: Amherst College Press, 2024); Sydney Calkin, *Abortion Pills Go Global: Reproductive Freedom Across Borders* (Oakland: University of California Press, 2023).

3. J Finley, *Sass: Black Women's Humor and Humanity* (Durham: University of North Carolina Press, 2024).

4. Center for Public Feminism, accessed January 10, 2024, https://www.publicfeminism.org.

5. Feminist Miniature Golf, https://www.feministminigolf.org.

6. Rickie Solinger, "Interrupted Life: Incarcerated Mothers in the United States: A Traveling Public Art Exhibition," *Meridians* 7, no. 2 (2007): 63–70.

7. https://www.feministminigolf.org/forced.

8. https://www.feministminigolf.org/shackled.

9. https://www.feministminigolf.org/criminalization.

10. https://www.feministminigolf.org/immigrantdetention.

11. https://www.feministminigolf.org/legitimatemother.

## APPENDIX

1. Erik Bleich and A. Maurits van der Veen, "Media Portrayals of Muslims: A Comparative Sentiment Analysis of American Newspapers, 1996–2015," *Politics, Groups, and Identities* 9, no. 1 (2021): 20–39.

# Index

*Italicized page numbers refer to figures.*

Founded in 1893,
UNIVERSITY OF CALIFORNIA PRESS
publishes bold, progressive books and journals on topics in the arts, humanities, social sciences, and natural sciences—with a focus on social justice issues—that inspire thought and action among readers worldwide.

The UC PRESS FOUNDATION
raises funds to uphold the press's vital role as an independent, nonprofit publisher, and receives philanthropic support from a wide range of individuals and institutions—and from committed readers like you. To learn more, visit ucpress.edu/supportus.

www.ingramcontent.com/pod-product-compliance
Lightning Source LLC
La Vergne TN
LVHW041309150826
845673LV00008B/2814

* 9 7 8 0 5 2 0 3 8 5 3 5 1 *